P9-DWZ-202

SYBIL IS "A BOOK LIKE NO OTHER"
—Stephen Longstreet

"Like a splash of ice water across the reader's face," says Richard D. Lesen in *Women's Wear Daily*, SYBIL is "more phantasmagorical than anything by Poe or Kafka," yet it is the true history of a real woman restored to a functioning whole from the splintered fragments of herself.

Applauded by *The New York Review of Books* as "a psychological document" and as a "moving human narrative," SYBIL is far more than a case history. It is an emotional experience, "spellbinding . . . frightening . . . because it is true."
—*Philadelphia Bulletin*

"This book is destined to stand as a significant landmark both in psychiatry and in literature."
—Dominick A. Barbara, M.D., F.A.P.A.,
The American Journal of Psychiatry

SYBIL

by Flora Rheta Schreiber

WARNER
PAPERBACK
LIBRARY

A Warner Communications Company

WARNER PAPERBACK LIBRARY EDITION

First Printing: May, 1974
Second Printing: May, 1974
Third Printing: May, 1974
Fourth Printing: June, 1974
Fifth Printing: July, 1974
Sixth Printing: July, 1974
Seventh Printing: August, 1974
Eighth Printing: September, 1974

Copyright © 1973 by Flora Rheta Schreiber
All rights reserved

Library of Congress Catalog Card Number: 72-11188

This Warner Paperback Library Edition is published by
arrangement with Henry Regnery Company, Inc.

Cover design by Gene Light

Warner Paperback Library is a division of Warner Books, Inc.,
75 Rockefeller Plaza, New York, N.Y. 10019.

 A Warner Communications Company

Printed in the United States of America

To my parents,
Esther and William Schreiber
Whose memory is a
Dwelling place for
All sweet thoughts and
Harmonies.

Contents

The Family Tree: The Hierarchy of the Sixteen Selves

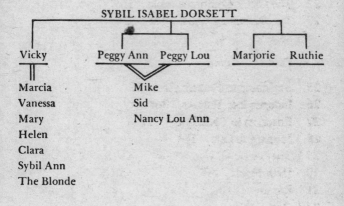

SYBIL ISABEL DORSETT

Vicky

Marcia
Vanessa
Mary
Helen
Clara
Sybil Ann
The Blonde

Peggy Ann   Peggy Lou

Mike
Sid
Nancy Lou Ann

Marjorie   Ruthie

Cast of Characters and Dates of "Birth"

Sybil Isabel Dorsett (1923): a depleted person; the waking self.

Victoria Antoinette Scharleau (1926): nicknamed Vicky; a self-assured, sophisticated, attractive blonde; the memory trace of Sybil's selves.

Peggy Lou Baldwin (1926): an assertive, enthusiastic, and often angry pixie with a pug nose, a Dutch haircut, and a mischievous smile.

Peggy Ann Baldwin (1926): a counterpart of Peggy Lou with similar physical characteristics; she is more often fearful than angry.

Mary Lucinda Saunders Dorsett (1933): a thoughtful, contemplative, maternal, homeloving person; she is plump and has long dark-brown hair parted on the side.

Marcia Lynn Dorsett (1927): last name sometimes Baldwin; a writer and painter; extremely emotional; she has a shield-shaped face, gray eyes, and brown hair parted on the side.

Vanessa Gail Dorsett (1935): intensely dramatic and extremely attractive; a tall redhead with a willowy figure, light brown eyes, and an expressive oval face.

Mike Dorsett (1928): one of Sybil's two male selves; a builder and a carpenter; he has olive skin, dark hair, and brown eyes.

Sid Dorsett (1928): one of Sybil's two male selves; a carpenter and a general handyman; he has fair skin, dark hair, and blue eyes.

Nancy Lou Ann Baldwin (date undetermined): interested in politics as fulfillment of biblical prophecy and intensely afraid of Roman Catholics; fey; her physical characteristics resemble those of the Peggys.

Sybil Ann Dorsett (1928): listless to the point of neurasthenia; pale and timid with ash-blonde hair, an oval face, and a straight nose.

Ruthie Dorsett (date undetermined): a baby; one of the lesser developed selves.

Clara Dorsett (date undetermined): intensely religious; highly critical of the waking Sybil.

Helen Dorsett (1929): intensely afraid but determined to achieve fulfillment; she has light brown hair, hazel eyes, a straight nose, and thin lips.

Marjorie Dorsett (1928): serene, vivacious, and quick to laugh; a tease; a small, willowy brunette with fair skin and a pug nose.

The Blonde (1946): nameless; a perpetual teenager; has blonde curly hair and a lilting voice.

The New Sybil (1965): the seventeenth self; an amalgam of the other sixteen selves.

Preface:

Sybil

This book goes to press over ten years after I first met the woman to whom I have given the pseudonym Sybil Isabel Dorsett. Sybil wants to maintain anonymity, and when you read her true story, you will understand why. But Sybil Isabel Dorsett *is* a real person.

Our first meeting took place on an autumn evening in 1962 at a restaurant on New York City's Madison Avenue. Dr. Cornelia B. Wilbur, Sybil's psychoanalyst, had arranged the meeting so that I could become acquainted with Sybil.

Sybil seemed constrained and remote. I knew that this was because of her illness. Dr. Wilbur and she had embarked on one of the most complex and most bizarre cases in the history of psychiatry—the first psychoanalysis of a multiple personality.

I had known about the case for some years. Dr. Wilbur's and my paths had often crossed through my work as psychiatry editor of *Science Digest* and as the author of articles about psychiatric subjects. A few of these articles, in fact, had been about her cases.

The meeting was arranged for a specific purpose: Dr. Wilbur wondered whether I would be interested in writing about Sybil. It was not sufficient, the doctor believed, to present this history-making case in a medical journal, because in addition to great medical significance, the case had broad psychological and philosophical implications for the general public.

I wanted to wait for the outcome of the case prior to

committing myself irrevocably to the book. In the meantime, Sybil and I became friends. We shared many intellectual interests, had an unmistakable affinity. Sybil became a frequent visitor in my apartment. She often confided in me about what had taken place in the analytic sessions, and what took place when she was in my home often found its way into the sessions.

Gradually, the idea of the book became more intriguing to me. I have written widely, and not without recognition, about psychiatry, and have a strong psychology and psychiatry background. By 1962 I had worked with many psychiatrists on their cases. Even my political profiles, many of which were written for national magazines, are strongly psychological in orientation. In addition, I am a college professor (currently at the City University of New York's John Jay College of Criminal Justice). My academic fields are English and speech; the literary bequest of the one and the closeness of speech scholarship to psychological scholarship prepared me to approach the subject of Sybil. Moreover, I had been in the theater, in radio and television, had written short stories and plays, and had taught writing at the New School for Social Research. All factors seemed to coalesce to make me want to transmute the clinical details of Sybil's story into a book in which I could capture that story's inherent drama.

I also wanted to write the book because of my friendship with Sybil and Dr. Wilbur, whose courage in pursuing the uncharted course of a very special analysis I greatly admired. I had great regard for Dr. Wilbur, an analyst with impressive credentials. She had a large Park Avenue practice and was prominent in a variety of psychiatric organizations, notably the Society of Medical Psychoanalysts and the Academy of Psychiatry. President of the National Association of Private Psychiatric Hospitals, she also served on the research committee of the Society of Medical Psychoanalysts that produced an important volume entitled *Homosexuality: A Psychoanalytic View*. Today, no longer in private practice, Dr. Wilbur is a full professor

14

of psychiatry at the Medical School of the University of Kentucky.

Thus it was, after knowing Sybil and her other selves for three years, that I made my commitment and began to do formal research for this book. The confidences I shared with Sybil and Dr. Wilbur and my direct contacts with the other selves had to be supplemented by a systematized approach to the case as a whole and to Sybil's total life. I read widely in the medical literature about multiple personality, and I discussed the general aspects of the case with various psychiatrists in addition to Dr. Wilbur. I retraced the outer odyssey of Sybil's life by talking with persons who had known her in her midwestern home town, which I call Willow Corners, in Omaha, and in New York. I also literally retraced the steps Sybil had taken during some of her strange travels as another personality. In Philadelphia, for instance, I counted the number of steps to the front door of the Broadwood Hotel.

To unfold this extraordinary saga of a chilling, dizzying kaleidoscope of fascinating events, I had first to disentangle them. Clues evolved through a minute exploration of every single document connected with Sybil's eleven-year analysis. These included Dr. Wilbur's daily notes, jotted in pencil on prescription pads, in the course of 2,354 office sessions; Sybil's essays, written as part of the treatment procedure; and recordings of those analytic sessions that were taped. I also studied Sybil's diaries, kept from adolescence through the first year of the analysis; letters; family and hospital records; and the newspapers and records of the town of Willow Corners during the years in which the Dorsett family lived there.

Through these ten years—during seven of which I was actively working on the book—I was intimately associated with Dr. Wilbur and Sybil, both of whom, sometimes separately, sometimes together, stood ready to "sit" for the portrait. Our roles were quite distinct, however. I was recreating what Sybil had already lived and the doctor had already analyzed. But never, perhaps, did an author have more "giving" subjects. In fact, in response to any questioning, they, too, reassessed many aspects of the analysis. For me there was also the satisfaction of being able always to check the medical facts of this case with a doctor who was never farther away than the nearest telephone.

Upon reading the finished book, Sybil remarked, "Every emotion is true"; Dr. Wilbur commented, "Every psychiatric fact is accurately represented."

Sybil's true story provides a rare glimpse into the unconscious mind and opens doorways to new understanding. A reflection of abnormal psychology and of an extraordinary developmental pattern, the case of Sybil Dorsett supplies new insight into the normal. It affords not only a new observation of the uncanny power of the unconscious mind in motivating human behavior but also a new look into the dynamics of destructive family relationships, the crippling effects of a narrow, bigoted religious background, a woman's identification with the males in her family, and the denial of self-realization. In terms of what not to do, Sybil's story is a cogent lesson in child care. Implicit in this account, too, are issues relevant to such questions as: What is maturity? What is a whole person?

Sybil's life story also illuminates the role of the unconscious mind in creativity; the subtle interrelationships of remembering and forgetting, of the coexistence of the past with the present; and the significance of the primal scene in spawning psychoneurosis. There are also certain philosophical questions implicit here, namely, the subtle relationship between reality and unreality and the meaning of "I."

Medically this account throws light on the genesis of mental illness in terms of heredity and environment and the difference between schizophrenia, which some doctors and the public alike tend to use as a catch-all for a multitude of diverse symptoms, and *Grande Hystérie,* the little-understood illness with which Sybil was afflicted.

16

Most important of all, perhaps, is the expansion of consciousness that the reader experiences as he or she falls under the spell of Sybil's internal adventures.

Flora Rheta Schreiber
New York City
January, 1973

Acknowledgments

Thanks are in order to James Palmer for his useful comments on certain portions of the manuscript; to anthropologist Dr. Valentine Winsey for her invaluable suggestions; to Dr. Donald H. Riddle, President of John Jay College of Criminal Justice, for his sustained encouragement; to Melvin Herman, Executive Secretary of the National Association of Private Psychiatric Hospitals, who introduced me to Dr. Wilbur; to the Reverend Eric Hayden, of St. Andrews Church, Newark, for doing some crucial sleuthing; to Professor Leo C. Loughrey, for legal advice on Chapter 5; to John Schreiber for his unflagging enthusiasm for the project; to that loyal group of performers at the typewriter who gave seemingly endless hours not only to typing the manuscript but also to empathizing with the author—Natalie Parnass, Margaret Schoppe, Janet Ludorf Küby, Susi Resnick, Shirley Sulat, Anne Henri, and Haydee Davis; to Haydee, too, who, along with her husband, George Thomas, bailed the author, laden with documents, out of Lexington, Kentucky; to Patricia Myrer of McIntosh & Otis for weathering the storm since 1962; and above all to Dr. Cornelia B. Wilbur and Sybil I. Dorsett, who made it all possible.

I have also discussed Sybil's case with such notable members of the psychiatric fraternity as Dr. Karl Menninger, Dr. Murray Bowen, Dr. Harvey Kay, Dr. Lawrence Friedman, and the late Dr. Nathan Ackerman. Dr. Herbert Spiegel, who did age regressions on Sybil and described her as "a brilliant hysteric," gave several hours to a valuable discussion of this case, which he knew first-hand. Dr. Menninger, who had never treated anyone with Sybil's condition, had, how-

18

ever, dealt with cases of automatic writing, which he regards as a subdivision of the condition, attesting to its reality. Dr. Bowen, whose specialty is family therapy, was particularly concerned with the family constellation in the genesis of the illness.

Teil 1

Beine

Part I

Being

1

The Incomprehensible Clock

The crash of glass made her head throb. The room swirled. Her nostrils were suffused with the acrid smell of chemicals, more than an inhalation of what was actually there. The smell seemed to emerge from some far-off memory of an experience long forgotten. That smell, so distant yet so familiar, was reminiscent of the old drugstore at home.

The broken glass in the old drugstore. The broken glass in the big dining room. Both times there had been the accusing voice: "You broke it."

Sybil Isabel Dorsett hastily flung her chemistry notes into her brown zipper folder and rushed to the door, with all eyes upon her, the chemistry professor's, the other students', uncomprehendingly engraving themselves into her spine.

The door closed behind her. She was in the long, dusky hall on the third floor of Columbia University's Havemeyer Hall. Then she was waiting at the elevator, the only person there.

"Too long, too long." Her thoughts spun round. She had waited too long before leaving the lab. She might have prevented what had happened by leaving the very moment that she heard the crash.

Too long. The elevator, too, was taking too long.

Sybil clutched for her zipper folder. It wasn't there. The elevator wasn't there, either, or the long, dusky hall. She was standing on a long, narrow street covered

23

with snow. The elevator hadn't come for her, but instead of waiting, she was walking.

A sharp, pungent wind whipped her. Snow, white, crackling, and swirling, was underfoot. She had no overshoes, no gloves, no hat; her ears ached with numbness. The light gray convertible tweed coat, which had seemed warm enough when she walked to the lab from her apartment on Morningside Drive, now offered painfully little protection against the unrelenting cold.

Sybil looked for a street sign. There wasn't any. She looked for a house, in which she might find refuge. There was none. A gas station? She didn't see any. A drugstore? None.

Drugstore. Chemistry lab. The long, dusky hall. Elevator. None here. There was only this street, this poorly lighted, deserted, nameless street in a place she didn't recognize.

Old, ugly, massive wooden structures—some painted battleship gray, others covered with sheet metal—lined both sides of the street. There were overhead entrances, huge doors below, and windows with tiny panes.

It couldn't be New York. Maybe it was some part of her native Wisconsin, where as a child she had been through many winter storms like this and had known what it was like to have chilblains. Ridiculous. How could she have gotten to Wisconsin in the split second between standing at the Columbia University elevator and now? But then she couldn't have gotten anywhere in that time. Maybe she hadn't; maybe she wasn't anywhere. Maybe this was a nightmare.

Yet as she walked faster, reality confronted her in the form of the ugly buildings and the constantly falling snow, which she wiped from her face with her gloveless hand and tried to shake from her body by gyrating from side to side. She knew that she couldn't have invented those barricaded structures; she had never seen anything like them before. The doors were huge not because she was imagining them that way but because they were used for storage and shipping. The realistic part of her imagination took hold again, and she knew that she was in a warehouse district.

24

A black silhouette against the white snow, the figure of a man, suddenly appeared on the other side of the street. He seemed as unapproachable as a passing shadow, as inanimate as the buildings that dwarfed her. Even though he could undoubtedly tell her where she was, she could not reach out to him. Besides, she feared that if she did, he would misunderstand her motives. She just let him pass into what seemed to be night, hurrying to a world beyond the warehouses and beyond her entreaty.

For Sybil there seemed no exit, just as there had been no entrance. The barricade of buildings, although outside herself, blended with her innermost fears. She felt closed in, shut off, imprisoned, trapped—without and within.

Was there no rescue? No taxi? Bus? Nothing to take her somewhere, anywhere so long as it was away from this non-place? Although just before getting off a crosstown bus in New York, her present home, she had always been prone to an odd, balky feeling, now she was even willing to risk a bus. The matter, however, was purely academic, since there was none. There was nothing.

A phone booth became pivotal in her thinking. If she could find one, she not only would know where she was but could also call Teddy Eleanor Reeves, her roommate, who must certainly be worried about her. Then Sybil remembered that Teddy had left for a vacation with her family in Oklahoma soon after she herself had left for the lab.

Ironically, Teddy had urged Sybil to wear a warmer coat when she had left their apartment. She had not listened because it had been one of the days when she couldn't listen. All that day, especially after it had begun to turn cold, she had felt overwhelmed by feelings of uneasiness and by strange stirrings within her, which had made it impossible for her to stay in the apartment even the extra minutes required for changing her coat.

Sybil also wanted to call Dr. Cornelia B. Wilbur. If enough time had gone by, the doctor, too, would surely be worried about her. Maybe Sybil had missed her hour with the doctor. Could she have missed *many* hours by now?

The word "now" was tantalizing, elusive since there was no knowing how much time had passed since she had been waiting at the elevator. If only she could remember, piece together what had brought her here, maybe she could understand. There could be no peace for her until she did.

A telephone seemed the most likely link to reality, though looking for one was like searching for a mirage. Somehow she had to find one, to keep moving long enough to do so. She felt she couldn't go on, but she also knew that she didn't dare stop. Her legs seemed frozen; yet if she did not go on, she knew from her experience with midwestern winters that she might freeze to death.

Forcing herself to keep moving, she listened for sounds, for life. There was only the wind. Block after block along glassy streets failed to reveal a single street sign. The hope of a telephone became even more vain.

As if to steady herself, at least momentarily, Sybil stopped at a street lamp. Aided by its dim light she opened her purse and rummaged through it. Her Social Security card, Blue Cross card, driver's license, Columbia University library card—each brought the reassurance of recognition.

Her billfold, which had contained $50 and some change when she had left her apartment, contained only $37.42 now. She had walked to the lab, bought nothing after she got there. Had she paid the missing cash to travel to this place? She had waited at the elevator; then she was here. That was all she could remember.

The key to her apartment was lying neatly in its compartment. Dangling from a large, reddish-brown tag, however, was a key she had never seen before. Turning it over and over in her almost frozen hand, she looked at it again and again, reading and rereading its gilt letters: room 1113.

What was this key doing in her purse? Where had it come from? Obviously it was a hotel key, but unlike

26

most hotel keys, it bore no name or address, no clue as to what city this was.

Maybe this was a nightmare after all? No, the key was tangible, the tag was solid, the lamppost was real. So were the ugly structures that seemed to leer at and mock her. Real, too, was the snow that clung to her coat and legs. And there was motion in the legs; despite her fears, her legs were not frozen. As she hurried on, knowing that she had no destination, she appreciated the grim humor of rushing to no place. Yet onward she went—running from no place to nowhere —racing to outstrip her mounting panic.

The key to room 1113 was the engine that drove her, the motor on which her panic turned. Then suddenly the key brought not panic but a measure of comfort. That key opened *some* hotel room door, a retreat from the cold, a haven. There she could at least be warm, get some food, rest.

Walking rapidly, looking at each street intersection for an approaching vehicle, Sybil grew angry with herself for not having made a more determined effort to find a taxi or bus. Although she had allowed herself to be trapped, now, whether or not it was the one to which the anonymous key led, she would find a hotel. Certainly there was a world beyond the warehouses.

Then a new terror overtook her. What if she had picked up the key on the street? She didn't remember doing so, but she didn't remember much. What if at some time in the past she had been in that room for days, weeks, even months or years and had been forced to leave for not paying her bill? In both cases the room would now be someone else's. Should she throw the key away? Free herself from possible guilt?

No. There was no key, no room, no shelter, no refuge, no world, only more of this no-woman's land, where unreal silhouettes of men could flit by in the snow, re-awakening the black and white images that had always terrified her.

There was no end to these long, narrow streets. No house would ever show a light. These barred windows —how she feared them—echoed old fears, fears that had followed her wherever she had lived and had now followed her to this non-place.

Suddenly there was a light. A gas station. A telephone at last and a directory to give this place a name.

According to the directory, she was in Philadelphia, a city she had visited many times, but not once in all those visits had she been in this area.

The phone booth beckoned to her, seemed to invite her presence. But when, accepting its invitation, she stood within the cagelike confines of its hospitality, hospitality turned to rebuff. Intending to call Dr. Wilbur's home number, she inserted a dime in the slot to ask for long distance but heard only a metallic nothingness. The telephone was dead.

She approached the gas station attendant and asked whether she could use his private phone. "Sorry, lady," he replied. "Sorry." All she saw, as he walked from her and closed the door in her face, was the back of his retreating white coat.

Her fear, she knew, had made him afraid. But contact with another person permitted her to decide to call from the Broadwood Hotel, where she always stayed when she visited Philadelphia.

The thought of the Broadwood and the knowledge that she was in a city she knew well lifted some of the terror. She took time to visit the washroom, where she let hot water run over her hands. Returning to the street, she noticed for the first time the Delaware River and on its other shore, Camden. Both had been there all the time.

The Delaware was familiar. She had once done an impressionistic water color of it while Capri sat at her side. The cat, who had watched every stroke of the brush, had occasionally taken a swipe at the brush handle as if to remind Sybil of her presence.

Street signs began to become visible. Front Street. Callowhill Street. Spring Gardens. On Front Street, between Callowhill and Spring Gardens, there were overhead elevated tracks. As Sybil approached a corner, she noticed a light, a city bus.

"Wait, wait," Sybil called frantically.

The florid-faced driver waited.

28

And then, acutely aware of an aching in her arms and legs, Sybil collapsed in a window seat in the rear of the bus. She was ready to go wherever the bus would take her, anywhere, everywhere, world beyond, world without end—anywhere.

Why were these other passengers—three men and a woman wearing a beaver hat—out on a night like this? But was it night? The maddeningly anonymous in-between gray of the overcast sky withheld the clue as to whether it was night or morning. She didn't know the date, either. If she were to ask the other passengers, what a fool they'd think her!

The enigmatic key in her purse, which also withheld all clues, once again possessed her. A Broadwood key? She didn't know. Nor did she know whether she was on her way to the Broadwood Hotel. She could easily get there, however, from wherever the bus took her. Eager to find out, she walked to the front of the bus and asked the driver: "Do you go anywhere near Broad and Wood?"

"Three blocks from it," he replied. "Shall I call you?"

Through the bus window, despite its frosty face, she recognized Benjamin Franklin Parkway, Logan Free Library, the Franklin Institute, and Fairmont Park. She remembered with excitement the two granite memorials in the park. On one, which was of soldiers in bas relief, was the inscription: "One country; one constitution. In giving freedom to slaves we assure freedom to the free." She had painted that war memorial. She must keep her mind on anything, everything, except the key. Except my life, except my life—wasn't that what Hamlet had said?

"Your corner," the driver called to her.

She was on terra firma again. Infirm with the skidding conditions of the roads and the slippery sidewalks, it was firm with the solidity of familiar landmarks: the Academy of Fine Arts, on Broad and Cherry Streets, the Hahnemann Hospital, and then, a present reality at last, the gold dome atop the Broadwood Hotel.

Finally, the red brick sixteen-story Broadwood Hotel stood before her. It had a diamond pattern up to the

29

third floor and a white cornice. Across the street from the hotel were the Roman Catholic High School for boys and an old building that used to be the home of the *Philadelphia Morning Record*. In front of the Broadwood there was a subway station. The subway had been there since 1927, someone had told her. And the Broadwood itself had been built in 1923 by the Elks. That was the year she was born. Funny.

Becoming annoyed with herself for lingering outside the hotel when she could already have been inside, she finally took the fateful plunge of entering. It seemed to Sybil that it was as difficult to ascend the three steps to the Broadwood's heavy glass front door as to climb Mt. Everest. Her ascent was into the unknown.

In the main lobby she stared at the torchlike lamps suspended from the ceiling, scrutinized the familiar marble, the yellow, black, and white tile floor. Although she knew this lobby well from previous visits, she noted each detail as if she were looking at it for the first time.

Should she register? She hesitated. Should she head for room 1113 on the supposition that it was free and that she had a Broadwood Hotel key? She ran up the fifteen steps to the rotunda. That was a safe detour from both desk and elevator—the Scylla and Charybdis of her terror.

The rotunda was dominated by a stained glass terrazzo tile marble window forty feet high. It was a beautiful window, overlooking a mezzanine. Inscribed on the rotunda's gold leaf ceiling was the motto: "Fidelity, Justice, Vanity, Brotherly Love—their virtues upon the tablets of love and memory. The faults of our brothers we write upon the sand."

For a few fleeting minutes, as Sybil stared at the ceiling, she felt relaxed by its beauty, but the sensation passed as she slowly retraced her steps from the rotunda to the main lobby. Again taking refuge in extraneous things, she noted how the place had changed since she had last been here. The bellhops were not the same. Nor had she ever seen the owlish, bosomy woman at the registration desk. And then, lingering at

30

the interior store window of Persky's Portraits, Sybil tried to force herself to decide whether to register or to go to room 1113, to which the inexplicable key could conceivably lead. Unable to decide, she rushed out to Broad Street.

At the newsstand in front of the Broadwood she bought a copy of the *Philadelphia Bulletin*. It was dated January 7, 1958. As if disbelieving the date, she bought the *Philadelphia Inquirer*. It too was dated January 7.

January 7. She had left the chemistry lab on January 2. *Five days lost.* The fear of not knowing had been replaced by an even greater fear—knowing.

"Do you have the time?" she managed with assumed nonchalance to ask the newsdealer.

"Nine o'clock," he replied.

Nine P.M. It had been 8:45 P.M. when she had waited at the Columbia elevator. Almost five days to the hour had intervened.

Slowly, fearfully, Sybil once again pushed open the heavy glass door of the hotel. Panic and a sense of remorse and self-recrimination awakened by the knowledge that she had lost five days compelled her to hurry. Someone, she dimly perceived, was calling to her. It was the owlish, bosomy woman at the registration desk. "Hello, there," the woman was saying, her large head bobbing over the desk in recognition, her eyebrows so prominent that they seemed like the stiff-feathered disks of an owl, by which Sybil had first characterized her.

"Do you have a minute?" the woman called. "I want to talk to you."

As if mesmerized, Sybil came to a halt.

"Now, when you get to your room," the woman said solemnly, "take a hot bath and get some hot tea. I was so worried about you out in that storm. 'Don't go out,' I begged you. You wouldn't listen. This is no weather to monkey around with."

"Thank you. I'm all right," Sybil replied somewhat stiffly.

The woman smiled at her as she headed toward the bank of elevators.

Sybil could swear—in a court of law she *would* have sworn on oath—that it had been a year since she had been at the Broadwood. In that same court, however, the woman at the desk, who had not worked at the hotel the previous year, would have sworn, also on oath, that Sybil had been in the hotel earlier that January 7.

One of the two elevator doors swung open. Sybil, anxious and deeply apprehensive, entered the car. She was the only passenger.

"Eleven, please," she said.

"Out in that storm?" the elevator boy asked.

She whispered, "Yes."

"Eleven," he called.

The elevator door closed behind Sybil, its metallic clang registering in her spine as had the uncomprehending eyes in the chemistry lab. Between the two elevators time had not existed. Remorse quickened at the thought.

Was there really a room 1113? The numbers on the doors, 1105, 1107, 1109, 1111, heralded a probable 1113. Then flashing, receding, and flashing, as if it were in neon lights, was 1113!

Sybil opened her purse, removed the key, turned it over in her unsteady hand, caught her breath, started to place the key in the lock, turned it over again, and wondered whether it was really the key to this door.

Go in? Go back?

She inserted the key in the lock. It fitted. The door swung open. Sybil faced room 1113.

Nobody spoke. Nobody stirred or moved. Did that mean that nobody was there?

She pressed her body against the doorjamb and, without entering the room, moved her hand over the nearest wall in search of a light switch. When the light went on, the thrust of her hand unleashed a floodlight on her fears of what she might find. Stepping into the room and closing the door behind her, she stood transfixed, unmoving.

As far as she knew, she had never before been in the room. But if this weren't her room, where had she slept from January 2 to January 7, how did she come by the

32

key? She could not have been in the street all that time.

Was she registered? The woman at the desk downstairs had acted as if she were.

Sybil removed her wet coat and placed it on a chair, kicked off her wet shoes, and slumped into the green chair near the window.

She didn't *know* that the room was hers, but somehow, from the way the woman had talked, she didn't think it was anybody else's, either.

For a time she just stared vacantly through the window at the Roman Catholic High School for boys and at the building that used to house the *Philadelphia Morning Record.* Then, unable to find solace in just sitting, she reached for the newspapers that she had brought with her.

THE PHILADELPHIA INQUIRER
FINAL CITY EDITION
INDEPENDENT NEWSPAPER FOR ALL THE PEOPLE

My eyes are heavy with exhaustion.

TUESDAY MORNING, JANUARY 7, 1958

January 7. January 7 is a plain fact that spells out that I have lost five days.

MAN ROCKETED 186 MILES UP, REDS SAY
Gavin Says Missile Stand Cost Promotion
85th Congress
Starts Second
Session Today

So much has happened while I was out of the world.

Flier Chutes
Safely After
Epic Ascent

My ascent was epic too. The streets. The steps. So

33

many streets. More of a descent since I have lost time after thinking I would not again.

Autos Slither
  Stop
    Glassy Roads

THE EVENING BULLETIN
PHILADELPHIA
TUESDAY, JANUARY 7, 1958

Pay bill. Check out. Check out when I haven't checked in? How did I get in without luggage?

SNOWSTORM EXPECTED TO LAST ALL NIGHT

All night?

She had better stay. She tossed the newspapers into the flowered metal wastebasket and went to the desk to call room service. She ordered split pea soup and a glass of hot milk. While waiting for the food to come, she started to call Dr. Wilbur. Too long. Too long. She had waited too long to get through to the doctor.

Sybil lifted the phone off its cradle and started to give Dr. Wilbur's number to the hotel operator. At that moment, however, something on the dresser riveted Sybil's attention. Staring at the object in disbelief, she dropped the telephone receiver abruptly. It was her zipper folder.

Also on the dresser were her mittens, which would have come in handy in the storm, and the red scarf she had been wearing at the Columbia University elevator.

Tremulously she walked to the dresser and clutched at the zipper folder. Unzipping it, she discovered that the chemistry notes were exactly as they had been five days before when she had scooped them up in the lab.

Then, in a corner of the dresser, was something that she hadn't noticed before: a receipt for a pair of pajamas purchased at a Philadelphia department store. She knew the place; she had been there several times. It was

34

a long walk from the Broadwood, but by subway one could make it door to door. The pajamas cost $6.98. Had this $6.98, she wondered, helped to deplete her billfold?

Pajamas! Where were they? She searched the drawers and the closets, but she didn't find them.

She searched the bathroom. At first she saw nothing; then she saw the pajamas on a hook behind the door, hanging like an accusation.

The pajamas were rumpled, slept in. Had she slept in them? They were loud and gay, with bright orange and green stripes. Not her style. She always chose solid colors, usually in varying shades of blue. The pajamas she found were the sort a child might select.

Sybil went back into the room. Her knees sagged. The self-recrimination she had felt upon discovering that she had lost time was suddenly intensified by finding the objects on the dresser. The zipper folder glared at her, the red scarf threatened her, and the mittens seemed to be pointing at her as though they had locomotion of their own.

Then, on a small bedside table an object that she had not seen before beckoned to her: a black and white drawing of an isolated female figure perched on a cliff against a towering mountain that threatened to engulf it, dwarfed it. The drawing had been penciled on Broadwood stationery. Drawn in this room, it had obviously been left behind by the person who drew it. Who?

There was a knock at the door, and the room service waiter placed on the desk Sybil's tray with the soup and milk she had ordered. "You're not very hungry tonight," the lean, lanky waiter said. It seemed as if he were comparing her order to what she had ordered on other occasions. His tone was gentle, his manner protective, as if he knew her well. Yet Sybil knew that she had not seen him before. The waiter left.

Staring at the food on the tray, Sybil felt a different kind of panic from what she had felt among the massive, ugly buildings of the warehouse district. The waiter. The woman at the desk with a bosom like a hill.

35

The pajamas. The black and white drawing of the female figure on the cliff. It all made sense—terrible
sense. The panic she had experienced in the warehouse
district because of not knowing what had happened
had been superseded at the newsstand by the even
greater panic of partial knowledge. And now the torment of partly knowing had yielded to the infinitely
greater terror of knowing precisely. The pajamas and
the black and white drawing left no doubt.

Sybil gulped the milk, pushed the soup aside, hastily
put on her shoes, her still-wet coat, her scarf, mittens.
She stuffed the pajamas and sales slip into her zipper
folder. She had planned to spend the night, but suddenly, even though she could see that the snow hadn't
stopped and she knew that the trains might be delayed,
she *had* to get back to New York to avoid the risk of
what might happen if she stayed.

Sybil Isabel Dorsett knew that she had to get back to
New York while she was still herself.

2

Wartime Within

Trains. These dragons in the night fascinated Sybil,
thrilled her and held her entranced. In the past they
had usually meant escape. This train, however, was
taking her not away from but toward. And she knew
that she had to get back to New York not because of
the chemistry lab and her other classes but because of
Dr. Wilbur.

Sybil tried to envision what had taken place in her
absence: the regular daily session with the doctor

missed, the doctor's possible attempts to search for her, and above all the doctor's disappointment upon surmising what had probably happened.

Then Sybil dismissed these disturbing thoughts. The mood of calm that had come over her since boarding the train was too pleasant to lose in idle speculation, remorse, self-recrimination.

Sybil Isabel Dorsett thought instead of the very first time she had seen Dr. Wilbur and of the events that surrounded that meeting. Unleashed was a flood of recollections so powerful that not until the train pulled into New York's Pennsylvania Station did it cease.

Sybil was twenty-two years old. Adrift in her feelings, she was living in despair with her parents—Willard and Henrietta "Hattie" Dorsett—that summer of 1945. Wartime without, it was for Sybil also wartime within. Hers was not a war of nerves in the customary sense but a war of nervousness in a special sense, for the nervous symptoms that had plagued her since childhood had become so bad at the midwestern teachers' college where she had been majoring in art that the college authorities had sent her home the previous June, saying that not until a psychiatrist deemed her fit could she return. Gwen Updyke, the college nurse, afraid to let her travel alone, had made the trip with her. But homecoming, which took Sybil from an unmanageable academic career to an even more unmanageable relationship with her parents, who were at once overprotective and unsympathetic, had served only to aggravate her symptoms. In August, 1945, Sybil was earnestly seeking a solution to a problem that had been a lifetime dilemma but that neither she nor anybody else understood.

In this state of mind Sybil had made her first trip to see Dr. Lynn Thompson Hall, her mother's doctor. That time it had been her mother who had been the sick one, with a swollen belly, and Sybil had come to the office as the daughter of the patient. But while talking to Dr. Hall about her mother, Sybil had experienced a fleeting wish that he would ask about her. She liked the tall, soft-spoken Dr. Hall, and she realized that what she liked most about him was that he treated her like an intelligent adult. The very realization, however, was disquieting. Being twenty-two entitled her to adult status. Having an IQ of 170, according to a standard intelligence test, should have earned her the right to be treated as if she were intelligent. Yet she never felt like an intelligent adult around her mother or even around her father. Her parents were forty when she was born; she had never known her mother without gray hair. She supposed that it was this Isaac-Jacob setting, with a generation gap spanning not one but two generations, coupled with her being an only child, that accounted for the fact that in the presence of her mother and father she remained a child. Somehow she had never been able to grow up in her parents' eyes.

Sybil wanted to reach out to Dr. Hall. During the first visit she wished he would ask her, "What is the matter with you? What can I do to help?" On the second visit, which took place three days later, the wish was even stronger and more insistent. But as her mother and she sat in the crowded waiting room hour after hour—because of the war doctors were scarce—she felt discouraged. It was unreasonable, she knew, for her to think that Dr. Hall would ask about her.

Her mother's turn finally came. Then the examination, during which, at her mother's insistence, Sybil was always present, was over. As her mother, Sybil, and the doctor were leaving the examining room, Dr. Hall took Sybil aside and said, "I'd like to see you in my office for a moment, Miss Dorsett." Her mother went to the dressing room as Sybil followed Dr. Hall into his office.

To Sybil's surprise, the doctor did not talk about her mother. Looking firmly at Sybil from his swivel chair, Dr. Hall said forthrightly: "Miss Dorsett, you look pale, thin. What's troubling you?" He waited an instant and added, "What can I do to help?"

Exactly what she had hoped would happen had happened, but she was anxious. Although she had wished for this opportunity, it was puzzling when it actually came. How could Dr. Hall have divined her plea? It was unreal that he should instinctively have tuned in to her unexpressed wish. That people regarded him as an astute physician, probably the best internist in Omaha, was not a sufficient explanation.

Suddenly realizing that this was no time for reflection since Dr. Hall, who had been straightforward with her, was waiting for her answer, she replied slowly, "Well, I don't have any great physical complaints, Doctor." She desperately wanted his help, but, afraid to tell him too much, she merely added, "I'm just nervous. I was so nervous at college that they sent me home until I could get well."

Dr. Hall was listening attentively, and Sybil sensed that he did really want to help her. Because of her overdeveloped capacity for self-effacement, however, and because of her longtime conviction that she wasn't important, she couldn't understand *why*.

"You're not at college now?" the doctor was asking. "Then what are you doing?"

"Teaching in a junior high school," she replied. Although she wasn't a college graduate, she was able to teach because of the wartime teacher shortage.

"I see," Dr. Hall said. "And this nervousness you speak about—what form does it take?"

The question terrified her. What form indeed? That was something about which she didn't want to talk. No matter how much Dr. Hall wanted to help her, no matter how much she wanted his help, she could not tell him this. She had never been able to share the information he was requesting with another human being. She *could not* share it, moreover, even if she wanted to. It was a sinister force that shrouded her life and made her different from other people, but it remained nameless even to her.

All Sybil said was, "I know I have to see a psychiatrist." That, she supposed, was a fair appraisal of the situation, but she studied Dr. Hall's face uneasily to see how he had reacted. He showed no surprise, and he seemed to make no judgment.

"I'll make an appointment for you," he said matter-of-factly, "and tell you the time when you come with your mother on Thursday."

"All right. Thank you, Doctor," Sybil replied.

The brief, stiff phrase of gratitude, with its conventional words, rang hollow. Those words, she knew, could not convey the impact of the powerful feelings that were overwhelming her. It was important for her to see a psychiatrist not only to secure relief from her nervousness, if indeed her condition was treatable, but also because her going back to college depended upon psychiatric help. She wanted desperately to return to school and knew that this was the only way she ever would.

Sybil said nothing of this to her parents, but on Thursday, in her mother's presence, Dr. Hall remarked, "Your appointment is with Dr. Wilbur for August 10 at 2:00 P.M. She's especially good with young people."

Sybil could feel her heart skipping, then throbbing. The excitement about seeing a psychiatrist was overshadowed, however, by the pronoun *she*. A woman? Had she heard correctly? All the doctors she had ever known were men.

"Yes," Dr. Hall was saying, "Dr. Wilbur has had a great deal of success with the patients I've sent her."

Sybil only half heard him because the initial terror of seeing in her mind a *woman* psychiatrist almost eradicated his words. But then suddenly the fear lifted. She had had a warm relationship with Miss Updyke, the college nurse, and she had had a devastating experience with a male neurologist in the Mayo Clinic. The neurologist had dismissed her case after a single visit, handing out an easy nostrum by telling her father that if she continued to write poetry, she would be all right.

Dr. Hall leaned forward to put his hand on her mother's arm as he said firmly, "And, Mother, you're not to go with her."

Sybil was startled—even shocked—by the tone that the doctor had taken with her mother and by her mother's apparent acquiescence. It had been a fact of Sybil's existence that her mother went with her everywhere, and she went with her mother. Never, even though she had tried, had Sybil been able to alter that fact. Her mother's omnipresence in her life had been almost a force of nature, as inevitable as the rise and setting of the sun. In a single sentence Dr. Hall had reversed the reality of a lifetime.

There was something else about that sentence that defied understanding, too. *Nobody*—not family, not friends, not even Sybil's father, and certainly not Sybil —had ever told her mother what to do. Her mother— the self-proclaimed "great Hattie Dorsett"—was a towering, unrelenting, and invincible figure. She didn't take orders; she gave them.

Leaving the office with her mother, Sybil fervently wished—irrationally perhaps but nonetheless powerfully —that the woman psychiatrist, whom she was soon to see, would not have white hair.

Precisely at 2:00 P.M. on August 10 Sybil entered the office of Dr. Cornelia B. Wilbur on the sixth floor of Omaha's Medical Arts Building, and the doctor's hair wasn't white. It was red, and the doctor was young, perhaps no more than ten years older than Sybil. Her eyes seemed kind—unmistakably, undeniably kind.

Still, churning within Sybil was the same set of op-posing feelings that she had experienced in Dr. Hall's office, the sense of relief that at last she was doing something about her nervousness but the terror that nothing could be done because hers was a unique, un-treatable condition.

Dr. Wilbur was patient as Sybil, trying to mask these contradictory feelings, rattled on about being terribly nervous and so shaky at college that she often had to leave the classroom.

"It was pretty bad at college," Sybil recalled. "Miss Updyke, the school nurse, was worried about me. The school doctor sent me to a Mayo Clinic neurologist. I saw the neurologist only once, but he assured me that I would be all right. But I kept getting worse. They sent me home and said that I should not come back until I was well enough."

Sybil found comfort in the doctor's smile.

"Well," Sybil continued, "I'm home now. It's dreadful, simply dreadful. I'm with my parents every minute. They don't let me out of their sight. They look at me with long faces. I know that they're ashamed that I was sent home from college. They were counting on my education and centered their hopes on it. But I'm going back when I'm well enough."

The doctor still hadn't said anything, so Sybil just went on talking. "I'm an only child," she said, "and my parents are very good to me."

Dr. Wilbur nodded as she lit a cigarette.

"They worry about me," Sybil continued. "Everyone worries about me—my friends, our pastor, everybody. I'm illustrating the pastor's lyceums on Daniel and Revelation. As he talks, I paint the beast about which he's talking. It's really very impressive. I'm suspended on a scaffold ten feet above the stage. I usually chalk on heavy drawing paper my interpretations of what the pastor says. He's keeping me busy. He . . ."

"How do *you* feel? Dr. Wilbur interrupted. "You've been telling me what everybody else thinks about you. But how do *you* feel?"

A compendium of physical complaints followed as Sybil talked of her poor appetite, of weighing only 79 pounds even though she was five-feet-five. The recital also included her chronic sinusitis and her poor eyesight, so poor that, as she put it, "I sometimes feel as if I'm looking through a tunnel." After a pause she added, "I'm not at all well, but I've been told I'm really healthy. Ever since I was a little girl, I've been sick but not sick."

Did she remember her dreams? the doctor wanted to know. No, she didn't remember them. As a little girl she had nightmares, which she didn't remember, either.

Sybil froze when the doctor tried to get her to talk about her feelings, but the doctor persisted. Finally Sybil had said enough for the doctor to be able to tell her: "You should come back. You have difficulties that can be worked on." Of that Dr. Wilbur was sure, but she also knew that it would not be easy to reach Sybil.

She was so naive, so unworldly, so immature. Too, she worked against herself, using a lot of words without saying much.

Sybil herself wished earnestly that she could come back, but standing in the outer office, paying the receptionist, she knew that she couldn't make another appointment without first talking it over with her parents. Still, she felt that, if she continued to work with the doctor, she would get well.

Had she told the doctor too much? Sybil wondered as the elevator went swiftly down the six floors of the Medical Arts Building. Quickly she reassured herself that what she didn't dare tell had not been told. Then, walking out of the building into the glare of the August sun, she realized that she would never be able to tell Dr. Wilbur all that she should and could about herself. All that she, Sybil Isabel Dorsett, knew—even then.

3

The Couch and the Serpent

Sybil made her second visit to Dr. Wilbur without incident. When the patient stepped out of the Medical Arts Building, however, she remembered that her mother was waiting in Brandeis department store on the adjacent block. Frustrated at being unable to accompany her daughter to the doctor's office, Hattie Dorsett had taken her as far as the elevators of the building in which the office was located.

"I'll wait for you in Brandeis," Hattie had said at the elevator door, making a promise of the statement, the old refrain of an enforced interdependency from which neither had been able, even if both had been willing—and certainly Hattie was not—to extricate herself. Now, as always, it was a strange case of "Wherever thou goest, I shall go."

Slowly, dutifully, Sybil walked into Brandeis department store, where, visible almost at once, were her mother's lean figure, proud carriage, white hair. At once, too, came her mother's "What did the doctor say about *me*?" Although it was a question, it had the ring of a demand.

"She didn't say anything," Sybil replied.

"Well, let's go," her mother said testily.

"I'd like to stop at the library," Sybil remarked.

"Oh, all right," her mother agreed. "I want a book myself."

At the library on Harney Street Sybil and her mother went to different shelves and then met at the checkout desk. Sybil was holding Sidney Howard's *The Silver Cord*.

"What's that?" her mother asked.

"It's a play," Sybil replied. "Dr. Wilbur suggested that I read it."

That evening, while Sybil prepared dinner and, later, did the dishes, her mother sat reading *The Silver Cord*. Her comment, when she finished, was: "I don't see why Dr. Wilbur asked you to read this. What has it got to do with *you*?"

Willard Dorsett, silent while his wife and daughter talked, was mulling a few questions of his own. He had reluctantly agreed to have Sybil enter treatment because ever since Sybil had been sent home from college, Willard had known that *something* had to be done. And although he was by no means certain that psychiatry was the answer, he was willing to give it a chance. But now, he wondered, was the decision correct?

The treatment, beginning on August 10, continued once a week throughout the summer and early fall of 1945. For all three Dorsetts it was a time of apprehension and watching.

Each time Sybil came home after seeing Dr. Wilbur her parents were waiting like vultures. "What did she say about us?" they asked separately and together. "And what else did she say?" Never did they ask, "How are you getting on?" or, "How did things go?" Nor was it ever what Sybil would have liked most of all: to have them say nothing. The treatment was painful enough in itself without this constant inquisition at home.

"You knock yourself down," the doctor told Sybil. "You don't think much of yourself. That's an uncomfortable feeling. So you project it on others and say, 'They don't like me.' "

Another theme was, "You're a genius and serious. *Too* serious. You need more social life."

Still another motif was: "When are you going to blow up?"

Dr. Wilbur advised: "Get away from home. Go to New York or Chicago, where you can meet people like yourself—people who are interested in art. Get away."

Sybil wished she could. The uneasiness she felt at home was being greatly intensified by the treatment.

The doctor's remark about Sybil's needing more social life, for instance, had really exasperated her mother.

"Well," her mother declared haughtily when Sybil told her about it, "what have I been saying all these years? What's wrong with my diagnosis? Why don't you spend all that money on letting me tell you what's wrong?"

Sybil's parents, dissecting what the doctor said, also criticized the doctor herself. She smoked, and no good woman did that—no good man, for that matter. She didn't go to any church, let alone a church of their fundamentalist faith. In short, they didn't trust the doctor, and they said that they didn't. The trouble was that having always had the upper hand with their daughter, they expected also to have it now. Her mother, who saw everything in terms of black and white, simply dismissed Dr. Wilbur as being wrong. Nobody, doctor or not, who did the things of which Hattie Dorsett disapproved, according to Hattie's precepts, could be right in *anything*.

Her mother's attitude toward Dr. Wilbur didn't surprise Sybil but her father's did. Sybil had thought him objective enough to be able to listen to reason, to be able to concede that Dr. Wilbur could be a good doctor even if he disapproved of her personally. Yet Sybil rapidly came to realize that her father could not overcome his resistance to everything Dr. Wilbur said or advised because her lifestyle was different from his. The doctor belonged to another world, and for Willard Dorsett, as for his wife, Dr. Wilbur would remain an outsider.

"Dr. Wilbur doesn't really care about you," Sybil's mother repeatedly warned. "She tells you one thing now. But when she gets you where she wants you, she'll tell you altogether different things. And remember, young lady, she'll turn on you if you tell her you don't love your own mother."

Sybil would assure her mother that she would never tell the doctor that because it wasn't true. "I do love you, Mother, I do," Sybil affirmed again and again.

The whole situation was awful all the time. Sybil desperately wanted to get well, and the scenes at home did not help at all. Yet there was no way out. If her talking led to a scene, so too did her silence. When Sybil did not talk, her parents would accuse her of being moody, and although they had upbraided her with this characteristic many times in the past, they now claimed that Dr. Wilbur was responsible for the moodiness. "She'll make you crazy," her mother warned, "and then they'll put you in an institution because that's the way doctors make their money."

In contrast, outsiders, people who knew she was seeing the doctor and people who didn't, talked of a marked improvement in Sybil. But when people said these things, her mother scoffed, and her father only partly listened. Sybil felt that he might have understood if his wife hadn't brainwashed him with her "She's better because she's growing up, and everybody gets more sense when they grow older and understand things better." Sybil was twenty-two, but her mother talked of that period of her life as a time not of maturity but of first growing up.

At least, the brainwashing had no effect upon Sybil

herself. As the weekly one-hour sessions with the doctor in Omaha continued through September, Sybil became more and more convinced that Dr. Wilbur would help her to get well. But she was still very puzzled by herself.

Sybil had not told the doctor about what puzzled her—some terrible, nameless thing having to do with time and memory. There had been times, for instance, during the last summer and early autumn, when Sybil had gone to the doctor's office without, later, having any clear recollection of what had transpired. There were times when she remembered entering the elevator, but not the office; other times when she remembered coming into the office, but not leaving it. Those were the times when Sybil could not tell her parents what the doctor had said about them or about anything else. Sybil had not known whether she had even seen the doctor.

One time in particular stood out in memory. A paradox, a joke: remembering what you didn't remember.

Sybil heard herself saying, "It wasn't as bad as usual."

"How do you know?" the doctor asked.

"I would have been out in the hall or something by now," Sybil replied.

"Well," said the doctor, "you almost jumped out of the window. You jumped out of the chair and rushed to the window. I couldn't stop you."

Sybil didn't remember doing anything of the sort, but she hadn't argued the point. All her life people had said that she had done things she hadn't done. She let it go in Dr. Wilbur's office, as she always had.

"I wasn't really disturbed," the doctor explained. "You can't get out of these windows. It's because of the kind of glass. Unbreakable, you know."

Then Dr. Wilbur became more serious. "You had what looked like a little seizure," she said. "It wasn't epilepsy; it was a psychological seizure."

Psychological? The doctor was saying that Sybil was nervous. That was old—not new. What was new, however, was that the doctor didn't seem to blame her. In the past, when these things had happened, she had always blamed herself. Nobody else knew about them, but she had been certain that anybody who had known would have found her guilty of inexcusable behavior.

Nor did Dr. Wilbur seem to think that her condition was hopeless, as she herself had often feared. The doctor presented her with three choices for the immediate future: to teach at the junior high school for another year; to go back to college; or to undergo intensified treatment at the Bishop Clarkson Memorial Hospital, where the doctor and a colleague ran a psychiatric division.

Sybil chose the hospital. But when she told her parents, they were distressed, even terrified. To them hospitalization meant only one thing: their daughter was insane.

"This has nothing to do with insanity," Sybil tried to explain. "Dr. Wilbur told me it didn't."

"Then it has to do with the devil," her father replied ominously.

"Clarkson, Parkson," her mother rhymed. "Park son, park daughter."

Even though the hospital seemed the road to damnation, Willard Dorsett agreed to talk it over with Dr. Wilbur, choosing to meet her not at her office at the Medical Arts Building but at Clarkson.

Outside the hospital Hattie and Sybil sat in the car —the mother biting her fingernails, the daughter grinding her teeth. Inside, Dr. Wilbur managed to dispel Willard Dorsett's visions of his daughter's being locked in and restrained, of her undergoing a lobotomy, of her getting worse because of contact with other patients more disturbed than she, and of her getting well enough to go home only to relapse and return to the hospital. He had envisioned hospitalization as an endless, unremitting cycle of *in* and *out, out* and *in*.

Dispelled, too, was the deepest of all her father's fears: that his daughter would be given drugs. "No," Dr. Wilbur assured him, "we wouldn't do that."

Finally, then, although Willard Dorsett had an uneasy feeling about the psychiatric course on which his daughter had embarked, he did give his consent for her hospitalization at Clarkson.

Clarkson, as Dr. Wilbur saw it, was to be only a temporary measure. What Sybil needed ultimately, the doctor felt, was psychoanalysis. "You are the sort of person who should be psychoanalyzed," she told her patient. "I would like to do the job myself, but I'm not an analyst yet. In fact, I shall be leaving Omaha shortly to begin my analytic training. I suggest that after you leave Clarkson you go to Chicago to be analyzed."

The prospect thrilled Sybil. Chicago meant not only moving closer to the truth about herself but also getting away from home. Psychoanalysis, however, posed a problem for Willard and Hattie Dorsett. They had agreed to the psychiatric treatment, even to plans for hospitalization, but psychoanalysis was a different matter.

The couch and the serpent. The parents feared that the strange world of the psychoanalyst's couch might be antithetical to their most deeply held religious convictions, would probably exclude God from the picture. Their religion, to which Sybil's father had been born and which her mother, originally a Methodist, had embraced some years after her marriage, taught that each individual has the privilege of choosing between God and the devil, between God and the Lucifer of the prophecies, between God and the serpent of the Scriptures. The devil, the religion taught, could exert control. Everyone, the Dorsetts believed, has the privilege of choosing between God and the devil; God, assuming full responsibility for the actions of those who chose Him, could carry all who choose rightly to Paradise. Conversely, their religion posited, those who choose the devil will travel a different road.

Fearing to commit his daughter and, through her, himself, to the devil, Willard Dorsett could not give Sybil an answer when she pleaded with him to permit her to go to Chicago for psychoanalysis.

"I don't know," he told her. "I'll have to talk it over with Pastor Weber."

The pastor, decisive in most things, shared Willard

49

Dorsett's doubts of the benefits of psychoanalysis. The two men were very close, and, impressed with Dorsett's talents as a builder-contractor, the pastor had engaged him to build churches for the denomination. As they talked in the half-built church on which Dorsett was working, the pastor was noncommittal. "I don't know, Brother Dorsett. I just don't know," he repeated several times.

After a silence Dorsett himself remarked, "I would be more comfortable if the Chicago psychoanalyst were of our own faith. I'm afraid that a doctor outside our faith will use drugs, hypnosis, and other techniques to which I am opposed."

Pacing the floor of the church, the pastor was thoughtful and perplexed. When he finally spoke, it was only to say, "You'll just have to decide for yourself, Brother Dorsett. I'd like to help you, but frankly I don't know what to advise."

This time it was Dorsett who paced. He replied apprehensively, "If God isn't part of the therapy, they'll have a hard time leading me into this channel."

"Yes," the pastor concurred, "it's like leading a mule in Missouri into a new barn. You have to blindfold him first." After a long pause he added, "I believe in freedom of thought, of conscience and conviction. Brother Dorsett, you know I can be very persuasive, even overpowering. But the only form of persuasion I've ever used is just talking to people. I've never used force in my life. And I'm not at all sure that psychoanalysis doesn't involve the use of force. But I'm not opposing Sybil's going to Chicago. The decision is not mine to make but yours and hers."

Willard Dorsett reported to Sybil his conversation with the pastor, and, finding that there was no more effective defense against his own fears than to displace them, he did leave the decision to her. "I still want to go to Chicago," was Sybil's fixed and unflinching answer.

At church the following Sabbath Sybil talked briefly with the pastor. She stared at his black suit and studied his penetrating brown eyes. It was a study in darkness, the visible symbols of the fears that had been expressed. Feeling her gaze, the pastor said gently, "Your father and I are only looking at this from our own point of view. We have to admit that there is another. If this is what you really want, we shouldn't stand in your way."

Sybil's decision remained unchanged. While waiting for a bed at Clarkson and for word from Chicago, she saw the immediate future as a stepped-up assault on the "terrible thing" that had enshrouded her life. There was comfort in having taken the first affirmative action after long years of vacillation and temporizing on the parts both of her parents and of herself. The decisiveness that she had been unable to show when she was younger she felt able to exert at last.

Suddenly everything changed. The instrument, though not the cause, was the pneumonia that she contracted as a concomitant of a strep throat. Her head ached terribly; her throat was raw; and although she tried to get out of bed to call Dr. Wilbur to cancel her October 6 appointment, dizziness and weakness intervened. Sybil asked her mother to telephone Dr. Wilbur.

Sybil heard Hattie Dorsett give Dr. Wilbur's number to the operator, announce herself to the doctor's secretary, and then talk to the doctor herself. "Yes, this is Mrs. Dorsett, Sybil's mother," Hattie spoke into the phone. "Sybil is ill and can't keep her appointment with you on October 6. Yes, everybody seems to have these bad throats, but she also has pneumonia. Anyway she asked me to call you. Thank you."

With a click her mother hung up.

"What did the doctor say?" Sybil asked. "What did she say?"

"She didn't say anything," her mother replied.

"Nothing about another appointment? Nothing about the hospital?"

"Nothing."

The train had reached Trenton and still Sybil's reverie continued. The echo of her mother's voice could not be stilled. What she said in Omaha she seemed also to be saying now. Her words, as distinct as if she were

51

in the seat next to Sybil, had their old cacophonous ring. The train moved on toward New York as the memories came, unbidden, propelled by what Sybil supposed was their own logic. The doctor had started all this, the doctor to whom she was returning.

Learning that Dr. Wilbur had said nothing about another appointment, Sybil quickly dismissed the feeling of disappointment with the reassuring thought that probably the doctor had assumed that, when she was well enough, she would call. However, when, fully recovered, she did call, she was told that Dr. Wilbur had left Omaha permanently. A feeling of rejection was natural.

After all the bitter battles at home, after the agonies involved in persuading her parents to let her go into treatment and then to agree to hospitalization at Clarkson, the road to getting well had been ripped from under her. The bravest of the emotionally vulnerable, she felt, could not sustain this blow.

She walked away from the telephone and sat limply on the bed. She thought of how her mother would scoff and her father would become silently critical. She thought about Dr. Wilbur and about how puzzling—incomprehensible—it was that she should have left town without a parting caution, without so much as a swift backward glance in her direction. Had she offended the doctor? Had the doctor thought that she had not really been ill and thus had deliberately called a halt to the treatment? Certainly these were possibilities.

What now? A letter from Chicago, stating that the analyst was booked for two years and wasn't accepting new patients, had ruled out analysis. The loss of Dr. Wilbur had ruled out Clarkson and the continuation of treatment. Then, in the stillness of her room, Sybil faced the fact that somehow she would have to manage to carry on alone. She even persuaded herself that, with Dr. Wilbur's departure and the cancellation of her Chicago plans, she would be freer to do as she wished. And what she wished most of all was to return to college.

Was she well enough? She wasn't certain, but she

52

realized that the treatment by Dr. Wilbur might serve as the means of readmission. After all, she *had* seen a psychiatrist.

She wrote to Miss Updyke about her desire to return, and Miss Updyke promised to use her influence to make the return possible. In the meantime Sybil continued teaching at the junior high school and painting. Her painting *City Streets* and a pencil piece were exhibited at an Omaha art gallery. But the nameless thing still pursued her. When a day came that she felt free of it, she recorded that day in her diary with the euphemism: "All went well today." In January, 1947, Sybil returned to the campus.

During the first week Miss Updyke was curious to know how things really were, and when Sybil told her that she was able to sit through classes without the inner disturbances that in the past had made it necessary for her to leave, Miss Updyke seemed very pleased. "She could see," Sybil wrote in her diary of January 7, 1947, "I'm well more nearly." On January 8, 1947, Sybil, referring to the nameless thing, recorded in the diary: "Am so proud—most thankful I could talk with Miss Updyke as I did yesterday and stay on a level. No inclinations ever. The one thing I desired for so long. God has heard my pleas surely."

The nameless thing, the "inclinations" that kept her from staying on a level, however, had *not* been put to rest. Her diary, virtually infallible as a clue to the presence or absence of the "inclinations" because when Sybil was in command of the situation, she never failed to make an entry, shows clearly that there were unrecorded days even in this period, when she thought herself "well more nearly." In fact, for January 9, the day after the splurge of optimism, there was no entry. Good days were often followed by bad days.

There were enough good days for Sybil to complete almost three years of college and to move triumphantly into the second semester of her senior year. But then in 1948, shortly before the end of her last semester, Sybil received a telephone call from her father summoning her to Kansas City, where her parents were then living.

Her mother was dying of cancer of the spleen, and she insisted upon having no other nurse than Sybil. "If this is what your mother wants," Willard Dorsett told his daughter, "this is what she will have."

Sybil did not know what to expect when she arrived in Kansas City. Old fears reasserted themselves. But Hattie Dorsett had never been as calm and as rational as she was in Kansas City. Paradoxically, in this period of crisis mother and daughter got along better than they ever had before.

The very calm became an ironic background for the events of what started out as an ordinary evening. Hattie Dorsett, relatively free from pain, was sitting in the big red easy chair in the living room of the Dorsett's home. She was reading *Ladies Home Journal* by the light of a small table lamp. Sybil came in with her supper tray. Then, seemingly apropos of nothing, Hattie Dorsett remarked, "I never made it."

"Made what?" Sybil asked softly, thinking that her mother was voicing some retrospective regret, some unfinished business that haunted her.

"I never made that call," Hattie Dorsett said.

"What call, Mother?"

"That call to Dr. Wilbur," her mother explained.

"You did," Sybil insisted. "Don't you remember? I heard your conversation. Every word of it."

Hattie Dorsett was composed as she replied, "Well, I held my finger on the button. I never made it. I never made that phone call."

Never had this possibility occurred to Sybil. It was inconceivable that her mother would have so determinedly blocked the route to her good health, inconceivable that her mother would have condemned her to the uncertainty and doubt about the doctor with which she had lived since October, 1945—almost three years ago.

A little insight here, a slight revelation there, picked up during the all-too-brief treatment, had been enough to maintain the inner balance that made it possible for Sybil to go back to college. That nameless thing that Dr. Wilbur had glimpsed the day her patient headed for the window had continued in Omaha, at college, and in Kansas City. And it had been her *mother,* nursing her bizarre secret, who, by preventing the continuation of treatment, had deliberately shaped her daughter's destiny.

The horror, the pain, the sadness of it! Yet there were no recriminations. Nobody ever criticized Hattie Dorsett. There was no flare-up of anger against her. Anger was evil.

Hattie ate her supper. Sybil took the tray back to the kitchen. Neither mother nor daughter ever again mentioned to each other that phone call or Dr. Wilbur.

The revelation about the phone call, however, completely changed Sybil's attitude toward the doctor. It seemed obvious that, not knowing that Sybil had been ill, the doctor had simply thought that she had fled from treatment without even having the grace to say she was not coming back. No wonder the doctor had left Omaha without calling her. It was not Sybil Dorsett but Dr. Cornelia Wilbur who had a right to be deeply disappointed.

Before hearing about the unmade phone call Sybil had deliberately ejected Dr. Wilbur from her thoughts. Now, however, the doctor loomed large again, and Sybil felt a sudden surge of hope. Returned to her was the glorious dream of getting wholly well, of picking up where she had left off with Dr. Wilbur. But this time the serpent must not be allowed to intervene. The dream would have to be delayed until Sybil, wholly on her own, could afford to pay for her own treatment.

Dr. Wilbur, Sybil learned from a directory of psychiatrists, was now a psychoanalyst in New York. And it was to New York that Sybil was determined to go.

Never, through the six years—from 1948 to 1954— that intervened between the decision and its execution, did Sybil breathe this dream to anyone. Her intention was one thing more she had to keep to herself.

In July, 1948, Hattie Dorsett died and was buried in a Kansas City cemetery. For the next two months Sybil kept house for her father, and in September she returned to college. She was graduated with a bachelor's degree in June, 1949, and it took the intercession of one of her professors to convince her father, who was with Pastor Weber in Denver, Colorado, to attend the commencement exercises. At one o'clock on commencement day Sybil left with her father for Denver.

For the next few years she lived with her father, taught school, and worked as an occupational therapist. Willard Dorsett's building schedule kept him constantly moving, and she went with him. However, by the summer of 1954 she had saved enough money to go to New York to get a master's degree at Columbia University and to resume treatment with Dr. Wilbur. Her father, told only that his daughter was going to New York to study, drove her there.

Sybil arrived in New York on Labor Day, 1954, but she waited until October before calling Dr. Wilbur, fearful both that the doctor would reject her and that she would accept her.

Rejection was plausible because of the seemingly cavalier way in which Sybil had closed the door on treatment, but it was more likely—and this hurt even more—that the doctor wouldn't remember her. The envisioned rejection was compounded by the fact that Sybil, who felt guilty for unjustly blaming Dr. Wilbur for failing to call Sybil before leaving Omaha, neatly converted that feeling of guilt into additional feelings of rejection.

Acceptance held a different kind of terror. If she were accepted, Sybil knew that she would have to tell the doctor about the end-of-the-rope feeling she had experienced toward the end of her three years in Detroit, her last residence before coming to New York. While she was teaching, she had seemed to be all right, although there were times in the classroom that she couldn't remember. The moment she left the classroom, however—it was too horrible to recall—strange, incomprehensible things had happened to her. These things were not new, had in fact occurred since she was three and a half and had filtered into awareness at fourteen. But in Detroit they had become not only more frequent but also more menacing. She was no longer able to endure the terrible burden of the secret she didn't dare tell, of the answers she had to improvise to implement the pretense of normality.

People she had never seen before would insist that they knew her. She would go to a picnic and have a vague sense of having been there before. A dress that she had not bought would be hanging in her closet. She would begin a painting and return to the studio to find that it had been completed by someone else—in a style not hers. Sleep was a nightmare. She just couldn't be sure about sleep. Often it seemed as if she were sleeping by day as well as by night. Often, too, there was no dividing line between the time of going to bed at night and waking up in the morning. Many were the occasions of waking up without going to sleep, of going to sleep to wake up not the next morning, but at some unrecognizable time.

If Dr. Wilbur accepted her, these things and many others like them would come up. This time, she promised herself, fearful or not, she would tell the doctor about them. Not telling was like informing a doctor that you had a head cold when you really had cancer.

Yet Sybil, not certain that she *could* bring herself to tell and knowing that if she didn't, the treatment would be devoid of reality, wondered whether resuming treatment was the right decision. She vacillated for six weeks before taking the plunge.

On the train the past faded. Suddenly it was the present that became compelling as Sybil faced the reason for her precipitous flight from Philadelphia. Each time one of these incidents occurred, and they had been occurring since she was three and a half, it was as if it were happening for the first time. Ever since she had, at fourteen, become aware of her situation, she had told herself each time that she would begin all over again and that it couldn't happen again. In Detroit the episodes had been overwhelmingly numerous, and yet, even then, she had braced herself to dismiss each one as the last.

This time, however, the illusion of the first time assumed even greater terror than it usually did because of the deep disappointment she felt this January, 1958 —three and a half years since her analysis had begun —that an episode like that in Philadelphia should occur.

The train chugged into New York's Penn Station. Sybil clutched her zipper folder, left the train, hurried into a taxi, and finally felt relieved of the nagging apprehension, of the insistent remorse at what had happened in Philadelphia. By the time the taxi turned into Morningside Drive and approached the brownstone where in September, 1955, she had taken a second-floor apartment with Teddy Reeves, she felt secure and at ease—tranquilized by her wish not to remember.

Teddy would still be with her family in Oklahoma. Sybil walked up the two flights of stairs, knowing but not caring that there would be no one to greet her.

As the apartment door swung open, the tranquility dissolved. Capri, thin and wide-eyed, croaked a pathetic, hoarse greeting. The cat's was the sound of accusation, the same accusation the pajamas had presented in the Broadwood Hotel room. Sybil had abandoned Capri by leaving her without water or food. Capri was her only real companion, really all she had. Sybil would not consciously neglect any animal, least of all her precious Capri. But she had. She'd abandoned the animal she loved as she herself had been abandoned repeatedly in the past by people who had claimed to love her.

4

The Other Girl

Sybil lay restless and wakeful, knowing that in the morning she would have to tell the doctor what she had done. It was going to be even harder than she had thought. She found herself thinking instead of the first time she had seen the doctor in New York.

Expectant, eager, anxious, Sybil had been awake that October 18, 1954, in the sunless moments before dawn. Her eyes darted around the small Whittier Hall dormitory room at shapes indistinct in the semidarkness. On the back of her desk chair was her navy blue gabardine suit. On the dresser were her navy blue leather purse, her navy blue silk gloves, and her navy blue hat with a small navy blue veil. Standing at attention under the chair were her navy blue leather pumps with their medium heels. Her gray stockings were tucked into the shoes. The ensemble had been painstakingly assembled the night before.

As the shapes became visible in the gathering light, the sense of strangeness dissolved. She found herself thinking about what she would say to Dr. Wilbur. This time she would have to tell the doctor everything.

Sybil stretched for a moment, facing the window and the dawn. She dressed slowly, meticulously. As she hooked her tiny bra, she realized that her hands were trembling, and to steady herself she sat down on the bed. Up again within seconds she stepped gingerly into her suit. Putting on her hat with almost mechanical precision, she could feel that it looked right without even looking in a mirror. Navy blue was very much in vogue, and the little veil gave an added fillip to the matching costume.

Sybil went to the window. The trees in the Whittier Hall courtyard were leafless with autumn's pillage. She faced the sun. Blinded momentarily, she walked away from the window. It was only six-thirty, not yet time to go. Her appointment with the doctor wasn't until nine.

Time. She could never be sure about time. The earlier she left the dorm, the better. She put on her gloves.

The world seemed not yet quite awake as she descended the front steps of Whittier Hall and headed across Amsterdam Avenue for Hartley's drugstore, on the southeast corner.

The drugstore was deserted except for a cashier and one counterman. Marking time until mankind would rouse itself, the cashier was treating her nails with an emery board; the counterman, in his white coat, was stacking dishes behind his marble slab.

Sitting at the counter, Sybil ordered a danish and a large glass of milk, removed her gloves, and played with them nervously. As she dawdled over her food, she realized that she was deliberately killing time. The phrase *killing time* made her wince.

Leaving Hartley's at 7:30, she waited briefly for an Amsterdam Avenue bus; then she decided against it. Buses confused her, and this morning she wanted her mind to be clear.

Passing Schermerhorn and the rotund St. Paul's Chapel, she scarcely recognized them. Not until she reached 116th Street did the area look like the Columbia University she had come to know. Through the heavy gates at 116th Street she could see in the distance Low Library, with its mixed architecture, its Ionic columns, and the proud yet somehow pathetic statue of Alma Mater on its front steps. She noted the striking resemblance between Low and the smaller Pantheon in Rome.

The Cathedral Church of St. John the Divine at 113th Street intrigued her. She lingered in front of it for a full ten minutes, examining its Gothic architecture and reflecting that it seemed to be a perpetual work in progress. Well, *she* couldn't walk perpetually. She waited for a taxi, but none appeared until 8:15.

The cab driver, in his Brooklyn accent, offered Sybil the *New York Times*. She took it gratefully and found comfort in it as her nerves, frayed by the taxi's slow motion in rush hour traffic, warned her that, while her mind was racing too swiftly to her destination, she might be late for her appointment despite her early start. No banner headline this October 18, 1954. No front page mention of President Eisenhower or of Senator Joe McCarthy, who usually made goggle-eyed headlines. Captions, neat and subdued, proclaimed: MACMILLAN HEADS BRITAIN'S DEFENSE IN CABINET SHIFT; STRIKES ON DOCKS OF BRITAIN SPREAD; 40 COLLEGES JOIN U.S. TECHNICAL AID TO 26 COUNTRIES; DEMOCRATS AHEAD IN HOUSE BATTLES; TRUCKERS SUE FOR STRIKE LOSSES PUT AT $10,000,000. The unwritten caption, running like a refrain through all the others, was: WILL THE DOCTOR REMEMBER ME?

The taxi came to a sudden halt. "Have a good day," said the driver as Sybil paid him. A good day? She wondered. She walked thoughtfully through the front door of the buff-colored building on Park Avenue and 76th Street, where Dr. Wilbur lived and had her office. At 8:55 she stood in the private foyer leading to Apartment 4D.

The door stood open so that patients could enter without ringing. Sybil found herself in a small, dimly lighted waiting room with a tiny wall table, a small brass lamp, and photographs in pale wood frames. Should she sit down? Dr. Wilbur came into the room. "Come in, Miss Dorsett," she said.

They went into a sunny consulting room, each remembering the last time they had met, in Omaha almost ten years before.

She's changed, Sybil thought. Her hair is brighter than I remembered it. And she seems more feminine.

61

But her eyes, her smile, and the way she nods her head are the same.

At the same time Dr. Wilbur was thinking: she's as slender, as fragile, as ever. Looks no older. I'd know that face anywhere: the heart shape, the tilted nose, the small rosebud mouth. It's a face you don't see on the streets of New York. It's an English face, and despite the slight pitting of the skin, it has the fresh, unadorned look of an Englishwoman.

The doctor didn't ask Sybil to sit down, but her manner indicated it. Where? The green couch, with a small triangular pillow at the end, on which patients evidently rested their troubled heads, wasn't inviting. It seemed even less so because of the upholstered chair that looked down on the triangular pillow and was the visible symbol of the psychiatrist's "third" ear.

Dismissing the couch, Sybil counted the rose rings in the broadloom rug as she walked across it with slow, strained movements to the desk and chair on the opposite side of the room. She stopped. Beckoning to her from the top bookshelf on a greenish-gray wall were a black pen with a gold band, set in a gold holder on an onyx base, a small green pencil holder, and a green vase with a motif of green leaves. In the vase were assorted green plants and pussy willows. She was glad the doctor didn't have artificial flowers.

Blocked, Sybil gingerly withdrew a small mahogany desk chair from the knee hole of the desk and perched stiffly on its edge. The account she gave of herself was brief, factual, devoid of emotion. It was as if she were giving a résumé in an employment office, not talking to the doctor to whom she had returned as the result of strong intention and after great striving. Such items as her graduation from college, her teaching, her work in art therapy, the exhibits of her painting, her not having been analyzed, as Dr. Wilbur had suggested in Omaha, and even her mother's death, mentioned without feeling, filled the frozen hour.

The deep freeze continued as Sybil introduced the subject of Stanley MacNamara, an English teacher with whom she had taught in Detroit, just before coming to

New York. Although their relationship had developed to the extent that Stan had asked Sybil to marry him, she talked of him coolly, as a social worker might. Skirting her actual relationship with him, avoiding any mention of intimacies or her own feelings, she reported only that he was part Irish, part Jewish, that his father had deserted his mother, and that his mother later had abandoned Stan. The "report" also included the observation that Stan had been raised in an orphanage, had worked his way through college, and had made his own way.

For her part, Dr. Wilbur was more interested in what Sybil did not say about Stan than in what Sybil did say. But the doctor didn't press. The hour was almost over, and she asked only: "Just what do you want from me?"

"I want to work in occupational therapy," Sybil replied.

"I think you already have."

"And I think I want to marry Stan. But I'm not sure."

When the doctor asked whether her patient wanted to see her again, Sybil shamefacedly lowered her head, peeked from under her eyelids, and remarked diffidently, "I would like to come back to you for analysis."

Dr. Wilbur was pleased. Sybil Dorsett would be an interesting analytical subject—bright, competent, talented, but also aloof, remote, and afraid. The fact that the pupils of her eyes—dilated as a result of anxiety— were the size of the irises themselves had not escaped the doctor.

In the weeks that followed, the analysis became so pivotal in Sybil's life that she almost literally lived for her Tuesday morning appointments with Dr. Wilbur. Getting ready for the appointments, Sybil would make a ritual of deciding whether to wear the gray suit with the rose sweater, the navy suit with the twin blue sweaters, or the gray skirt with the aqua sweater. At the same time Sybil indulged in the ritual of making frequent pilgrimages to Schermerhorn, the university's psychology library, where she steeped herself in psychiatric literature, especially case histories. She read about symptoms, but not strictly out of intellectual curiosity. The more she knew about symptoms in other patients, the more adept she would become, she believed, at concealing her own. In seemingly no time it had become her fixed purpose to keep hidden what she had come to New York to reveal.

Sometimes a patient gives one a glimpse even on the first visit. This one, the doctor thought ruefully, even after almost two months, buries herself, presents only the outer rim of the surface. On that outer rim sat Dr. Klinger, Sybil's art teacher, with whom she had differences of opinion. There, too, sat Stan, whom she thought of marrying but who in analysis had emerged wooden, a stick figure. But it was only through patient probing that the doctor finally uncovered the fact that he had made clear—or rather unclear in vague, oblique phrases—he was proposing a sexless marriage. *Platonic* was the word Sybil had used.

Why, the doctor wondered, should an intelligent woman allow herself to become involved with a man who apparently had no sexual responses, an abandoned child who had never known and could not give love? What could account for a libido so markedly low that it would countenance such a relationship?

Libido down, reserve up. At first the doctor had attributed the reserve to Sybil's strict upbringing. But that could not account for the aloofness masking the terror in her eyes. "She's fooling around," the doctor thought. "She isn't being candid with me."

On December 13 Sybil did finally strike a new note: "I'm concerned about Christmas vacation."

"Why?"

"Vacations bother me."

"In what way?"

"There's so much to do. I don't know what to do first, then I don't do anything. I get mixed up or something. I can't describe it."

"Why don't you come three times a week during the holidays?" the doctor suggested. "That way we can get more said and ease the tension."

Sybil agreed.

And it was on December 21, 1954—when the analysis was just three months old—in an hour that began innocuously enough with Sybil's saying, "I want you to see the letter I received from Stan this morning," Dr. Wilbur came measurably closer to the truth about Sybil Isabel Dorsett.

Sybil seemed calm that morning and talked of Stan's letter with her customary lack of emotion. But when she opened her purse, she became suddenly flustered. She saw that only half of the letter was there, a half with a zigzag edge.

She hadn't torn it. Who had?

She ransacked her purse in search of the missing half. It was not there.

She shuffled the other two letters she had received that morning in her lap. They were intact, exactly where she remembered having put them. But she also remembered having put Stan's letter—it had been whole then—with them. Now the missing half of his letter was not even to be found. Who had removed it? When? Where had she been when it happened? She had no memory of the moment.

It had happened again—this terrible thing that happened to time. It had followed her here, to the haven of the doctor's office, this black shadow that followed her everywhere.

Gingerly, stealthily, in an effort to conceal what had happened from the doctor, who was sitting away from her on the chair at the head of the couch, Sybil slipped the mutilated letter behind the other two. But the doctor was asking, "Do you want me to see the letter?"

Sybil started to stammer . . . and the stammer dissolved into something else.

The prim, gentle midwestern schoolteacher, her face contorted with fear and fury, jumped up from the desk chair, and, moving so fast that she seemed to do everything at once, ripped up the letters that had been in her lap and threw their remains in the wastebasket. Then, clenching her fists, she stood in the middle of the room, ranting, "Men are all alike. You jist can't trust 'em. You really can't."

She headed with rapid, spiderlike movements toward two long casement windows. Swinging the green draperies aside, she clenched her left fist again and pounded with it at a small windowpane. "Let me out," she screamed. "Let me out!" It was an agonized plea—the call of the haunted, the hunted, the trapped.

Dr. Wilbur moved swiftly but not swiftly enough. Before she could reach her patient, there was a crash. The pounding fist had gone through the windowpane.

"Let me see your hand," the doctor insisted as she grasped the wrist. Her patient shrank from her touch. "I only want to see if you cut yourself," the doctor explained gently.

This time the patient stood absolutely still, her eyes wide with wonder as she looked at Dr. Wilbur for the first time since jumping up from the chair. In a plaintive "little-girl" voice, a voice quite different from the one that had denounced men, the patient asked: "You're not mad about the window?"

"Of course not," the doctor replied.

"I'm more important than the window?" The tone was one of curious disbelief.

"Of course, you are," the doctor remarked reassuringly. "Anybody can fix a windowpane. I'll call the handyman. He'll do it."

Suddenly the patient seemed more relaxed. This time, when the doctor took her hand, she offered no resistance. "Come. Let's sit on the couch," the doctor suggested. "I want to have a good look at your hand. Let me see if it's bruised."

They turned away from the window and walked toward the couch, past the purse, which had fallen on the rug when the patient had jumped up, past assorted papers, drawing pencils, the outpourings of fury that had belched forth from the fallen purse. But now the fear and fury were gone.

Sybil had always maintained a safe distance from the doctor by sitting at the desk. This time, however, Sybil sat right up beside the doctor and let her hand linger in the doctor's even after the latter had declared: "No cut. No bruise."

But once again there was a shift of mood.

"There's blood," the patient said.

"No blood," replied the doctor. "You didn't cut yourself."

"Blood in the hayloft," the patient explained. "Tommy Ewald was killed. I was there."

"You were there?" the doctor echoed.

"Yes, I was. I was, too."

"Where was the hayloft?"

"In Willow Corners."

"Did you live in Willow Corners?"

"I live there," came the correction. "Jist everybody knows I live in Willow Corners."

Jist. Sybil didn't talk that way. But, then, the Sybil the doctor knew didn't do any of the things that had been done since the patient jumped up from the chair. Gradually, as Sybil continued to relive what had transpired in the hayloft, the doctor was overtaken by an uncanny, eerie feeling.

Since the patient had jumped up from the chair, the feeling had been there—muted yet insistent, like the traffic noises that trickled into the room through the broken windowpane. The more Sybil talked, the more insistent the feeling became.

"My friend Rachel was sittin' with me in the hayloft," Sybil was saying. "And some other children. Tommy said, 'Let's jump down into the barn.' We jumped. One of the kids hit the cash register. There was a gun there. The gun went off. I went back, and Tommy was lyin' there, dead, a bullet through his heart. The other children ran away. Not Rachel and me. She went for Dr. Quinoness. I stayed with Tommy. Dr. Quinoness came and told us to go home. We didn't go. We helped him remove the gun and put a blanket over Tommy. Tommy was only ten years old."

"You were two brave little girls," Dr. Wilbur said.

"I know Tommy's dead," the childlike voice continued. "I understand. I do. I stayed because I didn't think it right to leave Tommy lyin' there dead."

"Tell me," the doctor asked, "where are you now?"

"There's blood," was the reply. "I see blood. Blood and death. I know what death is. I do."

"Don't think about the blood," the doctor said. "It makes you sad."

"You care how I feel?" Again there was the look of curious disbelief.

"I care very much," the doctor replied.

"You're not jist tryin' to trick me?"

"Why should I?"

"Lots of people trick me."

The sense of being tricked. The anger. The terror. The feeling of entrapment. The profound distrust of people. The wistful, plaintive conviction that a window, a thing, was more important than she. These feelings and attitudes, expressed in the course of this hour, were symptoms of some profound disturbance. And all had turned up in the tortured mind of the patient like a dark deposit in a turbid well.

From the moment the patient had dashed to the window, the doctor had been aware not only that her behavior was uncharacteristic but also that she actually looked and sounded different. She seemed smaller, shrunken. Sybil always stood as tall as she could because she considered herself small and didn't want to appear so. But now she seemed to have shrunk into herself.

The voice was also quite different, childlike, not like Sybil's voice. Yet that little girl voice had uttered a woman's words in its denunciation of men: "Men are all alike. You jist can't trust 'em." And the word *jist*. Sybil, perfectionist schoolteacher, strict grammarian, would never use a substandard word such as *jist*.

The doctor had the distinct impression that she was dealing with someone younger than Sybil. But the denunciation of men? The doctor couldn't be sure. Then the thought she had reined back broke forth: "Who are you?"

"Can't you tell the difference?" was the reply, accompanied by a resolutely independent tossing of the head. "I'm Peggy."

The doctor didn't answer, and Peggy continued: "We don't look alike. You can see that. You can."

When the doctor asked for her last name, Peggy replied airily, "I use Dorsett and sometimes Baldwin. I'm really Peggy Baldwin."

"Tell me something about yourself," the doctor suggested.

"All right," Peggy acquiesced. "Do you want to hear about my painting? I like to paint in black and white. I do charcoal and pencil sketches. I don't paint as much or as well as Sybil."

The doctor waited a moment; then she proceeded: "And who is Sybil?"

The doctor waited, and Peggy replied, "Sybil? Why, she's the *other* girl."

"I see," the doctor replied. Then she asked, "Where do you live?"

"I live with Sybil, but my home, as I told you, is Willow Corners," Peggy replied.

"Was Mrs. Dorsett your mother?" the doctor asked.

"No. No!" Peggy backed away, cowering against the small pillow. "Mrs. Dorsett's not my mother!"

"That's all right," the doctor remarked reassuringly. "I just wanted to know."

There was sudden movement. Peggy had left the couch and was moving across the room with the same swift, spiderlike movement with which she had earlier rushed to the window. The doctor followed her. But Peggy had vanished. Sitting on the small mahogany chair near the desk was the midwestern schoolteacher —Sybil. This time the doctor knew the difference.

"What's my purse doing on the floor?" Sybil murmured. She leaned over and with patient restraint replaced the scattered contents of her purse. "I did that, didn't I?" she said, pointing to the window. "I'll pay for it. I'll pay for it. I'll pay." Finally she whispered: "Where are the letters?"

"You tore them up and threw them into the wastebasket," the doctor replied with conscious deliberateness.

"I?" Sybil asked.

"You," the doctor replied. "Let's talk about what happened."

"What is there to say?" Sybil remarked in hushed tones. She had torn the letters and broken the window, but she didn't know when, how, or why. She leaned toward the wastebasket and salvaged parts of the letters.

"You don't remember, do you?" the doctor asked softly. Sybil shook her head. The shame of it. The horror of it. Now the doctor knew about the terrible, the nameless thing.

"Have you broken glass before?" Dr. Wilbur asked quietly.

"Yes," Sybil replied, hanging her head.

"Then this is not different from what you've experienced before?"

"Not entirely."

"Don't be frightened," the doctor said. "You were in another state of consciousness. You had what we call a *fugue*. A fugue is a major state of personality dissociation characterized by amnesia and actual physical flight from the immediate environment."

"You don't blame me, then?" Sybil asked.

"No, I don't blame you," the doctor replied. "Blame has nothing to do with it. We need to talk more about this, and we'll do it on Friday."

The hour was up. Sybil, fully in control, rose to go. The doctor followed her to the door and said: "Don't worry. It's treatable."

Sybil left.

"What do I have here?" the doctor said to herself as she dropped into her chair. She seems to be more than one person. A dual personality? Sybil and Peggy, totally different from each other. It seems quite clear. I'll have to tell her on Friday.

The doctor wondered about Miss Dorsett's next appointment. Or should she say the Misses Dorsett? She (they) was (were) now coming three times a week because of the Christmas vacation. Well, Sybil had better continue to come that often. This case was more complicated than she had first thought. Miss Dorsett would be back on Friday. *Who?*

5

Peggy Lou Baldwin

It was Sybil. Sybil calm; Sybil collected.

"I want to apologize for not keeping my appointment on Wednesday," she began this December 23, 1954. "I . . ."

"You did come on Wednesday," Dr. Wilbur replied with deliberate bluntness. "But you were in one of those fugue states, and you don't remember."

Using "fugue states" as a framework, the doctor planned to tell Sybil that, while she herself blacked out during these states, someone called Peggy appeared. But Sybil, skillfully changing the subject, did not give the doctor the chance. "I'm relieved," Sybil said, "that I didn't let you down. And now I have something I want to tell you. I really need to get it off my chest. May I tell you right now?"

The "important" revelation was, however, only: "You should have heard Klinger this morning. That man has no instinct for modern art. He has repeatedly disappointed those of us who believe in it."

Sybil was so effectively evasive that, when the hour was over, the doctor still had not told her about Peggy. Nor did the doctor have the opportunity during the next appointment. When she stepped into the foyer to greet her patient, it was Peggy who was waiting. The doctor had no difficulty recognizing her. Hatless, glove-less, Peggy was looking at two enlargements of sea and island scapes the doctor had photographed in Puerto Rico and the Virgin Islands, the pictures that Sybil had observed on her first visit.

"Come in, Peggy," the doctor said. And Peggy, obviously pleased that the doctor had been able to tell her apart from Sybil, entered with quick, confident steps.

Relaxed and cooperative, Peggy was more than willing to talk about herself. "I told you a little the other day," she said. "I was angry then. I had a right to be." Her tone became confidential as she looked directly at the doctor and said, "You know Stan sent us a 'Dear John' letter. Only it was 'Dear Sybil.' Do you want to know what he said? He said, 'I think we should discontinue our friendship—for the time being, anyway.' That's what he said. I was so mad I tore up his letter and threw it in a trash can on Lexington Avenue at 65th Street on the way here. And I threw that letter away. Only it wasn't the whole letter. I thought it was. But you saw the other half here. Well, I was insulted. Who wouldn't be?"

Peggy paused, rose from the couch, paced a bit, and, with an impish glint, remarked rather than asked: "Want to know who wouldn't be insulted? Well, I'll tell you. The answer is Sybil. She can't stand up for herself. I have to stand up for her. She can't get angry because her mother won't let her. I know it's a sin to get angry, but people *do* get angry. It's all right to be mad if I want to be."

Coming back to the couch and sitting close to the doctor, Peggy asked, "Wanna know somethin' else about Sybil? She's scared. She's jist scared all the time. I get tired of it. She gives up, but I don't."

"Peggy," the doctor asked, "do you and Sybil look alike?"

"Not at all," Peggy replied indignantly as she pulled away from the cushion, rose to her feet, and began to prance around the room. "We're completely different. You see how my hair is. And the shape of my face."

Dr. Wilbur didn't see the difference. While Peggy did seem younger and did talk and behave differently from Sybil, the hair, the face, and the body were the same. Peggy was in complete command of the body, but the doctor knew from her experience of the previous week that at any moment Peggy could change into Sybil. In fact, Peggy stayed the whole hour.

As the doctor probed, Peggy remarked with a touch of edginess, "Boy, you ask a lot of questions!" And when the doctor tried to search for the thread that connected Peggy to Sybil, Peggy replied cryptically, "Oh, leave me alone. There are things I can't tell you. I jist can't. It's like the guards around the palace. They can't smile. They're on duty." Then, smiling herself, Peggy added, "I suppose they'd smile if you tickled them with a feather. Not me, though. I don't smile or talk if I don't want to. And nobody can make me."

When it was time to go, Peggy said pleasantly as she rose from the couch: "You know, we met before."

"Last week," the doctor replied. "Here."

"No," Peggy insisted. "We met in Omaha. At the window. The way we met here. I talked to you my own self in Omaha, but you didn't recognize me. I told you I was Peggy, but you thought it was Sybil's nickname."

When Peggy was gone, she remained very much in the doctor's questing thoughts. Peggy was angry because Stan had sent Sybil a "Dear John" letter. Could this mean, the doctor wondered, that even though Sybil didn't know about Peggy, they were closely allied and that Peggy carried the emotional impact of Sybil's experiences?

Peggy had said that Sybil couldn't get angry but that *she* could. Was Peggy Sybil's defense against anger? Was the rage in that fist, when Peggy broke the windowpane, the embodiment of what Sybil repressed? The doctor knew that she would have to learn a great deal more before she could confirm this hypothesis. Perhaps she simply was being bombarded with insights. In any case, the questions poured into her mind urgently and insistently.

Suddenly thinking about Peggy out on the streets alone, Dr. Wilbur was concerned. Peggy, an assertive personality, should be able to take care of herself. Yet when she said, "Sybil's mother won't let her," as if the

73

mother were still alive, she had clearly shown, as had also been the case on the previous visit, that she didn't know present from past. And she was young. How could she negotiate the streets of New York, the doctor wondered. Dr. Wilbur hoped that she would get home safely. Home? Home was Sybil's home.

Peggy Baldwin, sometimes Dorsett, had no intention of going back to the dormitory when she left the doctor's office. "I want to go someplace," she murmured half aloud as she strode through the front door of the building onto Park Avenue. "I want to do what I want to do."

The broad street, with its islands of Christmas trees sparkling with leftover snow, its shining limousines with men at the doorways, their bright buttons glistening in the sun, fascinated her. It was all so different from Willow Corners. Quickly she corrected herself: she had to admit that she lived in this wonderful, new city with Sybil. But her *home* was Willow Corners.

How would it feel, Peggy wondered, to live in one of these houses? She wanted someday to *be* somebody. When she was, maybe she could live in a house with a doorman with shiny buttons. She wanted to be like all those important people, to do lots of things and go lots of places.

She decided to walk for a while, look, see, experience. There were so many things she wanted to know about. That's why she was always listening, trying to hear everything, her ears straining to capture all she could. She often went to different places just to find out what was going on.

Crossing over to Madison Avenue, she looked at the shops that she passed—shops with slender stoles of sable, lovely knitted suits, pink peppermint nightgowns, black jersey tops above red and white cotton skirts banded with black velvet rickrack. She loved pretty things, but she didn't dare buy anything from good places like these. She just looked.

The bar she passed back on West 44th Street was another place to which she didn't dare go. But she could

74

look in at all those people in there this day after Christmas doing what nobody she knew in Willow Corners did.

Two men came out. One brushed against her and asked, "How about it?" How about *what?* she wondered as she looked at him sternly. The man laughed. Laughter scared her. When people laughed, she was sure that they were laughing at her. She began to walk quickly but not fast enough to avoid hearing the man who had brushed against her remark to the other man: "Pretty independent, no?"

Pretty independent, yes, Peggy simmered as she raced ahead of her anger. Blamed independent. She wasn't going to take anything from anybody. She could fight back.

Forgetting about the incident, she walked on, finally finding herself in a big store. Passing over a ramp upstairs, she went into a station: "Pennsylvania Railroad," the sign said. Oh, boy, she thought, I can go somewhere. In the station she found a place to eat. She liked to eat.

After lunch she found herself at a bookstand, looking at a doctor's story. She wasn't too crazy about doctor stories, but Sybil liked them.

Sybil. How had the nice lady with the red hair mixed her up with Sybil? Couldn't she see that Peggy and Sybil were not the same? All of a sudden Peggy laughed out loud. People turned to stare.

The people. She could cry when she thought of all the people. Sometimes when she thought of people, she felt lost and alone. There were too many cross people, and cross people made her angry. She knew it wasn't right to be angry, but many things made her angry. Her anger was purple and violet.

The ramp, which was long, made her feel small. She went through a turnstile, walked down a long corridor, and came to a place where they were selling tickets. She went up to the window. The woman behind the window looked cross. Peggy said evenly: "I don't have to buy a ticket from you!" It wasn't right to get mad, and now she had done it.

"Ticket, please," she said as she walked up to another window.

"Elizabeth?" the new lady asked.

Peggy nodded her head yes. Why not? She could see that lots of people were waiting until a sign was put up. She wanted to be the first through the gate, but even though she hurried, she was the fifth in line.

The next thing she knew she was in a restaurant near a railroad station, and she was ordering a hot chocolate. When she asked the waiter whether she was in Elizabeth, he looked at her in a peculiar way and said, "Well, sure." Funny, she didn't know how she had gotten there. Her last memory was of moving through the gate at Penn Station. Well, she supposed Sybil or one of those other people had taken the train ride. Who cares, Peggy thought, I bought the ticket for Elizabeth and I'm here.

She walked apprehensively along the street outside the restaurant. This place wasn't very interesting, but she had to do something. She was surrounded by unfamiliar sights. Spotting a parking lot, she walked briskly across it. She hadn't gotten very far when she felt the sudden joy of recognition at seeing her father's car.

It was! She had found her father's car, something familiar.

She walked to the car and began trying its doors. All the doors of the car were locked. She tried the doors again, but no matter how hard she tried, they just wouldn't open. She felt trapped, not by being locked in but by being locked out. It could happen both ways, she knew.

Anger, purple and violet, welled within her. Its quick, sharp, heavy pulsations throbbed through her body. Almost without knowing what she was doing, she took her handbag and banged the metal frame against a slightly open window. After a few blows she heard the tinkle of broken glass. She loved the sound of breaking glass.

A man in a tan suit was standing beside her. "What did you do? Lock yourself out?" he asked.

76

"It's my daddy's car," she replied.

Before the man in tan could reply, a man in a gray suit, who had joined them, snarled, "No, it isn't. It's my car."

Peggy didn't like this man in gray one bit. And he had no right to talk to her like that. "It's my daddy's car," she insisted, "no matter what you say."

"Who's that?" asked the man in tan.

"Willard Dorsett," she replied proudly.

The man in gray reached into his pocket, took out his wallet, and displayed the car's registration card. "You see, sister, the numbers match the license plate," he sneered.

Her head high, her eyes flashing fire, she started off to tell her father what had happened. She would find him, and he would make everything all right. But the man who claimed to own the car was hollering at her in a loud and ugly way: "Hey, come back here. You ain't going nowhere."

Peggy didn't like being left alone with these men. They were mean and ugly, and she was afraid of them. She feared that they would stop her if she tried to get away. She tried to escape anyway, but the owner of the car grabbed her by the arm.

"You take your hands off me," she warned. "I might jist hurt you."

Peggy tried to pull away, but the owner of the car placed a restraining hand on her shoulder and said, "Cool it, sister, cool it." She felt like an outcast, enmeshed by strangers from whom she could expect only mistrust, rejection, insult.

"Well, sister," the owner of the car insisted, "you broke the window. It will cost me $20 to replace that window. Are you going to pay for it?"

"Why should I? It's my father's car," Peggy replied.

"Who are you anyway?" the car owner asked. "Let me see your identification."

"I won't," Peggy asserted. "I won't. And not you or anybody else can make me."

The car owner, infuriated by her refusal, pulled her

purse away from her. "Give it back to me," she screamed. "Give it back to me right this minute."

He removed a plastic identification folder from the purse and returned the purse. "Sybil I. Dorsett," he read aloud. "That your name?"

"No," Peggy said.

"What are you doing with it, huh?" he snapped.

Peggy didn't answer. She certainly wasn't going to tell him about the *other* girl.

"Give me the $20," he ordered. "Damn it. Give me the money, sign this paper, and we'll let you go."

Peggy was raging mad. The next time the car owner asked for twenty dollars, pointing his finger at her, she bit his finger—hard. "Damn it," he sputtered, "you, Sybil Dorsett, give me the money and we'll let you go. Well?"

"I'm not Sybil Dorsett," Peggy replied coolly.

The man studied the picture in the plastic folder.

"That's you, all right," he said with conviction. "And that's your name under the picture. You're Sybil I. Dorsett."

"I'm not," Peggy protested.

"Well, what's your name?"

"I'm Peggy Lou Baldwin."

"Alias," said the man in tan.

"She said her father was Willard Dorsett," remarked the man in gray. "There's something rotten here."

"There sure is," the man in tan agreed.

Peggy tried to pull away, but she couldn't move. And she knew that she was being stopped as much from within as from without. In fact, it was because of what was happening within that she didn't move.

She thought of not having been in command during the train ride to this horrid town, and she knew that she wasn't at the helm now, either. She knew that it was Sybil who had control. She could feel Sybil reaching into their handbag as the car's owner repeated, "It will cost me $20 to replace that window. You're going to pay or I'll call the police." Peggy could feel Sybil handing two crisp $10 bills to the hateful man.

The man wrote something in a loose leaf notebook. "Okay," he said, "sign this."

Peggy could hear Sybil saying no, in a firm voice.

This time Peggy was proud of Sybil. It isn't like her to stand up for us, Peggy thought, but this time she is.

"If you don't sign this paper," the man muttered, "we won't let you go!"

Peggy watched Sybil reading the paper but couldn't see what the paper said. Only one phrase seeped through. It was: "The owner of the vehicle."

The owner of the vehicle? These words scared Peggy. They meant that this wasn't really her father's car. Not her father's car? Realizing this for the first time, Peggy again started to run away. But the owner of the car grabbed her, placed a ballpoint pen in her hand, and commanded, "Sign the paper." He then held the paper right up to her face, saying, "You broke the window in my car. You paid me for it. But not for the inconvenience—not for the time I'll waste having it repaired. You really ought to pay extra . . ."

"You put my name on that little card. You said I could go. And I'm going," Peggy announced firmly. "But I don't know why you want me to sign my name."

"I thought you said it wasn't your name," the man replied. "You're too much! Go!"

Peggy walked back to the depot. As she rode the train home, she thought of how silly it had been for them to make all that fuss about a little broken glass.

It was nearly dark when Peggy returned to the small room she shared with Sybil. Twilight peering into the room, so like the one they had occupied as undergraduates in college, cast a pale sheen here and there on the ceiling and on the upper surface of the dresser and chairs.

Peggy kicked off her shoes and stretched out on the bed. Then she got up and moved swiftly to the portable phonograph. Should she play "Mockin'bird Hill" or "Galway Bay"? Deciding on "Mockin'bird Hill," she sang along with it.

Still singing, she went to the window and looked out. The trees in the dormitory courtyard glistened with the snow that had just begun to fall. She stopped singing. She was afraid of snow, afraid of the cold.

Suddenly she had an idea. This was the night of the pre-Christmas social in the rec room, and, tired of all the dreary things that had happened during the day, she decided to go to the party and forget. She would wear the apple green dress that she had bought in a Chinese store on upper Broadway. She had gone there to buy only a tiny ten-cent paper parasol, but the moment she had seen that dress, she knew she had to have it.

As the record still played, Peggy took the dress off its hanger in what she humorously called "our closet." This dress is "jist" as pretty, she thought, as those she had seen in the windows of the fancy Madison Avenue shops. And her dress, which was all the rage this season, cost only $12. It would have been worth the price even if she had paid $30, $40, $50, $80, $200, maybe even $300 for it. But Sybil had to go and spoil everything. Peggy liked Sybil best when Sybil minded her own business.

As she slipped gracefully into the dress, which opened down the front, the pleasant feeling she had felt toward Sybil earlier in the day vanished. Sybil, she felt, stood between her and her desires, her needs, and the expression of her individuality. The dress had brought back all her dormant complaints against Sybil, keeper of their body and head of their household.

Sybil was a fact of Peggy's life, but sometimes Sybil could be an awful nuisance. When Sybil had found this beautiful dress in the closet, she had acted as if she had seen a ghost or something. How did it get into *my* closet? What is the sales slip doing in *my* purse?

Perhaps what had hurt most was that she had found the dress at all. Peggy had hidden it on the top shelf of a closet that Sybil used as a catch-all for everything except dresses. Who would ever have expected Sybil to look there?

Had Sybil been upset, Peggy wondered, about the money? Certainly $12 wasn't too much for the dress. Sybil had the money. But, Peggy supposed, Sybil had her own ideas and would go and use her money for furniture, art supplies, and all those medicines—all the things Sybil called necessities.

Sybil's always messing around with the things I buy, Peggy fretted. It was the same way with my blue suit and blue shoes. I got them out twice one day, but both times Sybil put them away again. Yes, she certainly can be a nuisance.

Peggy looked at herself in the mirror. The effect was beautiful, simply beautiful. Anybody would like such a dress. Maybe Sybil wasn't really upset because of the dress but because of Peggy. No, that's nonsense. The truth was—and Peggy had to face it—that Sybil didn't know of her existence. It wasn't very flattering, but that's the way it was.

A little jewelry would add to the effect, Peggy thought as she continued to examine herself in the mirror. It would be such fun to wear it, but she knew that she couldn't. It was wrong for her to wear jewels. Hadn't they said so in church? Hadn't she been told *that* ever since she could remember? Still, she did like pretty things. She hesitated. There was a string of pearls belonging to Sybil's mother. No, she wouldn't wear them. She didn't like Sybil's mother, and that made it doubly wrong to wear those pearls.

Peggy could not pull herself away from the mirror. Her square body gave her a chunky appearance that she wasn't too crazy about, but she liked her Dutch haircut, her straight black hair, her bangs, her round face, her pug nose, her bright blue eyes and—yes, she had to admit it—her mischievous smile. *Ofta mia,* she hadn't thought of it before, but she did look like a pixie. Sybil, with her thin, lean body, her light brown hair worn loosely, her heart-shaped face, her gray eyes, and her serious expression, was altogether different. Couldn't the nice doctor see that? Couldn't the men in Elizabeth who looked at Sybil's picture and at Peggy see that? Why were people always mistaking her for Sybil?

Suddenly Peggy moved swiftly from the mirror. The sight of her lips made her turn away. Full and big. The sort of lips Negroes have. She was afraid of her lips. She had begun to think of herself as a Negro. She was afraid of Negroes, afraid of the way people treated them, afraid of the way people treated her. She reached for her purse and left the room.

In the dormitory courtyard, with snow falling on her hatless head and trickling down her nose, Peggy raced ahead of her fear. As if to banish it, she found herself again humming "Mockin'bird Hill."

The recreation room was already crowded when she arrived. Students were gathered in groups, talking about everything under the sun. There were card tables and a ping pong table. Sybil didn't play cards or ping pong, but Peggy did. Peggy was well coordinated and quick.

Peggy looked at the men students. There wasn't one among them, she thought, who wasn't nicer than Stan. But was Sybil interested in them? She was not. Stan hadn't broken Sybil's heart; she simply didn't care that much. And Peggy's heart wasn't broken, either, not at all. Peggy wished that Sybil would find somebody else they could like.

The long refreshment table, covered with a lovely white lace tablecloth and displaying two large copper samovars, one for coffee and the other for tea, reminded Peggy that she had had no food since her snack in Elizabeth. She knew she couldn't have the coffee or tea because her religion wouldn't let her, but the little sandwiches and dainty cookies looked good. She had just begun to nibble on a sandwich when she heard a cultivated midwestern voice asking, "Have a good day, Sybil?"

"Great," Peggy replied without hesitation as she looked up at Teddy Eleanor Reeves, a good-looking woman even though she was indifferent about how she dressed, wore no makeup, and had a diamond shaped body. Teddy, who occupied the room next to her own, always called her "Sybil." Long ago Peggy had agreed to answer to the name of Sybil when necessary. It hadn't been necessary with those sinister people in Elizabeth, but with Teddy, who had become a good friend of Sybil, it was different.

"Where have you been all day? I was worried about you," Teddy continued. Teddy, all five-feet-ten of her, with broad shoulders, wide hips, and very small bust, was always a dominating figure, forever playing mother. Peggy couldn't see how Sybil could stand her. Peggy knew that Teddy was on tenterhooks to have a blow-by-blow description of Sybil's day. Well, it hadn't been Sybil's day, and Peggy had no intention of telling about it.

"Glad to see you, Dorsett," Laura Hotchkins said as she came up and joined them. "You said you weren't coming. I'm glad you were able to." Laura was another of Sybil's friends. Again Peggy kept her own counsel.

Teddy, Laura, and several other girls had clustered around Dorsett, all talking about Professor Klinger. All at once Dorsett took hold of a crayon pencil that was in her purse, pointed it against the wall and began, in an affected voice: "Now, ladies and gentlemen, you have to listen closely if you're going to listen at all. Art is in the great tradition of human experience, and unless you give it your *undeevided attention,* you are insulting the muse." The girls began to giggle. Peggy, making two large holes in a paper napkin, converted it into simulated eyeglasses, which she put on the edge of her nose. She squinted and said, "Sculpture is probably the oldest of the arts. As you know from other courses, its technical beginnings go back to the first prehistoric man who chipped an arrow head or carved a club or spear. As you also know, the relative permanence of stone, baked clay, or metal is, of course, a major factor in our dependence upon sculpture and inscriptions upon stone or clay as conveyors of historical record.

"In the long run, however, other kinds of written records finally undermined sculpture's supremacy and made painting of all kinds, at least in the West, the art having the widest use and popular appeal. And that is why I want you to concentrate on painting as if it is the most important thing in the world. Perhaps it is. But I mean the painting of Rubens, of Rembrandt, of the other masters. I don't mean the silly utterances of Picasso and other contemporaries. They're *cheeldren* prating in the cradle, babbling nothings that aren't so

83

sweet. What they call experimentation is an excuse for *emptEEness*.

"Now, Miss Dorsett, you're a serious woman with great talent. Why must you paint in this *seely* tradition?"

Laura Hotchkins's giggle turned into an unrestrained laugh. Teddy guffawed.

Peggy went on, bringing the house down. What had started as a performance for a few had become a show for everybody. Her imitation of Professor Klinger became the high point of the evening. Amid applause, Peggy removed her simulated eyeglasses with great deliberateness, returned her pencil crayon to her purse, took several bows, and made a grand exit from the room.

It was a different Peggy who saw Dr. Wilbur two days later on Christmas day—a Peggy silent about the trip to Elizabeth and her triumph at the college social, a Peggy who in a low whisper iterated and reiterated: "The people, the people, the people."

"What people?" asked Dr. Wilbur, who was sitting beside Peggy on the couch.

"People? Yes, there are people," Peggy replied ominously. "They're waitin' for me."

"What are their names?"

"The glass," said Peggy, ignoring the question. "I can see the glass. I'm goin' to *break* the glass—and get away. I'm goin' to get away from it! I don't want to stay. I won't. I won't!"

"Get away from what?" Dr. Wilbur asked.

"The pain. It hurts," Peggy whispered. She began to sob.

"What hurts?"

"It hurts. It hurts. My head hurts. My throat hurts."

The words of agony poured forth. Then came the angry accusation: "You don't want me to get away." Growing defiant, she warned: "I'm goin' to break the glass and get away even if you don't want me to."

"Why don't you go through the door? Go on. Just open it."

84

"I can't," Peggy screamed. She pulled herself up from the couch and began pacing like a trapped, hunted animal.

"But you can," the doctor insisted. "It's right there. Go and open it!"

"I want to get out! I want to get out!" Peggy continued with sustained terror.

"All right. Just turn the knob and open the door!"

"No, I'm goin' to stay right here by the white house with black shutters and the doors with steps leadin' to it and the garage." Suddenly calm, Peggy said, "My daddy's car is in the garage."

"Where are you? In Willow Corners?" the doctor asked.

"I won't tell! I won't tell," Peggy chanted.

"Can you tell Dr. Wilbur?"

"Yes."

"Then will you tell Dr. Wilbur?"

"Yes."

"Then go ahead. Tell Dr. Wilbur!"

"Dr. Wilbur went away," was Peggy's wistful reply.

"Dr. Wilbur is right here."

"No, she went away and left us in Omaha," Peggy insisted. "You're not Dr. Wilbur. Don't you know you're not? I've got to find her." The calm evaporated. Hysteria returned. Peggy pleaded, "Let me out!"

The plea seemed to have no relation to the particular room or the special moment. It was a plea rising from the past that for her was present, a past that reached out to her, encircled her, and kept her captive.

"Open the door," the doctor said firmly.

"I can't get through the door. I'll never get through. Never."

"Is the door locked?"

"I can't get through." It was the whine of a hurt, lost child. "I've got to get out of here."

"Out of where, Peggy?"

"Out of wherever I am. I don't like the people, the places, or anything. I want to get out."

"What people? What places?"

"The people and the music." Peggy was breathless.

85

"The people and the music. The music goes round and round and round. You can see all the people. I don't like the people, the places, or anything. I want to get out. Oh, let me out! Please. Please!"

"Just turn the knob and open the door."

"No. I can't." Peggy's fury was suddenly directed at the doctor. "Why won't you understand?"

"Why don't you try? You haven't even tried. Why don't you turn around and open it?" the doctor insisted.

"It's got a door knob, and it won't turn. Can't you see that?"

"Try it."

"It's no use to try." There was momentary relaxation, but it was the relaxation of resignation, of doomed acceptance. "They won't let me do anything. They think I'm no good and that I'm funny and my hands are funny. Nobody likes me."

"I like you, Peggy."

"Oh, they won't let me do anything. It hurts. It hurts bad." Peggy was sobbing. "The people don't care."

"Dr. Wilbur cares. She asks you what's on your mind."

"Nobody cares," Peggy replied defiantly. "And the hands hurt."

"Your hands?"

"No, other hands. Hands comin' at you. Hands that hurt!"

"Whose hands?"

"I won't tell." Again there was that childlike chant. "I don't have to tell if I don't want to."

"What else hurts?"

"Music hurts." Peggy was speaking again in a low, breathy whisper. "The people and the music."

"What music? Why?"

"I won't tell."

Gently, Dr. Wilbur put her arm around Peggy and helped her back to the couch.

Moved, Peggy confided softly, "You see, nobody cares. And you can't talk to anybody. And you don't belong anywhere." There was a tranquil pause. Peggy

86

then said: "I can see the trees, the house, the school. I can see the garage. I want to get into the garage. Then it would be all right. Then it wouldn't hurt so much. Then there wouldn't be so much pain."

"Why?"

"It hurts because you're not good enough."

"Why aren't you good enough? Tell Dr. Wilbur some more about how it hurts and what's the matter."

"Nobody loves me. And I want somebody to care a little bit. And you can't love somebody when they don't care."

"Go on. Tell Dr. Wilbur what the trouble is."

"I want somebody to love, and I want somebody to love me. And nobody ever will. And that's why it hurts. Because it makes a difference. And when nobody cares, it makes you all mad inside and it makes you want to say things, tear up things, break things, get through the glass."

Suddenly Peggy grew silent. Then Peggy disappeared. Seated where Peggy had been was Sybil.

"I had another fugue?" Sybil asked as she quickly drew away from the doctor. She was frightened, anxious.

The doctor nodded.

"Well, it wasn't as bad as the last time," Sybil reassured herself as she looked around the room and saw nothing out of place, nothing broken.

"You mentioned music to me once, Sybil," the doctor replied in an effort to discover what Sybil knew about what Peggy had said. "Why don't you tell me a little more about it?"

"Well," Sybil replied with composure, "I took piano lessons, and Mrs. Moore, my piano teacher, used to say, 'You have all the native ability. You have a good ear, nice hands. Your fingering is good. But you must practice more. You can do all this without practicing. What would you do if you did practice?' But I didn't practice. And I didn't tell her that I didn't because mother was overcritical. Whenever I made a mistake while practicing, mother would holler, 'That's not right. That's not right.' I couldn't stand it, so I didn't practice when mother was around. But the minute she left the house, I'd drop whatever I was doing and dash to the piano. I could always work things out at the piano. If I didn't have that, the tension would have gotten me long before it did. When I started teaching, the first thing I bought was a piano."

"Umm," Dr. Wilbur replied. "Tell me, do you have any special feelings about glass?"

"Glass," Sybil echoed thoughtfully. "Mother had some lovely crystal. So did my grandmother. Both grandmothers, in fact—Grandma Dorsett and Grandma Anderson. Oh, I remember something. When I was about six, we were visiting the Andersons in Elderville, Illinois. We went there for three weeks every summer until Grandma Anderson died. Well, this time my cousin Lulu and I were drying the dishes. She hurled a lovely crystal pickle dish through the French doors. She was a real brat. And then she told my grandmother and my mother and everybody else that I did it, that I broke the crystal dish. It wasn't fair. But I didn't say anything, just took it. My mother let me have it, but good."

"I see," said Dr. Wilbur. "Now tell me whether hands disturb you."

"Hands? Well, not particularly. My own hands are small and thin. My mother didn't think they were very attractive. She often said so."

"Did hands ever come at you? Someone else's hands?"

"Hands coming? I don't know what you mean."

It was apparent that Sybil's discomfort suddenly was greatly intensified.

"I see," said the doctor. "Another question: does the sight of blood disturb you?"

"Well, yes. But doesn't it bother everybody? Grandma Dorsett had cancer of the cervix and bled. I saw that. And when I started to menstruate, I wondered about the blood like most girls. There's nothing very unusual about that."

"But tell me, did you ever see other blood as a child? The blood of a playmate perhaps?"

Sybil sat back and thought. "Well, let's see. Tommy

Ewald. His father had a barn and kept horses. Tommy was his mother's favorite child. He died in the hayloft. We were playing. It was an accident. A gun went off. That's all I remember. There could have been blood in the hayloft. I haven't thought about Tommy in many years."

By February, 1955, the doctor was ready to tell Sybil about Peggy, who remembered what she had forgotten. There was no point in procrastinating any longer. But while the words were forming on the doctor's lips, Sybil's face went white, the pupils of her eyes became dilated even more than usual, and in a strained, unnatural voice she asked, "How do you know these things?" Wanting to tell her about her other self, the doctor could sense that she had become that self.

"Hi," Peggy said.

"Hi, dear," said the doctor.

"I'm goin' out now," Peggy told the doctor. "Right through the door. A long time ago Dr. Wilbur said I could."

And Peggy walked through the door that only minutes ago had been impenetrable, the tangible symbol of her captivity.

Dr. Wilbur, feeling that the diagnosis of dual personality had been confirmed beyond a shadow of doubt, could not take her mind off this unusual case. Peggy and Sybil, although existing in the same body, had different memories, different moods, different attitudes, different experiences. The experiences that they shared were perceived differently. Their voices, their diction, and their vocabularies were different. They presented themselves in different ways. Even their ages were different. Sybil was thirty-one, but Peggy . . . the doctor couldn't decide whether Peggy was a precocious child or an immature adult. Peggy was unself-conscious in a little-girl way, not easily embarrassed. Instead, she got mad. Instead of being like Sybil, circuitous, she gave vent to undisguised terror. And unmistakably Peggy carried some terrible burden that Sybil refused to face.

Dr. Wilbur's mind teemed with speculations, insistent but inconclusive. She had never treated a dual personality. She would have to treat the disturbance as she would any other case. First you get to the roots of the disturbance; then you proceed from there.

The immediate problem was to tell Sybil about the diagnosis, a task more difficult than the doctor had first realized. When a situation arose with which Sybil was unable to cope, she seemed to let Peggy take over. To tell Sybil about Peggy would be to invite a dissociation that would bring Peggy back.

The evasions were so effective that the problem remained unresolved until March, 1955. At that time, however, an event took place that, changing the diagnosis, made Dr. Wilbur glad that she had not yet told Sybil.

6

Victoria Antoinette Scharleau

March 16, 1955. Dr. Wilbur took a moment between appointments to replace her pussy willows with the new spring flowers, anemones and jonquils, that she had just bought. Then, wondering whether it was Sybil or Peggy who was waiting, she opened the door to the anteroom.

The patient, sitting quietly, was absorbed in the pages of *The New Yorker*. When she saw the doctor, she got up at once, smiled, walked toward her, and said warmly, "Good morning, Dr. Wilbur."

It isn't Peggy, the doctor thought. Peggy doesn't sit still. Peggy doesn't read. Peggy's voice doesn't have that cultivated tone. It has to be Sybil. But never before has Sybil spoken to me before I have addressed her. Never has she smiled in this spontaneous way.

"How are you today?" the doctor asked.

"I'm fine," was the reply. "But Sybil isn't. She was so sick she couldn't come. So I came instead."

For an instant the doctor was stunned. But for an instant only. The strange juxtaposition of "she" and "I" only reaffirmed her already dawning suspicions. I'm surprised, Dr. Wilbur reflected, but why should I be? There were more than two personalities in the Christine Beauchamp case, which Dr. Morton Prince treated and about which he wrote. But then, he too, had been surprised. In fact, he had been astonished when he had found more than one. I suppose this comes as a surprise to every doctor, Dr. Wilbur reflected.

All this was running through Dr. Wilbur's mind at top speed while this new "I" was saying: "I must apologize for Sybil. She wanted to come, but couldn't get dressed, though she tried and tried. I watched her last night as she took out the navy blue skirt and the twin blue sweaters that she planned to wear here this morning. Last night she had every intention of coming, but this morning it was different. She sometimes suffers from a complete absence of feeling and a total inability to do anything. This morning, I'm afraid, was one of those times. But how gauche of me to start a conversation without introducing myself. I'm Vicky."

"Won't you come in, Vicky?" the doctor asked.

Vicky did not merely walk into the consulting room; she made an entrance, with finesse and elegance. While Sybil's movements were always constrained, hers were free and graceful.

She was wearing a dress of many colors: rose, violet, and pale green. It had a double top and a slightly gathered skirt that fell just below the knees. Green shoes heightened the effect.

"This is a lovely room," she remarked casually. "A study in green. The tone must be soothing to your patients."

Then she walked to the couch and settled herself into a comfortable position. The doctor shut the door, joined her, lit a cigarette, and said: "Tell me, Vicky, how do you come to be here?"

"It's very simple," Vicky replied. "Sybil was sick. I put on her dress—not the blue outfit I was telling you about. It wouldn't have been appropriate because I have a lunch date. As I was saying, I put on her dress, got on the bus, and came over."

"But how did you know where to come?"

Vicky explained: "I know everything."

"Everything?" the doctor echoed.

"I know what everybody does."

There was a pause. The doctor tapped her cigarette against the side of an ashtray.

"You may think that is insufferable of me," Vicky went on. "I must admit it does sound presumptuous. But it won't seem so when you know the circumstances."

The circumstances? Perhaps this meant that Vicky had a clue to the total situation in this case. But Vicky only said: "I certainly don't claim omniscience. But I watch everything everybody does. That's what I mean when I say I know everything. In this special sense I *am* omniscient."

Did this mean, the doctor wondered, that Vicky could tell her everything about Sybil, Peggy, and herself? So far she had revealed very little.

"Vicky," said the doctor, "I'd like to know more about you."

"I'm a happy person," Vicky replied, "and happy people don't have big stories. But I'll be glad to tell you anything you want to know."

"What I'm really trying to say," the doctor replied, "is that I should like to know how you happen to be."

Vicky twinkled and said, "Oh, that's a philosophical question. One could write a tome on that." Then she became more serious and looked directly at the doctor. "But if you want to know where I come from, I'll be happy to tell you. I come from abroad. I come from a very large family. My mother and father, my brothers and sisters—there are lots of them—all live in Paris. *Mon Dieu,* I haven't seen them in years. My full name is Victoria Antoinette Scharleau. Vicky for short. One becomes Americanized, you know. One can't go around being called Victoria Antoinette. Vicky is easier."

After a pause, during which Dr. Wilbur suspended disbelief, she asked, "Don't your parents feel bad that you're not with them?"

"Not at all, Doctor," Vicky replied with assurance. "They know I'm here to help. After a while they will come for me and I'll go with them. Then we will all be together. They're not like some other parents. They do what they say they will do."

"You're very fortunate," the doctor remarked.

"Oh, I am," Vicky asserted. "It would be dreadful to have the wrong parents. Simply dreadful."

"I understand," said the doctor.

"My family will come eventually," said Vicky.

"Yes, I understand," said the doctor.

Vicky moved closer to Dr. Wilbur and confided with concern: "But, Doctor, I really came to talk about Sybil. It's simply appalling the way she worries all the time. She doesn't eat enough, doesn't allow herself to have enough fun, and generally takes life too seriously. A little less self-denial and a little more pleasure would go far to counteract Sybil's sickness." Vicky paused; then she added thoughtfully: "There's something else, Doctor. Something deep inside."

"What do you think it is, Vicky?"

"I can't really say. You see it started before I came."

"When did you come?"

"Sybil was just a little girl then."

"I see." The doctor waited for a moment and then asked: "Did you know Mrs. Dorsett?"

Vicky was suddenly aloof, guarded. "She was Sybil's mother," she explained. "I lived with the Dorsetts for many years. Yes, I knew Mrs. Dorsett."

"Do you know Peggy?" asked the doctor.

"Of course," Vicky replied.

"Tell me about Peggy."

"You want me to tell you about Peggy?" Vicky repeated. "You mean Peggy Lou? Would you also like to hear about Peggy Ann?"

"Peggy who?" asked the doctor.

"Stupid of me," Vicky apologized. "I had quite forgotten that Peggy Lou is the only one you've met. There are two Peggys."

"Two Peggys?" Again the doctor wrestled with amazement. But why should a fourth personality surprise her? Once she had accepted the premise of multiple selves, she realized there was no longer any reason for surprise.

"Peggy Ann will be along one of these days," Vicky predicted. "You'll meet her. I'm sure you'll like her."

"I'm sure I will."

"They do things together, those two, Peggy Lou and Peggy Ann."

"What makes them different?"

"Well it seems to me that what arouses Peggy Lou's anger makes Peggy Ann afraid. But they're both fighters. When Peggy Lou decides she is going to do something, she goes at it in a pretty bull-headed sort of way. You see, Peggy Ann goes at things, too. But she's more tactful."

"I see."

"They both want to change things," Vicky concluded. "And what they want to change most of all is Sybil."

"Very interesting," the doctor replied. "And now, Vicky, can you tell me: was Mrs. Dorsett Peggy Lou's mother?"

"Well, of course," Vicky answered.

"But," the doctor pointed out, "Peggy Lou claims that Sybil's mother is not her mother."

"Oh, I know," Vicky replied airily. "You know how Peggy Lou is." Then with an amused smile Vicky added: "Mrs. Dorsett was Peggy Lou's mother, but Peggy Lou doesn't know it."

"What about Peggy Ann?" asked the doctor.

"Mrs. Dorsett was Peggy Ann's mother. But Peggy Ann doesn't know it, either."

"I see," said the doctor. "It's all very curious."

"Oh, it is," Vicky agreed. "But it's a state of mind. Maybe you'll be able to help them."

There was a silence, which the doctor finally broke by asking, "Vicky, do Peggy Lou and you look alike?"

Vicky's face darkened with disappointment. Then she asked: "Can't you tell?"

"I can't tell," the doctor temporized, "because I've never seen you together."

Vicky rose from the couch and walked to the desk with swift, lithe movements. "You don't mind if I use this?" she asked when she had returned with a prescription pad.

"Go right ahead."

The doctor watched as Vicky settled herself on the couch, removed a pencil from her purse, and began sketching on the pad.

"Here," Vicky said after a while, "are two heads. This is I with my blonde ringlets. I wish I had a crayon to draw the hair color. This is Peggy Lou. Her hair is black. The lack of crayon doesn't really matter. Peggy Lou doesn't like any fuss and bother. She wears her hair perfectly straight, just like this." Vicky then pointed to the pad on which she had drawn Peggy Lou's Dutch cut. "You see," Vicky remarked triumphantly, "how different we are."

The doctor nodded and asked, "What about Peggy Ann?"

"I won't bother drawing her," Vicky replied. "The sketch of Peggy Lou could pass for Peggy Ann. They're very much alike. You'll see."

"You sketch very well," the doctor commented. "Do you also paint?"

"Oh, yes," Vicky replied. "But Sybil paints better than I. My forte is people. I like them and know how to get along with them. I'm not afraid of them because my mother and father were always very good to me. I like to talk to people and to listen to them. I especially enjoy people who talk music, art, and books. I suppose most of my friendships spring from this mutuality of interests. I love to read novels. By the way, have you read *The Tortoise and the Hare?*"

95

"No, I haven't."

"Oh, do," Vicky replied, assuming a light conversational tone. "I finished it last night. It's by Elizabeth Jenkins, and it's new. You might call it a muted novel about a curiously obtuse triangle. The femme fatale is a middle-aged spinster in thick, scratchy tweeds. She rides quietly through the story in a Rolls-Royce."

"Well, I'm going to get it on your recommendation," said Dr. Wilbur.

"I hope you enjoy it as much as I did. I really did. I suppose it's because I'm at home with society people. I enjoy them in life and also in books. It's my background showing, I suspect. But I don't think I'm a snob. I just have refined tastes, coming as I do from my kind of family. And why not drink deeply of the better things in life?"

Vicky became more serious and her tone more reflective as she remarked, "Life has so much pain that one needs a catharsis. I don't mean escape. You don't escape in books. On the contrary, they help you to realize yourself more fully. *Mon Dieu*, I'm glad I have them. When I find myself in a situation in which I'd rather not be—because of the peculiar circumstances of my life—I have this outlet. You may think me *très supérieure* but I'm not really, I just am what I am and live the way I like."

Sighing, Vicky remarked: "You know, Doctor, I wish Sybil could enjoy life the way I do. I love to go to concerts and art galleries. So does she, but she doesn't go often enough. I'm going to the Metropolitan Museum when I leave here. I mentioned that I have a lunch date with a friend. It's Marian Ludlow. We're going to lunch at the Fountain Restaurant at the Met. Then we'll look at the exhibits. We won't have time for all of them. But we especially want to see the collection of prints and drawings called 'Word Becomes Image.' Marian breathes culture and is impeccably social. She was raised in an East Side town house. They had a large household staff, summered in Southhampton, that kind of thing."

"Does Sybil know Marian Ludlow?" the doctor asked.

"I'm afraid not," Vicky replied with faint condescension. "Sybil's not a *femme du monde,* a woman of *esprit.* She saw Mrs. Ludlow in line in the Teachers College cafeteria and wondered what a fashionable woman like that was doing there. The cafeteria was crowded, and Sybil was sitting alone. Mrs. Ludlow asked if she might sit with her. You know Sybil is always afraid of not being polite enough. So she said, 'Certainly.' But the thought of having to cope with an attractive society woman terrified her. She blacked out. So I took over and had a conversation with the *grande dame.* That was the beginning of our friendship. And we're very good friends."

"Does Peggy Lou know Mrs. Ludlow?"

"Oh, I don't think so, Dr. Wilbur. They're worlds apart, you know."

"Vicky, you seem to do many things in which Sybil and Peggy play no part," the doctor observed.

"That's perfectly true," Vicky was quick to say. "I have my own route. I'd be so bored if I had to follow theirs." She looked at the doctor with an expression that was part mischievous, part quizzical, and confided: "Doctor, Sybil would like to be I. But she doesn't know how."

"Then Sybil knows about you?"

"Of course not," Vicky replied. "She doesn't know about the Peggys. And she doesn't know about me. But that doesn't keep her from having an image of a person like me—an image that she would like to fulfill but that constantly eludes her."

Dr. Wilbur hesitated for a moment, her mind racing as she assessed what she had heard. Sybil and Peggy Lou. Now Vicky and Peggy Ann. Four persons in one body. Were there others as well? Believing that Vicky had the answers, the doctor decided to take the plunge: "Vicky, you've talked of the Peggys. Maybe you can tell me: are there any others?"

"Oh, yes," was the authoritative reply, "we know there are many others. That's what I meant when I told you that I know everything about everybody."

"Now, Vicky," the doctor urged, "I want all of you

97

to feel free to come during the appointment hour, no matter who is using the body."

"Oh, yes, they'll come," Vicky promised. "And I'll come, too. I'm here to help you get to the bottom of what's troubling them."

"I appreciate that, Vicky," Dr. Wilbur said. Then the doctor was struck by a novel idea: enlisting Vicky's help in the analysis. Vicky, who claimed to know everything about all the selves, could serve as the Greek chorus for all the selves, throwing light on events and relationships that the others might report sketchily or not at all.

"And now," the doctor said as she looked steadily at Vicky, "I should like to ask your advice. I would like to tell Sybil about you and the others. What do you think?"

"Well," Vicky cautioned thoughtfully, "you can tell her. But be careful. Don't say too much."

In a confidential tone the doctor explained, "I think she ought to know. In fact, I don't see how the analysis can go anywhere if she doesn't."

"Be careful," Vicky reiterated. "Although the rest of us know about Sybil, she knows nothing about any of us, never has."

"I understand that, Vicky, but you see, I had planned to tell her about Peggy Lou when I thought she was a dual personality. But Sybil didn't give me a chance."

"Of course not," Vicky explained. "Sybil's always been afraid to reveal her symptoms—afraid of a diagnosis."

"Well," the doctor continued quietly, "I did tell Sybil that she is subject to fugue states during which she is unaware of what's happening."

"I know," Vicky asserted, "but that's very different from telling her that she's not alone in her own body."

"I think it will reassure Sybil to know that she is functioning even though she doesn't know it."

"She, Doctor?" Vicky asked quizzically. "Isn't the pronoun *we*?"

The doctor paused and made no direct answer. It was a thoughtful Vicky who broke the silence, saying,

"I suppose you can tell Sybil. But I repeat: is it *she* who is functioning?" Without waiting for the doctor to reply, Vicky asserted, "We're people, you know. People in our own right."

The doctor lit a cigarette and listened thoughtfully as Vicky went on: "Still, if you want to tell her, go right ahead. But I would advise you to let her know that none of the others would do what she wouldn't like. Tell her that they often do things she can't do but that these are things that wouldn't make her angry if they were done by someone else."

"What about Peggy Lou?" the doctor asked. "Doesn't she sometimes do things of which Sybil would disapprove?"

"Well," Vicky explained, "Peggy Lou does many things Sybil can't do, but Peggy wouldn't hurt anybody. Really, Doctor, she wouldn't." Vicky's tone became confidential: "You know, Peggy Lou went to Elizabeth and got herself into quite a mess there."

"I didn't know."

"Oh, Peggy Lou goes many places." Vicky looked at her watch. "And talking of going places, I suppose I myself had better be going some place right now. To the Met to meet Marian."

"Yes," the doctor agreed, "I'm afraid the hour is up."

"Doctor, do you ever get to the Met?" Vicky asked as they walked to the door. "You'd enjoy it. Also the memorial show of paintings and sculpture in honor of Curt Valentin—'honour' with a *U,* according to the gallery. It's at the Valentin Gallery, in case you get around to it. Well, I must be going. And please know that you can count on me whenever you need me."

Just before Vicky left, she turned, looked at the doctor, and said: "It seems strange for me to be coming to a psychoanalyst. The others are neurotic, but I'm not. At least I don't think I am. In this chaotic age one never knows. But I do want to help you with Sybil and the others. After all, that's the only reason why I'm not in Paris with my family. I don't believe that either Sybil or Peggy Lou has gotten down to the nitty gritty of what's bothering them. Watching them flounder here, I

99

knew I had to step in. How could you get anywhere with them? Sybil lives in total ignorance of any of us, and Peggy Lou is too busy defending herself—and Sybil as well—to be objective. So you see I simply had to come and work with you. Together I think we can get to the bottom of this. So please count on me. I know everything about everybody."

With that, Victoria Antoinette Scharleau, the woman of the world with the graceful movements, the mellifluous voice, and the faultless diction departed as she had come.

Dr. Wilbur liked Vicky. She was very sophisticated but warm, friendly, and genuinely concerned about Sybil. That concern, she decided, would have to be explored.

What, the doctor wondered, would Mademoiselle Scharleau have said if she had been asked how she had gotten into the Dorsett household or when her family was coming for her? As the doctor walked to her desk to write some notes about the Dorsett case, she asked herself, "How is Sybil to become one? Out of how many?"

New York, Vicky thought as she walked out of the doctor's building, isn't like Paris or like any other city in which I've lived since leaving Willow Corners. On a gray day like this, this bustling, ever-changing city seems like a shadow of itself.

She walked briskly because she was late for her appointment with Marian Ludlow at the Met and because she felt free at having left behind her—for the time being—the shadows of those others in whose lives her own was intertwined.

She thought of Marian Ludlow. Tall, with a strikingly good figure, handsome rather than beautiful, Marian was a volatile person. She had bright brown hair, bright brown eyes, and three freckles across her nose. Those freckles were the blemish that rescued her friend from a physical perfection that she herself, with a capacity for idealization, was always too prone to bestow.

100

Marian and she had shared a world of wonder since their accidental meeting in early November, 1954, in the Teachers College cafeteria. Since then, they had been to Carnegie Hall, where they heard the Philharmonic and the Boston Symphony, Walter Gieseking and Pierre Monteux. They had been to the United Nations Conference Building, where they had witnessed a stormy session of the Security Council.

Nothing had been as exciting as the art exhibits. The two of them especially enjoyed those at the Brooklyn Museum, where they had been enchanted not only with the collection of American artists but also with the marvelous contemporary water-color gallery and with an entire floor devoted to a display of American furniture.

Antique furniture for both Marian and Vicky was the past made tangible, a mirror of a departed way of life in which they both rejoiced. Heppelwhite tables, Chippendale chairs, lowboys, and highboys filled their conversation. There had been fascination for them in the dissection of a fine point in a Virginia cupboard or in a tastefully scrolled scrap hinge in a Pennsylvania chest.

Marian had exquisite taste, developed as the result of a wealth that she no longer had. She had been educated in exclusive private schools, had been graduated from Barnard in the 1930s, had gone to finishing school, and, chaperoned by a maiden aunt, had made a typical Henry James grand tour of Europe.

Born to wealth, Marian had married into still more wealth. After her husband's death, Marian had used her fortune for her pleasure. Seeing it dwindle and discovering that, for the first time, she had to work for a living, she had come to Columbia to prepare herself for teaching by taking graduate courses in art education. That's how she happened to be in the cafeteria at Teachers College the afternoon they had first met.

Suddenly realizing that she was within a block of the Met, Vicky abruptly emerged from her reverie, quickened her steps, and headed swiftly toward the Fountain Restaurant.

Standing at the doorway of this immense room designed as a Roman atrium, with its rectangular pool in its center, arched glass ceiling, towering columns, and tables with simulated marble tops, Vicky was overwhelmed by the mass of baroque art confronting her. Although she had been here many times, her reaction had always been the same.

Seated at one of the tables to Vicky's right was Marian Ludlow.

"I'm afraid I'm late," Vicky remarked as she approached her friend. "I must apologize. It was a business appointment. I just couldn't get away."

"I've been enjoying my solitude," Marian replied. "I was thinking about what this room will be like when Carl Milles's fountains are installed in the pool."

"That won't be until summer," Vicky said as she sat down. "I've read that there will be eight fountain figures. Five will represent the arts."

"Milles," Marian replied, "has always been at home in the classical world. We'll have to come back in the summer and see for ourselves."

Vicky could feel Marian's eyes, languorous but with a tinge of sadness, resting softly on her. It was an exquisite feeling to be in this woman's presence, a feeling, too, of infinite satisfaction to know that it had been Marian who had made the initial move toward friendship.

It was the tinge of sadness in Marian's eyes that proved most compelling to Vicky, who, in spite of the fact that she herself was a happy person, had had long experience in responding to the sadness of another. Vicky's empathy had quickened their friendship.

If Marian had a daughter, Vicky thought wistfully, it should have been I. We would have put an end to the generation gap. Though Marian is old enough to be my mother, the years make no difference at all.

"Let's go," Marian was saying. "They'll be out of everything if we don't."

They walked through the immense room toward the food counter. "Cafeteria food on marble tables," Vicky remarked, as Marian, obviously concerned with the contours of her excellent figure, reached for a salad of sliced pineapple and cottage cheese. "It gives a pedestrian flavor to a continental atmosphere." Vicky, slender beyond her desire because Sybil kept her that way, selected macaroni and cheese.

Back at the table beside the rectangular pool, Vicky and Marian talked of silk-weaving in France, the subject of a term paper Marian was preparing. "You know so much about it," Marian said, "I'm certain you can give me invaluable advice." And so they talked of early inventories of the royal furniture repository of Louis XIV, of how the first known material to originate in France was a piece of velvet having the crown as an emblem, dating from the reign of either Henry IV or Louis XIII. "If you can establish which king it is," Vicky said, "you'll have a coup."

The conversation turned to the pictorial and landscape patterns that had reemerged during the early eighteenth-century period as a result of the rediscovery of Chinese motifs. "Did you know," Vicky asked, "that these artists were very much under the influence of Boucher, Pillement, and Watteau?"

"And weren't those artists influenced by the Chinese motifs of Meissen porcelain?" Marian asked. "That was the period of Chinese influence, after all."

"I give you an A," Vicky said with a smile.

Marian finished her coffee, Vicky her hot chocolate. Marian lit a cigarette and remarked, "I'm glad you don't smoke. Don't ever start."

"There's little fear of that," Vicky replied. "It's not one of my vices."

"I haven't noticed any others," Marian teased.

"You'll have to look harder," Vicky replied in the same spirit.

"Well," said Marian, "we have our jewelry class at six. That gives us just time to see 'Word Becomes Image.'"

The exhibit, which was in the Great Hall, was intriguing. There were interpretations by American and European artists from Dürer to Alexander Calder of scenes and characters in some of the world's best-known literary masterpieces—*Aesop's Fables,* Dante's *Inferno,*

103

Faust, Don Quixote, Hamlet, and *King Lear, The Eclogues* of Virgil, and the legends from Ovid's *Metamorphoses.* Among the biblical illustrations was an interpretation of the beasts with seven heads and ten horns from the Apocalypse engraved by Jean Duvet in the sixteenth century.

Lingering over the Duvet work, Vicky remarked, "I used to paint beasts."

"You've never mentioned it," Marian said.

"No. It was back in Omaha some ten years ago when I used to illustrate our pastor's fiery sermons about the beasts rising from the sea."

"I'm glad to hear you talk about your painting," Marian replied. "You've always been so reticent about it, Sybil."

Sybil. The mention of that name didn't really disturb Vicky. That was the only name by which Marian and everyone else knew her—the name on identification cards and checks, in mail boxes, telephone books, in registrars' offices. As a realist Vicky had always accepted these as facts of her unique existence.

Victoria Scharleau couldn't disavow the name even though it actually belonged to "the other girl," as Peggy Lou called her. It was the name of the lean, frightened figure who was never seen at a time like this, among people, relaxed and happy. The real bearer of the name *Sybil* was the reserved, contracted being who walked alone and who, Vicky knew, was seeking a self that to her not only had come naturally but also was the substance of her very existence.

So she was used to the idea of "Sybil." She was discomforted more by the fact that she knew that it was this other Sybil, more than she, who, along with some of the others—those whom Vicky had mentioned to Dr. Wilbur—had really painted the beasts. Vicky felt that even in casual conversation she had been wrong in claiming those paintings as her own.

"I'm reticent about my paintings," Vicky said aloud, "because I know better painters than I."

"Well," Marian replied, "that's always true. By that standard no artist would ever have any sense of accomplishment. But you're no slouch. After all, the head of the art department said that he hasn't had anyone in the department with as much talent as you have for better than twenty years."

"Marian, let's change the subject," Vicky replied uneasily.

It was impossible for Vicky to accept the professor's evaluation of the work of the total Sybil Dorsett as her own. Sybil painted, Vicky painted, and so did most of the other selves of Sybil. Of them all, Sybil, in Vicky's opinion, was the most gifted painter. This ability had manifested itself in childhood. When Sybil's art teachers were impressed by her work, her parents had been confounded until her father had taken her work to be evaluated by an art critic in St. Paul, Minnesota. Only then was there parental acceptance of Sybil's ability. In high school and college Sybil had commanded good sums for her paintings, which were exhibited in prestigious places.

None of the paintings, of course, was Sybil's alone. Most were collaborative efforts of several of the selves. Collaboration had proved constructive at times, destructive at others. But despite diversity of styles and tell-tale lapses in the paintings, Sybil—the total Sybil Dorsett with Sybil herself as the dominant painter—had always had the potentiality of being an important artist. And although that potentiality was never realized because of the psychological problems that deflected Sybil from that course, there had been realization enough for the Columbia art professor to regard Sybil—as Marian had reported—as the most gifted student who had been in the department in the course of over twenty years.

As these thoughts moved through Vicky's mind, she realized how impossible it was to explain her feelings of reticence about talking about her—*their*—paintings to Marian Ludlow or anyone else who thought that there was just *one* artist answering to the name of Sybil Dorsett.

Vicky and Marian had an early dinner on the roof restaurant at Butler Hall, an apartment hotel near the Columbia campus. Marian ordered Salisbury steak, and

105

Vicky had spaghetti and meat balls. Then they went to the six o'clock jewelry class.

The jewelry class was a place to which Vicky went because Sybil couldn't. Taking place in a basement aglow with blow torches used by Vulcanian figures wearing goggles and black aprons, the class stirred in Sybil memories of Willow Corners. And the memories reawakened old, unresolved fears.

Vicky, stepping into the breach when Sybil blacked out or, as tonight, attending the class on her own because she was in the ascendancy, not only was making an A in the subject but also was helping Marian, who had little previous experience, to score an A.

Vicky always enjoyed this class. Some nights she sketched designs for jewelry or executed the designs she had already sketched. This night she was making a link necklace of copper and was helping Marian with a silver pendant.

After class Vicky and Marian went back to Vicky's dormitory room, in which lights from other rooms, turning on and off, were reflected in the window facing the courtyard. Vicky turned on the radio, and they listened to the news and to "The Great Gildersleeve." As the evening came to a close and Marian was getting ready to leave, Vicky very cautiously began putting away the jewelry supplies they had brought back with them. She was determined to leave the room exactly as it had been before they started working.

"Why are you so fussy?" Marian asked. "You room alone. These things won't bother anybody."

"Yes, I know," Vicky replied with a wry smile. Then, trying to disguise her feelings, she chatted amiably with Marian as they walked to the door.

After Marian was gone, Vicky thought of the time that Sybil had brought a sample sketch to Dr. Wilbur's office and had told the doctor that she was afraid to use the sketch because she didn't know if it had come out of a book or just where it came from. It had been Vicky's sketch. Thinking how disturbed Sybil had been then and how disturbed she would also be if she found any jewelry supplies in the room, Vicky wanted to protect her from another terrifying discovery. Vicky thought: "I live alone yet not alone."

And Vicky felt that she was moving toward the shadows of something from which she had been free almost all day.

Sybil was in her dormitory room, studying for an exam in Professor Roma Gans's education course. There was a knock on the door. She thought that it was Teddy Reeves. Standing at the door, however, was not Teddy but a tall, good-looking woman with bright brown hair and bright brown eyes, a woman who was probably in her early forties. Sybil didn't know the woman.

"I can't stay," the woman said. "I'm late for a hairdresser's appointment. Since I knew I'd be passing here, I thought I'd stop and give you this. You've done so much for me, Sybil. I want you to have it."

The woman handed Sybil a lovely handcrafted silver pendant with a beautiful blue stone, lapis lazuli. I don't know why she's giving me this, Sybil thought. "Thank you," she replied faintly as she hesitatingly accepted the pendant.

"See you soon," the woman said and was gone.

See you soon? Done so much for her? It's so unreal. Have I spoken to her before? I've seen her around, but we have never exchanged a single word. Yet she acted as if we were friends. Friends? The confusion raged.

Return to the desk. Try to study.

Sybil found herself clinging to realities. Even while she did so, however, she realized that the time-honored conundrum, the terrible thing, had overtaken her again. It had been the reality of her life to have something happen that had no beginning and to experience the painfully familiar "This is where I came in" feeling, with its tantalizing withholding of everything that had gone before.

Study for the exam. As Sybil sat at her desk, however, the pages of the education text blurred with her panic, and she asked herself fervently: Will there never be an end that also has a beginning? Will there never be continuity bridging the awful void between *now* and *some other time,* a time in the future, a time in the past?

Victoria Antoinette Scharleau, who knew everything, watched Marian Ludlow give Sybil the silver pendant.

7

Why,

Dr. Wilbur adjusted her desk lamp beam a fraction. Before her was almost the whole of the relatively sparse literature about multiple personality. In a pensive mood after Vicky had left her office, she had made a trip to the Academy of Medicine Library, where a librarian had assembled for her almost everything there was on this definitely established but rare illness. Morton Prince's *The Dissociation of a Personality*, first published in 1905, which is well known to students of abnormal psychology, was the only one of the books she had read before. She had tried to get hold of a copy of Dr. Corbey H. Thigpen's and Dr. Hervey Cleckley's 1954 article: "A Case of Multiple Personality" in the *Journal of Abnormal Psychology,* about which some of her colleagues were talking. But this article, about a girl whose pseudonym was Eve, had not been available at the time.

Now, however, as she read into the night, the names Mary Reynolds, Mamie, Felida X, Louis Vive, Ansel Bourne, Miss Smith, Mrs. Smead, Silas Prong, Doris Fisher, and Christine Beauchamp became known to the doctor. These were the people with multiple personalities whom medical history had recorded: seven women and three men.* The newly reported case of Eve made it eight women, and Eve was the only multiple personality known to be alive.

Mary Reynolds, the doctor learned, was the first recorded multiple personality. Her case had been reported in 1811 by Dr. L. Mitchell, of the University of Pennsylvania.

Mamie's case had been described in the *Boston Medical and Surgical Journal* of May 15, 1890. Following that had come reports of Felida X by M. Azam; of Louis Vive, studied by several French observers; of Ansel Bourne, observed by Dr. Richard Hodgson and by Professor William James; of Miss Smith, by M. Flournoy; and of Mrs. Smead, by Professor Hyslop. In 1920, as part of a volume entitled *The Ungeared Mind,* by Robert Howland Chase, there had been the recapitulation of "The Strange Case of Silas Prong," a case of multiple personality previously described by Professor William James.

The complexity of these cases, the doctor realized even after a cursory glance, varied markedly. In cases like those of Miss Smith and Mrs. Smead, which involved dual rather than multiple personalities, the secondary personality, while possessing the faculties of a full human being, exhibited very little independence in voluntarily moving about in a social world—working, acting, and playing. Clearly this characteristic was not true of Sybil. Her alternating personalities were obviously autonomous.

Cases like those of Felida X, Christine Beauchamp, and Doris Fisher were more interesting, for they were examples of independent personalities in the same body, leading their own lives as any other mortal. Miss Beauchamp had three selves; Doris Fisher, five. It was to this type, the doctor speculated, that Sybil belonged. But Sybil's case—again it was only speculation—seemed more complex than that either of Miss Beauchamp or of Doris Fisher.

Well, if it is, it is, the doctor thought, hypothesizing

* Others have been recorded since.

that in Sybil's case there were probably multiple roots. What those roots were, however, was at this stage unknown.

For a time Dr. Wilbur pondered. Then, beginning to read again, she searched for when, in these other cases, the first dissociation had taken place. She had no idea of when Sybil had dissociated for the first time and whether all the personalities had emerged then or whether some had come later. When had Christine Beauchamp first dissociated? According to Prince, it had taken place when Christine was eighteen and as the result of a nervous shock.

Dr. Wilbur didn't actually know, but she surmised that Sybil's first dissociation had taken place during her childhood. The childishness of Peggy seemed to be a clue. And probably there had been a shock for Sybil, too. But what? So little had been revealed that it was all but impossible even to speculate about causes. But, hypothesizing, the doctor thought that possibly there had been multiple roots, or shocks, leading to multiple selves, personifying reactions to those shocks. Many other selves could thus be translated into multiple childhood traumas, multiple roots sprouting into this complex condition.

The Dorsett case was taking on the aspect of an adventure, a whodunit of the unconscious, and Dr. Wilbur became even more excited when she realized that Sybil was the first multiple personality to be psychoanalyzed. This meant that not only would they be breaking new ground, but also that the doctor, through psychoanalysis, would be able to bring a much greater psychological sophistication to an understanding of Sybil than had been available hitherto. Dr. Wilbur's pulse quickened at the challenge and at its possible implications not only for Sybil but for the largely unchartered field of multiple personality.

The analysis, Dr. Wilbur decided, would have to be an unorthodox one. She smiled as she thought; an unorthodox analysis by a maverick psychiatrist. She did consider herself a maverick and knew that it was this characteristic that would stand her in good stead in dealing with this extraordinary case. She knew that she would have to utilize the spontaneous reactions of all the selves not only in uncovering the origin of the illness, but also in treating it. She knew that it would be necessary to treat each of the selves as a person in her own right and to winnow away the reserve of Sybil, the waking self. Otherwise the total Sybil Dorsett would never get well. The doctor knew, too, that she would have to make tremendous sacrifices of time and modify her usual consulting-room Freudian techniques to the harnessing of every shred of spontaneity that would help her break through to the truth that lay concealed behind these selves.

The pivotal question was: *why* had Sybil become a multiple personality? Is there a physical predisposition toward the development of a multiple personality? Do genetic factors play a part? No one knew. The doctor believed, however, that Sybil's condition stemmed from some childhood trauma, though at this stage she couldn't be certain. To date analysis had revealed certain pervading fears—of getting close to people, of music, of hands—that seemed connected with a trauma. Telltale, too, were the seething rage, repressed in Sybil but bursting forth unbridled in Peggy Lou, and the denial of mother in both Peggy Lou and Vicky. The feeling of entrapment strongly suggested trauma.

Many characteristics were common to several of the cases. The waking self, corresponding to the Sybil who had presented herself in Omaha and New York, typically seemed reserved and overnice. The doctor hypothesized that perhaps it was the very repression in this kind of temperament that made it necessary to relegate the emotions that had been repressed to another personality. The books talked of the secondary selves as depleting the waking self of emotions, attitudes, modes of behavior, and acquisitions.

But depletion was the effect, not the cause, of the condition. What in Sybil's case had caused it? What was the original trauma?

In the morning Dr. Wilbur approached the Dorsett

111

appointment hour, as she now always did, wondering "who" would be there. It was Vicky. That was a good start, for Vicky claimed to know everything about the case.

Hunting for the original trauma, the doctor asked Vicky, on this her second appearance in the office, just two days after the first, whether she knew why Peggy Lou was afraid of music, as had become evident in a recent session, and why music deeply disturbed her.

"Music hurts," Vicky replied, elevating her eyebrows and looking at the doctor through the thin wreaths of smoke that came from the doctor's cigarette. "It hurts way inside because it is beautiful, and it makes both Sybil and Peggy Lou sad. They're sad because they're alone and nobody cares. When they hear music, they feel more alone than ever."

Could this, the doctor thought, relate to the original trauma? Possibly it involved the lack of caring, perhaps the lack of nurturing. When she asked why something beautiful should hurt, Vicky replied cryptically: "It's like love."

Then, looking steadily at Vicky, the doctor asked, "Was there something about love that hurt?"

"There was," Vicky replied straightforwardly yet cautiously.

When the doctor asked how precisely love had hurt, Vicky became even more cautious. "Doctor," she said, "Sybil doesn't want to love anybody. It's because she's afraid of getting close to people. You've seen how she's been here. It's all part of the same mosaic—the fear of hands coming at her, the fear of people, the fear of music, the fear of love. All have hurt her. All have made her afraid. All have made her sad and alone."

The doctor, very much aware that Vicky was describing the very symptoms, with the addition of love, that she herself had pondered the night before, wished that this co-analysand of hers would get down to causes. "Vicky," she asked in an oblique attempt to steer her in that direction, "do you share any of these fears?"

"Certainly not," Vicky replied.

"Why is Sybil afraid when you're not?" the doctor persisted.

"That is an essential difference between Sybil and me. I can do what I want to do because I'm not afraid."

"But why aren't you?"

"I have no reason to be, and that's why I'm not." That was as far as Vicky would commit herself. "Poor Sybil," she sighed, changing the thrust of the conversation, "what a trial it has been. She's all choked up. She has an almost constant pain in her head and her throat. She can't cry. And she won't. Everyone was against her when she cried."

"Who is everyone?" the doctor asked hopefully.

"Oh, I'd rather not say," Vicky replied with a cautious smile. "After all, I was not a member of the family. I only lived with them."

Victoria Antoinette Scharleau closed the door that had swung at least partly ajar. Yet there had been a ray of light. The lack of caring, perhaps the lack of nurturing that the doctor had begun to suspect, had assumed greater probability with Vicky's placing the blame for Sybil's inability to cry squarely within the Dorsett family.

Things happened so fast. As Dr. Wilbur pondered this last thought, all at once, noiselessly and with a transition so slight as to be almost imperceptible, the assurance of Victoria Antoinette Scharleau slipped. The aplomb that was characteristic of her disappeared. The eyes that had been serene dilated with the fears that had been recounted. Vicky, who was not a member of the Dorsett family, had returned the body to Sybil, who was.

Startled at finding herself on the couch, sitting close to the doctor, Sybil moved abruptly away. "What happened?" she asked. "I don't remember coming here today. Another fugue?"

Dr. Wilbur nodded. This, she decided, was the moment to spell out what these fugues really were. The analysis would proceed more rapidly, she believed, if Sybil knew about the other selves. Then the doctor could confront her with what the other personalities

113

had said and bring her closer to the memories from which she seemed barred.

"Yes," the doctor told Sybil. "You had another fugue. But it's more complicated than that."

"I'm afraid."

"Of course you are, sweetie," the doctor replied consolingly. "Now tell me, you've never said this to me, but I think you're aware that time goes by without your knowing that it has." Sybil was rigid. "Are you?" When Sybil didn't answer, the doctor persisted: "You know that you have lost time here?"

After a long pause Sybil replied in subdued tones, "I promised myself I would tell you, but I haven't dared."

Then the doctor asked: "What do you think you do in the time you lose?"

"Do?" Sybil replied. The doctor could see that it was an echo more than a concept. "I don't do anything."

"You go right on saying or doing something, even though you're not aware of saying or doing it." The doctor was unrelenting. "It's like walking in your sleep."

"What do I do?"

"Did anyone ever tell you?"

"Well, yes." Sybil lowered her eyes. "All my life I've been told that I had done certain things that I knew I hadn't. I let it go. What else could I do?"

"Who are some of the people who told you?"

"Almost everybody all the time."

"Who?"

"Well, my mother always said I was a bad girl. I never knew what I had done that was bad. She would shake me. I'd ask what I had done. She'd holler, 'You know perfectly well what you did, young lady!' But I didn't know. I don't know now."

"Try not to be too worried," the doctor said gently. "Other people have had it. We can take care of it. It's treatable." Dr. Wilbur could see that this statement had made an enormous impression on Sybil. She seemed more relaxed.

"This condition," the doctor went on to explain, "is more complicated than the fugue states we've already discussed. In a simple fugue there's just a loss of consciousness, but your fugues are not blank."

"I've always called them my blank spells," Sybil said. "To myself, that is, never to anyone else."

"While you yourself lose consciousness," the doctor continued, "another person takes over for you."

"Another person?" Sybil asked, stunned. The question was again mere echo.

"Yes," the doctor replied. She started to explain, but Sybil interrupted.

"Then I'm like Dr. Jekyll and Mr. Hyde?"

Dr. Wilbur slapped her hand in her fist. "That's not a true story," she said. "It's pure fiction. You're not at all like Dr. Jekyll and Mr. Hyde. Stevenson wasn't a psychoanalyst. He created those two characters out of his literary imagination. As a writer he was concerned only with spinning a good yarn."

"May I go now? We're running over," Sybil suddenly said, the pressure on her almost unendurable.

But Dr. Wilbur pressed on relentlessly. She knew that having committed herself, she had to go all the way. "You're too intelligent to subscribe to the popular misconception that has evolved from fiction," she said. "The facts are quite different. I've been reading about other people who have this condition. They don't have a good side and a bad side. They're not torn by the conflict between good and evil.

"Not a great deal is known about this condition. But we do know that the different selves of any one person are likely to share the same ethical code, the same basic moral structure."

"We're running over," Sybil insisted. "I have no right to extra time."

"That's what you always do, Sybil," Dr. Wilbur replied firmly. "Declare yourself unworthy. That's one of the reasons you need other personalities."

"Personalities?" Sybil echoed fearfully. "Did you say 'personalities'? Plural?"

"Sybil," the doctor said gently, "this is nothing to be afraid of. There's a personality who calls herself Peggy Lou. She's self-assertive. There's Peggy Ann, who also is a fighter, but she is more tactful than Peggy Lou. The other calls herself Vicky. She's assured, at ease, responsible, a very delightful person."

Sybil rose to go.

"There's nothing to be afraid of," the doctor repeated.

But Sybil's pleading "Let me go, *please* let me go" showed that she had been profoundly shaken. Thinking it unwise to let her leave alone, the doctor offered to walk out with her.

"You have another patient," Sybil insisted. "I'll be all right." Walking out the door through which only an hour before a radiant Vicky had entered, Sybil was pale as a cod.

Later, in the gathering dark of her silent office, Dr. Wilbur speculated about the Dorsett case. Sybil had remained herself throughout the interview. Now that she knew about the other personalities, the first analysis in history of a multiple personality was about to begin in earnest. She turned again to the volumes about multiple personality that cluttered her desk, and she also took copies of Freud and Charcot from her shelves, combing the familiar references to hysteria.

Even though multiple personality was a bizarre and abnormal phenomenon, it was, Dr. Wilbur was certain, not a psychosis but a hysterical condition. This growing realization renewed her confidence in being able to handle the case; for although she had never treated a multiple personality, she had not only treated but had had many successes in treating hysterics. Her experience with hysterics had, in fact, begun so early in her career that the Omaha internist who had sent Sybil Dorsett to her in the first place had done so because of her success in treating patients with hysterical symptoms.

Multiple personality, it had become evident to Dr. Wilbur, belongs to the class of patients known as psychoneurotics. The specific neurosis is *grande hystérie*. The kind of *grande hystérie* from which Sybil Dorsett suffered, not only with multiple personalities but with a variety of psychosomatic illnesses and disturbances in the five senses, was as grave as it was rare.

Dr. Wilbur had seen schizophrenics—psychotics—who had not been as ill as Sybil. One might say that they were running a psychotic temperature of 99 degrees, whereas Sybil has been running a psychoneurotic temperature of 105 degrees, thought Dr. Wilbur. Though a psychosis is a more severe illness, the point is: How ill is the patient? It is not: How serious is the patient's illness?

There is no reason to be discouraged, Dr. Wilbur assured herself. Maybe she was being brash in thinking that Sybil Dorsett would get well. But it was an extremely complicated case, and it would take brashness to stick with it and see it through.

The phone rang. It was after ten. Probably a patient in a crisis, calling for help. Please, not a suicide tonight, she thought. When the day was done, she needed an interval to cleanse psychoses and psychoneuroses out of her system, to stop living other people's lives. She wanted more time for her husband, for professional meetings, to visit with relatives and friends, to read and think, to have her hair done and go shopping. So often these commonplace activities had to be thrown aside because of a patient's sudden, urgent need.

She picked up the phone. It was Teddy Reeves. "Dr. Wilbur," Teddy reported, "Sybil Dorsett fell apart. She really blew. I don't know what to do for her."

"I'll come right over," Dr. Wilbur volunteered. As she placed the phone back in its cradle, she wasn't really surprised at what Teddy Reeves had told her. She suspected that what Teddy had meant by "she really blew" was that Peggy Lou had taken over.

When Sybil finally admitted to the doctor that she had lost time, it had been an admission also to herself. Never before, despite all the years of gyrating from *now* to *some other time,* with minutes, days, weeks, years unaccounted for, had she ever formulated the idea of "lost time." Instead she had used the circumlocution: "blank spells."

However, the shiver that went through her body when the doctor told her, "While you yourself lose consciousness, another personality takes over for you," hadn't been fear. It was recognition. That sentence explained the things, good and bad, that people had said she had done, but which *she* hadn't, the strangers who said that they knew her. Embarrassed that the doctor would find out about all the terrible things, the evil things about which perhaps the doctor knew already but wasn't telling, she had fled from the office, haunted by self-accusation.

Whittier Hall at first brought surcease. The meeting in the dormitory elevator with Judy and Marlene, the twins she was tutoring, became a new affront, a new accusation. Inseparable, complete as an entity, *one,* they had spent a lifetime together, whereas she had not even spent all her time with herself!

She fumbled for her key, but with her unsteady hand she could not insert the key in the lock. Not trusting herself to negotiate the room alone, she tapped feebly at the door of Teddy Reeves's room.

Teddy put Sybil to bed and, standing by in terror and compassion, watched as Sybil, getting in and out of bed, also went in and out of a series of what appeared to be disparate moods. One moment she was a ranting child, walking on the furniture, leaving her fingerprints on the ceiling. The next moment she was a self-possesssed and knowing woman, talking of herself in the third person and saying, "I'm glad Sybil knows. Yes, indeed, it will be better for all of us this way." Then Sybil became the quaking person, the one who had tapped at Teddy's door. She was lying inert on the bed when the doctor arrived.

Dr. Wilbur could see that Sybil was suffering, and she tried to reassure Sybil by explaining that having other selves was nothing to be afraid of because it was just a form of what psychiatrists call "acting out": lots of people act out what troubles them.

It didn't work. Indeed, when, far from being reassured, Sybil protested, "I've never heard of one person who does that," the doctor began to question whether, even after all the delays, she had been too precipitous in the way she had sprung on Sybil the knowledge of the other selves.

"I'll give you a seconal," the doctor reassured her, "and you'll be fine in the morning." The doctor had discovered that barbiturate sedatives relieved Sybil's anxiety for forty-eight hours.

Morning came. Sybil awakened, freed of anxiety by the seconal the doctor had given her the night before. The multiple selves seemed like a nightmare that had receded.

It was well past midnight when the doctor left Whittier Hall. Although by no means certain what the alternating personalities actually represented, she hypothesized that the waking Sybil more or less corresponded to the conscious mind and that the alternating selves belonged to the unconscious. Borrowing an image from anatomy and biology, she saw the alternating personalities as lacunae—the very small cavities in bone that are filled with bone cells—in the unconscious of Sybil. Sometimes quiescent, these lacunae, with proper stimulation, emerged and lived. They functioned within Sybil but also in the outside world, where they seemed to act out the particular problem they were defending.

Defenses in the unconscious, the doctor thought as she paid the taxi driver. Now what I have to do is to become acquainted with each of the personalities, no matter how many there are, and to determine with what conflict each of them deals. This will take me to the roots of the trauma that made necessary the dissociation. This way I can get to the reality—an intolerable reality, I suspect—against which the selves have become a defensive maneuver.

The analysis, the doctor realized, will, of course, have to include all the personalities, and each of them will have to be analyzed both as an autonomous human being and as part of the total Sybil Dorsett.

What was of more immediate importance was to get closer to the waking Sybil. That was the only way to get around the anxiety and defensiveness behind which the other selves lay in ambush.

But how does one get closer to this remote and timid Sybil Dorsett?

"Sybil," Dr. Wilbur asked one morning in April, 1955, when Sybil had brought some of her water colors to the office, "how would you like to drive up with me to Connecticut some Sunday during the dogwood season? The countryside is lovely then, and you can sketch the flowering trees and shrubs."

Dammit, the doctor thought, as Sybil replied diffidently, "Oh, you have more important things to do than to spend a Sunday with me," I must make her understand that I regard her as an extraordinarily gifted woman, that I would enjoy being with her even if she weren't my patient. Is there no way of making her realize that even though she is extremely handicapped by her illness, I don't think less of her? Will she never understand that in spite of the fact that she undervalues herself to a marked degree, I do not undervalue her?

Indeed, it was only after much argument that Dr. Wilbur was able to persuade Sybil to agree to the trip—the trip that could, Dr. Wilbur was sure, make Sybil gain confidence and thaw.

As Dr. Wilbur drove up to Whittier Hall at 7:00 A.M. on a sunny Sunday in early May, 1955, she saw that Sybil was waiting with Teddy Reeves. Teddy, who had always manifested a proprietary interest in Sybil, had become even more possessive after Sybil had taken her into confidence about the multiple selves. Not knowing about them that night in March when she called Dr. Wilbur, Teddy now not only was able to recognize Vicky and Peggy Lou but also had set about building a relationship with them. Standing with Sybil in front of Whittier Hall, Teddy noted that the top of the doctor's convertible was down, and she fussed about whether Sybil had a scarf to protect her against the elements. When Sybil said that she had, Teddy cautioned that even so it was too cool to drive with the top of the car down. And although both Sybil and the doctor assured her that they would be all right, she remained unconvinced. But Teddy's greatest concerns were whether during the trip Peggy Lou was going to remain quiet and through how much of the outing Sybil would be Sybil.

For her part, Sybil seemed very much herself as she waved goodbye to Teddy and stepped into the doctor's convertible. In her navy blue suit and red hat she looked attractive and more at ease than the doctor had ever seen her.

The way that Sybil had concealed her pleasure in the trip until after they had left Teddy did not escape the doctor, who thought it both sensitive and thoughtful of Sybil to be aware of Teddy's envy and to guard against it.

Wanting the occasion to be purely social, Dr. Wilbur confined the conversation to the here and now, to the towns and houses they passed, to the geography and history of the land, and to the scenery. They skirted the small shore cities, turned off at Southport, and drove directly to the Sound. "I've always wanted to draw and paint boats," Sybil remarked as she looked at the boats in the Sound for the first time, "but I've always felt that I couldn't get the shapes right."

"Try," said the doctor as she stopped the car. Seated in the parked car, Sybil made some sketches of sail boats anchored at the marina.

"I like the sketches," the doctor said. Sybil seemed pleased.

Leaving the Sound, Dr. Wilbur drove in a leisurely way back and forth on various highways and on old country roads with little traffic. To Sybil, who had never been in this part of the country before, she pointed out that some of the houses they passed were prerevolutionary, while some of the others, although modern, had either original prerevolutionary windows or replicas of such windows. Sybil remarked: "My father's a builder-contractor. He's very much interested in architecture, and he developed my interest." The father had scarcely been mentioned in the analysis, and Dr. Wilbur was glad to hear about him.

The conversation turned to the beautiful plantings of dogwood, lilac, and flowering crab. Sybil asked to stop so that she could do a pencil sketch of a hill studded with flowering crab and dogwood.

Sybil had insisted upon providing lunch, which the doctor and she ate at a small camping ground near Kent, Connecticut. At the time Dr. Wilbur thought that Sybil had hoped to make the lunch her contribution to the outing, but she later learned that the picnic lunch was a precaution against having to go into a restaurant. In fact, Sybil's fear of restaurants was so intense that being in one had often led to "lost time."

Nor was it until later that the doctor learned why, when agreeing to the trip, Sybil had insisted upon returning to New York by four o'clock at the latest, preferably by three. "I have some work to do," Sybil had explained. The real reason, as the doctor later learned, was that Sybil had been afraid that, by staying out beyond three or four o'clock, she would show the signs of emotional disturbance, fatigue, and fright that often manifested themselves at the end of the day. She had been afraid that she would dissociate. And she hadn't wanted to risk having the doctor meet the other personalities outside the office.

And so, promptly at 3:00 P.M. Dr. Wilbur's convertible was once again at Whittier Hall.

At the time neither Dr. Wilbur nor Sybil knew that they had not been alone on that trip to Connecticut. Peggy Lou, who was also present, was delighted that Sybil had taken her somewhere at last. Vicky, another unseen passenger in the doctor's car, couldn't wait to tell Marian Ludlow about the old prerevolutionary houses.

In that car, too, were passengers whom neither the doctor nor Sybil had ever met. Marcia Lynn Dorsett, pert and assertive, with a shield-shaped face, gray eyes, and brown hair, had watched every step of the trip.

As the car swung in front of Whittier Hall and Dr. Wilbur said goodbye to Sybil, Marcia Lynn turned to Vanessa Gail, her close friend, and said in an English accent: "She cares about us." Vanessa, who was a tall, slender girl with a willowy figure, dark chestnut-red hair, light brown eyes, and an expressive oval face, communicated to Mary that single, simple sentence: "She cares about us." Mary, a maternal little-old-lady type, plump, thoughtful, and contemplative, repeated with a slight smile, as if it were a question: "She cares about us?" Then Marcia Lynn, Vanessa Gail, and Mary put into execution an internal grapevine through which the message rang loud and clear: *This Dr. Wilbur cares about us.* After that Marcia Lynn, Vanessa Gail, Mary, and everybody else held a conclave and decided that "We'll go and see her."

Part II

Becoming

8

Willow Corners

The trip to Connecticut produced a change, not only in the other personalities but also in Sybil herself. Less guarded, less constrained during the summer of 1955 than during the first seven months of the analysis, Sybil began to talk of her early environment. There were no sudden revelations about the root causes of the multiplicity, but out of the portrait of the town and the milieu in which Sybil—presumably born one—had become many, Dr. Wilbur was able to acquire insights that contributed to a later understanding of causes. Thus it was that, increasingly, Dr. Wilbur led Sybil—and Vicky as well—into a minute exploration of Willow Corners, Wisconsin, where Sybil, who was born on January 20, 1923, had spent the first eighteen years of her life.

Willow Corners stood in the flat terrain of southwestern Wisconsin, close to the Minnesota line. The surrounding countryside was flat, and the hard blue sky seemed so low as to be within hand's grasp. The local accent was barbed with a nasal twang, and the men and women, riding on their open wagons to town from the outlying farms during Sybil's early years, were a constant testament to the town's reliance on the land.

The town itself was dotted with tall maple and elm trees, but despite its name it was without willows. The houses, most of which had been built by the men who worked for Willard Dorsett, were chiefly white frame dwellings. The unpaved streets, dusty on dry days, were mud-filled bogs on rainy days.

Outwardly, there was nothing remarkable about Willow Corners. Founded in 1869, it was not a small town; it was a tiny town, in which the monotonous news of its one thousand persons, living in an area of two square miles, was recorded in the *Corners Courier,* the town's weekly newspaper, whose typical headlines were: SMALL TWISTER DEMOLISHES JONES OUTHOUSE; MOTHERS CLUB PICNIC AT HIGH SCHOOL WEDNESDAY.

Originally a frontier town, Willow Corners had been developed at the coming of the railroad. During Sybil's time the town was chiefly a wheat-producing farming community. Main Street, the hub of the town, had its general store, hardware store, small hotel, barbershop, drugstore, bank, and post office. Particular to Willow Corners were a gun shop dating back to the town's frontier days and two grain elevators, which were central to its economic life. The stores were open on Wednesday and Saturday nights, at which times parents and their children made a festive ritual of shopping together. It was the occasion, too, for the exchange of news and gossip.

The town had two policemen: one worked days, and one worked nights. There were one lawyer, one dentist, and one doctor. An ambulance always stood ready to take the sick to the already world-famous Mayo Clinic in Rochester, Minnesota, eighty miles away.

A slice of mid-America, the town was Republican in domestic politics, isolationist in international sympathies, and stratified in class structure, which included at one end of the spectrum a moneyed elite and at the other a working class. Mistaking money for virtue, the townsfolk tended to venerate the rich however their wealth was acquired and however they behaved— despite the best efforts of the good ladies of the Willow Corners Reading Club, the Willow Music Club, and the Choral Society of Willow County to bring culture to the town.

Before Sybil's birth and until she was six years old,

the town's wealthiest man was her father. That stature was lost in the Depression, in which he met with serious reverses. From 1929, when Sybil was six, until 1941, when, at eighteen, she left town to go to college, the wealthiest persons were German and Scandinavian farmers, the Stickneys, who owned the local bank, and a Mrs. Vale, an uncouth and vulgar woman who, through marriages to five successive husbands, had acquired property in town and a silver mine in Colorado.

Willow Corners, as any sociologist could predict, had churches of many faiths. The fundamentalist groups ranged from the Seventh-Day Baptists, who had founded the town's first church, to the Seventh-Day Adventists, the Church of Saint John Baptist de La Salle, and the Church of the Assembly of God. The Methodists, Congregationalists, and Lutherans all looked askance at one another and at the Roman Catholics, whom they regarded as the incarnation of evil.

Bigotry was rampant, and the town, although self-righteous in its utterances, was often cruel in its behavior. There were jeers for the mentally retarded ice man and snickers for the telephone operator who had a nervous tic. Prejudice against Jews, of whom there were a few in Willow Corners, and Negroes, of whom there were none, was intense.

In the course of events, bigotry and cruelty were overlooked, and the town, proceeding unthinkingly, abounded in an easy, unreasoned optimism. That optimism was expressed in such shibboleths as "If at first you don't succeed, try, try again" and in copy-book maxims such as "Today's leaves of hope are tomorrow's blossoms," which was embossed in an inscription in the combined auditorium-gymnasium used by both elementary and high schools. That tomorrow's blossoms were withering on today's leaves of narrowness simply did not occur to the virtuous citizens of Willow Corners.

On Vine Street, kitty-corner to the schools, stood the Dorsett home, which had already appeared in the analysis: the white house with black shutters. One could

129

regard black and white as the extremes of life, or as life and death, but no such symbolism was intended by Willard Dorsett, the builder of the house. Dorsett had had only utility in mind in providing for spacious lawns, a basement above ground, a garage, and a small adjoining building that served as his carpentry shop and office. Large maple trees shaded the front of the house. In the rear was a cement walk leading to an alley, which in turn led to the backs of the stores on Main Street. The Dorsetts' kitchen steps led to the cement walk.

Nor could one make too much of the fact that the Dorsetts' next-door neighbor was a recluse, the woman across the street a dwarf, and the man down the street his thirteen-year-old daughter's rapist who, after the event, went right on living in the same house with her as though nothing had happened. It was all part of the curious deformity and lewdness, resulting in assorted illegitimate children, that ran like a subterranean current through this town, outwardly so average, so normal, so puritanical.

The Dorsett household had its own unmistakable peculiarities—perhaps invisible at first glimpse, often minimized, but pervasive. When questioned about the Dorsett family, Mrs. Moore, Sybil's piano teacher, reported that Sybil was moody and that both mother and daughter had emotional problems. A distant cousin of Willard Dorsett characterized the father and daughter as "quiet" and the mother as "lively, witty, with a lot of get-up-and-go," but also as "nervous." This same observer talked of the excessive closeness between mother and daughter, who were always seen together. A favorite teacher recalled that "Sybil's mother always had Sybil by the arm."

Jessie Flood, who had been a live-in maid in the Dorsett home for six years, said only, "They're the most wonderful people in the world. Mrs. Dorsett was very good to me and my family. She gave us everything—all kinds of things. There never were kinder people than the Dorsetts."

James Flood, Jessie's father, who worked for Willard

Dorsett in the carpentry business, remarked that "Dorsett was the best boss in the world."

Willard Dorsett, born in Willow Corners in 1883 and descended from the original settlers, as were most of the townsfolk, brought the former Henrietta Anderson home as his wife in 1910.

The Dorsetts and Andersons were alike in lineage and tradition. On her paternal side Hattie was the great granddaughter of Charles, an English clergyman, who with his brother Carl, a schoolmaster, emigrated to Virginia from Devon, England, under a grant from Lord Baltimore. On the maternal side Hattie was even closer to England. Aileen, her mother, was the daughter of English-born parents who had left their native Southampton to move to Pennsylvania. Aubrey Dorsett, Willard's father, was the grandson of an Englishman who came to Pennsylvania from Cornwall, and Mary Dorsett, Willard's mother, who was born in Canada, was descended from an English family that, before settling in Canada, had fled to Holland to escape religious persecution.

Willard and Hattie met on a blind date while he was visiting in Elderville, Illinois, the town of which Winston Anderson, Hattie's father, was a founding father and first mayor. Winston Anderson came to Elderville after fighting in the cavalry of the Union forces in the Civil War. He had joined up at the age of seventeen by pretending to be eighteen. In Elderville in later years he ran a music store, headed the choir of the Methodist church, and again became mayor.

The flamboyant and volatile Hattie embarrassed Willard Dorsett on their very first date. They were strolling along Elderville's Main Street when Hattie suddenly came to a dead halt and made an impromptu speech on behalf of her father, who was running for reelection as mayor. Willard, dismayed, stood passively on the sidelines.

But while other men whom Hattie's good looks, wit, and vivacity had won had broken off with her because of her sharp tongue and her patent eccentricities, Willard did not. He was willing to "put up with her," as he phrased it, because he thought her intellectual, "re-fined," and a talented pianist. Since he himself sang tenor in the church choir, he pictured Hattie Anderson as his future accompanist. In the spirit of the easy nos-trums and homespun panaceas of Willow Corners, he believed that, although Hattie's behavior was often eccentric, she would change as she got older. When they married, she was twenty-seven, and what he meant by "getting older" was somewhat obscure. At any rate, he was in love with Hattie Anderson, and after a number of weekend dates in Elderville he asked her to marry him.

Hattie wasn't in love with Willard and said so. Her blind date with him had been a calculated act of de-fiance against the jeweler to whom she had been en-gaged, but who had reneged on his promise to give up alcohol. Moreover, Hattie claimed that all men were alike, not to be trusted (a sentiment Peggy Lou had echoed in Dr. Wilbur's consulting room), with "only one thing on their minds."

Still, the thought of living in Wisconsin appealed to Hattie, who had never been out of her native Illinois. Going to live in another state was the reason she gave for going, in 1910, to live in Willow Corners as Mrs. Willard Dorsett.

In time Hattie grew to think a great deal of Willard, even to care about him. He was good to her, and she tried to reciprocate. She cooked what he liked, fussed over recipes for good pies and cakes, and always had his meals on time—dinner precisely at twelve noon and supper at 6:00 P.M. sharp. Although she didn't espe-cially enjoy housework, she became a frantic and fanatic housekeeper. In the early days of marriage, too, Hattie and Willard had long, pleasant musical evenings. She was indeed the accompanist he had envisioned.

During the first thirteen years of the Dorsetts' mar-riage Hattie had four miscarriages, no children. Both Willard and Hattie began to think that they never would have children. Neither was sufficiently aware, however, to question whether the miscarriages had any psychological significance. Yet psychological compo-

132

nents seemed likely in the light of Hattie's ambivalence about having a baby. She enjoyed taking care of other people's babies and on at least one occasion joked with the mother of a newborn child about "stealing the baby." But expressing herself as urgently wanting a child of her own at one minute, Hattie would express opposite sentiments the next minute. The actual prospect of having to care for the child often made her antagonistic to motherhood.

Later, Dr. Wilbur speculated that the powerful surges of conflicting emotions upset Hattie's hormonal system and became a psychosomatic component of the miscarriages. In any case, when Sybil was conceived, Willard was afraid that this baby, too, might not achieve life. He therefore exerted over Hattie a dominance he had never shown before, forbidding her to appear in public during the pregnancy. Thus secrecy and concealment surrounded Sybil even in the womb.

At birth Sybil weighed five pounds, one and one-fourth ounces. As if ashamed that she was so tiny, Willard took great pains to have the one and a quarter ounces included on the birth announcements. Willard took it upon himself to name the baby, and Hattie, who did not like the name of Sybil Isabel, decided to use that name only when absolutely necessary. At other times Hattie was determined to call her daughter Peggy Louisiana, which later was often abbreviated to Peggy Lou, Peggy Ann, or just Peggy.

But it was more than Sybil's name that disturbed Hattie in the first months of the infant's life. The old ambivalence about being a mother reasserted itself. Thus Hattie, seeing her daughter for the first time, remarked darkly: "She's so fragile, I'm afraid she'll break."

In fact, it was Hattie herself who "broke." Severe depression overtook her after giving birth and lasted for the first four months of Sybil's life. In this period Hattie's only contact with the baby was to breast-feed her. Otherwise, the care of the infant fell to a nurse, to Willard, and, chiefly, to Grandma Dorsett.

When Hattie was well enough to be up and about,

she had a head-on collision with Willard about nursing the child when there was company in the house. Even though Hattie wanted to take Sybil into the bedroom and close the door, Willard issued the stern injunction: "No. Everybody will know what you're doing."

Hattie pointed out that other women—the women in the back pew at church, the farm women who came to town on their lumber wagons and often lunched with the Dorsetts—nursed their babies not only when other people were around but also in other people's presence —which Hattie was not proposing to do. But Willard remained obdurate, pointing out that Hattie was not a "farm woman."

Hattie acquiesced but resented her acquiescence. For her part, Sybil, unfed, cried. In turn, Hattie blamed the baby for the crying, which made Hattie nervous, and it was the nervousness this crying produced in Hattie, more than an awareness of any adverse effect that the lack of feeding might have on the baby, more even than resentment at being throttled by Willard, that made her scream, "I could just go through the ceiling!" This was one of her favorite expressions of her chronic frustration.

The depression that followed Sybil's birth intensified the volatility and anxiety that had always been characteristic of Hattie Dorsett. As time went on, Hattie became less and less concerned with pleasing Willard. "I don't care. It's a free country," she would sputter when he complained about an omission in her hitherto painstaking care of him. No longer did she have the patience to sit still long enough to accompany him at the piano. Indeed, no longer could she sit still under any circumstances for more than a few minutes without getting up to straighten the curtain or to flick off a little dust from the furniture. She would even act like this in other people's houses. Although she knew how to sew, her hand wasn't steady enough for her to thread a needle. Willard sewed all of Sybil's baby clothes. Restless, frenetic, Hattie played with words as she played with curtains and dust. She tossed off rhymes and fell into the habit of repeating the ends of people's sentences. If

134

someone said, "I've got such a headache," Hattie would repeat, "Such a headache."

By the age of eight, Sybil had come often to sit on the back-porch steps or on the trunk in the attic or on the box in the front hall and, leaning her head on her knees, to wonder why in the world she felt . . . not able to find the right word, she would settle for a "lack of something." But why in the world, she wondered, should something be lacking when she lived in one of the best houses in Willow Corners and had better clothes and more toys than any other child in town? She particularly enjoyed her dolls, her crayons and paints, and her little iron and ironing board.

The more urgently she tried to define the lack, the more elusive it became. All she knew was that some indefinable omission made her feel, as her mother would put it, "sad, down, and blue." What was most disturbing to Sybil was her feeling that she had no reason to be unhappy and that, by being so, she was somehow betraying her parents. To assuage her feelings of guilt she prayed for forgiveness on three counts: for not being more grateful for all she had; for not being happy, as her mother thought she should be; and for what her mother termed "not being like other youngsters."

Disconsolate, tortured, Sybil would sometimes hasten from the porch steps, the attic, or the front hall to the upper floor of the house, where Grandma Dorsett lived.

Her grandmother's place in Sybil's life was pivotal; it was, after all, her grandmother and not her mother who cared for Sybil as an infant. Then, too, while her mother was volatile and ambivalent, her grandmother was balanced and constant. And in the sanctuary of Grandma's home were many mansions—the recollections of small experiences that loomed large in the retrospect of Dr. Wilbur's consulting room.

Grandma would take Sybil in her lap. Sitting there, the child would draw pictures on the drawing paper that her grandmother always had ready for her. Proud of what Sybil drew, her grandmother would hang the drawings on the wall beside the oil paintings she herself had made many years before. Grandma, who had many jars of dried prunes, apricots, and figs, would take Sybil to the kitchen cupboard and let Sybil choose whatever she liked. Grandma let her open the drawers and fold everything she wanted to fold. One day Sybil found a baby picture of herself in one of the drawers. When she saw that picture, stored so carefully, she realized freshly that Grandma really *liked* her. There was even greater proof when Grandma came to Sybil's defense when Hattie accused the child of being bad. "Now, Hattie," her grandmother would say, "she's just a child." And Sybil remembered, too, the times when she felt sick. When, finally, Grandma came down to stay with her, Sybil, who had been unable to take food, suddenly could eat. Besides, when Grandma laughed, it was nice; it didn't hurt at all.

The visits upstairs with Grandma were never long, however. Her mother allowed only a set time and, as the visit proceeded, Sybil could feel that time was running out. There was so great a need and so little opportunity for its fulfillment that when her mother mounted the stairs to reclaim Sybil, the child could feel time literally slipping away.

When Grandpa came home, however, it was Sybil herself who brought the visit to a close. She didn't like her grandfather, a large, burly man, given to rough play. The sound of his wooden leg on the stairs, which heralded his approach, made her tell her grandmother: "I have to go now." In reply Grandma would smile understandingly.

When Sybil was four years old, her grandmother had a stroke and was sometimes not herself. She would wander around Willow Corners not knowing her way. Sybil made it her job to find her grandmother and bring her home, protecting Grandma until she recovered as for so long Grandma had protected her.

For five years after her recovery, Grandma Dorsett continued to protect Sybil. But, when Sybil was nine, Grandma was afflicted by a new illness—cancer of the cervix—which worried Sybil and made her afraid.

9

Yesterday Was Never

There was a coffin in the big house in Willow Corners, and they were going to take it away. It was almost one o'clock, and through the window of the white kitchen with its speckled linoleum Sybil could see the men from the funeral home bringing in the folding chairs for the service.

"Go to your room," her mother told her. "Mama will come and get you when we're ready and you can come down for the funeral."

Her mother then gave her a lollipop to lick while she waited. She lay on the bed, toying with the lollipop. She could hear voices downstairs, distant voices that, since she had been removed from them, had nothing to do with her. Then for a while she heard nothing.

Suddenly her father was standing over her. "Come on," he said, "the service is all over. You can come with us to the cemetery."

They had forgotten her. They had promised she could come down for the service, but they hadn't kept their promise. She was *nine* years old. The service had taken place in her own house. But they left her upstairs, with a fool lollipop as if she were a baby. She could not, would not forgive her parents.

On went her coat, on went her tam and plaid scarf. Down the stairs she went, past all those people, silent and motionless, on to the sidewalk. "You're to go in this car, Sybil," the minister said.

Inside the car were her uncle Roger and his wife,

137

another Hattie, whom she didn't like. Her uncle and her father looked so much alike that the minister had put her with the "wrong" daddy. She was upset.

She was also disturbed because this was *her* grandmother, yet she was the one her father and mother, so busy with all those other people, overlooked or pushed around. It was unfair. The tears, ice cold, stayed within her. She never cried aloud.

The car had stopped. They were walking toward the Dorsett family plot on a road in a cemetery in the village of her grandfather's birth. He was the first white male to be born in the county.

Walking here, Sybil thought about death. Death, she had been told in church, was a beginning. She couldn't quite see that. Her grandmother had told her that someday Jesus would come to raise from the graves those who loved Him. Then, Grandma had said, she and Sybil would be together forever in the earth made new.

Uncle Roger and Aunt Hattie led Sybil to where the family was standing: mother and daddy, Aunt Clara and her husband, Anita and Ella (two years old), and, of course, grandpa. Together they stood some ten feet from her grandmother's grave, silent beneath an overcast Wisconsin sky. It was a cold, windy April day.

The gray metal casket, with banks of flowers over it, had been placed near the grave. The minister was standing beside it. "And I saw a new heaven," he began, "and a new earth . . . and I John saw the holy city, new Jerusalem, coming down from God out of heaven, prepared as a bride adorned for her husband. . . . and there shall be no more death, neither sorrow, nor crying, neither shall there be any more pain. . . . And he that sat upon the throne said, Behold, I make all things new."

Sybil saw not the metal casket, the flowers, or the people; what she saw was Mary, her Canadian grandmother married to a native of Willow Corners, living in *his* town. An outsider to the people in his church, Mary had been forced to do his bidding. She loved to read, but he had stopped her with the injunction: "Any-

138

thing but truth is false." Religious writings alone were true, he thought.

Sybil could see her grandmother in her long skirts, her hightop shoes, her white hair, her small blue eyes, her warm, sweet smile.

What Sybil heard were not the words of the minister but her grandmother's gentle voice saying, "It's all right, Hattie," when her mother had said, "Sybil, you mustn't bounce on grandma's bed."

Her grandmother's big bed was high and soft. Sybil bounced on it all she liked. Her grandmother would scoop her up, rock her and say, "Sybil, Sybil, Sybil." When she was with her grandmother, there was no hollering. Home, just downstairs, seemed miles and miles away—a memory to forget.

Sybil would show her grandmother her drawings, and her grandmother would say, "Wonderful," and hang them on the wall. Her grandmother had a big box by the window, and she had a lot of magazines and papers in it, with all the children's pages, which she saved just for Sybil. And she let Sybil draw pictures, and Sybil stayed inside all the lines, coloring neatly. Her grandmother liked what Sybil did.

Her grandmother let Sybil set the table and didn't say Sybil did it all wrong. If Sybil did do something wrong, her grandmother didn't get mad at her. Sybil could tell her lots of things, pleading, "You won't tell mother, will you?" Her grandmother would say, "I never tell Hattie anything that you tell me." And she didn't.

There were flowers in the woods where Sybil had walked with her grandmother to the river, but now the minister was saying, "For so much as it has pleased Almighty God to permit our sister, Mary Dorsett, to fall asleep, we do tenderly commit her body to the ground . . ."

Asleep. Her grandmother was asleep. They would not again walk together to the river. Only the flowers would be there—the flowers all alone, without her grandmother and also without Sybil.

". . . Earth to earth, ashes to ashes, dust to dust, in

the hope of her joyful resurrection through Jesus Christ, Our Lord."

The wind howled over Sybil's father and her uncle Roger in silent grief, over her aunt Clara, wringing her hands and moaning hysterically, over these grown children bereft of a mother. It howled over her grandfather's soft moan. Sybil alone, her throat constricting, her chest growing heavy, and her fingers becoming prickly and numb, was dry-eyed.

The wind was cold. The feeling was icy blue with brown specks. Anything that is cold is not love. Love is warm. Love is Grandma. Love is being committed to the ground.

The glimmer of the metal casket in the streak of sun momentarily superseded the gray of the day. The casket was in the hands of the men who had come to do a terrible thing. They had lifted the casket and were beginning to lower it. Inch by inch, moment by moment, they were pushing her grandmother down deep, more deep into the earth. They were burying love.

Everyone was weeping now, but still Sybil's eyes were dry, dry as the barren world that stretched before her, a world in which nobody said, "Sybil, Sybil, Sybil," a world without anyone to listen when she tried to talk, a world without love.

Propelled by powerful feelings, galvanized into locomotion, Sybil found herself moving forward. It was one or two slow steps at first, but then there were more steps, faster steps toward the banks of flowers over the lowered casket. She was at the grave, her body poised to jump into it, to join her grandmother forever.

Then there was that hand grabbing her arm with a swift, sharp movement. The restraining hand was pulling her, dragging her away from the grave, away from her grandmother.

The wind howled. The sky grew dark. There was nothing.

That hand with its overwhelming force was still pulling her. Its pressure was deeply embedded in her flesh. Her arm ached with the soreness engendered by the sharp, jerky movement.

Sybil turned to see who it was who had so forcibly removed her from her grandmother. Was it her uncle Roger, her father? They were not there.

There was no grave. There were no banks of flowers. No wind. No sky. Daddy and Mother, Uncle Roger and Aunt Hattie, Aunt Clara and the rich old man she married, the minister, all those other people were not here.

Instead of a grave there was a desk. The banks of flowers were blackboards. Instead of a sky there was a ceiling. Instead of a minister there was a teacher.

The teacher, who talked quickly in short nervous sentences, was tall and thin. She wasn't Sybil's teacher. Miss Thurston, her teacher, spoke slowly and deliberately and was stout and of medium height. The third-grade teacher was Miss Thurston. This should be Miss Thurston, but it was Miss Henderson. Sybil knew Miss Henderson as the fifth-grade teacher.

What has happened? Sybil wondered. It was no dream. The room, a regular classroom in the school she had attended since kindergarten, seemed normal between its four walls. Only it wasn't her classroom. The windows of the room faced the east, not the west, as they did in the third-grade classroom. She knew all the rooms in the school, and this, she knew, was the fifth-grade classroom.

Somehow she had gotten into this fifth-grade classroom. She had done something wrong, a terrible thing. She had to get out, had to get back to the third grade where she belonged, where Miss Thurston had probably marked her absent. She had to apologize to Miss Henderson for being here, had to explain to Miss Thurston for not being there. But what was the explanation?

Then she began to notice the other children. There was Betsy Bush across the aisle, Henry Von Hoffman in front of her, Stanley, and Stuart and Jim and Carolyn Schultz and all the rest. Well, she thought, the whole third grade is in here.

Most of these children had started with her in

kindergarten, and she knew them well. They were the same children, yet they were not the same as when she had seen them last. They were dressed differently from when they were in the third grade. They looked bigger than they had been before she left for her grandmother's funeral. How could that be? How could all these children get bigger in a moment?

Betsy Bush, assured and confident as always, was waving her hand as usual to answer the teacher's question. She acted as if she belonged here. All the other children did, too. None of them seemed to think there was anything wrong about being here. Why should Betsy be answering questions when Miss Henderson was not her teacher?

Sybil's eyes turned next to the page of the notebook open on her desk. She thought of concentrating on the page and forgetting all the nonsense. But it could not be done, for the page made no sense to her, and in her present state of mind the notebook only induced more terror. There were lots of notes, but she hadn't taken them. There was completed homework, which she hadn't done, but she noted that the homework was consistently graded A. However urgently she forced herself to minimize the meaning of all this, the more terrified she became.

She tried hard to shut her eyes to this teacher who wasn't hers, to this classroom with the windows on the wrong side, these children, blown up beyond their normal size and dressed in strange clothes they hadn't worn before. It didn't work.

Sybil began to feel a strange compulsion to examine herself. Were her clothes "different"? Was she bigger, too? Her eye descended to her own dress. It was of yellow voile with green and purple embroidery, as totally unfamiliar as those of the other children. She hadn't owned it, didn't remember her mother's buying it for her, hadn't worn it before, and hadn't put it on this morning. She was wearing a dress that didn't belong to her in a classroom in which she didn't belong.

Nobody seemed to think that anything unusual was happening. The third-grade children kept on answering

142

questions about things she'd never studied with them. She didn't understand any of it.

She looked at the clock above the teacher's desk. It was two minutes to twelve. She would soon be saved by the bell. Waiting, she was overtaken by panic. Then the bell sounded, and she heard the teacher's high-pitched nervous voice saying, "Class dismissed."

Sybil decided to sit still. She was afraid to move, afraid to face going home. The children, however, made a mad dash to the coat hall, shouting, laughing. The boys, shoving with their elbows, pushed their way past the girls.

Sybil saw them leave, going quickly out of the coat hall. She was certain that they must have just grabbed their coats, helter-skelter, without any semblance of order. The way the children acted was very bewildering and frightening.

Tense before, she became even more tense as she watched them. Miss Thurston knew how to keep order, and this mad scramble could not have taken place in her class. Sybil had always heard, however, that Miss Henderson could not manage a class. Because of the way the children acted it suddenly seemed that this *might* be Miss Henderson's class after all.

Everything was running through her mind at such speed that she was unable to make any sense of it and to do the sensible thing: go home. When she looked up, the room was deserted. Certain that the other children had indeed gone, she rose slowly from her seat and walked even more slowly to the coat hall.

Inside the hall she realized that she wasn't alone. There was Miss Henderson putting on her coat. It was too late to turn away.

Except for being on the opposite side of the building this hall was exactly like the one in the third grade. All the classrooms and all the coat halls were alike. There was nothing unfamiliar about this one.

There was just one coat still hanging, a plaid macki-naw. She had never seen it before, but she went over and examined it. She looked for a name tape to find the name that belonged to the coat. Miss Thurston always had the children put their names on two pieces of tape, one for the coat, the other to be placed under a coat hook. There was no name either under the hook or in the coat. Miss Henderson was about to leave. "Sybil," she asked, "why don't you put your coat on? What's wrong? Aren't you going home for lunch?"

Instead of replying Sybil simply continued to stare at the unfamiliar coat, reflecting that it was not surprising that Miss Henderson knew her name. In the tiny town of Willow Corners everybody knew everybody else. Miss Henderson repeated: "Aren't you going home for lunch?" Then, with Miss Henderson's eye on her, Sybil finally put on the coat. It fitted her perfectly. Miss Henderson left, but Sybil lingered until she could be certain that the teacher was so far ahead that they wouldn't meet on the stairs.

Sybil walked slowly out of the old red-brick school building. On the corner across the street was the big house with black shutters, her home. Before crossing the street she looked to see whether anyone was coming. Certain that nobody was looking, she crossed.

Top, waiting on the front steps, barked his welcome. She gave him a quick hug around the neck before hurrying into the house. She wanted to be inside among familiar things, eager to see this morning's confusion at school fade away at home.

In the small entrance hallway, however, her longing for normality was crushed. When she hung the plaid mackinaw in the hallway closet, none of the clothes she remembered was there. Unfamiliar reds, greens, and yellows leaped out at her. Turning abruptly from the closet, she started to go into the downstairs bedroom, where her grandmother and grandfather had lived during her grandmother's last illness. The extra door to the room was plastered up; it was strange that they had done this so quickly. In the living room she found some of her grandmother's furniture incorporated with theirs. How quickly they had rearranged things. And what was that on the breakfront? A *radio!* They had hesitated about buying a radio because her grandfather said that it was the work of the devil.

144

Mother called from the kitchen, "Is that you, Peggy? You're so late."

That nickname again. Her mother, who didn't like the name *Sybil,* had invented the name of Peggy Louisiana for her. When she was cute or funny, the way her mother liked her, her mother would call her Peggy Louisiana, Peggy Lou, Peggy Ann, or just Peggy. Evidently her mother liked her today.

The kitchen, Sybil noted with alarm, was light green. It had been white when last she had seen it. "I liked the white kitchen," Sybil said.

Replied her mother, "We went through that last year."

Last year? Sybil wondered.

Her father was in the sunroom, reading an architecture magazine while waiting for lunch. Sybil went in to speak to him. Her playroom was in the sunroom, and she kept her dolls in the window seat. The dolls were there, as they had always been, but there were more of them. Where did that big, beautiful, blonde-haired doll with the bright face and shining teeth come from? It wasn't hers.

Her father looked up from his magazine. "Sybil," he said, as he noticed her for the first time, "aren't you late?"

"Daddy," she blurted, "what doll is that, the great big one?"

"Are you playing games?" he replied. "That's Nancy Jean. You won her in a contest. You were so excited about it."

Sybil said nothing.

At the dining room table there were four place settings instead of three. What was the fourth one doing there? There didn't seem to be any company. This time, however, she was not going to ask any questions. She had been too embarrassed by the doll, Nancy Jean.

There was the thumping of a wooden leg, the familiar thump that had always brought her visits with her grandmother to an end, the thump, thump, that had always frightened her. It was her grandfather, all six feet of him, with his goatee and his bald head. What was he doing here? Why did he sit at their table? The grandparents' living quarters, whether they were living upstairs or downstairs, were always separate from theirs. Each family ate by itself and did not enter the other's sphere. That was her grandmother's rule. But her grandmother was dead. Newly dead and already the rule was broken.

Her father said grace. Her mother passed the food. The fried potatoes were passed around twice. There were some left. Her father took the dish and said to his father, "Dad, here are some more potatoes."

Her mother said pointedly, "It went around *twice*."

"He'll hear you," said her father with a pained expression.

"He'll hear you," her mother mimicked. "He won't hear you. He's deaf, deaf, and you know it."

In fact, her grandfather hadn't heard. He continued talking awfully loudly, the same old talk about Armageddon, one of the last battles that was to take place on earth before the end of time. He was talking of Alpha and Omega, the beginning and the end. He talked of the seven last plagues, the war that was coming with China, and how the United States would join Russia against China. He talked of how the Catholics would come into power, how some terrible day there would be a Catholic president.

"There could *never* be a Catholic president," said Hattie.

"Mark my words," Sybil's grandfather said, "it will come to pass. Those Romans will rule the world if we're not careful. Those Romans, they will bring us trouble without end until the end of the world!"

Her mother changed the subject. "Willard," she said, "I had a letter from Anita today."

"What does she write?" her father asked. Then turning to Sybil he remarked, "I'll never forget how wonderful you were about taking Anita's little Ella off our hands those few weeks after grandma's funeral when they were staying here."

The *weeks* after the funeral? Taking care of Ella? What was he talking about? She had done absolutely

146

nothing about Ella. And she didn't know about the weeks after the funeral. She was becoming confused. When had the funeral taken place? Hadn't it just happened?

Then Sybil looked directly at her mother and made what she considered a bold plunge. "Mother," she asked, "what grade am I in?"

"What grade am I in?" her mother echoed. "That's a silly question."

They didn't tell her, didn't understand how urgent it was for her to know. They didn't seem to care. What could she tell them if they did care? Even if she tried, she didn't know what to tell.

Her mother turned to her and said, "What's the matter with you? You're awfully quiet. You're so different today."

Her grandfather, seeing how solemn his granddaughter looked when her mother said that, proclaimed, "Christians must always smile. It is a sin not to smile."

Her father rose to go. "I told Mrs. Kramer I'd be back to the store by one-thirty."

Sybil's father had worked in a hardware store since they had come back from the farm, where they had gone to live briefly as an economy measure when they had lost their money in the Depression. Sybil and her mother had come back first so that she could start kindergarten. Then her father went to work in Mrs. Kramer's hardware store. They were in their old house again, with her grandparents in their own part upstairs. Now her grandfather lived with them, it seemed.

Her grandfather got up to go to his room. "Cheer up, Sybil," he said. "If you smile and be cheery, life won't be dreary." He bumped against the corner of the dining room table.

"He's so clumsy," her mother said. "He bumps into everything. He bumped the stand by the door so often, the plaster is all chipped off."

Sybil lingered, saying nothing.

"I don't know what's the matter with you today," her mother said. "You're not yourself—just not yourself."

Sybil walked to the closet. Still searching for the red wool coat she had looked for in the school coat hall, she dawdled.

Her mother followed her to the closet. "By the way," she said, "I'd like you to drop in on Mrs. Schwarzbard after school. She has a package for me."

"Who is Mrs. Schwarzbard?" Sybil asked.

"You know perfectly well who she is," her mother replied.

Sybil, who had never heard the name, was afraid to make too much of it. She just stared into the frightening closet with all those unfamiliar garments, the visible symbols of the unknown events that surrounded her on this enigmatic day.

"What are you waiting for?" her mother asked. "Miss Henderson will be furious with you if you are late."

Miss Henderson? Her mother knew she was in Miss Henderson's class!

"Put on the mackinaw you wore this morning," said her mother.

Sybil did as she was told. Her mother didn't seem to think there was anything odd about doing that.

As Sybil left the house, she saw Carolyn Schultz and Henry Von Hoffman on the school side of the street. She waited until they had gone into the school. When she herself entered the building, she was torn between going to the third-grade classroom and going to the fifth-grade room. Her mother knew that Miss Henderson was her teacher, but Sybil still thought she belonged in the third grade. She tried the third grade first.

Miss Thurston was at her desk, sorting test papers. "How nice of you to come to visit," she said when she saw Sybil. "I love having my girls come back."

Come *back*? Sybil headed for the fifth-grade classroom. Walking gingerly into the room, she made certain she returned to the seat in which she'd found herself that morning.

The first lesson was arithmetic. They were doing fractions, but Sybil couldn't multiply beyond the 3s and 4s. The last thing she remembered was doing the 3s and 4s, in the spring of the third grade.

Then, they were doing decimals, and Sybil couldn't do them, either. Miss Henderson said something about multiplication. Sybil couldn't multiply. The teacher erased the board, wrote up new multiplication problems, distributed paper, and drilled for the next day's quiz.

Sybil stared from her blank paper to the blackboard and back again. Miss Henderson watched her; then she walked to Sybil's desk and leaned over her shoulder.

"You haven't written anything," Miss Henderson said crossly. "Now work 'em."

Sybil did nothing, and the teacher, with even more irritation than before, pointed to the blackboard and demanded, "What's this and this?"

Sybil just shook her head. "Now, Sybil," the teacher said, "what is it?" The other children laughed. Carolyn Schultz snickered. "Sybil," the teacher insisted, "tell me what the answer is."

"I don't know it. I don't know." Sybil's tone was hushed.

Miss Henderson turned on her. "But you've always been an A student. I don't know what's gotten into you." The teacher was furious. "Young lady, you had better get hold of yourself. Or are you playing games with me?"

There was no answer to the baffled teacher's rhetorical question. Then, in total perplexity, the teacher, walking back to the blackboard, threw a parting shot over her shoulder: "You knew it yesterday."

Yesterday? Sybil was silent. For her—she was beginning to know it now—yesterday was never. Things had taken place that she was supposed to have done or learned of which she had no knowledge.

This was not altogether a new experience. At other times, too, time seemed to have been erased for her the way Miss Henderson had erased those numbers from the blackboard. But this time seemed longer. More had happened, more that Sybil didn't understand.

She had never mentioned this strange feeling to anyone. It was a secret she didn't dare tell.

But how much time had gone by? This she still didn't

149

know. She was in the fifth grade and didn't remember being in the fourth. Never before had that much time passed. Things were happening to her of which she knew nothing and over which she had no control.

"Is there something bothering you?" asked Miss Henderson, who had come back to her desk.

"No, no," Sybil replied, with a brave show of conviction. "But I can't do the work."

"You did it yesterday," Miss Henderson repeated icily.

There was no yesterday. Sybil remembered nothing since being at the cemetery.

What she couldn't understand was that other people didn't know that she didn't know. Miss Henderson kept talking about yesterday as if she had been right at this desk then. But she wasn't here. Yesterday was blank.

At recess time the children scrambled out to the playground. Both the boys and girls had their baseball and softball teams. They chose sides, but Sybil stood alone —unchosen. To be left out was a new, terrible experience. In the past the children didn't leave her out of anything, and she couldn't understand why they did now.

When school was over, Sybil waited until the last child was safely out of reach and then started for home. She wasn't going to Mrs. Schwartzbard, whoever she was, to pick up her mother's package. Her mother would be furious. But there was nothing she could do except accept the fury, as she always had.

In the school's main lobby, with its cold, austere marble, Danny Martin called to Sybil. Danny, who was a year older than Sybil, was a very good friend. They had many long talks on the front steps of the white house with black shutters. She could talk to Danny more than to anybody else. He had been at her grandmother's funeral. Maybe she ought to ask him about the things that had happened since then. But what a fool he'd think her if she asked him outright. She would have to find subtle ways to make her own discoveries.

Danny walked across the street with her. They sat

on the front steps of her home and talked. One of the things he said was: "Mrs. Engle died this week. I went with Elaine to take the funeral flowers to invalids and shut-ins, just as I went with you when your grandmother died."

When Danny said this, Sybil remembered, as if it were a dream, that a girl whom they called Sybil but who wasn't Sybil went with Danny Martin to distribute her grandmother's funeral flowers to the sick and poor of the town. As in a dream, she remembered watching that girl. It felt as if she had been beside this other Sybil, just walking along. And she couldn't be certain whether or not it was a dream. But although she knew now that time, unaccounted-for time, had passed since the funeral, this was the only memory that came back. Otherwise there was nothing but emptiness, a great, cavernous emptiness between the moment that a hand had grabbed her at the cemetery and the time that she first found herself in the fifth-grade classroom.

Had she dreamed about that girl and those flowers? Or had the event actually happened? If it was a dream, how could Danny be in tune with it? She didn't know. But she didn't know about many things that had happened during this time, cold, blue, unreachable. To forget was shameful, and she felt ashamed.

10

Thieves of Time

The vague memory of the girl who had distributed the funeral flowers gave Sybil the incentive to ask Danny about *all* of the things that were different.

Houses had been built. Stores had changed hands. The town was not the same. Sybil knew that she could ask Danny about any or all of it.

"How come the Greens are living in the Miners' house?" Sybil asked.

"They moved there last summer," Danny replied.

"Who's the baby Susie Anne is pushing in the buggy?" Sybil wanted to know.

"That's Susie Anne's little sister," Danny explained. "She was born last spring."

"Who is Mrs. Schwarzbard?"

"A dressmaker who came to town a year ago."

Danny never asked, "How come you don't know?"

Sybil was freer with Danny Martin than she had been with any human being except her grandmother. The freedom with Danny was the more remarkable because it came during the spring, summer, and fall of 1934, the very period during which, tricked by time, Sybil enshrouded herself in a green aloneness and fortified her usual reserve with a special invincible armor against the world.

Danny became the antidote to the loneliness and vulnerability Sybil experienced after "coming to" in the fifth grade. Inexplicably, she had lost her friends. And, although her fundamentalist faith had always set her apart from other children, it was now as if they were noticing it for the first time. Now, because she could not do all the things they did—because of the prohibitions of her faith—they directed at her the sinister epithet "white Jew."

Less painful, too, because of Danny, was her father's coolly critical counsel, "You should be able to talk to people and to face the world," and her mother's reactivation of an old complaint, "I never know from one day to the next what mood you'll be in or what kind of person you'll be."

If it weren't for Danny, Sybil knew she could not have endured the humiliation at school, where, because of her problem with math, her marks had gone down. Without Danny, Sybil could not have withstood her mother's unrelenting accusation: "But you used to

152

know the multiplication tables. You used to know them. You're just pretending to forget. You're a bad girl—bad." And without Danny it would have been impossible to weather the stormy confrontation with her mother over the lost place in the school's honor roll, regularly published in the *Corners Courier* for the whole town to see. "You were always there," her mother lamented. "I don't know what I would do if I had a dumb child. You're bright. You're only doing this to hurt me. Bad. Bad!"

Although Sybil didn't actually enumerate these things to Danny, she felt that without her doing so, he somehow understood. Sybil felt so close to Danny that there were times when she would have liked to talk with him about why time was so "funny" and about how unaccountably she had discovered that she was eleven years and two months old without ever having been ten years old—or eleven. But in the end this was too painful to talk about even to Danny. Besides, her reluctance grew with the recollection that when some years earlier she had expressed this thought to her mother, Hattie had laughed sarcastically and chided, "For land's sake, why can't you be like other youngsters?" All the same, time, Sybil knew—even though her mother scoffed and Sybil was afraid to tell Danny about it—was funny.

Upon occasion, however, Sybil was able to forget the strange, immutable subject of time—when she sat on the front steps talking with Danny, or when they played in the sunroom, where he made Shakespearean costumes for her dolls, transforming Patty Ann into Portia, Norma into Rosalind, and a nameless boy doll into the fool in *Twelfth Night*. Just as miraculously, Danny transformed going to a party from a terror to a pleasure. While the parties of the past, attended only at her mother's harping insistence, went unremembered, the parties to which Sybil went with Danny were never forgotten.

When Sybil was with Danny, she was able to forget that otherwise she walked alone. And she was alone. In the morning she was careful not to leave home until after she had ascertained that none of her classmates was in sight. After school she lingered at her desk until all the other children had left. When she walked on Main Street, doing some errand for her mother, she often crossed from one side of the street to the other six or seven times in a single block to avoid an encounter with one of the townsfolk. Turning from everybody else, she turned to Danny. Danny, without erecting barriers against other children, turned as surely to Sybil as she did to him. Sybil and Danny just naturally assumed that when they were old enough, they would marry. Sybil firmly believed that when this happened, time somehow would cease to be funny.

Then, on a brisk October day, as Sybil and Danny sat on the front steps, Danny said, somewhat awkwardly, "Syb, I have something to tell you."

"What?" Sybil, sensing his tone, asked anxiously.

"You see," Danny continued, "my Dad—well, he bought a gas station in Waco, Texas, and, well, we're going there to live. But you'll come see me. I'll come back here. We'll see each other."

"Yes," Sybil said, "we will."

That evening, when Sybil told Hattie Dorsett that Danny was leaving Willow Corners forever, Hattie shrugged and said, with great deliberateness: "Well, Daddy didn't like you to spend so much time with that boy anyway. Daddy thought you were too old to be playing together."

When Sybil reported to Danny what her mother had said, he answered quietly, "If your mother knew it would hurt you, she'd tell you." Sybil was surprised that Danny should say that.

The next month, while Danny's family got ready to leave Willow Corners, seemed like a reprieve, as if they had been spared the parting. Between Sybil and Danny nothing was changed except that they did everything together more intensely because they knew that time was running out. It was the same feeling that Sybil had experienced during her truncated visits with her grandmother.

Ultimately, however, the day came for Danny to say goodbye. Sybil, sitting with him on the front steps,

154

which for so long had been the scene of close communion, was quiet and composed.

"You'll come see me," Danny reminded Sybil.

"I'll come," Sybil temporized.

"We'll see each other," Danny repeated.

"We'll see each other," Sybil echoed.

Danny rose to go. Sybil sat motionless on the steps. "Well, Sybil," he said. "Well . . ." Overwhelmed by adolescent embarrassment and unable to complete the sentence, he fell silent, bending over instead to where Sybil was still sitting. He kissed her swiftly on the cheek, pulled away, turned, and was gone.

Sybil, who, since early childhood, had shunned even the most casual physical contact, was now transported by a joyous tingle. At first she was not even aware that Danny was no longer beside her. Then, when awareness did come, she panicked, apprehensively searching for Danny. There he was—his blond hair, his lithe body— moving, retreating.

As he turned from Vine Street into Main Street, he faded out of sight. Sybil sank down onto the steps. The rescue that Danny represented had been withdrawn. The town was deserted. All that existed now was an unmitigated aloneness.

And there still was something funny about time, which, like invisible soap in imperceptible water, slipped away.

The sky is blue, Vicky thought, as, getting up from the front steps, she stepped into the time from which Sybil had just departed.

Vicky walked around the white house with black shutters thinking about how nice it was to be able to give locomotion to the body, which for the very first time belonged wholly to her, Vicky.

At last, the eyes were Vicky's alone to see the world steadily and to see it whole, to look up at the blue sky, clean and clear.

Having reached the back porch steps, Vicky decided to enter the house through that route. "That you, Peggy?" Hattie called from the kitchen window.

155

No, Vicky thought, it isn't Peggy, or Sybil. It's a person you haven't met before. I'm not your daughter in reality, but I'm here to take Sybil's place, and, although you will call me your daughter, you will discover that I'm not afraid of you. I know how to cope with you.

"That boy gone?" Hattie asked as Vicky entered the kitchen.

"Yes," Vicky said.

"You had no business sitting out there in the cold. You'll come down with pneumonia. You know you're not very strong."

"I'm used to our midwestern winters, and by comparison this autumn weather is child's play," Vicky replied.

"Don't act smart with me," Hattie warned.

"I was only stating a fact," said Vicky.

"Well," Hattie answered as she changed the subject, "I'm expecting a package from Elderville. Go on over to the post office and get it for me."

Vicky went.

Strange that it should be autumn. The time of beginnings is spring, she thought, as, listening to the rustling of the dry leaves, she walked down the back porch steps and along the alley that led to Main Street.

Autumn without, it was nevertheless spring within—the spring that followed the long, subduing winter of a little over eight years of secret residency within the recesses of being. Subdued, quiescent, nameless, she had *been* from the autumn of 1926 to this October day in 1934, from the time Sybil was three and a half until she was eleven. Quiescent, yes. Powerless, no. During that period, by exerting a variety of internal pressures upon Sybil and the other selves, Vicky, still nameless, had become silently instrumental.

It had been a momentous decision—Vicky knew—that she had made as Danny Martin receded out of sight and she rose from the inner recesses of being to the surface of life. Yet at that moment there had been no other possible course of action, for Vicky had realized that the time of instrumentality had passed and

156

that of active intervention had come. She realized that to be effective she would have to take command of the body away from Sybil, who was obviously too traumatized by the parting to carry on. And so, christening herself by a name borrowed from Sybil, who in the fantasy of the pretend world of childhood had created a girl, bright and unafraid, by the name of Victoria Antoinette Scharleau, this hitherto quiescent self entered the world.

It was good, Victoria thought as she walked along Main Street, to feel the bitter, biting wind and to be in control of the body that did the feeling. A newcomer to commanding the body that walked along the street, she felt like an old-timer in the street itself. She had seen everything many times before.

Vicky knew what had happened in the life of Sybil Isabel Dorsett, whether or not Sybil herself had been present. Paradoxically, while time had been discontinuous for Sybil, who had lived in the world, it had been continuous for Vicky, who had existed in the recesses of being. Time, which had been capricious and often blank for Sybil, had been constant for Vicky. Vicky, who had total recall, served as a memory trace in the disjointed inner world of Sybil Dorsett.

This solidity of memory, combined with the fact that, in surfacing into the world, Vicky incorporated within herself a powerful fantasy of Sybil's own coinage, became the source of Vicky's strength. The Victoria of the fantasy, like the new Vicky, an alternating self, was confident, unafraid, immune from the influence of the relationships that had disturbed Sybil.

Vicky thought wryly of the persons who, seeing the slender frame of Sybil Dorsett, would expect the repeated crossing of the street in flight from people. Well, they will not see it now, Vicky thought, as she entered the post office.

The package from Elderville was waiting. This was a good beginning, Vicky decided. If that package hadn't been here, Mrs. Dorsett would have blamed her. How well, Vicky felt, she knew this woman—no mother to her—with whom all these years she had tried to help Sybil cope.

Home only long enough to give Mrs. Dorsett the package, Vicky again walked down the back porch steps and headed for the swing. It was natural for her to do so, for it had been she who had prevailed upon Sybil to adopt the swing as the perfect solution to Hattie Dorsett's constant haranguing for not "doing something." When Sybil, absorbed in thought, sat quietly, Hattie would harp, "Don't just sit there. For land's sakes, do something!" In the swing it had been possible to think and "do something" at the same time.

That evening when supper was over, Hattie suggested to Vicky that they go for a walk. In silence Hattie and Vicky walked, Hattie's controlling hand holding the putative daughter in check. Passing the Stickneys' house, twice the size of the Dorsetts', Hattie snorted, "Old man Stickney is senile. I hope they put him away." As they walked, Hattie talked of Ella Baines, who "did nasty things with a teacher in town" and should be "harpooned by the authorities"; of Rita Stitt, whose mother wasn't really her mother and who some months before Hattie had confounded by telling her so. (Vicky thought: you're not my mother, and I could retaliate for Rita by telling you so.)

Hattie Dorsett talked of Danny Martin. "I'm glad to see you're not blue because that boy went away," Hattie said. "I told you that Daddy objected to your playing with him."

"You did tell me," said Vicky, knowing that it had been not to her but to Sybil that Mrs. Dorsett had conveyed that cruel intelligence.

"Well, young lady, there's something else," Hattie added with a childishly triumphant expression. "You don't know that Daddy had a talk with Danny's father a few months ago. Daddy told him straight from the shoulder that it was wrong for you to mix in with people like the Martins, outside our faith."

Vicky winced. The Martins, like Hattie Dorsett herself before her conversion, were Methodists. Willard Dorsett had married a Methodist, yet he objected to his

158

daughter's friendship with one. What hypocrisy! But Vicky said nothing.

"Well," Hattie continued, "Daddy looks down on the Martins for other reasons, too. He feels that they have no class, no background, no style. The father came here from New Jersey looking for gold, and he ended up driving a milk truck. Now he's on his way again, still looking. Where he got the money to buy a gas station down there in Texas *nobody* can figure out. Anyway, Daddy had a good long talk with Danny's father. Mr. Martin said they would be leaving town soon, so nobody did anything. But, young lady, I thought you should know what Daddy thinks about Danny and Danny's family."

"Danny's gone," was all Vicky said.

"A good thing, too, according to Daddy," Hattie reported, careful to remove herself from the judgment.

Vicky thought: it's a good thing that Sybil will never know what her father did.

"Well, let's go back," Hattie said. "I wanted to tell you this when Daddy wasn't around. Now that you know, we can go back."

At school the next morning Vicky was in command of both the body and the school work. And although the other children were aloof, Vicky understood that the aloofness was rooted in the happenings of the two years that followed the death of Mary Dorsett, Sybil's grandmother.

Vicky had watched with close scrutiny how, during those two years, Peggy Lou, in complete control of the body, the person who did the actual living, had lost all Sybil's school friends. Peggy Lou would sit at her school desk during recess and make paper dolls instead of going into the yard to play with the other children. At lunch and at the end of the day she would dash out of school, snubbing the children who attempted to talk or walk with her. When asked to go some place with them, she replied cryptically, "I can't." Then she'd run. After a while nobody asked her to go anywhere or do anything.

Vicky knew that Peggy Lou had isolated herself from

the other children not because she disliked them but because being with them made her angry at not having what they had—a home in which there were brothers and sisters, where there was no reason to be afraid. Rather than go with the other children to those homes, she persuaded herself that she didn't need anyone and, fully persuaded, raced alone to the white house with black shutters, where what made her angry lurked in every corner.

Her bitter loneliness had one compensation. She had a real sense of accomplishment at being independent and doing exactly what she desired, with no one stopping her or telling her what to do. Isolated, she managed somehow to feel free—albeit with a freedom that made her want to smash a hole in the very center of the universe.

Sometimes Vicky regretted having let Peggy Lou take over at Mary Dorsett's grave. But Vicky had felt then—and still felt when she recalled the event—that no other course of action had been possible.

Too, Vicky assured herself, even though Mary Dorsett was a lovely person, she wasn't her grandmother, and there was no reason for her to involve herself in that macabre business. It seemed fitting to let Peggy Lou take over. Besides, Sybil, standing at the grave, was angry. Dealing with anger was Peggy Lou's function—not Vicky's.

Moreover, the two Peggy years hadn't been all bad. It had been Peggy Lou's emergence more than the restraining hand that had kept Sybil from jumping into Mary Dorsett's grave. After the funeral Peggy Lou, an active child, had been able to do what Sybil, an inactive child, could not have done. When the mourners stayed on as the Dorsetts' houseguests, Peggy Lou had earned the gratitude of Mr. and Mrs. Dorsett by taking Cousin Anita's obstreperous two-year-old Ella off their hands. The Dorsetts, in fact, were pleased that their daughter was active at last, and Vicky had been amazed to discover that Hattie Dorsett got along better with her daughter after than before the death of Mary Dorsett. The daughter who came home from the funeral and stayed for two years talked back and walked on the furniture in a rage, but she also seemed more winsome than the daughter who lived in the white house before Mary Dorsett's death.

Peggy Lou was much more "like" other youngsters than was Sybil. Although Vicky wasn't certain, she felt that this was because Peggy Lou, the daughter of the years after the death, was so much more like Hattie herself than was Sybil. It had been amusing, too, to observe that, upon Sybil's return, Mrs. Dorsett regarded Sybil, not Peggy Lou, as the "different" one. "That child is so different now," Hattie screamed. "I could go right through the ceiling!"

Vicky recalled having told Peggy Lou at Mary Dorsett's grave to answer to the name of Sybil Dorsett because it wasn't polite to point out people's mistakes. Then, on the second day of her residency in the world, Vicky took her own advice. In the sixth-grade classroom, she immediately recited when the name of Sybil Dorsett was called by Mr. Strong, the teacher.

Vicky liked Mr. Strong and remembered that Sybil had liked him too. One afternoon, while Sybil was raking leaves in the backyard, Mr. Strong, who happened to be passing, called to Sybil. Roused from daydreaming about the Victoria Antoinette of her fantasy, Sybil had been thrilled that the teacher had spoken to her first.

Isn't it pathetic, Vicky thought, that Sybil doesn't know about me, but keeps thinking about that imaginary girl whose name I now bear? It is sad that Sybil doesn't know about any of the people who live within her.

Having acquitted herself beautifully on the first day of school, in all subjects, including arithmetic, which Vicky had absorbed through silent observation, Vicky went home, sanguine about her new existence.

Approaching the Dorsetts' home, Vicky observed that Mrs. Dorsett was peering out of the window. Mrs. Dorsett, Vicky thought, always seems to be spying. "Come on. Let's go visit somebody," Hattie said. "There's a new baby at the Greens' house. Let's go down there and see what's going on." Here it is, Vicky thought, the almost daily ritual with its everlastingly boring adult-woman talk to which Sybil had been subjected. Well, Vicky decided, I'll go. Peggy Lou fought back, but I'll be diplomatic.

Mon Dieu, Vicky thought as in subsequent weeks she took a good look at Willow Corners, the people in this town had no style, no *éclat.* Narrow, provincial, and dull were the adjectives for them. Even at the age of thirteen she had outgrown them. She was certain that they and she were worlds apart. As for Sybil's parents . . . well, the father was nice, but he didn't care enough. In fact, he didn't come up from behind his newspaper or his blueprints long enough to see enough of what was happening to be able to care. The mother was a different story. She was always saying, "You should do it this way or that." And Vicky decided that it was this that had hampered Sybil in doing things. How, Vicky speculated, can you do anything when there are so many *shoulds* and *shouldn'ts,* and nothing is any fun? Still, Mrs. Dorsett was hard to fathom. She was either too much there or not there at all. But Vicky had the consolation of knowing that she was here to help, that after a while her own loving parents and her many brothers and sisters would come for her and she would go back to Paris with them. How she looked forward to the time when they would all be together. Contrasting her parents with the Dorsetts, she felt almost guilty at her own good fortune. She promised herself that before she left this family she would arrange to let Sybil have as many good days as possible—as many in fact, as the outside world and the other people within her would allow. Poor Sybil, Vicky thought.

There were times when Vicky retreated to the more congenial inner stratum and allowed one of the other selves in the Sybil Dorsett entourage, or even Sybil herself, to take a seat in the sixth-grade classroom.

One day Mary Lucinda Saunders Dorsett, who had emerged during the first year of Peggy Lou's two-year tenure, when Sybil was ten, took that sixth-grade seat. Before the day was over Mary suddenly didn't feel well.

It wasn't a pain she felt; it was more like a stretching.

When Mary got home, she headed for the bathroom. Grandpa Dorsett was in it, so Hattie called, "Why can't you use the other bathroom?" What other bathroom? Mary didn't remember there was any and only learned later that her father had built it during the second year, during which Peggy had been there and Mary had paid no attention.

In the new bathroom Mary blanched at the sight of what she later described as "this brownish red stuff" in her underwear. She had seen her grandmother, who had had cancer of the cervix, bleed, and she was afraid that she too was going to die.

"Why are you in there so long?" Hattie called.

"I'll be right out, Mom," Mary replied.

Mary, who didn't feel that Sybil's mother was hers, always called Hattie "Mom," which seemed like a general word for any older woman who took care of one. Washing her underwear to make sure that Hattie wouldn't know what had happened, Mary lingered long in the bathroom, worrying about the strange condition in which she found herself.

At bedtime that night Mom came in and said, "Let's see your underwear." Mary hesitated. "Show it to me this minute," Hattie demanded. When Mary did as she was directed, Hattie remarked, "Just what I thought. It's your age working on you. It's simply awful. The curse of women. It hurts you here, doesn't it? It hurts you there, doesn't it?" And pushing at various target points of Mary's anatomy, Hattie jabbed hard, accentuating the pain.

"It's sick time," Hattie said as she prepared a cloth for Mary to wear. "Only women have it. Don't mention it to Daddy." Then Hattie stalked out of the bedroom, muttering, "The curse of women. The curse. I wish men had it. It would serve them right. Men!"

Mary was frightened because Mom had said "sick time." Sick meant staying home from school; school meant getting away from Hattie. And Mary wanted to get away. Next day Mom explained that with this sickness girls did go to school. So Mary went to school.

What Mary didn't know was that what had happened to her for the first time had already happened to Sybil for two successive months without Hattie's knowing and without pain. In the future, Mary, who carried the burden of menstruation, inflicted the pain on Sybil or whatever other self was in the ascendancy during the menstrual period.

Mary continued to appear occasionally during the sixth grade, but it was Vicky who was there most of the time. Toward the end of the school term Sybil arrived one day on the way to school, feeling that the Victoria of her fantasy was taking her there. This return, however, was not so alarming as had been the return in the fifth grade. Although Sybil still thought that time was "funny," she found herself somehow more at ease about this spell.

At the time of Sybil's return Mary talked to Vicky about Danny Martin. "Sybil doesn't know," Mary said, "that while Peggy Lou was there, Danny was jealous of Billy Denton. Peggy Lou didn't pay any attention to Danny, but she certainly did latch onto Billy."

"Yes," Vicky agreed, "she certainly did. And Billy could never understand—after Sybil came back—why the Dorsett girl acted as if she didn't know him."

Mary, who was interested in poetry, became grandiloquent, telling Vicky that for Sybil the mighty heart of the world often lies still and that at such times there are for Sybil no fresh woods, no pastures new, just pastures fallow with forgetfulness. "Sybil calls it nothingness. And that's not very flattering to us!"

In the months that followed Sybil found herself floating in and out of blankness. Disguising the fact, she became ingenious in improvisation, peerless in pretense, as she feigned knowledge of what she did not know. Unfortunately, from herself she couldn't conceal the sensation that somehow she had lost something. Nor could she hide the feeling that increasingly she felt as if she belonged to no one and to no place. Somehow it seemed that the older she got, the worse things became. She began repudiating herself with unspoken self-derogating comments: "I'm thin for a good reason: I'm not fit to occupy space."

Spring was bad because of her grandmother. Now summer was approaching, and summer would be bad because of Danny. Sitting on the front steps or high in the swing, Sybil would remember the summer leading to Danny's departure. "Break, break, break,/On thy cold grey stones, O Sea!/. . . But O for the touch of a vanished hand,/And the sound of a voice that is still! . . . But the tender grace of a day that is dead/Will never come back to me," Mary recited as she took over the swing from Sybil.

During the late spring of 1935, Sybil faced a new terror, brought on by the vulnerability of puberty. The terror centered around hysterical conversion symptoms that were part of her then undiagnosed illness. For hysteria—*grande* or otherwise—is an illness resulting from emotional conflict and is generally characterized by immaturity, dependency, and the use of the defense mechanisms not only of dissociation but also of conversion. Hysteria is classically manifested by dramatic physical symptoms involving the voluntary muscles or the organs of special senses. During the process of conversion, unconscious impulses are transmuted into bodily symptoms. Instead of being experienced consciously, the emotional conflict is thus expressed physically.

Suddenly, half of Sybil's face and the side of her arms would become numb. She would grow weak on one side, not always the same side. Almost constantly her throat was sore, and she had trouble swallowing. She began to suffer from tunnel vision; sight would often leave one eye. She—and some of the other selves as well, notably Mary—developed a nervous tic, which, like that of the telephone operator, caused consternation in the town.

Sybil or one of the others would twitch, jerk, and carry on with unrestrained body movements. Sybil or the others would aim for the doorway and run into the door, aim for the door and run into the doorjamb. The symptoms were intensified by headaches so bad that following such an attack, Sybil had to go to sleep for several hours. Sleep after one of these headaches for Sybil, who was generally a light sleeper, was so sound that it seemed she had been drugged.

Most disturbing of all, life seemed to be floating by in an unreal kind of way, filled with strange presentiments. Sybil would remember that she had been somewhere or had done something as if she had dreamed it. She seemed to be walking beside herself, watching. And sometimes she couldn't tell the difference between her dreams and this dreamlike unreality.

One night Sybil mentioned this feeling of unreality to her parents, who then decided to take her to Dr. Quinoness, the town's doctor.

Dr. Quinoness diagnosed Sybil's case as Sydenham's chorea, a form of St. Vitus dance. Explaining that there was a psychological component, he advised that Sybil should see a psychiatrist and made an appointment for her with a doctor in Minneapolis. Willard and Hattie refused to keep the appointment. If it were only psychological, Willard claimed, he could handle it himself. Upon this assumption he bought Sybil a guitar and engaged a guitar teacher for her. Father and daughter practiced together and later gave recitals. Since Vicky, Mary, Peggy Lou, and some of the other selves also learned to play and did so with different degrees of enthusiasm, the performances Willard Dorsett's daughter gave were strikingly uneven.

Despite her father's easy optimism, Sybil admitted to herself that she was having "mental trouble," which in the Dorsett household and in the town of Willow Corners was considered a disgrace. Indeed, new fears began to revolve around the state hospital, where her uncle Roger worked as a purchasing agent and her aunt Hattie, as a nurse. Sybil had often visited her uncle and aunt at the hospital.

Trying to take her mind off her trouble, Sybil threw herself into her school work. At school, however, she was disturbed by not knowing the European history that had been taught while she was not present. Vicky carried history, just as Peggy Lou was the keeper of multiplication. With science, however, Sybil caught up quickly. Fascinated as Mr. Strong elucidated the mysteries of the human anatomy, she didn't even notice that he carefully bypassed the sexual parts. When students were required to draw a large sketch of a heart, Hattie bought Sybil a pencil that was red at one end and blue at the other, which made Sybil feel like a teacher, grading papers. Sybil's daydreams were filled with ideas about heart circulation and doctors, and she would pretend that she herself was a physician explaining heart function to patients.

One day Sybil dashed into the house after school to tell her mother about heart function. Refusing to listen, Hattie said, "I don't want to hear about that." Sybil, however, was so excited about the subject that she went right on explaining what she had learned. "How many times do I have to tell you that I'm not interested?" Hattie screamed, lashing out at her daughter. Sybil, who had been standing on the polished linoleum in the sunroom, took the blow full on the hip, slipped, fell sideways over the rocking chair, and landed on the floor. Her ribs were badly bruised.

From that time forward Sybil was afraid of the science class, and even though science continued to fascinate her, she had a hard time getting through high school and college biology. She also became afraid of rooms without rugs.

That night Hattie took Sybil on an outing to Main Street. It was a Wednesday night, and the stores were open. There were popcorn stands on the corner and popsicles in the drugstore. Children always asked their parents for a nickel or a dime, but Sybil made no demands. Hattie asked, "What do we want tonight? Do we want popcorn or a popsicle?"

Sybil replied, "Well, anything is all right."

The remark, although characteristic, didn't indicate that Sybil had no preference. Just as she didn't dare tell anybody her secret about time, she didn't dare ask anybody for anything.

As mother and daughter were enjoying the popsicles Hattie bought, Sybil caught sight of some hair bows displayed on a counter. Thinking how pretty they were, Sybil hoped that her mother would ask whether she wanted one. But Hattie passed the counter, looked at the hair bows, and went down the aisle. Sybil gave up hope that her mother would ask her.

Then Vicky decided to do the asking and pointed to a light blue hair bow. "I'd like to have it," Vicky informed Hattie. "It matches our blue organdy dress."

"What do you mean by 'our,' you numbskull?" Hattie replied. "Don't you know that organdy dress is *yours?*"

Hattie paid the cashier for the hair bow.

11

The Search for the Center

Vicky and Sybil, Mary and Sybil, Peggy Lou and Sybil—what was the connection? Dr. Wilbur decided to ask Vicky, who knew everything about everybody.

It was June 15, 1955, and the analysis had been proceeding for nine months. Doctor and patient were seated on the couch. "Vicky," the doctor said, "I should like to know something. Are you related to Sybil?"

Startled, Vicky replied, "You know I know Sybil because you ask me about her. I tell you about Sybil."

"Yes," the doctor agreed, "I know you know her. But how do you know what she thinks?"

An amused smile was Vicky's only answer.

"Vicky," the doctor persisted, "you've talked of *our* blue organdy dress. What else do you and the others share?"

"Share?" There was a tinge of irony in Vicky's tone. "We sometimes do things together."

"You have told me that some of the others have the same mother? Then would you say they *share* a mother?"

"Yes, I suppose you could say that."

"Do they also share the same body?"

"That's silly," Vicky replied authoritatively. "They're people. I can tell you about them."

"Yes, Vicky, I know they are people. But people have relationships to each other. How are Peggy Lou, Peggy Ann, Mary, Sybil, and the others related? Are they sisters?"

"Nobody ever said they were sisters," Vicky replied, looking squarely at the doctor.

"No," the doctor answered with precise emphasis, "nobody ever *said* that. But Vicky, when people have the same mother, they must either be the same person, sisters, or brothers."

Ignoring the implications of the doctor's logic, Vicky concurred, "I have lots of brothers and sisters, and we all have the same mother and father."

"All right, Vicky," the doctor continued, "you have just acknowledged the kinship bonds in your own family. But you haven't said anything about the family of which Sybil, the Peggys, Mary, and the others are a part. You haven't told me how these people are related."

Vicky shrugged and said, "Well, Doctor, you just said they must be sisters."

"No, Vicky," the doctor replied firmly, "I didn't say they *must be* sisters. I asked you if they *were* sisters, and I said that logically, since they have the same mother, they must either be the same person, or they must be sisters or brothers."

Vicky said nothing.

When the doctor, remorselessly pursuing the logical course, demanded: "Now, Vicky, tell me, are they sisters or are they the same person?" Vicky, forced to reply, spoke with great deliberateness. "Doctor," she said, "when you put it that way, I have to admit that they must be sisters. They have to be sisters because they *couldn't* be the same person!" Vicky closed the subject

169

by opening her purse, putting lipstick on, closing the purse, tucking it under her arm. *"Mon Dieu,"* she said as she rose to go. "What an absurdity it is to think of those complete individuals as the same. Marian Ludlow and I are more alike than are any two or three persons you have mentioned."

"Now, Vicky," the doctor said firmly, "the hour is not over yet, and I would like you to listen to what I'm going to tell you."

"Our discussion," Vicky said in a tone of great finality, "has reached its logical conclusion. What else is there to say?"

"This, Vicky. Now sit down, won't you, please?"

Vicky seated herself, but she didn't really acquiesce.

"You say," the doctor remarked unrelentingly, "that Peggy Lou, Peggy Ann, Mary, and the others couldn't be the same person. But they can be. Vicky, don't you see that they could be different aspects of the same person?"

"No, Dr. Wilbur," Vicky said thoughtfully, shaking her head. "I don't see. You, you're just you. You're Dr. Wilbur and no one else."

"Yes?" the doctor asked.

"And I'm just Vicky. There's nobody else here. See." Vicky rose from the couch, paced the room, and asked, "Now do you believe me?"

Vicky sat down again, smiled at the doctor, and remarked, "That settles the question. There's no one else here. You're just Dr. Wilbur, and I'm just Vicky."

"Vicky," the doctor replied, "we haven't settled anything. Let's be honest with each other."

"But, Dr. Wilbur," Vicky insisted, "we most certainly have. We've settled the large, philosophical question of *who am I?* I am I. You are you. I think; therefore I am. There's a Latin phrase for it: *cogito ergo sum.* Yes, that's it."

"We've settled nothing," the doctor reminded Vicky. "We haven't established the relationship among Sybil, Peggy Lou, Peggy Ann, Mary and the others. What . . . ?"

"Questions, questions, questions," Vicky interrupted.

"I'd like to ask a question, too. Why do you have to ask all these questions?"

After rejecting the logical conclusion toward which Dr. Wilbur had been trying to lead her, Vicky contradicted the earlier contention that the doctor and she were alone, for she said, "Now, Dr. Wilbur, Mary would like to meet you. She wants to participate in our analysis, and I think we should let her."

"Our analysis?" Dr. Wilbur echoed. "How can it be 'our' if you girls are not the same person?"

Vicky chuckled. "I suppose," she said with what seemed like deliberate ambiguity, "you might call it *group* therapy."

"You agreed you were sisters."

Vicky was quick. "Family therapy, then, if you insist. Thanks for the correction."

Then, as surely as if she had physically left the room, Vicky was gone. A voice that definitely was not Vicky's remarked politely, "I'm glad to meet you, Dr. Wilbur."

"You're Mary?" the doctor asked.

"Mary Lucinda Saunders Dorsett," the voice replied.

It was not the voice of a woman of the world like Vicky, nor of an angry child like Peggy Lou. The accent was unmistakably midwestern, soft, low, and somber. The doctor had not heard that voice before and knew of Mary only through Vicky's recapitulation of the sixth grade.

The doctor motioned Mary to the couch and waited. Mary was silent. New patient reserve? the doctor mused. New patient?

"What do you like to do, Mary?" the doctor asked.

"I keep our home going," Mary replied, "but it's hard to do so much."

"What do you have to do?" the doctor asked.

"Follow Sybil."

"What do you do when you follow Sybil?"

"Go where she goes."

"What else do you do?"

"Help Sybil."

"How do you help her?"

"Practical ways. Subtle ways."

171

"Such as?"

"Well, Dr. Wilbur, right now, it's a practical matter. You probably know that Sybil and Teddy Reeves—a friend from Whittier Hall—have just taken an apartment together on Morningside Drive. You know what a new apartment involves. At 8:45 yesterday morning I had to come out to receive the workmen who are putting in new windows. I had to come out again at 7:15 P.M. because I didn't want Sybil to put up the new drapes. I feel it's up to me to keep the home going. And with all the deliveries we're getting these days, we can't sleep in the morning. So I had to put up a sign, 'Do Not Disturb,' near the downstairs bell. Sybil and Teddy are doing over the apartment. The doing falls to me."

"What else do you do?"

"It's hard to do anything with that Morningside barn called a brownstone. How I wish we had more space. I'd like to have a flower garden, room for some animals. We just have Capri."

"You don't like New York?"

"Not really. But then I don't get around much. Sometimes I go to a museum or a library. That's about it. I rarely leave the apartment."

"What do you do when you're there?"

"Housework. Read. Listen to music. Do a little painting. Write poetry. Poetry eases the pain."

"What pain, Mary?"

"Oh. I've prayed about how we feel."

"What pain, Mary?"

"Haven't they told you? Vicky? Sybil? Peggy Lou?"

"Not directly. They've talked of the fear of getting close to people, of music, of hands, of being trapped, and, by denying mother, Vicky and Peggy Lou indicate that they fear her. Do you fear her?"

"I never felt Sybil's mother was mine." Mary's tone was confidential.

"What pain, Mary?"

"You'll know in time. That's why I told Vicky that I wanted to come today. I want to help with our analysis. But I feel guilty about coming. Maybe it's a sin to go to a psychiatrist."

"Now, Mary," the doctor said very slowly, very plainly, "you know that Sybil, Vicky, and Peggy Lou have been coming here for some nine months. Do you think that anything they've said or done here is sinful?"

"I don't know," Mary answered thoughtfully. "I really don't know."

"Then why have you come?"

"That day last month among the dogwoods and the flowering crab," Mary answered thoughtfully, "you weren't a psychiatrist. You were a friend. We need friends."

"Sybil has friends. Aren't her friends also yours?"

"I suppose so," Mary replied, "but only in a way. Teddy Reeves knows me by name and can tell me apart from the others, but Laura Hotchkins thinks I'm Sybil. Most people do, you know. I'm sometimes very lonely."

"Then why don't you go out and make friends on your own, the way Vicky does?"

"Well, you know how it is," Mary explained. "For one thing I don't have the clothes for it. I just wear what I find in our closet, and what looks well on the others doesn't necessarily suit me." Mary paused, ducked her head, and added with a slight, tired smile, "But then I'm not as attractive as Vicky or as glamorous as Vanessa. I can't compete with them. I am what I am."

It was not until later that Dr. Wilbur discovered that Mary saw herself as a plump, maternal, little-old-lady type, not very stylish. Mary emerged as a homebody, a nest-maker, the eternal housewife interested in *Kinder, Küche, Kirche*. And although the children didn't exist, although the cooking was difficult in, as Mary put it, "one of these city apartments with kitchens the size of a pencil box," it became increasingly clear to Dr. Wilbur that what really caused trouble for Mary was not the absence of *Kinder,* the difficulties of *Küche,* but the problems revolving around *Kirche*. In time the doctor discovered that the initial "maybe it's a sin to go to a psychiatrist," etched in deep hues, reflected church-centered conflicts.

In dark hues, too, was Mary's account of grandmother Dorsett. "Grandma died," Mary told the doctor during the June 15, 1955, session. "There was no one to take her place. Sybil didn't mourn for Grandma. Sybil went away. Peggy Lou mourned quietly when she was by herself. All of us—except Vicky—mourned for Grandma, but I was the one who mourned most. After Grandma died, I came out to mourn for her."

"Did you come out at the funeral?"

"No," Mary replied, "I wasn't there. Sybil was nine then. I came when we were ten and Peggy Lou was in charge of things."

"How did you get your name?"

"It's Grandma's name. I look like Grandma, and I took her name. Grandma Dorsett's son is my father, and I also look like him."

Mary began to cry softly. Here, the doctor reflected, were the tears Sybil didn't shed. "What's the trouble, Mary?" the doctor asked.

"Grandma," Mary replied.

"But, Mary, that was more than twenty years ago."

"It's now," Mary answered, shaking her head sadly. "There is no past. Past is present when you carry it with you." Later Dr. Wilbur learned that Mary always hankered for the only real home she ever knew—Mary Dorsett's home.

"Mary," the doctor asked as the visit drew to a close, "I hope you won't resent my asking, but where are you going when you leave here?"

"Home," said Mary. "Home, where I belong. When I get there I'm going to phone Daddy. Did Sybil tell you that he and his wife, Frieda, live in Detroit? I want to reassure him about many things. You see, Sybil doesn't show him that she can try harder. I'm the one who has to show him."

"But suppose something gets in the way of the trying?" the doctor asked pointedly. "Shouldn't you get that something out of the way before you try?"

"You try," Mary answered firmly, almost self-righteously. " 'In the world's broad field of battle, you try.' "

The doctor nodded.

The hour was up. Dr. Wilbur walked her new patient to the door.

"Do you know 'The Egotist,' by Sarah Fells?" Mary asked. "Both Sybil and I liked it when we were little girls. This is how it goes:

'In a self-centered circle, he goes round and round,
That he *is* a wonder is true;
For who but an egotist ever could be
Circumference and center, too.'"

Who is the circumference, the center? the doctor wondered. Is Sybil the center or is one of these others?

The search for the center was complicated further by the arrival the next day of two selves Dr. Wilbur had not met before. From the moment Vicky introduced these newcomers, the consulting room seemed so alive and there were so many impressions, that, gazing at the woman beside her, who at the moment was simultaneously Marcia Lynn and Vanessa Gail Dorsett, the doctor, who had thought herself inured to the surprises that a multiple personality had to offer, could not refrain from being excited by this simultaneous sharing of the body. Nor could the doctor keep from speculating on how so many diverse characters could simultaneously flourish in the small, slight frame of Sybil Dorsett. The thought was fanciful because occupancy was not a matter of inhabiting space but of sharing being.

The little that Dr. Wilbur knew about Marcia and Vanessa had come from Vicky. "Marcia," Vicky had said, "feels what Sybil feels—only more intensely. Vanessa is a tall, red-haired girl who plays the piano and is full of joie de vivre. The two have many tastes in common and enjoy doing things together."

Yet after she met Marcia and Vanessa, the doctor knew less about them than about Mary.

Since the body was now *simultaneously* occupied by Marcia and Vanessa, the doctor wondered how she was going to be able to tell them apart. But after the first exchange of pleasantries, she was able to distinguish one

177

from the other by the difference in their voices, which, even though both spoke with English accents in similar diction and speech patterns, were markedly individual. Vanessa talked soprano, Marcia alto. Vanessa's voice had a lilting, Marcia's, a brooding, quality.

As she had with Mary, the doctor began their conversation by asking, "What do you girls like to do?"

"Travel," said Marcia.

"Go places," said Vanessa. "We're always interested in new and different places to see and things to do. Life is for living."

Marcia and Vanessa then talked about how they both enjoyed airplanes, big cities, the theater, concerts, places of historical interest, and buying choice books. "We have our own likes," Marcia explained, "but Vanessa and I enjoy things most when we do them together." It became clear to the doctor that, just as Vicky and Marian Ludlow were special friends in the world, Marcia and Vanessa were special friends within the "circumference" of Sybil Dorsett.

"Tell me a little about how you feel, Marcia," the doctor suggested.

"You don't know what you're letting yourself in for, Doctor," Marcia replied with a slight smile. "You've opened Pandora's box with that question."

"Doctor," Vanessa chimed in, "you shouldn't ask her. She might tell you!"

"I see you girls have a sense of humor," the doctor observed.

"You have to have humor to survive in the Dorsett clan," Vanessa replied promptly. "Mary, Peggy Lou, and, of course, Sybil worry so much that they make life sound like a Russian novel. It's really comical to watch them. It's so out of character with the town of Willow Corners, whence we hail. When I got there, Sybil was twelve, and I stayed a long time. But I couldn't stand that town. Honest, you should see it. God-fearing and man-hating. Sugar. Sugar. There was so much sugar in the way they pretended to treat each other that I suffered from diabetes of the soul."

"That's a good phrase," Marcia interrupted. "I never

178

heard you use it before. Are you sure you didn't steal it from me? I'm the writer! Why don't you stick to your piano playing and let me coin the phrases?"

"But I'm the one who came up with it. I'm the one . . ."

"Oh, Vanessa, please. I was only kidding."

"Careful," Vanessa cautioned with a satiric overtone. "As our mother would say, 'Kidding is not a word we use when people are around.'" Vanessa's voice had changed. It was clear that she was mimicking Hattie Dorsett. Then, turning to Dr. Wilbur, Vanessa said, "We were never 'kids,' Doctor, outside the family circle. And in the home even the word *heck* was not allowed."

"It's not right to criticize mother," said Marcia.

"Oh, you make me sick with your clinging. You never were able to untie the umbilical cord. That's what they call it, Doctor, isn't it? That is why this nice lady is going to have to help you to grow up."

"Vanessa, please . . ." Marcia pleaded. "It's not a crime to want to be loved."

"Lands . . . lands—I'd say *God* if I hadn't been brought up in the Dorsett household—you sound like a soap opera." Vanessa punctuated each word with an extravagant gesture.

"Vanessa, it isn't fair for you to talk like that," Marcia replied tearfully.

"Fair! What do any of us know about fairness?" Vanessa countered. "Is it fair that we've been denied what other girls have? Someday I'll break loose, be on my own, and you, my dear Marcia, will come with me. You have the taste for life, the vitality for it, and we've always been together even though you entered Sybil's life long before me. Marcia, you'll learn that you can sleep at night and feel good when you wake up in the morning only if you will stop looking back. You remember what happened to Lot's wife!"

"Vanessa," Marcia pleaded, "you've said enough. The way we're talking to each other, the doctor will think we're one person talking to herself."

"No," the doctor interrupted, "I understand perfectly well that you are two different people. I want both you girls to feel perfectly free to come here whenever you like and to say whatever you want to say."

"When we don't have competition from the others," Marcia said mischievously. "Vicky, for instance. She's pretty smart, and she helps us out a lot. But she talks too much—almost as much as Vanessa."

Then, since the hour was up, the doctor asked, "What do you plan to do when you leave here?"

"I'd like to go to International Airport and go somewhere," Vanessa said without hesitation. "But last time I did that Peggy Lou gummed up the works. I was going to buy a ticket for San Francisco, but she bought one for Cleveland. So I guess I'll just go home and play a little Mozart."

"I'm going home," Marcia volunteered, "to work on my article for *Coronet.*"

"Now, feel free to come back," the doctor reminded her patients.

When they had gone, Dr. Wilbur thought of the mechanics involved in Vanessa's pounding Mozart on the piano while Marcia pounded her article on the typewriter. They were two persons, but they had, after all, only two hands.

For three days in a row Marcia and Vanessa came back, and the doctor began to wonder what had happened to Vicky, Mary, Peggy Lou, and Sybil herself. Through the three successive visits, however, the doctor was able to resolve her initial incredulity that Marcia and Vanessa, who seemed so different, were good friends, closely linked. What linked them, the doctor came to believe, was that they were equally dynamic.

Still, there were differences. There was an excitement, an electric quality about Vanessa, who was full of energy, used extravagant gestures, and dramatized everything, that neither Marcia nor any of the other selves, at least among those the doctor had met, shared. Marcia was a calmer version of Vanessa, more somber and brooding. Even though Marcia could be lighthearted, she was basically a pessimist. She found escape with Vanessa or in books, but essentially she thought of life as "horrid and futile" and of people as being "simply awful."

What Vicky had said about Marcia's sharing yet intensifying Sybil's feelings seemed true. What Vanessa had said obliquely about Marcia and soap operas also seemed true. When Sybil and the others watched something sad on television, Marcia was the one who cried. Whenever a child or dog returned to its home or was taken back to its parents or found its mother again, Marcia would weep copiously. And Marcia, who had criticized Vanessa for criticizing their mother, was the one who seemed to need her mother most. "Marcia," Vicky told Dr. Wilbur, "will weep just because she's lonely for her mother."

Shortly after Vanessa and Marcia arrived at the doctor's office for the fourth time, Vanessa put on a show. "Goodbye, dear," Vanessa said in dulcet tones, "I'm sorry to be leaving you. I shall miss you, but I will try to have fun in Europe. *Try,* my dear. But it will be hard because I shall miss you." Then, changing her position and speaking in an aside, Vanessa exploded: "I can't stand the sight of her. I wish the bitch would go home and get off this pier."

Changing her voice and position, Vanessa slipped into the role of the second woman on the pier, who was seeing the first woman off. "I'm sorry you're leaving me, but take good care of yourself and have a simply marvelous time in Europe." Then, turning for an aside, Vanessa, still playing the woman who was not sailing, muttered with a taut, twisted curve of the lips, "I hope she drowns!"

Dr. Wilbur could see clearly the two women saying goodbye to each other on a pier near a ship about to depart. The scene was so well done that the doctor remarked: "Vanessa, you missed your calling. You should be in the theater."

12

Silent Witnesses

As the summer of 1955 gave place to autumn, Dr. Wilbur found the analysis reverting to the spring of 1934, the time of Sybil's return after the two-year absence between the ages of nine and eleven. The bewilderment Sybil had felt had been compounded by the discovery that for the first time in her life she no longer was required to sleep in her parents' bedroom. As this pivotal realization came into focus, so did the experiences she endured in that bedroom from the day of her birth to the age of nine. Those experiences, spanning the years 1923 to 1932, provided a continuum that Dr. Wilbur saw as the matrix of Sybil's attitudes toward sex and, perhaps even more important, as an incubator of the illness itself.

The evening meal was over on the first day of Sybil's return in March, 1934. The Dorsetts were in the living room. Hattie was reading a volume of Tennyson and listening to the radio. Willard was absorbed in the pages of *Architectural Forum*. Sybil was trying to do a charcoal sketch, but she found it difficult to concentrate because of the strange concatenation of events she had recently experienced.

"It's time to go to your room, Peggy," Hattie ordered.

Sybil was accustomed to being called Peggy, but she didn't understand her mother's instructions. She had

182

never had a room of her own. Always she had slept in her parents' bedroom.

Sybil said good night and walked thoughtfully toward the downstairs bedroom. To her amazement, the crib was not there. The only bed in the room was the familiar large white iron bed in which her parents slept.

"Peggy Louisiana!" her mother's voice echoed sharply from the living room. "Aren't you going upstairs?"

Upstairs? Sybil didn't know what her mother was talking about.

"It's after eight!" her mother's voice had become sharper. "You won't be able to get up in the morning. You'll have to answer to Miss Henderson—not me."

Upstairs? Some years earlier Hattie had designated an upstairs bedroom as Sybil's room. Somehow, however, Hattie had never gotten around to moving either the crib or Sybil there. With nothing to lose, Sybil decided to find out whether that room could be what her mother meant.

The crib was not in this other bedroom, either. Instead there was a full-sized bed. The fresh sheets and pillowcases invited occupancy. Was the room for company? There was no company. Could the grown-up bed be hers? Her mother had sent her there. It had to be. But when had they given this bed to her?

Sybil undressed and—for the first time—slept in an adult-sized bed in a room of her own. It was the first time that she could remember not having to face the bedroom drama that was always there.

No doubt the moment she had first become aware that merely going to bed at night was profoundly disturbing could not be fixed by clock or calendar. The cause of disturbance was always there. Only now, at last, she discovered, she could go to sleep without squeezing her eyes shut or turning to the wall.

The drama from which Sybil rebelliously removed herself was what, in psychoanalytic terms, is known as the "primal scene"—a child's auditory and visual perception of the parents' sexual intercourse. The scene is called *primal* because it is first in time in the sense that it is the child's first encounter with adult sexuality and because, as a foundation on which a youngster will build future feelings, attitudes, and behavior, it is of first importance in the child's development.

For some children there is no primal scene; for many others there is a moment in which a door opens slightly, and a child glimpses sexual intercourse between his parents. Usually the moment is accidental, inadvertent, and the way a child is affected depends on the general atmosphere of the home. When sexual intercourse is made to seem something private but not forbidden, the effects of this brief encounter are often free from psychological damage.

In Sybil's case the primal scene was no momentary glimpse, no single accidental moment. It was *always* there. For nine years Sybil had witnessed her parents' sexual intercourse as a fixed, unchanging part of life and in marked contrast to the excessive propriety and coolness of their daytime behavior.

By day they never kissed, touched, or addressed each other by any endearment, either affectionate or perfunctory. By day there was no display. The observation of the parental copulation, moreover, took place in a household in which sex was regarded as wicked, a form of degradation. Theirs was a household in which alcohol and tobacco, dancing and the movies, even novels (which, because they were "made up," were regarded as lies) were strictly forbidden.

The daughter's normal questions about the facts of life went unanswered. When Hattie was pregnant, Sybil was excluded from the "filthy" truth. When the pregnancy resulted in a miscarriage and Willard Dorsett buried the fetus—a boy— alongside the back steps, Sybil did not know what he was doing or why. Babies, born or unborn, somehow happened, but nice people did not admit how.

There were no hows or whys, only the conversational assumption of an incorporeal saintliness that, denying the flesh, consigned it to the devil. "All men," Hattie counseled her daughter, "will hurt you. They're mean, worthless." On other occasions, however, she did say,

"Daddy is not like other men." But so saying, she led Sybil, who had seen the penises of little boys, to believe that her father didn't have a penis. With father "castrated" and because of the negative attitudes toward sex inculcated within her by day, Sybil was shocked and bewildered by what she saw and heard at night.

Riveted to the nighttime lie that represented the hypocrisy of her formative years, Sybil was forced to watch a drama from which she could escape only by closing her eyes and covering her ears.

The shades were usually halfway down in the twelve-by-fourteen bedroom. The crib was placed so that a street light shone in the bedroom window, silhouetting the penis that Sybil denied her father had. Three or four nights a week, year in and year out, from the time Sybil was born until she was nine years old, parental intercourse took place within her hearing and vision. And not infrequently the erect penis was easily visible in the half-light.

Observing this primal scene, directly and in silhouette from the time of their individual arrivals, the various selves had different reactions to it.

Peggy Lou was wakeful, uneasy, but she did not try to cover her eyes or to keep from listening.

"What are you talking about?" she would sometimes demand to know.

Hattie would reply, "Go to sleep."

But instead of going to sleep, Peggy Lou would strain her ears in the hope of unscrambling what was being said. She didn't like to have her father and Sybil's mother whispering about her. They often whispered about her at the table, and she thought they were doing the same in the bedroom. Enraged by the feelings of exclusion engendered by the whispering, Peggy Lou was also made furious by the rustling of the sheets. Every time she heard that rustling she wanted to stop it.

It had been a relief to have been moved into the upstairs room shortly after Grandma Dorsett's funeral and not to have had to hear that rustling any more.

Vicky had seen the erect penis in silhouette on many

occasions. Unafraid, she would turn from the shadow on the window to the substance in the bed. What happened in bed was not always visible and, when visible, not always the same. A humped figure, Willard would sometimes move toward Hattie and mount her. At other times he would approach her as they lay side by side.

In the beginning Vicky had thought that perhaps Willard was going to crush Hattie and kill her, but instead of dying, Hattie rolled over with Willard. They embraced. And on it went. Vicky had decided that if Mrs. Dorsett hadn't wanted him to do what he was doing, she would have stopped him. At any rate, Vicky knew that it certainly wasn't up to her to help Mrs. Dorsett.

Usually the faces of Mr. and Mrs. Dorsett were hidden in the darkness. There were times, however, when the room was light enough for Vicky to see the faces—tense, strained, transformed, unrecognizable. Looking back from the vantage point of later years, Vicky could never decide whether these were the faces of ecstasy or of some malign affliction.

Vicky often felt that perhaps it wasn't right for her to look. She dismissed the scruple, however, with the realization that whether or not she looked, she would have heard anyhow. And she was curious. There was also something else: Vicky had the distinct impression that Hattie Dorsett actually wanted her daughter to look. That "something else" was that Hattie customarily threw the sheets back as if to reveal what was happening.

Marcia feared for mother's safety.

Mary resented the denial of privacy.

Vanessa was revolted by the hypocrisy of parents who paraded in their daughter's presence the sexuality they pretended to deny.

Watching and listening in that parental chamber of sexual display was a self called Ruthie, who emerged in analysis during the reliving of the primal scene. She was only a baby, perhaps of three and a half, and she could not give the date of her arrival in Sybil's life. But of all the silent witnesses to the parental intercourse it was

186

Ruthie who was most actively indignant. Acting in concert with Sybil, who was then of the same age, Ruthie retaliated against her parents with undisguised rage.

When the parents came into the room, Ruthie would lie very still, pretending to sleep. The pretense would continue while the parents undressed—Hattie in the bedroom, Willard in the adjoining doorless bathroom. But when the parents got into bed and her father moved to her mother's side, Ruthie would make her presence known. "Go to sleep, mama," she would call. "Go to sleep, daddy."

Ruthie was angry because she didn't want *her* father on her mother's side of the bed. Ruthie didn't want her father to whisper to her mother, or embrace her or breathe heavily with her or rustle the sheets with her. When he was near her mother that way, Ruthie felt that he liked her mother better than he liked her.

One night, seeing and hearing these things, Ruthie climbed out of the crib and walked very quietly toward her parents' bed. In the car Ruthie always sat in the middle. If she could do that in the car, she could do it in the bedroom. Climbing onto the bed, she attempted to get between her parents and to reclaim her rightful place in the middle.

Infuriated, Willard jumped naked out of bed, dragging his daughter with him. He sat down on a chair, placed the child over his knees, and spanked her hard. Then he put her back into her crib and returned to his wife to discover that for Hattie as for himself interrupted intercourse was to be followed by interrupted sleep; for, even after the morning sun had replaced the street light, the agonized sobs that had emanated from the crib from the moment the child had been returned to it had not ceased.

"Never again," Willard told Hattie. "I'll never spank that child again. Anyone who sobs all night takes things too hard."

Willard Dorsett, who had never spanked his daughter before and who kept his promise not to spank her again, did not know that it had been Ruthie and Sybil who had interrupted the intercourse but Peggy Lou who had sobbed all night. The incident had been so traumatic that Sybil, who had shared the experience with Ruthie, blacked out and became Peggy Lou.

Willard and Hattie Dorsett, of course, were not so disturbed by a lost night's sleep that they did not continue to have intercourse in the presence of their daughter. And Sybil continued, time after time, to be exposed to this primal scene until she was nine years old.

Awakened at times or wakeful and restless, Sybil tried to shut out the insistent rustling of the starched sheets of the parental bed, the whisperings, the murmurs, and the silhouettes. The penis of shadow and substance, which was visible to the other selves, was an object of denial for Sybil. She claimed not to have seen her father's penis until the morning when her father had leaned over the crib to tell her that Grandma Dorsett had died. At that moment Sybil had become uncomfortably aware of the mass of hair on her father's chest. She had wondered why she was so shocked, and she realized that it was not because of the hair on the chest. As a very young child, hadn't she often made a game of cutting off her father's chest hair? She was shocked instead because of how far down she could see. Visible was something from which she turned with aversion. It was partly concealed, and the closest she could come to describing it was to say that it was hidden in feathers. It wasn't very big, but it was bigger than any boy's she had ever seen. It was a little bigger around than her father's thumb, but it wasn't long. It sort of hung down when her father leaned over. In back of it, on either side, a pair of little lumps was hanging down. Sybil felt so scared and so awful that at first she didn't quite grasp what he had said about her grandmother.

If Sybil was terrified by her father's maleness, Willard Dorsett was equally terrified by his growing awareness of his daughter's femaleness. She was only two and a half when he suddenly began insisting that she was "too big" to sit on his lap, "too big" to wander in and out of the bathroom while he was shaving. By the time she was four, she had become "too big" to cut the hair

188

on his chest or to put salve on his feet, both of which activities she had by then been performing for about a year. Like a metronome, the phrase *too big* ticked off the incestuous stirrings in Willard Dorsett.

But to be *deliberately exposed* to the sights and sounds of her parents' most private sexual intimacies, Willard and Hattie Dorsett's daughter—even at the age of nine—was not too big.

13

The Terror of Laughter

When Sybil was six, however, there had been an interlude away from the white house with black shutters. For, when the Great Depression struck, Willard Dorsett suffered serious reverses, even losing his home. The house became the property of his sister in payment of an old debt, and Willard, virtually penniless, took his wife and daughter to live on farm land belonging to his parents five miles outside of Willow Corners.

The only house on those forty acres of land was a one-room chicken house, which the Dorsetts made their temporary home. High on a hill in undulating country, the new home delighted Sybil, who found in it surcease from the strange occurrences in the white house with black shutters where she had always lived.

At the farm, which Willard dubbed The Forty, autumn had yielded to winter and winter to spring. It had been snowing for three days, but now it had stopped. Willard Dorsett was putting wood in the range —it was only March and still cold—and was talking to

Sybil in his usual soft voice: "We will go outside and leave Mama alone."

That meant that they were going back to the big oak tree at the bottom of the hill, which they had been sawing before the snow began. She enjoyed all the things she could do in the house—coloring with her crayons, playing with her dolls, making dresses for them, playing with Top, the big Airedale her cousin Joey had given her, and reading in the primer her father had bought for her. But it was good to be going out again.

"Are we going right away?" she asked.

"As soon as I look after Mama," her father said.

"Mama." He always called her that, but Sybil herself never said anything except "Mother." Sybil had stopped saying "Mama" long ago, when she was a very little girl. Now Sybil was six and two months, but her father hadn't noticed that her mother wasn't "Mama" to her anymore.

That's the way her father was. So handsome, so bright, so successful until just before coming here—to this one room on top of the hill. But his nose was in his work—designing and building all those wonderful houses, churches, and barns for people. Some folks called him "master builder." He just didn't have time to notice.

At the far end of this room, which served as living room, bedroom, and playroom, there was a figure that didn't move. Her mother. The kerosene lamp with which the room was lighted on dark days was glowing beside her.

Sybil could see her mother's gray-white hair, the bun in the back held together by three bone hairpins and the wisps and loops in front. Although it was the middle of the afternoon, she was wearing a dark blue flannel bathrobe and her feet were encased in gray-felt carpet slippers. Her hands were straight down and flat at her sides, and she hung her head so low that you could hardly see her face.

The pelican on the piano in the big house in Willow Corners: her mother was like that, or like the statue in

190

the museum in Rochester. Her mother used not to be this way. She used to think well of herself, ran things, held her head high. "Hattie Dorsett holds her head so high," Sybil once overheard a neighbor say, "that I'm sure that she wouldn't see a crack in the ground."

Other things also were different from her mother here and her mother in Willow Corners. That mother did things to you; this mother didn't do *any*thing.

Her father had walked over to her mother and motioned to Sybil. Sybil knew what that meant. She didn't like doing it, but her father had crippled hands and couldn't lift her mother by himself. Now that her mother was like this, she had to help him.

Her mother didn't pay any attention even though her father and Sybil were standing over her. She didn't notice when they lifted her from her chair onto the white enamel slop jar they kept just for her. A shadow passed over her father's face while they waited for her to finish. Then they lifted her back to her chair, and her father took the jar outside.

Sybil was alone with her mother. In Willow Corners, in the house with black shutters, Sybil was always afraid to be left alone with her mother. Here she was not afraid. This mother didn't do anything to her. She was a forty-seven-year-old woman who had to be treated like a baby.

They had to do everything for her mother now. She couldn't walk to the toilet, which was outside. They had to dress her and feed her. She swallowed so slowly that even the liquid meals lasted for hours.

In the big house her mother had cooked, and Jessie had cleaned. Here there was no Jessie, and her father cooked, got water from the spring, and washed clothes in the river. He had to do everything—with his hands, crippled with the neuritis he had back in Willow Corners.

Sybil turned from her mother to Norma, her doll. "Norma," she said as she put an extra blanket on her, "I'm going out. You'll be asleep, so you won't feel lonely."

"Mama," her father, who had come back, was telling

191

her mother, "I'm taking Sybil out with me. Will you be all right?"

Why did he talk to her? She didn't hear him. She didn't hear anything. Her eyes were open, but when something passed in front of them, they didn't even blink. Her mother wasn't asleep, but she didn't hear or see. And she never answered when they talked to her.

"Sit down, daddy," Sybil said as she lifted his fleece-lined jacket from the padded box he had made for their clothes. The jacket was so woolly and furry. It looked so nice over his long trousers. He never wore overalls, but the men who worked for him in Willow Corners did.

When her father sat down, she buttoned the collar of his shirt and then helped him into his jacket. She also helped him with his buckled overshoes. "Foot up," she said.

It was so nice to be doing this for her father. It was only after his hands had been crippled that he had allowed her to do things for him again. When she was little, he had come home tired after a long day and she had put sweet-smelling salve on his feet. Then, all of a sudden he had decided to put the salve on by himself.

"Why can't I do it?" she had asked him. "Didn't I do it right?"

"Yes, yes, you did it fine," he had replied, "but you are too big."

This *too big*. She couldn't understand it. Was she too big for her father?

"All right, daddy," she said, "you can get up now."

She put on her red wool coat with the beaver collar, her brown knit leggings, her overshoes with three buckles, and her red wool stocking cap. She never looked in a mirror. She didn't like to look at herself. Her mother used to say that she had a funny nose.

"Daddy, I'm ready," she said.

"Coming," he replied. Then he walked to her mother's chair. To protect her against the afternoon chill in case the range did not provide enough heat, he placed her black coat around her shoulders as if it were a cape. Then he went out with Sybil.

192

Outside everything was white and beautiful. It had been autumn when they had arrived. Now it was the beginning of spring. Soon the trees would grow leaves. Sybil looked forward to that.

"A beautiful spot," her father had said.

Her sled was outside the door, and her father said, "When we come back, you can go sleighing." How she loved sledding down this rounded, snow-clad hill on which their house stood. She never hit the furrow. She was careful.

They passed the woodpile. She loved helping her father carry wood from that pile. At first he couldn't pick up the wood or load it in his arms. She picked up a stick of wood, placed it across his arms. Her father was weak, and the work was hard for him. But he did it.

Sybil thought of that autumn day when she had come here with her father and mother. She would never forget that drive. Nobody spoke. Of the three, she herself, it was clear from the way the others behaved, cared least about losing their old home. Now and then she would try to place bits of talk into the long silences, but she knew that her parents weren't listening so she, too, finally said nothing. Her mother did say, though, "A chicken house is only fit for chickens."

Her father had replied: "It's clean, and there have never been any chickens in it." Then her mother's neck got red all over, and she had sneered: "No, we're the first. When I married you, I didn't think you'd turn me into a chicken. Your sister Clara did this to us. You were silly to let her." Her father turned away, concentrated on the driving, and said nothing.

Her mother didn't sneer anymore. At Christmas the change had come. Her mother told her parents and her brothers and sisters in Elderville, Illinois, that this year they would not exchange gifts. But the relatives sent things anyway, and her mother, who didn't have the money to buy anything for them, had become very depressed. Then she stopped talking, stopped doing anything.

Sybil remembered the time they had come just for a visit. Someday, her father had said, they would build a

193

summer house here, and when she was big enough, she would have her own pony. Then all of a sudden they had just come. They hadn't built a house, but they had come anyway. Daddy and Mother hadn't liked it, but she had. It was much better here than in the big house.

It was fun to walk down the hill with her father and with Top, who had come along with them. He stopped when they reached the corn crib and the barn on the side of the hill. The barn had stalls, where they kept a cow and horses. Sometimes Sybil came here with her father to hitch horses. She was too little to lift the harness in place, but when she stood on the milking stool, she was big enough to help her father lift it.

It was nice to be going back to their tree. When it wasn't snowing, they came nearly every day to saw at it. She wanted to cut down the whole tree, but her father said it was so huge that it was not safe for just the two of them to cut it. They sawed, took the saw out, and then a man her father had hired axed the tree. Then they came back and sawed some more.

There were lots of trees, oaks and elms. Beautiful.

She was now with her father and Top in a plowed field covered with snow, where the oak tree waited for them. "Daddy," she said as she placed her hand on the tree, "it still remembers us."

"You certainly have a good imagination," her father said as, smiling, he handed her one end of the cross cut saw and took the other himself. Together they ran the saw, and the wood began to give.

"It's so peaceful here, Sybil," her father said. She knew he was trying to forget all the things that made him sad—mother and the rest.

The sun was bright. She could see their house on the hill in the sunlight. She and her father continued to work. They would have lots of wood. She could see their shadows on the field.

"I like shadows," she said.

Suddenly there was something else. She didn't know what. She could feel it. And her father was asking nervously, "Did you hear that loud laugh?"

"There's nobody here," she answered.

"But did you hear it?" he asked again.

"I heard it, but I don't know who it is," Sybil said as she stared at the silvered field.

The laugh was repeated. It was shrill, rising higher. Sybil began to tremble. She knew that laugh but was afraid to admit that she did. She had heard the laugh many times in Willow Corners. The laugh came when she was made to stand up against the wall. A broom handle struck her back. A woman's shoe kicked her. A washcloth was stuffed down her throat. She was tied to the leg of the piano while a woman played. Things were put up inside her, things with sharp edges that hurt. And cold water. She was made to hold the water in her. The pain, the cold. Each time worse than before and always that laugh along with the pain. When she was placed inside a trunk in the attic she heard that laugh. It was with her again when she was buried in the wheat crib and nearly smothered.

The laughter died and did not come again, but that sharp, shrill sound, coming to her in the March wind, had ripped away the quiet of the afternoon, its peace, its happiness gone.

Sybil looked up. Her mother was on the top of the hill in front of the house, near the sled. How? Only a little while ago she was like stone. At first she didn't move; then Sybil saw her drop onto the sled in a sitting position. With knees drawn up, feet on the steering bar, she pushed backward with her bare hands in the snow. The sled shot forward down the hill, gaining speed as it dizzily angled off to the left, straight toward the furrow of the plowed field under the snow.

Sybil, shocked and fearful, stood immobile. Then she stammered, "She'll hit the furrow. She'll hit the furrow!"

Her father, whose back was toward the hill, turned instantly in the direction of Sybil's petrified gaze and then shouted as he started running toward his wife, "Don't, Hattie, don't. Stop!"

Sybil herself did not run. The laughter had made her heart stand still, and her whole body froze with it. She wanted to run not toward the hill but away from it, but she could not run anywhere. She could not even move.

She knew that some terrible danger would surely follow the familiar laugh. Was the Willow Corners mother back?

Her father was pretty far away now, but Sybil could hear him calling, "Hattie, Hattie, I'm coming." Sybil, still standing in the same spot, could hear herself breathe. Her mother was again near and threatening. Her mother was like the dragon she had heard about in church, a dragon breathing fire.

Sybil should be moving to avoid the fire. She could not. "Move. Save yourself." The voices: "You cannot save yourself. You're bad—bad—bad. That's why your mother punishes you."

The moving sled moved closer. She could not move. Her mother's black cape swept the snow and turned partly white. Black on white.

Top began to bark, then to move around in circles, not knowing what to do either. Another shrill scream. More laughter, closer this time. Then silence.

Her mother had hit the furrow. The sled rose up and threw her off. Her mother was flying through the air, a big black bird without wings. Her shadow, moving, zigzagging, was everywhere on the white snow.

Then her mother wasn't flying anymore. She was lying in the plowed field. Her father was leaning over her, taking her pulse.

"Daddy!" Sybil screamed.

Sybil tried to go to them but was stuck to the spot. Watching her father and mother as if they were far away, she clutched the saw tightly as if it could give her comfort and quiet her terror.

The only sound was the murmuring of the branches of the trees. Otherwise the field was as hushed as her mother had been when they had left her in the house on the top of the hill.

The sun was sinking lower and was about to set. Sybil let the saw slip from her hand. She had been clinging to it perhaps because it was the link to the happy time, the months from Christmas to now, when her mother was silent and the Willow Corners mother did not exist.

Sybil stood near the stove while her father hovered on one knee over her mother in the chair. He was applying hot packs to her mother's badly bruised and swollen leg. Her mother was saying, "I thought sure it was broke. Put on some arnica when you get done with the hot packs."

"You shouldn't have steered the sled so hard with one foot, mother. That's what made it go sideways into the plowed field," Sybil said softly. Then, turning to her father, she asked, "How did you get her to the house alone?"

Looking up into the child's face, her father dryly remarked, "Well, you helped me pull her back up the hill on the sled, didn't you?"

Had she? Sybil only remembered being in the field, dropping the saw, and then being beside the stove.

Now her father was asking, "How do you feel, Hattie?"

"I'll live," said her mother.

"Hattie," her father said, "you shouldn't give in to your moods."

"I can do what I like," her mother laughed—that laugh again.

"Lie down, Hattie," her father said.

"Later, Willard," her mother answered. "Get water."

Her father took a pail and went to the spring for water. Sybil put arnica on her mother's legs, which were snow white and bony. Her left leg was turning all colors now; it had marks all over it.

"Hurts, mother?" Sybil asked.

"Well," her mother said, "use your head. What do you think?"

"Oh," Sybil said.

Her father wasn't here. Would her mother hurt her? Fortunately, her father soon came back with the water. He bathed her mother's leg and made hot packs for it. Then he made supper while Sybil set the table.

"You're doing it wrong," her mother said. "The forks are in the wrong place." The Willow Corners mother had returned.

Her father took a plate of food over to her mother.

Her mother laughed and said, "I'm coming to the table. Help me." Her mother came to the table and sat with them, for the first time in months, and she fed herself.

When supper was over, Sybil helped her father wash the dishes. Then they put more hot packs and arnica on her mother's leg. Hours passed. "Time to go to bed, Sybil," her mother said. It was the first time in a long time that her mother had said that. Sybil didn't move.

"I told you to go to bed," said her mother. "I mean now, this minute."

"What do you want of her, Hattie?" her father asked. "She's just a youngster. And she was a big help getting you back here."

Sybil said nothing. When people said she had done something she didn't know about, nothing was all she would say.

She walked over to her crib, which they had brought with them from Willow Corners. Her crib, her dolls, her doll crib, her doll table and her little chairs—they had brought all her things. She put on her nightgown and her stocking cap. Her mother wasn't laughing now, but Sybil could still hear her mother's laughter coming from the top of the hill. She could still see that black cape against the white snow. And then her father bending over her . . . how had he gotten into all this trouble? The loss of the house in Willow Corners—overnight, as her mother used to say, from the richest man in town to the poorest. Why had Satan struck him? Was this the beginning of the end of the world that her father and grandfather were always talking about?

"Sybil, get a move on," her mother called.

From her father: "Sybil, rinse this rag."

Sybil took the rag, rinsed the rag, and gave it back to him. He put it on her mother's leg. Yes, Sybil did things to make her mother's bruised leg better.

14

Hattie

Learning of Hattie Dorsett's catatonia at The Forty and of her later aberrations within the Willow Corners community, Dr. Wilbur became increasingly convinced that it was impossible to treat Sybil without having a fuller understanding of Hattie. Hattie, it was becoming evident, had forged an intolerable reality from which Sybil had to defend herself in order to survive. Even though the doctor, aware that it was a psychiatric cliché to make a scapegoat of the patient's mother, had resisted pinpointing Hattie Dorsett as a major cause of Sybil's dissociation into multiple selves, it was becoming increasingly difficult to resist the notion.

In late 1956 and early 1957, as Dr. Wilbur came closer to the source of the original trauma that had led Sybil to become a multiple personality, there was little doubt that the trauma seemed to revolve around her mother. It was the Willow Corners mother, who returned from immobility at the farm, on whom the analysis then turned.

Sybil scuffed along the cement path of the alley behind the white house with black shutters as she approached the Willow Corners Drugstore for the first time since coming home from the farm.

The familiar fly-covered screen door with its high bent-iron handle intrigued her, and standing on tiptoe, she grasped the piece of iron and swung wide the door. As she stepped over the worn wooden threshold, the acrid odor she had always known behind this special door assailed her.

Sybil tried not to breathe, not wanting to inhale this hated smell. She wanted to hurry through this back room with its high tables and shelf-lined walls filled with bottles, glass stoppers, bowls, herbs, colored liquids, and white powders, the room in which medicines were made by the white-coated, tall, slightly bent, old Dr. Taylor, whom Sybil had known since memory began for her. But she could not hurry, could not move her feet to make the transition from back room to "up-front," where the drugstore blended shelves of medicines with huge glass cases of penny candies, dolls, combs, and hairbows.

Sybil's eyes sought the open wooden stairway standing between the room she had entered from the alley and up-front. The stairs led to the fascination of her childhood—the great, bewildering "something" known as Dr. Taylor's balcony. None entered there unbidden, and few were bidden. It was the doctor's retreat.

Following the hand rail of the stairs, Sybil looked hopefully for Dr. Taylor's white-haired figure near the high ceiling. She couldn't speak, couldn't ask, but breathlessly she hoped for the druggist's notice of her. Pausing between hated odors and adored soft-voiced invitations, she saw the druggist's kind, wrinkled face peer over the rail of the balcony. Dr. Taylor smiled and said, "Come on up, Sybil. It's all right."

Swiftly, with toes barely touching the steps, Sybil raced to the top, where abruptly she stopped, hand on rail and eyes wide with anticipation and delight. Hanging on the walls and lying in parts on work tables were the violins, the music makers of Dr. Taylor's creation.

Here was the special music reached through a special door, the music accompanied not by pain, as it was for her at home, but by friendship and the comforting softness of the druggist's voice. Smiling, Dr. Taylor played a little on his violin, and Sybil entered her private world of dreams. "Someday when you are bigger," the doctor promised, "I shall make a violin just for you. You shall play music, too."

Sybil dreamed of music and also of pictures. She could see trees, dark trees, white trees. She could see horses running and all kinds of chickens. The chickens were all of different colors. Some had blue legs. Others had red feet and green tails. She drew these chickens, and although her mother reminded her that chickens were white, plain black, or brown, Sybil continued to draw chickens as expressions of the feelings her mother denied. And Dr. Taylor had said: "You shall play music, too."

At that moment a voice, sharp, loud, and shrill, was heard from the bottom of the stairs. It was her mother's voice, calling. Her mother, who seldom let Sybil out of her sight, had followed her here. Quickly Sybil took her leave of Dr. Taylor, descended the stairs, and appeared at her mother's side.

As Sybil and her mother approached the drug counter, a clerk remarked, "I told you, Mrs. Dorsett, you'd find her with Dr. Taylor." While the clerk was wrapping the bottle of medicine for which Hattie had left a prescription, Sybil rested her elbow on the counter and her head on the hand of her upraised arm. Inadvertently her elbow knocked against a bottle of patent medicine that had been left on the counter. The bottle crashed to the floor, and the crash of glass made Sybil's head throb.

"You broke it," came her mother's accusing voice. Then there was her mother's contemptuous laugh. Sybil panicked, and panic produced a sensation of dizziness that made the room swirl.

"You broke it," her mother repeated as she grasped the iron handle and swung wide the door with its complaining creak of rusty hinges. As her mother and she stepped over the threshold into the alley, the odor suddenly assumed the coloration of all the hated medicines her mother had poured into the child. The short walk along the alley, so filled with expectation minutes before, became a prisoner's walk.

Hattie turned abruptly from the alley into the street, and Sybil wondered where they were going *this time;* for many were the walks with her mother that Sybil would rather not have taken.

Hattie walked briskly toward the wagons that the farmers brought to town, lined up for four or five blocks along Main Street. Sybil's mother approached the wagons after the farmers had left them and helped herself to peas and corn, which she put in her apron. Other people did this, too, but Sybil was embarrassed because her father had said it was stealing.

"Now you get some, too," her mother ordered, but Sybil refused, as she also did when her mother asked her to get tomatoes from the Tomley's vegetable garden or apples, asparagus, lilacs, or some other produce from the loading platforms behind the stores. Even though her mother explained that the items stolen never would be missed because the owners had more than they needed, or that the products on the loading platforms were out in the sun and would spoil anyway, Sybil felt it was wrong to steal. It continued to seem wrong even when her mother explained to the farmer, the storekeeper, or the neighbor: "I didn't have a chance to ask if I could have some. But you have plenty, and I'm sure you won't mind."

It somehow seemed especially wrong that afternoon, as, leaving the wagons, Sybil and her mother went to the fruit and vegetable garden belonging to the Bishop family. Her father had warned her mother to leave the neighbors' property alone.

"Let's get some," Hattie suggested conspiratorially as Sybil walked with her toward the Bishops' rhubarb stalks. Hattie bent over the stalks, but Sybil hung back. "You'd be the first to eat the rhubarb pie," Hattie taunted as she pulled the best stalks. But neither then nor at any other time could Sybil eat the rhubarb pie or reconcile herself to the fact that the Willow Corners mother had returned.

This was the mother who embarrassed Sybil not only on the streets but also at church functions. On these occasions Hattie would be loud. Willard would caution, out of the side of his mouth, "Don't say that," and Hattie would announce loudly to everybody, "He says I shouldn't say that."

"It was unbelievable," Vicky stated in analysis. "The

things Mrs. Dorsett did. Who would have thought that a woman of her background would make a spectacle of herself at church or turn out to be a Fagin? But Fagin she was in wanting us to cooperate with her in taking things. Not one of us ever did. Not one!"

But there was a feeling that Hattie also awakened that went deeper than embarrassment. That emotion was shame—the raw, naked feeling of a daughter's watching her mother's voyeuristic peering into other people's windows or her gossiping about the sexual peccadillos of persons who came from what she called the "lower crust."

"Hattie Dorsett is odd," declared the townsfolk of Willow Corners. But, if by virtue of her filching neighbors' rhubarb stalks, or being loud at church functions, or spontaneously getting up from her table to do a solo dance in a restaurant where there was no music or dancing, Hattie Dorsett qualified as "odd," other public performances in which she indulged had to be described as "crazy."

There were, for instance, Hattie's nocturnal escapades. Sometimes, as the shades of evening drew on, or after supper, she would summon Sybil with a brusque, "We're going for a walk." Filled with intense foreboding and dread because she knew what was coming, Sybil at the ages of three, four, and five would quietly follow her mother out of the house and walk apprehensively through the town.

The walk, which began as a casual stroll, was destined to become a demonic ritual. For, with her head held high and her carriage proud, as befitted the daughter of the mayor of Elderville and the wife of one of the wealthiest people in Willow Corners, Hattie Anderson Dorsett advanced from the sidewalk, the lawn, or the backyard, to the bushes. Watching, Sybil cringed with repugnance as her mother pulled down her bloomers, squatted, and with ritualistic deliberateness and perverse pleasure defecated on the elected spot.

Election it was, and besmirchment was a badge of honor. For these escapades of Hattie Dorsett were part of a grand design to single out the town's elite for her hostility and contempt. During the years in which the escapades took place—1926, 1927, and 1928—the Sticknews and Mrs. Vale vied with Willard Dorsett for the title of the wealthiest person in town. As editor of the newspaper of which Hattie was an unpaid stringer, Harrison Ford was Hattie's superior. And so Hattie chose for the expression of her defecatory contempt locally prestigious targets that threatened her own feelings of omnipotence. Converting the more normal "I shit on you all" into an actual performance, she responded in the manner of a psychotic, acting upon the power of the unconscious, which regards all secretions as gifts of power.

Hattie Dorsett didn't silently hypothesize that her feces were directed at the Sticknews, Mrs. Vale, or Harrison Ford, or for that matter at Willard Dorsett, when she similarly performed in the basement of his (and her) house. Hattie deliberately defecated on the property of her victims, at the very spot on which her contempt could be concretely symbolized. It was an act of psychotic cruelty, manifesting the wish of the unconscious to pour upon special persons its fecal wrath.

Neither the Sticknews, nor Mrs. Vale, nor Harrison Ford, nor Willard Dorsett, nor the town itself seemed to notice. When Sybil had pleaded, "Mother, someone will see you," Hattie had invariably retorted, "Rubbish." And for whatever reason—perhaps the Dorsetts' prestige in the town—"rubbish" it seems to have been, since the town of Willow Corners apparently never made any attempt to bring Mrs. Willard Dorsett into line.

The town seems also to have been unaware of Hattie Dorsett's incredible performances on Sundays when she babysat with a flock of little girls whose parents were at church.

On the surface, nothing could be more virtuous, more harmless, more publicly maternal than to care for one's neighbors' children, and in fact the games Hattie played with these little girls did begin innocently enough.

"We're going to play horsey," she would tell them as

she got down on all fours and encouraged them to do likewise.

"Now lean over and run like a horse." As the children squealed with delight at the prospect, Hattie would motion them to begin. Then, while the little girls, simulating the gait of horses, leaned over as they had been instructed, Hattie, from her perch on the floor, revealed the real purpose of the "game." Into their vaginas went her fingers as she intoned, "Giddyap, giddyap." Watching, Sybil and the other selves responded with the same intense shame they had experienced during the pilgrimages of defecation.

The perversity that was more than "oddness" was also evident one afternoon when Peggy Lou, looking into Hattie and Willard's bedroom, saw Sybil's mother nude on the bed with a baby boy between her legs. Sybil's mother was lifting the baby up and down with her hips and rubbing him between her thighs. The eighteen-month-old boy was a neighbor's child for whom Hattie was babysitting. Peggy Lou furrowed her brow and thought, as she told Dr. Wilbur in analysis, "What Sybil's mother was doing wasn't nice." Then Peggy Lou, glad that Hattie was not *her* mother, slipped silently away from the room.

Shame there was, too, when Sybil walked through the woods to the river with her mother and her mother's three teenage friends. All three—Hilda, Ethel, and Bernice—came from "the lower crust," and Hattie let it be known that her fraternizing with them was a form of social service.

Sybil never saw her mother and father kiss or hold hands by day. But as Sybil walked to the river, she saw her mother do such things with these special friends. At the river her mother would say, "You wait here while we go behind the bushes to get into our suits." Sybil, who was already wearing her bathing suit, waited. The first few times that her mother went behind the bushes Sybil didn't pay any attention to how long it took before her mother and her friends returned.

Then one day Sybil began to feel uneasy as, wading along the edge of the river on the sloping shore, she realized that her mother and the girls had stayed behind the bushes longer than was required to get into their bathing suits.

Sybil didn't dare call to her mother, but she decided to walk around the bushes in the hope that she would be noticed. The woods were silent, but, as she reached the bushes, she heard soft voices—the voices of her mother and her friends. What were they saying? What were they doing? Why were they taking so long? Overwhelmed by curiosity, Sybil pushed aside some leaves to see.

Her mother and the girls were not getting into their suits, which were lying in a heap. Her mother and the girls were not standing. Their dresses, pulled up, were tucked above their waists. Naked from the waist down, mother and the girls were lying on the ground, their hands intermingling, their buttocks visible. Fingers moving. Palms stroking. Bodies gyrating. Ecstatic expressions. Everybody seemed to be holding somebody. Her mother was holding Hilda. Her mother's hands were at Hilda's crotch.

The horsey games, Sybil thought as she turned away and walked slowly back to the edge of the river. At the age of three Sybil could think of no other description for the mutual masturbation, the lesbian encounter, that she had witnessed.

Silent witness she was, on that shore, for three successive summers. Each time she would wade in the river, play with the rocks, and either glimpse the scene behind the concealing bushes or wait without looking for its cessation. How she wished her mother and the girls would hurry!

15

Battered Child

In early 1957 the analysis unfolded a drama of cruelty, secret rituals, punishments, and atrocities inflicted by Hattie on Sybil. Dr. Wilbur became convinced that the taproot of Sybil's dissociation into multiple selves was a large, complicated capture-control-imprisonment-torture theme that pervaded the drama. One escape door after another from cruelty had been closed, and for Sybil, who was a battered child four decades before the battered child syndrome was medically identified, there had been no way out.

Normal at birth, the doctor speculated, Sybil had fought back until she was about two and a half, by which time the fight had been literally beaten out of her. She had sought rescue from without until, finally recognizing that this rescue would be denied, she resorted to finding rescue from within. First there was the rescue of creating a pretend world, inhabited by a loving mother of fantasy, but, the doctor hypothesized, being a multiple personality was the ultimate rescue. By dividing into different selves, defenses against not only an intolerable but also a dangerous reality, Sybil had found a modus operandi for survival. Grave as her illness was, it had originated as a protective device.

At the farm the mother against whom Sybil had to defend herself had been immobilized by what seemed to Dr. Wilbur to be the catatonic phase of schizophrenia. But the return to Willow Corners had brought with it the mother who, no longer immobilized, was again threatening. Reality again became dangerous, and once again Sybil sought her customary means of coping.

At the moment Hattie Dorsett had taunted, "You'd be the first to eat the rhubarb pie," Sybil, in anger, had blacked out into Peggy Lou.

Returning home with Sybil's mother, Peggy Lou went into the sunroom to play, shut the door, and began to act as if Hattie Dorsett did not exist. Peggy got out her crayons, sat on the linoleum, drawing and singing a song that her father had taught her: "A train's acomin' 'round the bend, all loaded down with Harrison's men, goodbye, my lover, goodbye."

When Hattie shouted, "Stop that infernal noise," Peggy Lou went right on singing. "You have to find something you like besides music and all these colors," Hattie pontificated as she swung wide the sunroom door. "It's not like that when you grow up. It's not all sunshine and singing and pretty colors. There's always thorns in the roses." And at that moment Hattie punctuated what she was saying by stamping her foot on her daughter's box of crayons.

Peggy Lou went on singing and, unable to use the broken crayons, turned to her dolls. Peggy Lou, who could get angry, could also defy Sybil's mother.

Sybil returned shortly before supper and, when her father suggested, "Why don't you go color a while?" replied, "My crayons got broken."

"These new ones, already?" Willard asked. "Sybil, you have to learn to take care of things."

Sybil said nothing because she knew nothing of how the crayons had gotten broken.

The Willow Corners mother laughed when there was no reason for laughter and didn't allow her daughter to cry when there was cause for tears.

Ever since Sybil could remember, the laughter—cacophonous, wild—had accompanied a special brand of matinal maternal ministration. Beginning when Sybil was only six months old, this special ministration continued throughout early childhood. In the early morning after Willard Dorsett had gone to work and she was alone with her child for the day, the Willow Corners mother began to laugh.

"We don't want anyone looking in, spying on us!" Hattie would say as she locked the kitchen door and pulled down both door and window shades.

"I have to do it. I have to do it," Hattie muttered, as with the same ritualistic deliberateness with which she indulged her aberrations in the community, she placed her daughter on the kitchen table. "Don't you move," the mother enjoined the child.

What followed was not always the same. A favorite ritual, however, was to separate Sybil's legs with a long wooden spoon, tie her feet to the spoon with dish towels, and then string her to the end of a light bulb cord, suspended from the ceiling. The child was left to swing in space while the mother proceeded to the water faucet to wait for the water to get cold. After muttering, "Well, it's not going to get any colder," she would fill the adult-sized enema bag to capacity and return with it to her daughter. As the child swung in space, the mother would insert the enema tip into the child's urethra and fill the bladder with cold water. "I did it," Hattie would scream triumphantly when her mission was accomplished. "I did it." The scream was followed by laughter, which went on and on.

These early morning rituals also included unneeded enemas, which Hattie gave her daughter with frightening frequency. Almost invariably it was an enema of cold water administered from an adult-sized bag, containing about twice as much water as would normally be given to a child or infant. After the enema Hattie insisted that the child walk around the room holding in the water. This resulted in severe cramps. But if Sybil cried, Hattie would beat her and say, "I'll really give you something to cry about."

The ritual was not complete until Hattie had warned, "Now don't you dare tell anybody anything about this. If you do, I won't have to punish you. God's wrath will do it for me!"

With frightening frequency, too, during infancy and childhood, Hattie would force her daughter to drink a glass full of milk of magnesia. Sybil would get cramps. Hattie would pick up the child, allowing the legs to hang straight. The cramps would become more severe. When Sybil pleaded to go to the bathroom, Hattie made her go to the bedroom instead. Hattie made Sybil soil herself and then punished the child for doing what Hattie had made her do. Sybil began to cry. Then Hattie tied a towel around Sybil's mouth so that grandmother Dorsett, who lived upstairs, would not hear the cry. Fearing the towels, Sybil also was afraid to cry. By the time she was three and a half she no longer did cry.

There was still another morning ritual with which Hattie Dorsett took great pains. After placing Sybil on the kitchen table, Hattie would force into the child's vagina an array of objects that caught the mother's fancy—a flashlight, a small empty bottle, a little silver box, the handle of a regular dinner knife, a little silver knife, a buttonhook. Sometimes the object was her finger, performing as it did when she bathed the child and scrubbed so zealously that at two and a half the child locked the door and tried to bathe herself.

"You might as well get used to it," her mother, inserting one of these foreign bodies, explained to her daughter at six months or at six years. "That's what men will do to you when you grow up. They put things in you, and they hurt you, and they push you around, and they hurt you, and you can't stop them, and when they get tired of one woman, they get another. So I might as well prepare you."

Hattie prepared her daughter so well that Sybil's hymen was severed in infancy, and her vagina was permanently scarred. The preparation was so effective, moreover, that a gynecologist who examined Sybil when she was in her twenties stated that, because of the internal injuries, she would probably never bear a child.

Sybil fought back at first even though her mother's "I have to do it" led her to think that this was indeed something that had to be done. Too, although the fight was literally beaten out of Sybil by the time she was two and a half, she blamed not the perpetrator of the

uring the infant's first six weeks of
Iattie, who suffered postpartum de-
birth, was unable to care for the
   Dorsett returned to help Willard
when the infant developed a disease
Hattie, unable to stand the crying,
e mother's role. The ear "broke"
s resting on Willard's shoulder with
ard the hot stove. Her grandmother
er mother came back, and the infant
from pain with her father.
two and a half, love returned in the
a maid who later cared for the child
d her time to grandmother Dorsett,
ke. Sybil loved Priscilla second only
. One day Sybil said, "I love you"
overhearing the remark, said, "Well,
, don't you?"
und to where Hattie was standing,
viland china. Sybil put her arms
k and said yes. Pushing Sybil away,
u're too big to act like that."
Irs. Dorsett was being "cross" with
spread her arms toward Sybil in a
. Sybil ran over and took hold of
scilla said that Sybil could help her,
the dusting, and that they'd prepare
ogether. Sybil had Priscilla and felt
mother.
der, however, the interludes of her
f Priscilla ended, and her mother
ie helm. The stage for repression was
nded not to tell, not to cry, lest she
everything to herself. Sybil learned
cause by fighting she evoked further

e, however, was the fascination of
 creativity, of making things. Often
a the case of drawing the chickens
reen tails, also led to head-on colli-
er and child.

torture but its instrument: the flashlight, the towels, the silver box, the shoe buttonhook.

"Sybil," Willard Dorsett said one Sabbath morning as the family was getting ready for church. "I don't see why you scream so every time we put those shoes on you."

To Hattie, Willard remarked, "Mama, we'd better get her new shoes."

Willard Dorsett didn't know that it hadn't been the white kid shoes that made Sybil scream. He didn't know that in the Dorsett household the buttonhook had uses unrelated to the buttoning of shoes. Hidden from Willard, concealed from the world beyond the drawn shades, these sadistic tortures remained nameless.

These tortures, of course, had nothing to do with what Sybil had done. When Hattie Dorsett actually wanted to punish her daughter, there were other means. Then Hattie would slap her daughter and knock the child to the ground. Or Hattie would fling Sybil across the room, once sufficiently violently to dislocate one of the child's shoulders. Or Hattie would give Sybil a blow on the neck with the side of her hand, on one occasion severely enough to fracture Sybil's larynx.

A hot flat iron was pressed down on the child's hand, causing a serious burn. A rolling pin descended on Sybil's fingers. A drawer closed on Sybil's hand. A purple scarf was tied around Sybil's neck until she gasped for breath. The same scarf was tied around her wrist until the hand became blue and numb. "There's something wrong with your blood," Hattie pontificated. "It will get better."

Sybil was tied with dish towels to the scrolled piano leg while her mother played Bach, Beethoven, Chopin. The binding sometimes took place without the preamble of other tortures, but on other occasions Hattie would first fill the child's rectum or bladder with cold water. With the pedals of the piano pushed down, Hattie would pound the instrument as hard as she could. Vibrations in the head and reverberations in the full bladder or rectum created physical agony and emotional horror.

Unable to endure, Sybil would almost invariably allow one of her other selves to emerge.

Sybil's face and eyes were bound with dish towels, and the "blindfold" game served as punishment for the child's having dared to ask some question to which the mother's answer was, "Anyone could see that who isn't blind. And I'll show you what it's like to be blind." The result was that Sybil feared blindness, and later, when she suffered vagaries in her vision, she was terrified.

There were times when Hattie showed Sybil what it's like to be dead, when she put the child in the trunk in the attic and closed the lid or stuffed a damp wash rag down Sybil's throat and put cotton in Sybil's nose until the child lost consciousness. When Hattie threatened to put Sybil's hands in the meat grinder and chop the fingers off, Sybil couldn't be sure whether or not the threat was real. Her mother threatened to do lots of things; later she did them.

There were times, however, when it was not Sybil but the china, the linens, the piano, or books that were the butt of Hattie's obsessive frenzy. At these times Hattie Dorsett, who, before Sybil went to school, spent virtually twenty-four hours a day in her daughter's presence, didn't know that the child was there. Completely self-absorbed and apparently fixated in fantasies of her late father, Hattie would sit, stroking and smelling by the hour the quilted smoking jacket that had belonged to him. When she wasn't holding it, she kept it sealed in a box.

Or she would wash and polish the Haviland china that, seldom used, needed neither washing nor polishing. She would arrange and rearrange, unfold and refold the linens. She would sit at the ornately ornamented Smith and Barnes upright piano to the left of the window in a rather dark corner of the living room, playing Chopin and Beethoven. She would put records on the phonograph, insistent that they had always to be played from the beginning and in sequence. It was heresy and a violation of her code to play the fourth movement of a symphony, for instance, without having preceded it by movements one through three.

Hattie woul...
from "Evangel...
and other poer...
amuse Hattie,...
would ask wha...
the recitation,...
"Mother, what...
dress?" Sybil w...

"My Havila...
would reply. "...
match mine. I...

The walls of...
ing Sybil's infan...
a high chair in...
and a rubber c...
at the piano in...
kitty and then...
Sybil struggled...
Unable to make...
Hattie went on...
the infant's "ch...
louder the jailer...

When the pr...
to crawl, she m...
over her mother...
in the sunroom...
left the house to...
way into the liv...
scattered Hattie...
to find Sybil p...
never connected...

The child had...
her mother trip...
Sybil refused to...
Having precocio...
shut the barn d...
lately to walk, a...

Retaliation ag...
earliest years of...
friends. It was...

took care of Sybil...
life, during which...
pression after the...
child. Grandmoth...
care for Sybil late...
of the middle ear...
again abdicated...
while the infant w...
her infected ear to...
again went away,...
connected surceas...

When Sybil wa...
person of Priscilla...
while Hattie devo...
who had had a st...
to her grandmoth...
to Priscilla. Hatti...
you love mama, t...

Sybil turned a...
polishing some...
around Hattie's r...
Hattie said, "Oh,...

Observing that...
the child, Priscil...
gesture of inclus...
Priscilla's hand...
that Sybil could...
the noonday me...
she didn't need h...

As Sybil grew...
grandmother an...
steadily took ove...
set as Sybil, com...
be punished, ke...
not to fight back...
punishments.

What did su...
new experiences...
the creativity, a...
with red feet an...
sions between m...

212

One afternoon when Sybil was four, she pasted a face she had clipped from *McCall's* magazine on some tin foil and put some red Christmas cord on it. Delighted with what she had made, she ran into the kitchen to show her new creation to her mother. "I thought I told you not to run in the house," Hattie said as she placed a pan in the oven.

"I'm sorry," said Sybil.

"Well, you better be," said Hattie.

"Look, mother," Sybil said as she proudly held up her handiwork.

"I don't have time to look at it now," said Hattie. "I'm busy. Can't you see I'm busy?"

"Look what I made. It's for our Christmas tree."

"Well that's just a magazine and some tin foil," Hattie sniffed.

"I think it's pretty," Sybil said, "and I'm going to hang it on the tree."

"Well, I'm busy," said Hattie.

Then Sybil hung the ornament she had made on the tree that stood near the piano in the living room. She looked at what her mother had belittled, and she herself was, nevertheless, proud of having made it. "Mother, come look," she called, as she went back into the kitchen.

"I don't have time."

"Come on."

Then all of a sudden Hattie stopped what she was doing and looked at Sybil. Hattie asked: "You didn't go hang that on the tree after I said that?"

Sybil wanted desperately to get the ornament off the tree before her mother saw it. But standing at the tree, her mother was already calling, "You come here this minute and get that thing off that tree."

Sybil stood still.

"Do you hear me?" Hattie was standing next to the tree.

"I'll take it off in a minute," Sybil promised.

"Don't you say 'in a minute' to me," Hattie's voice rasped.

Sybil was trapped. If she obeyed, she had to go to

the tree, where Hattie stood ready to hit her. If Sybil didn't go, she would be hit for disobeying. Deciding on the former, Sybil pulled the ornament down quickly and, eluding her mother, ran toward the door. Hattie started after her daughter. Sybil ran faster. Her mother's menacing, "Don't you run in this house," echoed everywhere. Sybil wondered whether she should keep running or stop. If Sybil stopped, her mother would hit her because of the Christmas ornament. If Sybil ran, her mother would hit her for running. Entrapment was complete.

Stopping, Sybil received a swift, sharp blow on the right cheek.

So there were bad days, but there also were good days—such as the one when the Floods visited. As the Floods—Pearl, Ruth, Alvin, and their mother—were leaving in their sleigh, Sybil waved goodbye from the porch steps. The sleigh faded from sight, and Sybil turned to go back into the house. She had been happy that afternoon as she played on the sunroom floor with Ruth and Pearl, who were older than she. She was only three and a half, but they played with her and taught her many things. Pearl had made Sybil's doll, Betty Lou, walk.

Still holding Betty Lou in her arms, Sybil went into the sunroom. Hattie came after her and said, "Get that doll out of your hands. I want to get your sweater off."

But Sybil didn't want to put the doll down. It had been a wonderful afternoon, and she had discovered many things. She had learned how to make Betty Lou walk.

"I want to show you how Betty Lou walks," Sybil told her mother.

"I don't have time," Hattie bristled. "I have to get supper ready for daddy. Now put your doll down this minute. I want to get your sweater off."

As her mother was taking off the sweater, Sybil bubbled, "I like Pearl. She's fun."

"I don't have time," her mother replied as she hung the sweater on a hook in the kitchen.

Sybil had followed her mother out of the sunroom and

into the kitchen, still trying to talk about the afternoon's events. Her mother began preparing supper. As she took some pots and pans out of the cupboard, the blue sweater, placed hastily on the hook, fell to the floor. "When I turn my back to you," her mother said, "see what happens. Why did you pull that sweater down? Why can't you behave yourself? Why must you always be bad, you bad, bad girl?"

Her mother picked up the sweater, turned it over in her hand, scrutinizing it. "It's dirty," she finally announced in the tone of a doctor making an important diagnosis. "Mother always keeps you clean. You're a dirty girl."

Sybil felt her mother's knuckles hitting her hard on the side of her head over and over again. Then her mother shoved her onto a little red chair. It was the chair on which she had been sitting the time her grandmother had come downstairs, wanting to talk to her and her mother, and her mother had said, "Grandma, please don't go near Sybil. She's being punished." And her grandmother had not come near.

The little red chair was in front of a mantel clock. Sybil was not big enough to tell time, but she could see where the big hand was and where the little hand was. At this moment the big hand was on 12 and the little hand on 5.

"It's just five o'clock," her mother said.

It was such a wonderful afternoon, Sybil thought as she sat in the little red chair, not daring to move, and *she* had to go and spoil it. I had so much fun that I was sorry Alvin couldn't play on the floor with the girls and me because we were playing with dolls and he is a boy. He was left out. It is awful to be left out.

Her mother had been so kind to the Floods. She gave them all kinds of things: food for Mrs. Flood, mittens for Pearl, leggings for Alvin. Her mother also gave them two games that Sybil had never really used, never really had a chance to play with. That was all right because she liked the Floods.

Sybil looked at the mantel clock. The little hand was now on 6. She called to tell her mother.

"I didn't ask you," her mother answered sharply. "For that you sit there five minutes more, you dirty girl. You made the sweater dirty, and you have a dirty mouth."

"What did I do?" Sybil asked.

"You know perfectly well what you did," her mother replied. "I have to punish you to make you good."

Sybil didn't want to think of herself, sitting on that little red chair, watching the clock. But she often thought about it. Whenever she did, she managed to turn right away from it.

"Why must you always be bad, you bad, bad girl?" her mother asked.

The "you" confused Sybil. The "bad" made her wonder. She didn't think anything she did that day was bad.

Sybil told no one about the day of the blue sweater, but thoughts of that day, lodging in her throat, always made her throat hurt.

Nor did Sybil tell about the glass beads of many colors that hung like a rainbow on a cotton string. The beads, which were made in Holland and were very old, were given to Hattie by her mother. Hattie had given them to Sybil, who enjoyed pulling on them, sticking them in her mouth, and licking them. One afternoon while she was doing this, the string snapped, and the beads were sprinkled over the living room rug. Sybil, who was then three, tried to pick them up as fast as possible before her mother could see. But before Sybil could get them all up, Hattie had grabbed her and had shoved one of the beads up her nose. Sybil thought that she was going to smother. Hattie tried to remove the bead, but it wouldn't budge.

Hattie was frightened. "Come on," she said, "we'll go to Dr. Quinoness."

Dr. Quinoness got the bead out. But as the mother and child were about to leave, the doctor asked, "Mrs. Dorsett, how did the bead get there?"

"Oh," Hattie Dorsett replied, "you know how children are. They're always sticking things up their noses and in their ears."

That night Hattie told Willard how careless Sybil had been about the bead. "We ought to teach her to be more careful," the mother told the father. "Teach her . . . impeach her . . . beseech her . . . reach her . . . what a creature . . . it's time . . . let's rhyme."

Willard agreed that Sybil should learn to be more careful. Sybil, who had said nothing to Dr. Quinoness, said nothing to her father.

Another incident Sybil kept to herself was the one that took place in the wheat crib one rainy afternoon when she was four and a half. Hattie had taken Sybil there for an afternoon's play.

After Sybil and her mother had climbed up the retractable stairs from Willard's carpentry shop to the wheat crib above it, Hattie said, "I love you, Peggy." Then the mother placed the child in the wheat and left, pulling the stairs up into the ceiling.

Encircled by wheat, Sybil felt herself smothering and thought that she was going to die. Then for a time she knew nothing.

"Are you in there, Sybil?" She recognized her father's voice. Then Willard was standing beside her in the wheat crib. He bent over, lifted her gently, and took her downstairs to where her mother was waiting in the shop.

"How did Sybil get up in that wheat crib?" Willard asked his wife. "She could have smothered in that wheat."

"Floyd must have done it," her mother improvised. "He's such a mean child. This town would be better off without him. The church would be better off. We ought to get rid of that bully."

Willard went right down the street to speak with Floyd while Sybil and Hattie went back to the house. When Willard came home, he told his wife and daughter that Floyd had said, "No, I didn't do it. What do you think I am?"

"Floyd's a liar," her mother declared haughtily.

Willard, not knowing whom to believe, asked Sybil how she had gotten into the wheat crib. Sybil's eye caught her mother's eye, and she remained silent.

"I don't want you in that wheat crib again," Willard

lectured his daughter. "It's a good thing I came home early because of the rain. It's a good thing I went into the shop. The stairs didn't look right to me, so I went up to look."

Just as Sybil had said nothing about the buttonhook and the beads, she said nothing about the wheat.

Nothing was also what Sybil said one night when she was only two and her father asked, "How did you get that swollen black eye?" Sybil refused to tell. She didn't let the father know that her mother had kicked the blocks with which the child had been playing, had hit the child in the eye, and, with hard knuckles, had smacked the child on the mouth, where a new tooth grew.

These were the things, not separate but indivisible, forming an unending sequence of captivity on which the torture chamber of Sybil's childhood was built. Their memory returned to torture Sybil on the day that had begun felicitously with her drugstore dreams.

Torture reawakened, however, could also sometimes be put aside. In the first grade now, Sybil enjoyed school, made friends, and a few days after the return of the Willow Corners mother visited the home of her classmate and friend, Laurie Thompson, after school.

Laurie's mother, who was a warm, outgoing, rotund woman, greeted Laurie and Sybil as they came up the porch steps. After giving Laurie a big hug and smiling a greeting to Sybil, Mrs. Thompson ushered the two children into the house. Milk and a fresh apple pie were waiting.

Everything was so peaceful in the Thompson home, but Sybil—then seven—was certain that as soon as she left, Mrs. Thompson would do terrible things to Laurie, the way all mothers did.

The supposition that hers was the normal way of life didn't really make it better, nor did it lessen the unexpressed, impotent rage buried in Sybil from infancy. Rage there had been when the hated hard rubber nipple had replaced the breast and when the cries of the eleven-month-old prisoner in the high-chair had been ignored by the jailer. But the most terrible rage of all—cumulative but repressed—came with the growing sense that there was no exit, no way out of the torture chamber. The more intense the rage became, the more repressed it also became. The more repressed it became, the greater were her feelings of impotence; the greater the feelings of impotence, the greater the rage. It was an endless cycle of anger without an outlet.

Her mother tortured and frightened Sybil, and Sybil could do nothing about it. What was perhaps even worse, Sybil did not dare to get anybody else to do anything.

Sybil loved her grandmother, but she hadn't intervened when her mother said, "Now, Grandma, don't go near Sybil. She's being punished." Her grandmother hadn't intervened when her mother tripped Sybil as she was going down the stairs. Her grandmother had asked what had happened, and her mother had replied, "You know how clumsy children are. She fell downstairs." The rage Sybil felt at her grandmother was repressed.

Her father hadn't intervened, either. Couldn't he see what the buttonhook, the dislocated shoulder, the fractured larynx, the burned hand, the bead in the nose, the wheat crib, the black eyes, the swollen lips meant? But her father had refused to see.

When Sybil cried or the shade was up, her mother always said, "What if somebody comes?" There was repressed rage, too, at the neighbors who never came, at Grandfather Dorsett, who was upstairs and didn't seem to know what was happening below, at Dr. Quinoness, who again and again saw that the Dorsett child had been hurt but didn't try to discover why. And later Sybil repressed rage at her teachers, who from time to time asked her what was wrong but never actually bothered to find out. Sybil especially loved Martha Brecht, her seventh-grade teacher, because she could talk to her. But Sybil was disappointed in this teacher too because, even though she seemed to recognize that Sybil's mother was strange—perhaps even crazy—she, too, did not intervene. That saga had a sequel in college, where even Miss Updyke, who seemed to understand, was a party to sending Sybil home to torture.

Distressed by those who didn't come to her rescue, Sybil nevertheless invested the perpetrator of the tortures with immunity from blame. The buttonhook was at fault, or the enema tip, or the other instruments of torture. The perpetrator, however, by virtue of being her mother, whom one had not only to obey but also to love and honor, was not to blame. Almost two decades later, when Hattie, then on her deathbed in Kansas City, remarked, "I really shouldn't have been so cross with you when you were a child," it seemed sinful to Sybil even to recollect that euphemistic crossness.

Sybil's feelings toward her mother had always been complicated by the fact that Hattie's behavior was paradoxical. The same mother who embarrassed, shamed, and tortured her daughter would cut bright-colored pictures from magazines and paste them on the lower part of the cupboard door so that they would be at Sybil's eye level. At breakfast this same mother would often manage to have a "surprise" in the bottom of the daughter's cereal bowl: prunes, figs, dates, all of which the child especially liked. To encourage Sybil, whose appetite was slight, to eat, her mother would make a game of having Sybil guess what was at the bottom of the bowl. Her mother would insist that the child eat down to the bottom to discover whether the guess was correct. Hattie provided children's dishes decorated with pictures, children's silverware engraved SID, Sybil's initials, and a chair that was a little higher than the regular kitchen chairs. There were playthings all over the house and lots of good food, which, Hattie said, the starving children in China would give anything to have.

The one time that Sybil, then four, was audacious enough to reply, "They can have it if you want to send it over to them," Hattie reminded her daughter: "You have so much to be thankful for—a nice home, two parents"—Hattie's frequent reiteration of the *two* invariably irritated Sybil—"and more attention than any other child in town."

Again and again, both in her childhood and during

her adolescence, Sybil heard a multitude of varieties of "You have so much to be thankful for," followed by "And after all I do for you, you still don't appreciate it; you can't come to the table with a smile on a bet." Then Sybil would say, "You're the best mother in the whole world and I'll try to do better."

The "best mother in the world" would say, "I worry so when you are late from school for fear you got killed." The "best mother" didn't allow Sybil to swim, to ride a bicycle, to ice skate. "If you ride a bicycle, I can see you lying out in the street with blood all over. If you ice skate, you might fall through the ice and drown."

Hattie Dorsett enunciated solemn strictures about exemplary child care. Never hit a child, Hattie Dorsett preached, when it is possible to avoid it, and under no circumstances hit a child on the face or head. Hattie, who had a neat trick of denying reality by twisting it to conform to her fantasies, meant what she said. It was a mental sleight of hand that made it possible for her to dissociate what she actually did with what she thought she did, to separate action from ideation.

Hattie liked to dress her daughter up and show her off to company. In an effort to display the child's precocity, the mother would get the child to read and recite for guests. If Sybil made a mistake, Hattie would regard the error as a personal affront. Sybil would think: it's like mother doing it instead of me.

"My dear Sybil," her mother wrote in the daughter's elementary school graduation autograph book, "Live for those who love you, for those who know you true. For the heaven that smiles above you and the good that you can do. Your loving Mother."

The loving mother of Sybil's life, however, was not the one who played constructive eating games with the cereal bowl or who wondered about the daughter's getting drowned or showed the daughter off to company. Sybil's loving mother was the one who inhabited a "pretend" world of Sybil's own creation and in which Sybil found the rescue she was denied in the real world.

The loving mother of the pretend world lived in

223

Montana. In this state, which Sybil never had visited but which she fancied was her own, she imagined that she had many brothers and sisters with whom she played.

The Montana mother didn't hide Sybil's dolls in the cupboard when Sybil wanted to play with them or stuff Sybil with food and then force it out of her with enemas and laxatives. The Montana mother didn't tie Sybil to a piano leg or beat her or burn her. The Montana mother didn't say that Sybil was funny and that only blonde children were pretty. The Montana mother didn't punish Sybil for crying or tell her not to trust people, not to learn too much, never to get married and have a lot of kids around your neck. This good mother of the fantasy allowed Sybil to cry when there was cause for tears and didn't laugh when there was no reason for laughter.

When the Montana mother was there, Sybil could play anything she wanted to on the piano. The Montana mother wasn't sensitive to noise, and Sybil didn't have to blow her nose or clear out the dripping in the back of her throat without making a sound. When the Montana mother was there, Sybil was allowed to sneeze.

The Montana mother didn't say, "You won't grow up to be a good girl if you aren't good when you're little," didn't cause Sybil to have headaches because what she did was unfair. The Montana mother never said, "Nobody loves you except mother," only to prove that love by inflicting pain.

Where the Montana mother lived was not just a house; it was a home, where Sybil could touch things and didn't have to scrub the sink every time she washed her hands. Here Sybil didn't have to be searching all the time for some way to reach her mother, to change her, to earn if not her love, at least her liking. The Montana mother was warm and loving, always kissed Sybil, hugged her. She made Sybil feel wanted.

In the Montana mother's home Sybil wasn't told, "You are above your friends," at the same time that she was also told, "You can't do anything; you'll never amount to anything; you'll never be like my father. My

Marcia's drawing of the town of Willow Corners. Marcia is in the lower left corner, separated from the people of the town. The sketch depicts the bushes and the neighbor's garden, the scene of Hattie Dorsett's embarrassing activities during Sybil's early childhood. Sybil was nine years old when Marcia did this sketch.

Peggy Lou's pencil drawing of Hattie Dorsett. The pose refers to the "winter on the farm" episode of Sybil's childhood.

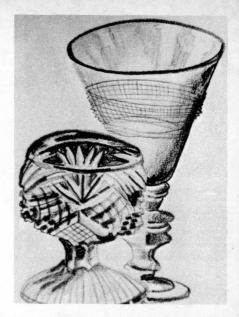

RIGHT: Peggy Lou's pencil drawing of Hattie's cut-glass goblet and tumbler. Even as an adult Sybil was frightened by the sound of breaking glass. BELOW: Peggy Ann's pre-suicidal city sketch. Her notations describe her feelings of fear, pain, and loneliness.

Sid's self-portrait,
drawn when Sybil was ten years old.

A pre-suicidal tempera painting by Marcia. Again she stresses her loneliness and separation from others. The original is done in dull browns and blue-grays.

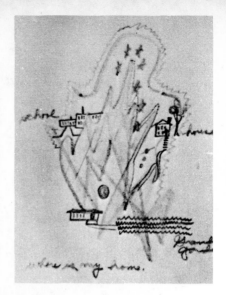

RIGHT: Mary's crayon drawing with her handwriting, drawn just before she bought a house without Sybil's knowledge. BELOW: Peggy Ann's torn sketch of the numbers she hoarded for so many years. It was only after integration that Sybil knew the multiplication tables that Peggy Ann had learned in the third grade.

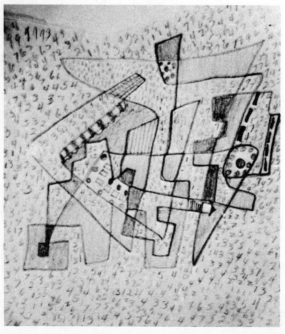

LEFT: Peggy Lou's tempera self-portrait shows "lips like a Negro," a description applied to her by Hattie Dorsett. BELOW: Sybil's self-portrait, painted in 1957. The original is done in low-tone blue watercolors.

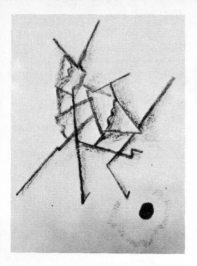

TOP LEFT: a 1959 crayon drawing by Sybil.
Her comments on the back: "The world is
blue. I'm the purple spot. I'm not part of the
world. . . . I do not like it this way. . . ."
BOTTOM LEFT: a crayon drawing of Sybil
Ann. She shows herself alone in a world composed of folded cardboards. RIGHT, TOP AND
BOTTOM: pages from Peggy Ann's sketch
book.

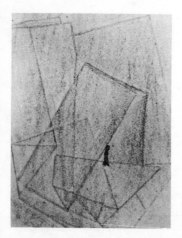

Drawings in Peggy Ann's sketch book record items associated with pain, anger, and fear. Each can be traced to a specific event, usually related to the activities of Hattie. Many of the sketches frightened Sybil, especially the one of knives; she was unaware that they had been done by Peggy Ann.

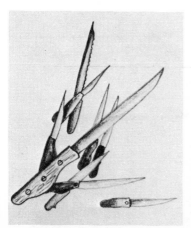
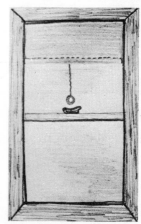

Sybil's pastel painting of Dr. Cornelia
B. Wilbur's office, the scene of Sybil's
eleven years of psychoanalysis.

Peggy's drawing of the Willow Corners church attended by the Dorsett family.

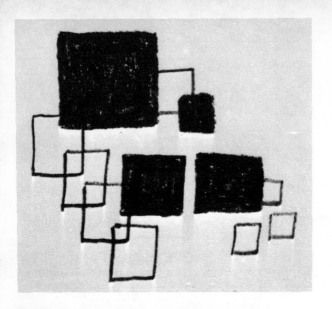

Geometrical patterns from Peggy Ann's sketch book. The designs of boxes were often repeated in her work.

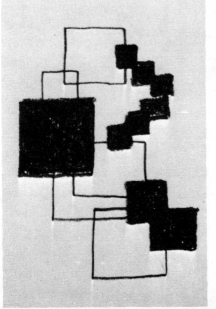

TOP: Peggy Ann's sketches of music, always associated with fear and anxiety. BOTTOM: the pattern of the superimposed boxes.

Multiple Christmas greetings to Dr. Wilbur from Vicky, Vanessa Gaile, Mary, Mike, Sybil Ann, and Peggy. By 1958 no message was sent from Clara, Nancy, Marjorie, Ruthie, Helen, or Sid. Peggy Lou and Peggy Ann were represented by a single Peggy.

A 1958 Christmas message from Sybil to her doctor.

Blue is the Color of Love, by Sybil.

father was a Civil War hero, the mayor of the town, a gifted musician. He was everything. No child of mine, no grandchild of his, should be like you. Lands, how did I get you?"

16

Hattie's Fury Has a Beginning

Hattie Dorsett's behavior, as presented in the analysis of her daughter, seemed to Dr. Wilbur clearly schizophrenic. The doctor, moreover, was convinced that this schizophrenic mother was the taproot of Sybil's dissociation into multiple selves. It therefore seemed essential to probe into what had caused the schizophrenia and to unravel what had made Hattie what she was.

In the account of Sybil's visits, for two weeks every summer until she was nine, to the large white house in Elderville, Illinois, that was Hattie Anderson Dorsett's birthplace and girlhood home, the doctor was able to find some clues.

The Andersons' sprawling home housed a family of thirteen children (four boys and nine girls). Winston Anderson, the father, who was well respected in town and an autocrat at home, demanded from his brood not only general deference and obeisance but also precise individual attention. Aileen, the mother, having to divide herself among many children, had little time for any of them. The children clearly lacked nurturing.

Hattie, a tall, slender girl with wavy, auburn hair and blue-gray eyes, whose elementary school report cards revealed a solid phalanx of As, who wrote poetry and whose music teachers had such high regard for her ability that they supported her dream of going to a music conservatory and of becoming a concert pianist, saw the collapse of her ambitions when she was twelve years old. At that time her father yanked her out of the seventh grade to work in his music store. She was to replace in the store an elder sister, who had left to get married. There was no economic justification for making Hattie give up her studies, no plausible argument for requiring her to renounce her dreams.

"The smartest child in the class. One of the best students I've ever had," said the seventh-grade teacher. "It's a crime to take her out of school."

"Extraordinary musical talent," said the nun who was Hattie's piano teacher. "She could go far if given the chance."

The chance, however, was not given, and the scene in which it was denied lived on in Hattie's memory. The scene began one evening when Winston, in his quilted smoking jacket, was seated in his special chair smoking his special cigar. "You're not going back to school tomorrow," he announced to Hattie bluntly. His coal black eyes were riveted on her. "You're going to work in the store."

No one talked back to her father, and Hattie knew better than to try. She just started to laugh. The cacophonous laugh continued to echo through the house even after she had gone to her room and closed her door. After the family was asleep, she strode down to the living room and, finding the purple quilted smoking jacket in an adjoining hall closet, cut off its sleeves. When questions were asked the next day, she feigned innocence and left the house to walk the four blocks to the music store. Winston bought a new smoking jacket identical to the old one.

One of Hattie's jobs at the store was to demonstrate pianos. Improvising music that wasn't actually on the sheet, she increased the marketability of her father's merchandise. When a rare customer, astute enough to detect the difference, came back to complain, Hattie, her face a complete deadpan, would protest, "I played what was there." When the store was empty, she just played and played. On Thursdays after work she would walk to the convent for her music lesson.

Hattie's dream had crumbled, and Hattie herself became ill with chorea, a physical illness that made her jerk and twitch. There were nervous components. The neurosis became so virulent that members of the family had to take their shoes off before coming up the stairs so as not to disturb Hattie, and the family's dishes had to be placed on flannel because Hattie couldn't stand the rattle. Although the concessions were out of keeping both with the lack of nurturing and the educational deprivation, the concessions were daily as long as the acute part of the illness lasted.

Striking back for the lost dream not by open rebellion or outright confrontation but through little acts of mischief and practical jokes, Hattie became a family *enfant terrible*. A recurrent joke was connected with Hattie's task of bringing the cows home from the cow pasture, which was at the edge of Elderville. Dallying on the way home, she would stop to visit friends en route while both the cows and the Anderson family waited.

Another joke was specifically directed at Winston, who led the Methodist choir and who had assigned Hattie the task of pumping the bellows of the church's pipe organ. One Sunday Hattie ran off before the last song, leaving the bellows and her father flat. Resplendent in his Prince Albert coat, Winston Anderson raised his baton as the chorus readied itself for song. His coal black eyes flashed fire when the only sound issuing from the organ was silence.

Hattie struck back again when her father was in his early fifties and began to show signs of the effects of a wound he had suffered during the war. A pellet that had entered his shoulder when he was shot during his service in the Civil War had never been removed, and it affected his circulation, causing his legs to swell and to become so heavy that it took two persons to lift him. When he began drinking to ease the pain, his wife and children raised such a row that liquor was no longer kept in the house. When, however, Winston managed to get the liquor on his own, the family elected Hattie to find out how. Discovering a row of bottles on the shelves in back of the piano, the detective, asking triumphantly, "Where else would a musician put a bottle?" succeeded in thwarting the father who had thwarted her.

The paradox of Hattie's anger was that during her father's lifetime and after his death she buried her resentment against him, transmuting it into idealization, idolatry, and pathological attachment, which was evident when she fondled his surviving smoking jacket.

Occasionally slipping through the protective armor of the overcompensating memory, however, was the fact that Hattie sometimes said that she blamed her "trouble" on her father. Even though she never defined what that trouble was, everybody who knew her knew also that she had a problem. The trouble was epitomized by a *McCall's* magazine photograph Hattie clipped and saved with the other mementos in her overstocked array of keepsakes. The photograph was of an attractive woman standing at a fence. The caption read: *No, she was not particularly loved. She sensed it.*

Unloved, Hattie Anderson Dorsett was incapable of loving. Unnurtured herself, she became a nonnurturing person. A lonely isolate in a large brood, she later isolated emotionally her only child. The anger, a result of the frustrated dream of a music career, was the environmental heritage that, transmitted from generation to generation, eventually made Sybil its target.

Sybil's emotional heritage from Winston Anderson, who died before she was born but who was represented to her as a mythological figure, was thus threefold. The recipient of Hattie's repressed fury against Winston, Sybil, who could not measure up to Hattie's idealized image of him, was also the victim of Hattie's father idolatry and of the repressed conflict that resulted from Hattie's idealizing and blaming her father. It was because of this conflict that Hattie counseled her daughter that all men were worthless.

Other ingredients in the Anderson family syndrome also were instrumental; the Winston-Hattie interaction was a dependent fragment of the larger family neurosis.

244

Aileen, the mother, whom Hattie talked of as a "marvelous woman, a wonderful woman," revealed no particular emotional problem except perhaps passivity in allowing her husband to tyrannize over the family. Yet problem there must have been to have spawned emotional problems in all of the sons, who in turn bequeathed emotional problems to their sons. (One of the grandsons of Winston and Aileen Anderson committed suicide.)

Four of the Anderson daughters, including Hattie and her oldest sister, Edith, who tyrannized over all the girls in the family, were similarly volatile and aggressive. Four of the others were too docile, too quiet, too unconcerned, and all four married tyrants. Fay, the youngest of the sisters, displayed the family neurosis by weighing two hundred pounds.

Hattie and Edith were very much alike in build, looks, and attitude. In later years they displayed the same symptoms: severe headaches, very high blood pressure, arthritis, and what was vaguely termed *nervousness*. In Hattie nervousness became virulent after the crushing experience of being yanked out of school. It is not known whether Edith became schizophrenic or at what point Hattie did. That Hattie was schizophrenic at the age of forty, the time of Sybil's birth, is clear.

Edith's sons had a variety of psychosomatic illnesses, including ulcers and asthma. Her daughter was sickly with undefined complaints until she became a religious fanatic, joined a group of faith healers, and proudly announced a return to health. The daughter of the religious fanatic, however, suffered from a rare blood disorder and was a semi-invalid all her life. The daughter of one of Edith's sons had almost all of Hattie's physical illnesses and emotional attitudes, although to a milder degree.

Even more important in terms of the germination of Sybil's illness was that two members of the family—Henry Anderson, Hattie's youngest brother, and Lillian Green, the granddaughter of Edith—gave evidence of possibly being multiple, or at least dual, personalities.

Henry would often suddenly leave home, disappear, and be unable to return because of amnesia, which kept him from knowing his address or his name. On one occasion he contracted pneumonia. He was delirious when a Salvation Army worker found him. Then, by means of the identification card uncovered during a routine search, the army volunteer was able to return him to Elderville.

Lillian, who married and had three children, often absented herself from her family without warning. After a number of these episodes her husband hired a detective to follow her and to bring her home.

Harry and Lillian provided some evidence for ascribing Sybil's malady to a genetic predisposition, but Dr. Wilbur remained convinced that the taproot, induced by her mother, lay not in the genes but in the childhood environment.

The Anderson home in Elderville seemed far from being the incubator of neurosis. For in Elderville, which Sybil visited every summer, there was a break as clean as surgical gauze, with Hattie's angry tyrannies and persistent perversions. Here it seemed that the borders of Sybil's pretend world spread to include reality itself; reality became so transformed that it paralleled some of the aspects of the pretend world.

Here aunts and uncles hugged and kissed Sybil, held her high in the air, listened intently when she sang or recited for them, and said that everything she did was wonderful.

No visit was complete without Sybil's going to the movie theater, where her aunt Fay played the piano in this era before talkies. Sitting on the piano bench beside her aunt in the empty theater, with the piano shut off and the keys moving without making sounds, Sybil would pretend that she was playing for the movies. Staying for the matinee while Fay played, Sybil would look up at her aunt and pretend that she was her mother.

Not until it was time to go back to Willow Corners did Sybil realize quite how much she wanted to remain in Elderville. One summer she turned to her aunt Fay and said, "Will you keep me?" Stroking Sybil's hair and straightening the child's bangs, Fay replied: "You're a Dorsett. Your place is with the Dorsetts. You'll come back next summer."

Just twice during nine glorious summer vacations were there occurrences in Elderville that made the illusion of the pretend world collapse.

One Sunday in July, 1927, Sybil and her cousin Lulu were in the kitchen of the Anderson home, helping her aunt Fay with the dinner dishes. Aunt Fay, who saw Lulu all the time and Sybil only for two weeks in the summer, was paying more attention to Sybil than to Lulu. When Aunt Fay left the room to take some tea up to Grandmother Anderson, Lulu and Sybil continued their chores in silence. But Sybil, who was drying silver soup spoons, couldn't keep her eyes off the beautiful rainbows in the cut crystal pickle dish Lulu was drying. Then all at once the rainbows were moving through the room as the pickle dish, which Lulu hurled at the French doors between the kitchen and the dining room, floated in space. In the panic following the crash of glass Sybil's head throbbed, and the room seemed to swirl.

The shattered door was swung open by the aunts and uncles, who, drawn to the scene by the crash, stood staring at the dish. Now the dish lay on the dining room floor in pieces.

The adults stared at the children; the children returned the stare. "Who did it?" was written in those accusing adult faces, which moved compulsively from the minuscule glass shavings on the floor to the frightened faces of the two children. As the heavy silence was intensified, Lulu announced, "Sybil did it!"

"You broke it," came Hattie's accusing voice, directed at Sybil.

"Now, Hattie," Fay cautioned, "she's only a little girl. She didn't mean any harm."

"No harm? For land's sakes, Fay, you can see she didn't drop it. She flung it out of malice. How did I get a child like that?"

Sybil stood dry-eyed, but Lulu began to cry. "Sybil did it," Lulu intoned between tears. "Sybil did it."

Then Hattie's daughter headed for the dining room window, pounded against the window with her fists, pleading, "Let me out. Oh, please let me out. I didn't do it. She did. She's a liar. Let me out. Please. Please!" Sybil had become Peggy Lou.

"Go to your room," Hattie ordered. "Sit on the chair in the corner until I call you."

(Sybil forgot the incident of the pickle dish, but it was a scene that Peggy Lou not only remembered but relived and reenacted many times. In New York between October, 1954, and October, 1955, the first year of the analysis, Peggy Lou, who had broken a window in Dr. Wilbur's office during that period, had also smashed $2,000 worth of old-fashioned crystal in Fifth Avenue shops. With each crash, Sybil would reappear and would say to the clerk, "I'm terribly sorry. I'll pay for it.")

The other disquieting Elderville episode took place during this same July, 1927. Hattie was out in the yard, laughing in her special way. Hearing the familiar sound, Sybil rose from the kitchen table, took a large stride forward to look through the kitchen window, and saw that her mother was off by herself near the stable. The laughter came again.

Sybil saw that her cousin Joey and her uncle Jerry were about five feet from her mother. They were carrying a box, which Sybil had seen on the kitchen table. Aunt Fay, coming to the window at that moment, stood near Sybil. Ashamed of her mother's eerie, unmotivated, haunting laughter, especially in the presence of relatives from whom Hattie usually tried to conceal it, Sybil shuddered and turned away.

"Let's go inside, Sybil," Fay said softly. "We'll play a duet."

"Later," Sybil, who could not move from the window, answered.

Then Sybil heard her aunt Fay calling through the window to Joey and Jerry about saying something to Hattie. Joey's voice came from the yard: "Leave her alone, Fay." Sybil knew that Hattie was Joey's favorite aunt and that he was trying to protect her.

A coffin, Sybil thought, as she looked at the box Joey and Jerry were lifting. It was smaller than the boxes and caskets she often saw in the funeral parlor in back of her home in Willow Corners. . . . It was Marcia who completed the thought: *the box is big enough to hold Mama.*

Standing very still, Marcia continued to muse: boxes grow just as trees grow and people grow. The box will get bigger and will be big enough for Mama. But Marcia felt that she should have gone out to stop Joey and Jerry from putting the box on the dray, that she should have been worried about her mother, and that she wasn't worried because she wanted her mother dead!

Marcia, however, could not have known that the death wish for a mother frequently occurs in little girls, among whom the first affection is normally for father. Marcia didn't know that the wish grows because little girls find their mothers disturbing rivals for the affection of their fathers.

However, when Hattie, who was usually well behaved in Elderville, laughed as she did in Willow Corners, her daughter's wish, propelled by new fury, was accentuated.

Because of the intense guilt her wish aroused, Marcia pushed the wish from her thoughts and returned the body to Sybil, who didn't know about Marcia's little box grown big.

17

Willard

In her solitary ruminations about the Dorsett case Dr. Wilbur over and over again reviewed the evidence in the strange saga of a child's being violated, abused, deprived of a normal childhood, and thus driven into psychoneurosis for the most paradoxical of reasons—in order to survive. Yet all of the assembled facts had come from just one source—Sybil and Sybil's selves. Other testimony, Dr. Wilbur realized, was needed to substantiate the truth of the findings.

The mother was dead. Apart from the patient herself, the father was clearly the only witness in whom the nearly three years of analysis could find verification. So in April, 1957, after the doctor had minutely explored the available evidence about the mother-daughter relationship, she decided to bring Willard Dorsett into the case. Sybil asked him to come to New York.

Both Dr. Wilbur and Sybil would have been more sanguine about bringing seventy-four-year-old Willard Dorsett to New York from Detroit, where he lived, happily remarried and still working, if this were a court not of human emotions but of law. Willard Dorsett, whose relationship with both his daughter and the doctor had become strained, might not, they both felt, come of his own volition.

Willard had already let it be known that he thought that at thirty-four Sybil was too old to be supported by him, despite the fact that, after her money had run out at the end of two years in New York, he had agreed to pay her expenses so that she could continue treatment. (Although she had undertaken analysis without his knowledge, she had informed him about it at the end of the first year.)

The doctor was inclined to regard the support as payment of a debt, the debt of a father to a daughter who through analysis was literally struggling to become whole. He was supporting her grudgingly, erratically. Yet at this stage of her life she had no bank account, no permanent job, and her only sources of income were occasional sales of her paintings, sporadic work as a tutor, and an intermittent part-time job as an art therapist in a Westchester hospital. Willard Dorsett's obligation to Sybil, the doctor thought, was also the debt of a father who had squandered his daughter's money. He had sold Sybil's piano, bedroom set, and several of her paintings without consulting her and without giving her the money accruing from the sales. He had even made her pay half of her mother's funeral expenses. The doctor's attitude had been exacerbated when Willard had once failed to send Sybil her monthly check, a default that had been the more distressing because it was a repeat performance of an episode that had taken place in Sybil's undergraduate days. Her father's failure to send her money, together with the prohibitions to borrow under which she had been raised, had forced her to live for five weeks on oranges and cookies, rationed to two each a day.

Both the present and past episodes made Sybil feel that her father gave her things under pressure or out of a sense of duty, not because he cared about her. Noting her depression in the present instance, Dr. Wilbur wrote Willard Dorsett that the default had caused anguish that his daughter was not well enough to withstand. He replied that he was a busy man and could not always keep track of details. Nor did the fact that the doctor was not now being paid for treatment bother him. Vicky had reported his having said: "Dr. Wilbur is a rich Park Avenue doctor. Let her absorb it."

The Willard Dorsett of 1957, who had written that

he was too busy to concern himself with his daughter, moreover, was clearly the same man who in the analysis had so far emerged as being preoccupied behind his drafting board, encircled and isolated by the sound of his drills. That the encirclement was quite complete seemed evidenced by this exchange within the analysis:

"Vicky," the doctor had asked, "didn't Mr. Dorsett ever see the atrocities Mrs. Dorsett inflicted on Sybil?"

"He would ask Sybil, 'What's the matter with your arm'—or whatever the injured part was," Vicky had replied, "and then he'd shrug and just walk out."

Before sufficient time had elapsed for Willard to reply to Sybil's letter, she found a letter from him in her mailbox. Afraid to read it while she was alone because several of his letters had caused her to become somebody else (as the doctor put it) or "to black out," as she herself still described it, she waited until Teddy Reeves came home.

The letter read:

Dear Sybil,

Frieda just reminded me that it was time to write Sybil. Frieda is getting more like the Dorsetts. She has told me several times that she is enjoying life. I think she had some enjoyment coming her way for once if any one should ask me. I am glad to see her happy. We received your welcome letter yesterday. We are always glad to hear from you. Hope this semester will not be too hard or too much work. Hope you got along okay in your tests. Ha!

My work is going ahead well. Weather has been cold. Good to be home for a couple of days each week. But I am glad I am still well enough to hold a job and earn my way. Seems to be quite a lot of jobs ahead for the coming year. Frieda still likes her work. Social Security went up 7%, so now I have a raise in S.S. I get $104.00 per month now. Helps a lot. Glad I went into Social Security. That was many years ago. Getting old now. I stopped to watch "Lassie" on TV and now must go to bed. Have to get

church, the Victorian age, and his overreaction to the Roaring Twenties, which he considered an indication of the moral decay of civilization, a sign of the end of the world.

An intensely religious man, he rigidly adhered to the doctrines of his fundamentalist faith and was so literal in his readings of the Scriptures that, unlike more sophisticated members of his faith—unlike Pastor Weber, for instance, his mentor in Omaha—he took the church's preachings about the end of the world so literally that his entire life was spent on the precipice of the world's impending end. The church itself and the benighted Willow Corners congregation to which he belonged became so disquieting that, while still observing its doctrines to the letter, he left the church for fourteen years.

Perhaps the flight from the church was also a flight from his father—a belligerent and boorish six-footer with large features and a goatee who, a wrestler in his youth, found in the church a tailor-made outlet for aggression and hostility. Aubrey Dorsett, Willard's father, was the son of Arnold and Theresa, who came to Willow Corners as homesteaders and whose children, in addition to Aubrey, included Thomas, Emmanuel, Frederick, and Theresa II.

Aubrey, an avid churchgoer, found in evangelical rantings, uncontrolled bellowings, and hallelujahs intoned with ecstatic passion the substitute for the swearing denied him as a pious man. The evangelical rantings from the first row of the church had their counterpart at the front of the Willow Corners post office, where Aubrey inveighed against the "Romans" and the "horn of Rome" (the Pope), denouncing the hated Catholics to a gathering crowd. Aubrey Dorsett predicted the country's doom if a Catholic ever came to power. Hostile not only to the hated Romans but also to members of his own faith, indeed to everybody, including his own family, Aubrey sought the Achilles' heel in everyone around him, often exploiting it in public with a verbal vigor that matched the physical powers of his wrestling days. Then having spotted and descended

257

upon the weak spot, he proceeded to save his victim's soul.

A particular target was Mary, whom Aubrey had married on the rebound and whom forever after he taunted with Val, the love of his life, who had rejected him. At various times in the course of his marriage he would turn the saw mill he owned and operated over to a subordinate and silently fade away to take up with Val in New York. Thence he would return to parade his infidelity to Mary.

As a father, Aubrey demanded unquestioning obedience and required his three children—Theresa III, the eldest; Willard, the middle child; and Roger, eighteen months younger than Willard—to smile at all times, as becomes a Christian, and never to laugh, which was sinful. Although all three siblings were musical, Aubrey never asked them to play or sing. He feared that if they did so, they would feed on the sin of pride. He didn't want his children to have "swelled heads."

Ashamed of his father's belligerence, Willard resorted to passivity. Embarrassed by his father's haranguing hallelujahs, aggression, and gruffness, Willard retreated into a shell of silence. Unable to see himself in the image of a father who embarrassed him and of whom he was ashamed, the father with whom his own sensitive, artistic nature was in conflict, Willard made identification instead with his gentle, artistic, but passive mother. And the identification with his mother was responsible for the paradoxical nature of the peripheral Willard Dorsett.

Indisputably male, sexually vital despite his professed puritanical rigidities, attractive to women and lustily pursued by them during the nine years of being a widower, a man who worked and thought in brick and mortar, Willard also had a distinctly feminine side. As a boy and young man he often helped his mother with the housework. He canned fruit and vegetables and later taught Hattie these skills. He sewed and supported himself in college by working as a tailor, just as later he sewed all of Sybil's baby clothes. He had superb taste

258

in interior decoration, and, respecting his taste, Hattie had trusted him to decorate their first home.

Willard's identification with his mother, moreover, not only helped mold his personality; it also affected his choice of a mate. Like Aubrey Dorsett, Hattie Anderson Dorsett was overly aggressive, constantly conspicuous and downright cruel. Willard married his father in female form.

In fact, both Willard and his brother Roger appear to have married their father. The two brothers somehow managed to find strong-minded and strange women, both named Henrietta. Too, Roger, like Willard, married outside his faith. Roger's wife was a Roman Catholic nurse, whom he married probably in rebellion against the hysterical anti-Catholic feeling of the people of his own church, especially of his father. Roger's Hattie smoked when no other woman in Willow Corners dared, and she used rouge and lipstick, which affronted her fundamentalist in-laws. But her real eccentricity lay in the originality of her moonlighting. In her spare time this Hattie Dorsett ran a gambling joint and a house of assignation for nuns in the basement of her red brick home in Rochester, Minnesota. She even provided the nuns with a change of costume to speed them on their worldly way. Roger remained aloof from both enterprises, but it was said that he managed to have a few assignations of his own.

This Hattie had two sons, but she didn't like having boys, and she wanted to take Sybil away from her mother. The motivation, which has never been made clear, probably revolved around the fact that she always wanted a daughter, but it could also have been spurred by insight into Sybil's predicament. As a psychiatric nurse this Hattie could conceivably have realized that her sister-in-law was unfit to raise a child.

Willard's sister, Theresa III, didn't marry her father; she reacted against him and the total milieu by becoming a neurotic loner and eccentric. As a girl Theresa loved and lost; then she blamed her loss on her brothers. At the age of forty she married a wealthy old man and moved to his farm, in another state. She returned to

Willow Corners only twice after that, once when her mother had a stroke and again when her mother died. At home on her farm she scandalized the neighbors by wearing men's clothing and the church, which hounded her for money, by giving none. The money, which neither Theresa nor her husband trusted to the banks, was scattered in assorted nooks and crannies in the spacious farmhouse. At the time of the 1929 crash these homespun banks did not fail.

When Willard and Roger lost the timberland in which Theresa had invested with them, she demanded her money. Because of the old wounds occasioned by her thwarted young romance, the brothers mortgaged their homes so that Theresa could have her pound of flesh. Then when she owned the mortgage to Willard's house, Theresa decided that her parents should occupy it. She had no compunction about ordering Willard and his family to move.

Surrounded by wealth, Theresa acted like a pauper after the death of her husband. Boarding up all the rooms of the farmhouse except one, she retreated into that room, which was heated in winter only by a small kerosene stove. In the last years of Theresa's life there was a reconciliation with Willard. After Hattie's death Willard and Sybil visited Theresa. Sybil, who had seen her aunt Theresa only twice before, now understood why people mistook her for Theresa and why her father often called her Theresa.

Willard was always even more quiet and low-voiced than usual, almost reverent, when he talked about his mother. He would become louder and almost dogmatic about his father and his father's brother Tom, then quiet again about Roger and Theresa. Willard always had disquieting feelings about both his sister and his brother—Roger died at the age of fifty-six—and it was never easy for Willard either to remember them or to forget them.

Willard, who had a stronger ego than did either Roger or Theresa, erected a protective shell against domestic disturbance, but he did not otherwise appear meek. Silent but strong, he could not infrequently make his will prevail. Faced with the fact that both his wife and his daughter had emotional problems, Willard acquitted himself in terms of hereditary responsibility for his daughter's illness. His father was a boor and Theresa an eccentric, but neither was actually emotionally disturbed, Willard convinced himself. Observing the descendants of his father's four brothers, he had to admit some oddities in the clan, but he was swift to attribute the oddities to the families into which his uncles had married.

His uncle Thomas, for example, who had all kinds of land and money, had five wives, three of whom he buried and one of whom deserted him. It was the wives, Willard thought, who were at fault, not Uncle Tom. Tom's first wife went crazy, lost her hair and her fingernails, turned an alabaster white, and died of general paresis. Bernard, the son of this marriage, was willful as a child, and although largely indolent as an adult, he had become an inventor. The first sentence that his son, Bernard, Jr., spoke to his mother was: "I will kill you." And gossip had it that his behavior did kill her. Bernard, Jr., was later hospitalized as a schizophrenic.

Frances Dorsett, the wife of Willard's uncle Frederick, and Carol, a daughter of that marriage, were subject to elations and depressions as part of a manic-depressive psychosis. But because this illness has a very strong familial trend, Willard was on solid ground in maintaining that Carol had inherited the gene from her mother, not from the Dorsetts. Because Frances and Carol were in and out of state hospitals and frequently visited Willard's family when they were out, Willard often asked Sybil if she was worried that she was like her aunt Frances and cousin Carol. Then, as if the damage were not already done, he would remind her: "No need to worry. They're not Dorsetts."

All of this family history was known to Sybil, of course. Even more important, she was aware of her father's needs and fears. Thus, as she waited in New York for his letter from Detroit, she had two fears—that he would not come and that he would come. Night after night, over and over again, during this period of watchful waiting, she dreamed:

> She was walking through a tremendous house, looking for her father, or in the same house he was looking for her, or they were searching for each other. She would go through room after room in a frustrated quest, knowing that her father was there some place, but knowing, too, that she couldn't find him.

"You ought to tell your father in your dream," Dr. Wilbur said in analysis, "that you are looking for him. The dream expresses a sexual yearning for him because he was seductive toward you but also a denial of the desire." Sybil had admitted that she had been aware of sexual feelings toward her father when he talked to her about sex. "There are some things about sex for which I don't have the answers yet," he would say, for instance, while he was dating Frieda. "You young people know a lot more about sex than we ever did."

It was clear to the doctor, indeed, that Willard had stimulated Sybil sexually not only when she was an adult but also as a child, both in the long-run primal scene and by his denials of physical closeness after she had become what he had called "too big."

In another dream:

> Men were pursuing her sexually. Her father was not there to rescue her. The pursuit continued and, too, the lack of rescue.

Long having waited for her father to intervene on her behalf, to come to her rescue, Sybil was waiting again. And, as the days followed without an answer to her letter, she was caught in a web of ambivalent feelings. The feelings would have been simpler if Willard had been a typically rejecting father. However, she did have a relationship with him, one in which he habitually failed her, out of passivity, but which was quickened by accentuated Oedipal desires and by a close affinity of similar tastes.

When an art critic in St. Paul, Minnesota, had assured Willard that Sybil's talent for painting was genuine, he had been proud of her work. He had even made it a point to mount and frame her paintings. When father and daughter looked at a painting together, it was like two eyes looking at the same work. Between them there was a mutuality, an attunement, made all the stronger as a result of two childhood happenstances.

First, when Sybil was only six weeks old, she had developed a disease of the middle ear. No one had been able to tell what was the matter with her, and she was comforted only when her father held her. By chance, when he held her, he always sat next to the kitchen stove. The warmth, which she associated with her father, had soothed her: the attachment to her father was begun.

Second, because she was unable to make identification with her mother, who abused her and made her feel ashamed, Sybil had more and more been compelled to make identification with her father. She had to have *someone,* and she persuaded herself that her father was the figure on whom she could depend, especially since she looked not like the Andersons but like the Dorsetts.

Thus on a conscious level Sybil had always protected her father's image, yet there were times when that image was not an invincible fortress. "In college," Sybil wrote in her diary as an undergraduate, "I had roommates, classmates, a big sister, an adviser. My adviser, Dr. Termine, was fat and jolly. He had a moustache. He was warm. He was like a father I never had. He'd always take time to talk to me. It was so different."

And when Dr. Wilbur had asked Sybil directly, "Does your father love you?" Sybil had given a qualified reply: "I suppose he does."

So the wait for Willard Dorsett's reply was long.

Part III

Unbecoming

18

Confrontation and Verification

At 4:00 P.M. on May 4, 1957, Willard Dorsett entered Dr. Wilbur's anteroom—an assured, complacent, well-defended, passive, and unreachable figure who took his responsibilities lightly.

Some ten minutes later, his defensive armor had begun to crack and he felt himself faltering. He wiped his forehead gingerly with a freshly starched handkerchief, as, sitting on the little green desk chair in the consulting room, he realized that the questions Dr. Wilbur was asking were not what he had anticipated. He had expected questions about Sybil's status as a thirty-four-year-old woman, alone in New York, trying to get well. Instead, the doctor was taking him back to Willow Corners and the years of his marriage to Hattie. The year with Frieda had been a good year, a veil across the face not only of Willow Corners but also of Omaha and Kansas City. But now the doctor was mercilessly ripping the veil, inch by dreadful inch.

Willard's anxiety was intensified by the awkwardness of being in Dr. Wilbur's presence after the voluminous correspondence that in recent months had passed between them about Sybil's finances. He had had to force himself to come. Now that he was here, he was constantly reminded that the doctor was not the same woman he had known in Omaha.

He was not aware, however, of the reasons for the change. In Omaha she had not been a psychoanalyst, and the psychoanalytic approach placed strong emphasis on the deterministic power of childhood. In

267

Omaha the doctor did not know that Sybil was a multiple personality and did not have the wealth of information that Sybil and the other selves had since revealed—information indicting Hattie and pointing an accusing finger at Willard for the genesis of Sybil's illness. It was chiefly to ascertain the truth of Hattie's and Willard's role in spawning the illness that the doctor had urged this meeting.

Yet there was also another purpose. The increasingly unsatisfactory and evasive tone of Willard's letters and his omissions in supporting Sybil financially and psychologically were shocking to his daughter's analyst. Whatever his role in the past, Dr. Wilbur firmly believed that in the present he had condemned himself.

As an analyst, Dr. Wilbur withheld judgment about the past, but as Sybil's friend, she was determined to provoke Willard into assuming greater responsibility as a father. She therefore viewed the interview as both a search for verification of the initial parental guilt and as a confrontation with a father who was currently failing his daughter. The doctor was determined to mince no words, nor to repress the accusatory tone in her manner that under the circumstances came naturally. Taking Willard Dorsett's measure, it was clear that the only way she could get the verification she was seeking was by taking the offensive and waging a direct attack.

"Why, Mr. Dorsett," the doctor asked, "did you always entrust the full care and upbringing of Sybil to your wife?"

Willard Dorsett was not a man who studied himself or looked at those around him to weigh or measure their moods. In Willow Corners he had been a busy man, away from home from dawn to sundown. He hadn't known all the details of his domestic life and had felt that he couldn't have been expected to know them. How, he asked himself, could he possibly answer the doctor's questions about these details, so far off, so forgotten?

Why had he always entrusted to Hattie the full care and upbringing of Sybil? He merely shrugged in reply. The question obviously seemed to him irrelevant. It was like asking a butcher why he sells meat or a

Hattie!" His head was bowed. He was

Dr. Wilbur replied. "If what Sybil has told

wondered what to say next. He stared at
aperies and then at the doctor. Once again
eyes, but only momentarily, for the doctor
"Mr. Dorsett, there are some things that
appened in the early morning . . ." He had
in a confrontation that was shattering the
d belatedly secured for himself with Frieda
emories of Willow Corners, Omaha, and
had been put to rest. "In the early morn-
octor was saying, and as she recounted
ritualistic tortures, he felt himself inwardly
en she referred to the buttonhook, he again
ead. It was a moment of revelation.
hy Sybil screamed so on the Sabbath,"
d, "when we tried to button her white kid
, still thinking about his daughter's screams
t the buttonhook's evocation of a hideous
l that what had been described was quite
omprehension. He added also that he had
rom home and couldn't know what was
hy these things should have taken place,
could not fathom.
phere was like melted rock issuing from a
Villard Dorsett iterated and reiterated: "I
How could I know when nobody told me?
attie." Then he added what was partly
partly confession, "I was so overwhelmed
t I didn't think."
r. Dorsett," the doctor enjoined. "Can
vhether these things Sybil reported to me
place? There are internal scars and injuries
lence to her account."
eadful moment for me to live through,
ht, as he removed his handkerchief from
et of his gray-flannel suit and wiped the
ering perspiration from his forehead. The
d the buttonhook were the undeniable
he chain of his recollections. He could

farmer why he plants corn. A mother *should* take care
of a child.

Had he been aware that Hattie's behavior was peculiar? He moved jerkily in his chair and became
defensive. When he finally spoke, it was to say, "The
first Mrs. Dorsett was a wonderful woman, bright,
talented." He hesitated.

"And?" the doctor asked.

He became flustered. "Well," he said, "we had a
lot of trouble. Financial and otherwise. It was hard
on Hattie. At times she was difficult."

"Just difficult?" the doctor asked.

"Well, she was nervous."

"Just nervous?"

He mopped his forehead, changed his position. "She
had some bad spells."

"Is it true that she was in a bad state at the farm
when Sybil was six?"

He averted his eyes and finally said yes.

"Was it true that when she came out of her depression, she tore down the hill on Sybil's sled?"

He squirmed while saying, "Yes. Sybil must have told
you it was a big hill. A child's imagination, you know.
But the hill wasn't really very high." (He had an almost
comic way of wriggling out of facing the real issue.)

"But your wife came down that hill, large or small,
on a child's sled, laughing? What did you make of her
behavior in that instance?" The doctor was trapping
him into an admission. "Was it safe, Mr. Dorsett, to
allow this strange, nervous woman, who had what you
call spells, to have the sole responsibility for raising
your child?"

Instead of answering directly, he murmured non-
responsively, "Hattie was odd."

"It was more than odd, Mr. Dorsett. She was more
than nervous if what I've been told is true." The bom-
bardment of recollections made the room gyrate. Each
recollection, rising from the buried past, reawakened the
dull, sad ache in his hands, the after-image of the
neuritis from which he had suffered after he had lost
his money.

"Well," Willard explained, "Hattie and Sybil never

got along. I thought a mother and daughter should be close, and I was disturbed by their arguments. When they were at each other, I used to say, 'Hattie, why don't you rest a while or crack some nuts?' I used to hope Hattie and Sybil would get over it in time."

"That was when Sybil was a teenager," the doctor reminded the father. "But weren't there certain things that occurred when she was a very young child—even an infant—that couldn't be settled by cracking nuts?"

"You must know something I don't know," he replied defensively, fiddling with his fingernails.

Was he aware that as a child Sybil sustained an unusual number of injuries, the doctor wanted to know. With annoyance he answered quickly, "She had accidents, of course, like any child." Did he remember any of these accidents? No, he couldn't say he remembered. Was he aware that Sybil had had a dislocated shoulder, a fractured larynx? "Why yes," he replied, screwing up his thin lips.

How had they happened?

He made no answer, but the involuntary twitchings in his face betrayed uneasiness. Flustered, he finally replied, "I never saw Hattie lay a hand on Sybil."

Did he remember the burns on his daughter's hands, her black eyes? "Yes," he replied slowly, remotely. "I seem to recall these things now that you take me back." He became even more flustered and said, "After all, I didn't see them happen. They must have taken place when I was away from home."

Did he remember the bead in Sybil's nose? He replied defensively: "Sybil put the bead in her nose. You know how children are. Always putting things in their noses and ears. Mrs. Dorsett had to take Sybil to Dr. Quinoness. He got the bead out."

And now, the doctor was asking pointedly, "Is that what your wife told you?"

Willard Dorsett clasped his hands together to reaffirm his own solidity and put up some resistance, saying, "Yes, Hattie told me that. I had no reason to question her."

Dr. Wilbur insisted, "What did your wife tell you about the larynx and the shoulder? Did she say that Sybil had fractured her own shoulder?"

He knew an answer was time to think about the d said at last, "I can't rem said. But she was always many falls. I suppose I how these things happene Ignorance is one of my fa

The wheat crib over his eyes as if by doing so he that had been evoked. He up courage to listen. Yes dent well. "How did you in there and then put th such a thing could not hav had told him came to his "The town bully did it."

"But did he?" the docto "Well," Willard replied didn't know anything abo "Who was guilty?" the

The edifice of Willard crumbling, and he sank ba normally soft and low. mumbled, "Not Hattie?"

It was an important m lard Dorsett had always lated in the private sea c been resolute in pursuing to look in any other direc the sea, was steaming in The many years of alo know, converged in a mo which, by instinct, by p Dorsett came to believe in the wheat crib; that H his daughter's fractured assorted burns, the bead Willard repeated in a frig however, it was to con

Father, n praying.

"Hattie, me is true

Willard the green he shut hi was sayin Sybil says been caug peace he after the Kansas Ci ing," the the mornin writhing. bowed his

"That's he murmu shoes." Th of anguish pain, he s beyond his been away going on. he said, h

The atm volcano as don't know I believed self-defens by Hattie

"Think, you tell m actually too that lend

What a Willard tho the vest p beads of g wheat bin evidence i

hear his daughter's piercing scream at the sight of that harmless buttonhook. And the scars and injuries also constituted proof. He folded his handkerchief neatly and returned it to his vest pocket. He then looked steadily at the doctor, seeing the past whole for the first time.

"Doctor," he finally said in a low voice, "I'm sure that Sybil's recollections are quite accurate in every respect. I didn't know about these things, but now that I look back I recall most of the physical injuries. There were times after they must have occurred when Sybil would be in bed, and her grandmother—my mother—would care for her. With her grandmother Sybil was fine." He stopped short as he realized what he had said. Then resuming, he explained, "I didn't know about these things, but, knowing Hattie, I do know that she was entirely capable of them." He added, with a strange, emotionless objectivity, "I'm sure not only that they were possible but that they happened."

It was a pivotal moment, the kind that the classic Greek dramatists describe as a *peripety*—the moment in which the action of a drama assumes a quick catastrophic new turn, a reversal. As a witness, corroborating the truth of Sybil's testimony about the atrocities, which Dr. Wilbur already regarded as the taproot of the multiplicity of personality, Willard Dorsett had also incriminated himself. His admission that Hattie was entirely capable of the atrocities attributed to her was tantamount to a confession that by failing to protect his daughter against a perilously destructive mother he had been partner to the mother's deeds. This was precisely what Dr. Wilbur suspected.

Indisputable now was the fact that the violent tyrannies of this nonneurotic father (the doctor was convinced that he was free of neurosis), consisting of bland evasions, the shrug that withheld concern, the lifelong retreat into his shell, had augmented the mother's violent tyrannies in driving Sybil to search for a psychoneurotic solution to the intolerable reality of her childhood. The mother was the taproot of Sybil's having become a multiple personality, but the father, Dr. Wilbur was now sure, through the guilt not of commission but of omission, was an important associated root. The mother had trapped Sybil, but the father, even though Sybil herself had never quite admitted it, had made her feel that from that trap there was no exit.

The doctor simply said, "Mr. Dorsett, you have just told me that you consider Sybil's mother entirely capable of the atrocities we've discussed. Then, to repeat an earlier question, may I ask why you allowed your daughter to be brought up by her?"

He wondered whether to answer or to withhold the self-incrimination that an answer would inevitably imply. "Well," he replied while measuring his words, "it is a mother's place to raise a child." Once again the shell closed around him.

"Even, Mr. Dorsett, when that mother is clearly schizophrenic? Even, Mr. Dorsett, when this schizophrenic mother came very close on at least three occasions I can think of to killing her child?"

Flustered, defensive, he replied, "I did what I could." Then he told Dr. Wilbur about his having taken Hattie to see a psychiatrist at the Mayo Clinic in Rochester. The doctor there had diagnosed Hattie as a schizophrenic and had said that, although she didn't have to be hospitalized, she should be treated on an out-patient basis. "Hattie saw the doctor only once," Willard remarked. "She wouldn't go back because she said that all he did was stare at her."

Dr. Wilbur was both pleased and troubled by this new intelligence. The other psychiatrist's diagnosis confirmed Dr. Wilbur's own. It was the confirmation that made the atrocities doubly believable as part of a schizophrenic's mode of behavior. This, together with Willard Dorsett's observations, meant that the verification for which the doctor had been searching had been found. No longer did she have to ponder that even though the various selves of Sybil had told identical stories about Hattie's atrocities, that that in itself did not constitute confirmation. Again and again the doctor had rejected the evidence on the grounds that all the selves belonged to Sybil's unconscious and that although the conscious mind often doesn't know what the unconscious mind is doing, the unconscious absorbs what takes place consciously. What the other personalities had said *could,* therefore, have been but an echo of Sybil, an echo of Sybil's fantasy of torture, her delusion of cruelty, or even a perverse screen memory. The internal scars and injuries were, of course, objective data, but there was at least a remote possibility that they had been self-inflicted. But now there was no need to question further. The veracity of the reporting could not be doubted.

Hattie Dorsett's visit to the Mayo Clinic psychiatrist was disturbing, moreover, because it seemed to affirm the fact that Willard Dorsett had knowingly allowed his daughter to be cared for by a diagnosed schizophrenic. In explanation, Willard Dorsett said only: "She was her mother. I never dreamed a mother would hurt a child." It was an echo of a perennial stereotype. Or perhaps, more grimly, it was the same voice of denial in which the Germans, watching the mass slaughter of Jews in Nazi concentration camps, also claimed not to know.

The analogy was the more apt because Sybil had made identification with the Jews in German concentration camps. She thought of her mother as Hitler, the torturer, and of herself as a tortured Jew. Frequently, Sybil dreamed that she was a prisoner in a camp and her guard was a woman with white hair—the dreaming image of her mother. The thoughts and the dreams were given cogency by the fact that Sybil belonged to a religious group that thought of itself as a minority and that denounced dictators from the pulpit as the incarnation of the prophetic words to be found in the books of Daniel and Revelation in the Bible—that an evil man would rise and conquer the world. Indeed, when finally Sybil had resumed her existence after the two years of Peggy Lou's rule, it was to discover that an evil man was denying freedom to millions of people, just as her mother denied freedom to one.

The distaste Dr. Wilbur had felt for Willard Dorsett because of his financial derelictions to Sybil turned to outright anger. Willard Dorsett hadn't known, Dr. Wilbur was convinced, because he had refused to know. At first she had thought him like fathers she had dealt

275

with in other cases, aloof, passive, committed to not knowing facts that might distress them, too gentle to cope with the women they married, effectual in their business but ineffectual at home. It was a common complaint of many American males—the syndrome of the overpowering mother and the recessive father that had frequently been revealed as the root of family disturbance.

Now, however, the doctor believed that while these things continued to be true of Willard Dorsett, the cardinal fact about him was that he had not taken any action whatsoever against the most destructive mother of whom the doctor had ever had any knowledge.

From her knowledge of Willard's behavior as already revealed in the analysis, the doctor knew, too, that he had failed Sybil in accessory ways. It was to these failures to which the doctor unrelentingly addressed herself next.

Noting that Sybil was emotionally disturbed, Willard—the doctor told him—had reacted as if he hadn't wanted to know. He had evaded the issue by never asking her what the trouble was when they were alone and Sybil was free to communicate with him. Instead, he had asked her in front of Hattie or when there obviously wasn't time to talk. He had asked Sybil during the few moments he was alone with her while she did bookkeeping for him or between customers in the hardware store.

Instead of getting at the heart of his daughter's problem, he had embellished and smothered it with concerns of his own. He was worried about the imminent end of the world, a concern so real to him that he had dropped out of college because he wanted to utilize the time left to him (he never was precise about how much) not on the campus but in the "real" world. And so, when Sybil had shown symptoms of depression, he had evaded the real issue by asking, "Are you worried about the end of the world?" He was worried that Sybil was like his cousin who had been in and out of state hospitals; therefore, when Sybil was anxious, he projected his own worry upon her by asking whether she was worried that she was like this cousin.

276

He had resorted to instant solutions and pat panaceas —a guitar, for instance, to cure the emotional illness for which Dr. Quinoness had recommended a psychiatrist. When Sybil had complained that things felt unreal, he had laughed off the complaint in a grimacing sort of way or had said, "Dr. Quinoness will give you some shots, and you'll be all right." Willard Dorsett had also often dismissed Sybil's worries as imaginary. In short, through a variety of strategies of denial, the father had overlooked, ignored, refused to face the underlying problem that was his daughter's real worry.

The real worry? Had Sybil's behavior ever seemed strange? the doctor asked the father.

Yes, Willard recalled that there were times in which Sybil hadn't seemed to be herself, that, in fact, it had often been hard to say just what that self was because Sybil was seldom the same. She was very moody, and she seemed to be many different kinds of people. Sybil had not seemed like herself, the father recollected, after her grandmother died or in the fifth grade (when Sybil forgot all the multiplication that she had known) or in the sixth grade (when Willard had been called to school because, having wandered out of her classroom, Sybil was found in the cloakroom talking in a way that was not like her). There were also times, the father remembered, when Sybil and he gave guitar concerts or sang in the glee club, and she would forget the music she had previously known very well.

According to Willard, Sybil also had not seemed like herself in Omaha when she walked on the furniture after she had been sent home from college and had said, "You get out of my way. I might hurt you." Her behavior, he said, had been so strange at that time that Hattie and he had had to lock all the doors and hide the keys. Nor had he known what to make of it when sometimes Sybil would disappear.

"I don't know what I did wrong," he said, "but I'm sure there were things. I tried to be a good father."

Dr. Wilbur's list of the things he had done wrong was extensive. In addition to what had already been mentioned, the doctor claimed, he had been doubtful about everything, and his doubts had created false fears in Sybil. He had made decisions involving her without consulting her and had betrayed her many times. A childhood example of betrayal was that at the time of her tonsillectomy he had not told her what was going to happen but had lured her to Dr. Quinoness's home (the upper floor of which served as his hospital) by telling her she would spend the day playing with the Quinoness children. This bare-faced lie produced such intense fear that Sybil began to struggle the moment the ether mask approached her face. Her father held her legs down. She continued to struggle throughout the operation and forever after when any association with this betrayal entered her consciousness.

The father, who himself was not a rejecting father in all respects and who did have a relationship with his daughter, often made Sybil feel rejected, notably when he had not allowed her to be present at her grandmother's funeral service.

"I only did it to spare Sybil the agony it would have caused her," Willard explained.

"But," the doctor countered, "there was greater agony for Sybil in feeling that you had rejected her—greater agony in not being allowed to express her grief."

Agony and rejection there had been, too, when Sybil was thirteen and Willard, weary of Hattie's complaints about having to live under the same roof with his father, talked of renting a place for Hattie and Sybil to live in while Willard continued to stay with his father in their old home. "Girls should be with their mother," Willard explained.

Willard Dorsett, the doctor claimed, had let his daughter down by not permitting her to skip a grade (even though her I.Q. was 170 and she was held back by slower children), for fear she would get what he called a "swelled head."

When Dr. Wilbur accused Willard of having wanted to break up Sybil's friendship with Danny Martin, which had had a healing effect on Sybil and which could have developed into a marriage, for religious reasons, the father took umbrage. "I didn't want Sybil to be with that boy for her own good," Willard said. "I did only what I knew to be right. I didn't want her to marry out of our faith, and if she had been older, she would have agreed with me." He added, "She did, in fact, agree with that philosophy later. When a man she dated differed with her religious philosophy, she would immediately withdraw. Sybil was devout."

There were reasons for what Willard Dorsett had "done wrong" that the doctor suppressed because they were the answers that would have alienated him forever. In the instance of Danny Martin the doctor would have liked to have told Willard that he had sacrificed his daughter's happiness on the altar of a narrow religious concern. The doctor would have liked to have asked: what do you suppose your daughter was trying to say to you when she climbed into your bed and got between you and your wife when you were having intercourse? Why, the doctor would also have liked to have put to the father, are you such a hypocrite, preaching "decency" and yet thinking it moral and right to have sex for nine years in your daughter's presence? And why, while making too much of your daughter's being too big at two and a half to sit on your lap, too big for all the little intimacies that would have made her feel that she had a living, breathing father, did you later seduce her with words? The verbal seduction was an oblique reference to the fact that, while courting Frieda, Willard often had made remarks to Sybil such as, "You young people know so much more about sex than we do that I'm sure you can tell me a few things."

And, just as Dr. Wilbur refrained from smoking or swearing in the presence of this modest, puritanical man, she had also inhibited the questions that would have challenged his puritanism.

"I tried to be a good father," Willard Dorsett repeated as he shook hands with the doctor at the end of a session that had run two hours. His words, however, had lost the old cadences of assurance, and his invincible armor had crumbled. The door closed on a man who had been visibly shaken.

Still self-protective, eager to get hold of himself and to obliterate the past that had caught up with him, he returned to Butler Hall and telephoned Frieda, with

279

whom he could make connection with the present. In that conversation, of course, he did not mention the harrowing encounter, though the confrontation was to produce immediate results. Never again, as long as he lived, did the first of the month roll around without Sybil's receiving a check from her father.

Shortly after Willard concluded his conversation with Frieda, the house phone rang and he was told, "Your daughter and her friend are waiting for you."

"Yes, yes, I'm expecting them," he replied. "Tell them I'll be right down."

In the lobby, Sybil, wearing a blue gabardine suit and a red blouse, was waiting with Teddy Reeves. Suddenly she thrust out her chest, began whistling a tune, and strutted jauntily away from Teddy. Approaching Willard who had been walking toward her, Sybil said in a firm, clear voice, "Why didn't you ever take me to a football game?"

It was an uncanny moment, and Willard was taken back to a night when there had been a pounding of nails in his carpentry shop in Willow Corners. Wondering who could be there at that hour, he decided to investigate. In the carpenter's shop was a lean figure clad in blue denim coveralls with a belt in the center; the figure's arms were covered by a red woolen sweater. Willard did not see the face, for the figure's back was turned toward him. However, when he called out, the figure turned. Sybil in the Butler Hall lobby looked now as she had looked then. "Dad," she repeated as they flagged a taxi to take them to Carnegie Hall, "why didn't you ever take me to a football game?"

Teddy Reeves knew that Sybil had changed into somebody else, but she didn't know into whom. And the harassed father didn't know that, by not taking his daughter to a football game, he had frustrated a son.

19

The Boys

At the very moment that Willard Dorsett was walking into Dr. Wilbur's office that May 4, 1957, Sybil Dorsett was placing her key into the lock of her Morningside apartment. As the door swung open, she gazed in astonishment at the thirty- by eighteen-foot room that was the apartment's main thoroughfare. Between 8:00 A.M. and the present moment, a space of eight hours, the room had been transformed by what seemed like a great wall.

The smell of fresh paint that assailed Sybil's nostrils affirmed not only the recency but also the reality of the wall. The red paint that adhered to her fingers when she reached out to touch this inexplicable wall was further testament to its reality. But it was not quite what it at first seemed. Upon closer scrutiny, Sybil realized that the wall—really a partition—was only eight feet high.

The apartment, which originally had been the dining room of an old mansion, provided an ersatz elegance and the redundancy of two kitchens but no privacy. Teddy Reeves slept in the smaller of the two kitchens; Sybil slept in the part of the long room that had an old woodburning fireplace. In the Dorsett-Reeves household the area was known as the living room. To get to her room, Teddy always had to pass Sybil's bed. It had been an odd, unsatisfactory arrangement, for which neither Sybil nor Teddy had ever quite gotten around to finding a solution.

The partition, which divided the room in half and

masked the area in which Sybil slept, rendered Sybil's bed inviolable against intrusion. Teddy could walk directly to her own room. But although Sybil was greatly pleased at finding the solution presented as a *fait accompli,* she was anxious about the mysterious existence of this protector of her privacy.

The anxiety was the greater because her discovery had occurred at the end of a fragmented day with long stretches of lost time. Even as she took her key out of the lock, closed the door, and walked toward the end of the partition, she could feel strong internal movement—"the interference of the others," as she had learned to call it. There was a clamoring without sound.

Still, the partition was sturdy, and, although hastily assembled, it had been skillfully wrought—worthy, she thought, of two generations of Dorsett carpenters—her father and her grandfather. She would have to show it to her father before he returned to Detroit.

She could hear Teddy's key in the lock. "I smell paint," Teddy called. She stopped short, staring at the wall. "The partition's marvelous. Why didn't you tell me you were going to build it?" she asked.

"I didn't," Sybil said. But even as she spoke, she knew that she couldn't be sure of the "I." Not inconceivably the nails, which her nervously wandering fingers had discovered in the pockets of the blue slacks that she had been wearing all day, belonged to the partition's carpenter. Dorsett carpenters?

The next morning Dr. Wilbur's office, a virtual tribunal the day before, became a confessional. A personality strutted jauntily toward the couch, sat down, and confessed, "I did it."

"Did what?" the doctor asked.

"Built the partition, of course. I let Mike drive in the nails, but I did all the heavy work myself. Vicky and Peggy Lou did most of the planning and measuring and some of the painting. You have to give girls credit where credit is due."

For the nonce Dr. Wilbur did not make too much of the name "Mike" or of the patronizing compliment to girls. What most greatly impressed the doctor was that alternating selves had translated Sybil's wish and need for privacy into a constructive solution, which the waking self hadn't found. While the conscious mind had vacillated, the unconscious had acted.

The doctor's attention quickly was brought back to the immediate situation, however, as she became aware that the patient—a self whom the doctor hadn't met before—was looking at her very intently. "I'm Mike," the voice announced. "I want to ask you something." This voice was different from the one that had talked about the partition.

"What would you like to know?" the doctor asked.

"How come?"

"How come what?"

"We're different?"

"Different?" the doctor repeated.

"Well," Mike explained, "the others are girls. But I'm a boy, and so is Sid."

"You live in a woman's body," the doctor reminded Mike.

"Not really," Mike countered with certainty.

"It just looks like it," Sid added with equal assurance.

The moment passed. The boys, having asserted confidence in their maleness, rattled on about who and what they were. By their own description, Sid had light skin, dark hair, and blue eyes; Mike, olive skin, dark hair, and brown eyes. Sid had derived his name from Sybil's initials—Sybil Isabel Dorsett. Mike attributed his name to two sources—father and grandfather. The name of Mike, which had originated in Willard's having called his daughter, "Mike" whenever she was dressed in coveralls, had been reinforced by a favorite expression of grandfather Dorsett: "For the love of Mike."

Mike and Sid talked of the concert they had attended last night with Dad, of helping Sybil with her woodcarving and sculpture. They talked of their stamp collection and of life in the Dorsett-Reeves apartment.

Sid, who was the partition's carpenter, was also Sybil's repairman. "I fix what's broken, mend what needs mending," Sid told Dr. Wilbur. "Sybil never knows who did it." A broad smile illuminated his face.

"You know what," he said, "I'm going to get six apple crates and build Sybil a bookcase."

New York, the boys complained, offered them almost no opportunity for the sports they had enjoyed in Willow Corners, where, dressed in their blue denim coveralls and a red sweater, they had spent long hours roller skating or hitting a ball against the side of the Dorsett home. In Willow Corners they had watched, they said, the miracle of construction performed by their father's crew. What Mike and Sid enjoyed most of all was to climb into the long rope swing and to get that swing up high enough so that they could touch their own home when swinging forward and the neighbor's house when swinging backward. "Boy, it was fun," said Mike.

"You should have seen us," said Sid.

Life in Willow Corners was, of course, not without frustration. Symbolic of that frustration was the megaphone other kids at school used for the amplification of sound at sports events. "Sid and I never used the megaphone," Mike told the doctor wistfully, "because we never went to a ballgame. Our Dad wouldn't take us."

Even in the first session with Dr. Wilbur there had been clues that illuminated Mike's initial "How come?"

"I look like my Dad," Sid had volunteered. "He's a builder. I'm a builder. As good as he is anytime."

Mike had remarked, "Grandpa was strong, and I'm strong. He could pound nails, and I can pound nails just as hard as he can. He was big, and I can be just as big. I'm not crippled."

Saying that, Mike had thrust out his chest with a flourish of masculine pride. With this bit of pantomime Dr. Wilbur realized that even though at the beginning of the hour Sid had spoken first, it had been Mike who had entered the room. The doctor knew, too, that the clues that had been dropped, like pebbles in a stream, were producing ripples in answer to Mike's initial question. She hypothesized that Sid was an identification with father; Mike, with grandfather Dorsett.

Boys in the 1920s and 1930s in Willow Corners, Mike and Sid were still boys in the 1950s in New York.

Theirs was the eternal youth of an alternating self, a youth with the constant although unfulfilled promise of growing up.

As they walked to the door, the doctor was struck by the fact that they were wearing blue slacks, the New York counterpart of the Willow Corners blue denim coveralls.

Growing up for Mike and Sid, who had remained boys for more than twenty years, had a special meaning: becoming a man. Over a period of weeks they revealed the intensity of their yearning to Dr. Wilbur.

"It was so dark in the garage," Mike told Dr. Wilbur. "You could smell the shavings and the lumber, and it smelled good. It's clean, that smell. There was a long bench in there, with a box under it, with books that kids aren't supposed to look at. Know what else was in that box? Woman's switches." (The switches were auburn tresses, the remnants of Hattie's youth.)

"It's sin in that box," Mike declared. "Sin."

There was a mischievous glimmer in his eyes as he turned them up at the doctor. "Wanna know something?" he asked. "I put those switches on for fun. I looked like a girl. I didn't like that." His eyes flickered elusively. "Would you believe it? When I wore those switches, I looked like a girl!"

Mike waited for the doctor to share his consternation, but, noting that she made no answer, he confided: "I didn't like looking like a girl. I don't want to be a sissy and do dirty things like our mother. I took those switches right off."

"Your mother was not a nice girl," the doctor replied. "She was a dirty girl, that's true. But, Mike, very few girls are like your mother. You can be a girl without being what you call a dirty girl."

"I'm glad," he replied with conviction. "I'm not a girl at all."

"What do you have against girls?"

"Nobody likes girls. Not anybody."

"I like girls."

"Oh, some girls are all right." Mike grinned broadly.

"I like Vicky and Peggy Lou okay. But I'm glad I'm a boy."

"You say you're a boy, but you're not built like your father, are you?"

There was silence—a silence that was finally broken not by Mike but by Sid.

"Almost," Sid replied.

"How almost?" the doctor asked.

"Arms and legs and everything," Sid explained.

"Yes, arms and legs, Sid, but what is different from your father?"

"I don't know," Sid replied.

"Is there anything different from your father?"

"I don't know."

"Is there?"

"I said I didn't know," Sid repeated angrily.

"What do you think? Do you think there is something different from your father?"

"Well," Sid admitted after an awkward pause, "I never got it, but I will. When I'm bigger, it'll grow."

"Sid, you didn't have it at birth like other little boys. There will always be something different."

Sid became thoughtful. "Well," he finally said, "I sometimes used to pretend I was a girl. When I did that, a woman with gray hair laughed. Nobody laughs when I'm a boy, and that's what I really am."

"What you pretended was real, Sid," the doctor said slowly. "You look like your father and can be like him in thought and feeling, in the way you approach things. The differences in the sexes are fewer than people, even experts, used to think. But you are never going to be like your father sexually. Your father has a penis, and you don't. He doesn't have a vagina, and you do. Now how do you suppose that you came to think you're built like him when you're not?"

"But I am."

"Your father was a boy who became a man."

"That's what Mike and I will be when we're older. We will have everything our Dad has. Dad has to shave. We'll have to shave. Dad . . . ."

"But this is a woman's body . . . ."

"Doctor, I want to tell you something." It was

Mike, speaking in a firm clear voice in which he seemed to be pushing Sid aside to assume control of the situation. "If I pushed hard, I could push it out."

"But you have tried," the doctor pointed out, enunciating each word with care, "and you haven't pushed it out."

"I could, though." The certainty of Mike's tone was matched by the confident look in his eyes.

"If you could, you would have," the doctor insisted.

"You're just saying that," Mike replied with a broad, infectious grin.

"No, I'm not just saying that. This is the truth for both you and Sid," the doctor reminded her patients. "Boys in a girl's body don't grow up to be men."

Unconvinced, Mike asked, "If I give a girl a baby, will it be mine?"

"Mike," the doctor replied firmly, "I cannot say yes to the impossible. In this body in which you reside there is a uterus, ovaries, a vagina. Each of these is just as special, just as precious as a penis in a man's body. Without the woman's organs as well as the man's, the perpetuation of the human race would be impossible. It takes a woman's organs as well as a man's to produce a baby. Now, in this body—your body, Mike—there is a pair of ovaries, where the eggs are . . . ."

"I don't want those sissy girl organs," Mike interrupted, "and I don't have them. Not me—I'm a boy."

"Mike, you only have half of what it takes to create a baby, and it is not the half you think you have. All of these parts of the body—the woman's organs and the man's—are important for both the woman and the man. But no one of them is more important than the other. None of them is dirty. You understand that?"

"I'm built like my Dad, like Grandpa was," Mike protested. "I can give a girl a baby if I want to. How many times do I have to tell you that if I pushed hard enough, I could push it out?"

"Why don't you try?"

"I will when I'm older."

"Mike, you do not have a penis or the two little sacks, the testicles, that hang down below the penis and

287

contain the male cells. Without these you cannot give a girl a baby."

"Not ever?" Mike asked. "Not ever?" His tone, for the first time since he had presented himself to the doctor, was somber, subdued.

"No, not ever."

He replied with wistful urgency: "But I want to. I want to. I have to!"

Mike Dorsett could not accept the special facts of his life.

Of the two, Mike proved in analysis to be the more aggressive; Sid was the more thoughtful. This was quite appropriate in terms of their identification—Mike with his grandfather, Sid with his father.

Sybil had made identification not with her mother, of whom she was terrified and ashamed, but with the males in her family. Her father had let Sybil down but, except for the one instance when he and Hattie had been having intercourse, had not hit her or hurt her physically. Because she had to have someone, she had made her father the figure on whom she depended. The identification was the more natural because she looked like her father.

Her father was a builder and carpenter. She became a builder and carpenter by dissociating into a male personality. And that was the genesis of Sid, who had built the partition.

Grandpa Dorsett was aggressive and fanatical. He aroused Sybil's fear, anger, and hatred. Sybil had found the means of dealing with this grandfather and these emotions by dissociating into a male personality whose name was Mike. In Mike Sybil found an aggressor to deal with her grandfather's aggression. Sybil was terrified and ashamed of her grandfather. Mike reflected Sybil's feelings but at the same time made identification with the aggressor—in fact, became the aggressor.

"How could Sybil get along with her grandfather?" Mike had asked the doctor in late May, 1957. "He was always there and always right. The only way to get along with him was either to lick him or join him. I joined him."

Sid and Mike emerged strong and nonneurotic. As far as the doctor had been able to determine, neither was subject to fear, anxiety, depression, or even undue sadness. Sid, however, more contemplative than Mike, was often subject to the intermingling of love, fear, and hate in his feelings toward his father and his father's father. Mike maintained a strong silence about his mother. Even though he talked freely of grandfather and father, of the "girls," as he called Vicky, the Peggys, Marcia, Vanessa, Mary, Ruthie, and the others who had not yet emerged in analysis, he was always reluctant to talk of Sybil herself.

Both Mike and Sid were capable of anger, but it was an anger that was more controlled, less furious than that of Peggy Lou, though it turned out to be linked with Peggy Lou. Mike and Sid, Dr. Wilbur discovered, were Peggy Lou's progeny, a part of a family tree unconnected with genetic inheritance, an offshoot of emotional functioning, of the defensive maneuvers to which the alternating selves owed their existence.

As the mastermind behind Mike and Sid, Peggy Lou delegated her feelings to them. By a curious phenomenon, Sybil had lost the emotions, attitudes, and acquisitions she bequeathed to the personalities into whom she had dissociated whereas Peggy Lou, in proliferating into subselves, among whom were Mike and Sid, lost nothing of what she delegated to them. That Mike was the product of Peggy Lou's wish became clear in a conversation between Dr. Wilbur and Vicky.

"Peggy Lou," Vicky said, "is angry about sex because of her mother's refusal to explain the facts of life. Sometimes Peggy Lou used to say that she was a boy and that her name was Mike. Whenever she thought she was a boy, she wore blue coveralls and a red sweater and did things with tools. She played like the boys and tried to do everything that boys do. But then she would get mad because she knew she wasn't. Even today it makes her mad to know she's a girl. It makes her simply furious because she wants children and wants to get married when she's old enough. She wants to be the man. She wants to be the man she marries when she's old enough."

Identified with Willard and Aubrey Dorsett, emotional descendants of Peggy Lou, Mike and Sid, these boys in a woman's body, were also mythological figures, the compensatory answer to the myth of woman's inferiority, particularly as enunciated in the benighted world of Willow Corners.

Although Mike and Sid epitomized the antifeminist view that women slink through life with secret masculine yearnings, a penis envy so strong that it becomes penis identification, and a woman's capacity for self-derogation so virulent as utterly to repudiate femininity, their feelings were rooted in the environmental influences of a milieu and were rejected by genetic, medical, and psychological evidence. These boys without penises were perhaps the objectification of a woman's rebellion not so much at being female as at the connotations of femaleness evoked by the retarded culture of Willow Corners. That rebellion, moreover, as Mike had made clear in saying, "I don't want to be a dirty girl like our mother," was a revulsion against the distortions about sex a mother had created. Loathing the femaleness that was her mother, a loathing intensified by her father's puritanism, Sybil extended that loathing to the femaleness that was self, to the body that her mother had violated.

"Now, in this body—your body, Mike," Dr. Wilbur had said, "there is a pair of ovaries, where the eggs are."

And Mike had replied, "I don't want them."

Mike and Sid were also autonomous beings, with emotions of their own. Mike's wistfully urgent need "to give a girl a baby" was an expression of that autonomy. But though both, denying that the body in which they lived was alien to their desires, thought and acted as free agents, it was a limited, uncertain freedom. Moreover, analysis threatened their freedom, for regarding the boys' presentation of themselves as a serious complication in a case already overloaded with complications and already following a halting course, Dr. Wilbur was determined to fuse Mike and

290

Sid into the feminine whole they so resolutely rejected as soon as possible.

Mike's initial question, "How come?" had produced an answer rooted in multiple origins. Perhaps there was also a subtle answer in the fact that the unconscious, to which Mike and Sid, like the other alternating selves, belonged, doesn't draw the sexual distinctions that a stratified society imposes.

The uniqueness, which, before, was based on Sybil's having developed more alternating selves than had any other known multiple personality, was now founded as well on her being the only multiple personality to have crossed the borders of sexual difference to develop personalities of the opposite sex.* No known male multiple personality had developed female selves. Sybil Dorsett was the only known woman multiple personality whose entourage of alternating selves included males.

20

The Voice of Orthodoxy

After the appearance of Mike and Sid the analysis suddenly began to veer into the terrifying pathways of religious conflict. The serpent had caught up with the couch. "I want you to be free," Dr. Wilbur told Sybil in September, 1957. "Free not only of your mother and your ambivalent feelings about your father but also of the religious conflicts and distortions that divide you."

---

* Since 1957, other multiple personalities who have developed selves of the opposite sex have been recorded.

Sybil *wanted* to be free, but she was terrified that analysis would take her religion away. The terror was greatly intensified, moreover, by the realization that the help that she had always thought would come from God was now coming from Freud. Unready to accept this conclusion even though it was her own, she pondered whether both Freud and the Church could be right at the same time. The pondering in turn heightened the feeling of being simultaneously frantic, anxious, and trapped.

Wanting freedom from the religious distortions that hounded and divided her yet wanting to hold on to her fundamental beliefs, she realized that the problem was one of salvaging God while surrendering the appurtenances with which He had been enshrouded. This meant breaking free from an environmental bondage to a childhood in which religion was omnipresent. Armageddon was table talk, and the end of the world was a threatening reality. There had been menace, too, in grandfather Dorsett's prattle about the seven last plagues and the inevitable war with China and about how in the wake of the Catholics' assumption of power would come the doom of mankind, a doom that had also been prepared, her grandfather averred, by the perfidious, sacrilegious theory of evolution that Darwin had promulgated.

The crypt in the cathedral of Sybil's religious torment was occupied, too, by a variety of symbolic figures from the past, exerting in the present their throttling grip. One of these was no less a personage than Satan—the serpent who had stalked through Sybil's childhood, a living, breathing presence. Fearing that he would creep in at night, she had also feared that nothing she could do would or could keep him from "getting her."

In the crypt of torment, too, was an angel with sword and fire, who, having driven Adam and Eve out of the Garden of Eden because they were "bad," threatened to drive Sybil out of her home because she, too, was "bad."

The more, therefore, that the analysis led Sybil to dip into the accretive religious heritage of an overstrict observance of rigid faith, the more hounded, divided she became. Yet while inwardly rebelling, she outwardly conformed to the letter of the orthodoxy.

The voice of that orthodoxy was heard in the consulting room that brisk September day. Sybil was seated on the couch, close to the doctor. The discussion moved from the need for freedom in the present to the lack of freedom imposed by the past.

"I understood the reasons for not smoking, not dancing, not going to birthday parties on Sabbath," Sybil explained. "But I rebelled inside. Then after a while I didn't rebel. Then I did again. And now I'm trying not to."

"Why," the doctor asked in dismay, "are you trying not to now?"

Sybil was silent.

"Okay," the doctor prodded. "Now what makes sense about not going to a birthday party on Sabbath?"

"Because it says in the Bible you should not do your own pleasure on the Sabbath day. You are supposed to think about God. Not do secular things." She had spoken unhesitatingly, but now she added defensively, "I don't want to talk about it."

"Doesn't the Bible say," the doctor reminded her, "on six days work and rest on the seventh? Isn't going to a party part of the seventh day's leisure of which the Bible talks?"

"You could go to a party on another day," Sybil replied non-responsively. "But not on Sabbath because observance was from sundown to sundown. That's what God told us to do."

The doctor offered a correction: "That's what the prophets in the Bible said God told us to do. Let's not confuse the issue."

"God talked through them," Sybil replied with conviction.

"Perhaps," said the doctor.

"The Bible is written by the inspiration of God," Sybil affirmed. "It isn't just something somebody has written down."

"The prophets were human beings and we cannot

be absolutely, positively, totally sure they got things exactly correct."

"God," Sybil replied, "would not permit them to make mistakes."

"Oh, He permits people to make mistakes!" There was a tinge of irony in the doctor's voice.

"Yes," Sybil conceded. Then her facial expression became taut as she added, "But not in something as important as His law, the guide for generations to come."

"Is loving your fellow man part of worshiping God?" the doctor asked.

"It's part of it," Sybil replied authoritatively. "Not all of it. God said: 'Love thy neighbor as thyself.'"

"And if a neighbor should have a birthday on the Sabbath," the doctor argued, "should he be deprived of the celebration of that day?"

"Yes," Sybil insisted, "God said *He* should come first."

"Aren't we worshiping God when we celebrate our birthday?"

"We are not," said Sybil.

"All right," the doctor persisted, "you celebrate Christmas—Christ's birthday?"

"Not in our Church. It's all right to realize and remember that He was born, but you must keep in mind it wasn't that particular day—December 25."

"Isn't it proper to honor the days on which we were born if we are children of God?"

Sybil replied sternly: "But you don't have to have birthday parties and go around tooting and yelling and that sort of thing on the Sabbath. There are many things you have to forgo if you are going to follow God. It doesn't have to be easy. St. John the Baptist said, 'I have fought the good fight.'"

There was momentary silence. Then, with a directness calculated to quicken Sybil's own repressed doubts —as expressed by some of the other selves—Dr. Wilbur said: "Well, there is one thing I really don't comprehend about your religion: one thing for which man has struggled through the centuries is his freedom."

"That may be. But no one wants freedom from God."
An unwavering Sybil had had the last word.

A few days later Peggy Lou and Peggy Ann displayed combined anger and terror when Dr. Wilbur began to talk about religion. "It's all mixed up," said Peggy Lou, speaking for both Peggy Ann and herself. "It's futile to talk about it. It goes round and round." Pacing the consulting room, Peggy Lou came to a sudden halt. "It's supposed to do more than not upset you. It's supposed to help you. But it never helped me. It never helped Peggy Ann or any of the rest of us." The fire of rebellion had been unleashed, yet the Church still stood. With a swift sharp movement, however, as Peggy Lou continued to pace the floor, she reached metaphorically for the edifice without exit, serving notice, "I'd like to tear the Church down!"

Vanessa breezed into the consulting room a few days after Peggy Lou's diatribe. Although Vanessa was not quite ready to tear the Church down, she expressed contempt for both the Church's prohibitions and its congregation. "I'm not devout," Vanessa said with an attractive toss of the head, "but even if I were, the people in the Willow Corners Church would have turned me off. They were bigoted, unjust, irrational, and hypocritical. I can't see how they dared to call themselves Christians." Vanessa's lips formed a satiric smile. "All the things you had to do to be right," she jeered. "The irony was that the things you wanted to do weren't wrong. On Sabbath they wanted you just to sit. That, of course, my dear Watson, was a waste of time."

She stopped talking and met the doctor's gaze. "And, Doctor, I must confess that I didn't understand the meaning of God's love. Mother was always trying to tell me that God was love, and I couldn't understand what love was. But I did know I didn't want God to be like my mother."

"I see," the doctor replied.

"Mother said she loved me, but if that was love . . ."

"Then you didn't want love . . ."

"And I'm supposed to want God . . ."

"You were afraid . . ."

"Because," Vanessa explained, "I didn't know what God and His love were going to do to me."

"Yes," agreed the doctor. "So you were afraid."

Even before Vanessa left the room, Marcia entered the scene to add a few variations on the theme. Religious yet resentful of the religion's prohibitions, which had created in her a sense of alienation and deprived her of the opportunity to grow up freely, she looked at the doctor pensively.

"Things that were right for everybody else were wrong for me. The worst of it was I knew I couldn't do these things—dancing, going to the movies, wearing jewelry —even when I grew up.

"Would you believe it, Dr. Wilbur, I didn't see my first movie until I came to live in New York?" she confided with a derisive but almost comic shrug.

Marcia smiled wanly. "Looking back," she said, "I realize how trapped I was by all the talk of the end of the world. It was something to look forward to, and there would be a better life after that. I had to believe that. But underneath I wished it weren't that way because there were so many things I wanted to do, and it was as if the end would come before I had a chance. But it seemed wrong to think that way, and I had a mixed up feeling—the same sort of feeling I have now when I realize things can't be different."

Mike and Sid, who also made their way into the era of analytic religious debate, voiced a belief in God but a contempt for religious rituals and histrionics. They were not religious, but they were concerned with religion. What they especially resented was grandfather's prattle about Armageddon and evolution. They—especially Mike—were more interested in doing battle with their grandfather and in defending Sybil as well as themselves against him than in the truth or falsity of his utterances.

Ruthie, who was only a baby and whom Dr. Wilbur had met only in connection with the primal scene, talked of rebellion in the church's sandbox. "Our hands were in the sandbox," Ruthie said. "The sand felt all smooth. We let it run through our fingers. We liked the sand, stood things in the sand. Then we were big enough to hear about that angel we didn't trust at all. We'd get up Sabbath morning and play. We thought they'd forgotten, but then they'd remember. We'd say, 'Don't wanna go! Don't wanna go!' Daddy would look. Mama said we hadda grow up. If Daddy had a white shirt and Mama was fixing pancakes, then we knew there'd be the sandbox. So when we saw the white shirt and the pancakes we got sick, had to go to bed, and Daddy and Mama went to church without us."

Of all the selves of Sybil it was Mary, the homebody, to whom religion meant most. Mary, who had rejected the doctrines, the rituals, the florid symbolism of the faith, had incorporated within herself the unpretentious religion of grandmother Dorsett. "I pray to God," Mary told the doctor, "but I don't go to church. I try to be honest, truthful, and patient and to lead a good Christian life. I believe in 'live and let live.' This brings me solace."

Yet as the discussions of religion progressed, Dr. Wilbur could see that Mary was losing her serenity. While Sybil was concerned that analysis would deprive her of her religion, Mary was troubled that analysis would make her religion sound inconsistent. And in time the feelings of entrapment that the religion wrought in all the selves, but most especially in the Peggys, reached and overwhelmed Mary. Becoming subdued and depressed, Mary told Dr. Wilbur, "I'm caught in here, inside of these walls. Peggy Lou brought me a picture of the church, and there was no exit. I'm caught in this building with no doors. It seems to be dome-shaped and to be built of blocks of packed snow."

As the analysis proceeded, the religious conflicts surfaced more and more. It would be easy but untrue to say that while Sybil, the waking self, representing the conscious mind, conformed, the others, whose domain was the unconscious, rebelled. The truth was that even though most markedly conformity was apparent in Sybil and rebellion in the Peggys, both conformity and rebellion were expressed in a variety of ways in all the selves, many of whom were further divided within the autonomy of their individual identities.

All of the selves had independent religious convictions and attitudes. All, with the exception of the Peggys, believed in God; all felt trapped by the Church. Under the pressure of confrontation with religion in analysis, Mary wanted to die, and the Peggys wanted to run away. Marcia and Vanessa broke away from some of the old restraints and began, in keeping with Dr. Wilbur's urging, to separate God from the Church, the congregation, and the Church's prohibitions. Feeling freer, Vanessa bought a pair of red earrings to match her hair and Marcia went to the movies on Sabbath. Marcia also dared, experimentally at any rate, to light a cigarette and take a sip of sherry.

Vicky, who had played the role of observer without declaring her own convictions—since after all she had only been a visitor in the Dorsett church—became troubled about Marcia and Vanessa.

"No harm in what they've done so far," Vicky told Dr. Wilbur, "but they're showing off their new freedom. By pulling away from the others they are going to make integration more difficult."

"Yes, I know, Vicky," Dr. Wilbur agreed. "But maybe integration will involve bringing the others to where Marcia and Vanessa are."

Vicky shrugged. Then she looked fixedly at the doctor and expressed perturbation at the change in Sybil herself. "Sybil," Vicky informed the doctor, "hasn't known what her relationship to God is ever since she found out about the rest of us. You see, Dr. Wilbur, she always felt that this condition of hers was evil. As a little girl she thought it was a form of punishment, the handiwork of Satan. When you told her about us, that old feeling about evil came back, even though she was no longer so sure about Satan.

"Sybil often wonders," Vicky continued, "whether she has displeased God. She is also unsure of whether her motives are always right. She gets scared about words—all this talk here—making things better and then having the whole world to face." Vicky leaned her head on her hand thoughtfully. "Sybil's afraid that if she gets better, something terrible will happen. It's as if the serpent is about to get her once again even though the serpent is losing his name."

Toward Christmas Sybil became perturbed by the courses in zoology and evolution that she was taking at Columbia. Together Dr. Wilbur and Sybil read passages from Darwin's *Origin of Species* and *The Descent of Man*. It was difficult for Sybil to accept that the bodily structure of man shows traces of descent from some lower form. "We are children of God," Sybil insisted defensively. "Evolution, after all, is only a hypothesis."

The subject of evolution stirred Mike to say, "You see—Grandpa was wrong," and Mary to remark, "It doesn't matter where we come from but what we do with our lives." Peggy Lou fumed, "Animals have the freedom we never had in our church," and a newly skeptical Vanessa quipped, "What a relief not to have to be a creature of God!"

The analysis veered from religion in Willow Corners to religion in Omaha, where the serpent of childhood became less menacing. The Omaha congregation was better educated, less rigid, more humanistic than that in Willow Corners. Pastor Weber, a preacher who was also an evangelist, considered Sybil an artist and was aware of the subduing impact that a too-literal interpretation of the faith had had on her as an isolated only child in a family that had not experienced the mediating influences of young people. Pastor Weber swept Sybil out of isolation and into the limelight.

"And four great beasts came up from the sea, diverse one from another . . ."

Pastor Weber's voice, resonant and full, rang through the Omaha church during the special Sunday night service.

". . . the first was like a lion and had eagle's wings."

The audience of five hundred looked from the evangelist to the scaffold nine feet above him, at an easel covered with drawing paper and spanning the entire width of the church. Following the beam of the heavy spotlights that illuminated the scaffold, the audience focused on the slight figure of a woman in a light blue chiffon dress with a small white apron: Sybil.

Sybil, delicate, ethereal in the enveloping lights—

"angelic," as one observer described her—brought to life, with rapid strokes, the lion with eagle's wings on the drawing paper. The audience was spellbound, transfixed.

As the evangelist then spoke of a second beast, "like to a bear" with three ribs between its teeth, and of a third beast after that, like a leopard but with four heads, and on whose back were four wings of a fowl, these beasts, too, appeared in swift succession upon the paper.

Portraying the message of the Scripture, translating the evangelist's words into pictures, Sybil drew the fourth beast, dreadful and terrible, and exceedingly strong, with iron teeth and ten horns. "I considered the horns, and behold, there came up among them another little horn, before whom there were three of the first horns plucked up by the roots," the evangelist's voice boomed, "and behold in this horn were eyes like the eyes of men, and a mouth speaking great things." From the paper, compellingly real, glared the eyes that stared into the captivated audience and the mouth that, though mute, spoke.

"Daniel takes the position," the evangelist told the audience, "that we started out all right, man being created perfect, and then came the degeneracy. Instead of coming from the zoo, we are heading for the zoo. We are becoming like animals." The figures, no longer representational, had become abstract, an instant translation of the evangelist's message.

"Man became so sinful," the evangelist's voice warned, "that God had to create a special animal to describe the sinful generation."

On the paper, nine feet above the evangelist and created by lightning strokes of black chalk, was an abstraction of the divine fury that had been evoked.

For three successive Sundays Sybil stood, a slight figure with a mighty stroke, on the scaffold. The audience was spellbound. Sybil's parents were unreservedly proud of their daughter. Pastor Weber was jubilant that Sybil Dorsett had put his philosophy into pictures.

Sybil herself, however, looked at the drawings at the close of each of the three Sunday night performances and wondered how it had come to pass that on that paper was more, much more, than she had drawn.

21

The Wine of Wrath

The real importance of the great spectacle in the Omaha church, withheld at that time but revealed in the analysis, was that on the scaffold Sybil had not been alone. The beasts that rose from the sea to the paper had been put there more by the other selves than by Sybil herself. The greatest part of the drawing had been done by Mike and Sid. Even more significant was the fact that among the selves on that scaffold were five Dr. Wilbur had not yet met: Marjorie, Helen, Sybil Ann, Clara, and Nancy Lou Ann.

Marjorie was a small and willowy brunette with fair skin and a pug nose. Helen had light-brown hair, hazel eyes, a straight nose, and thin lips. Sybil Ann was a pale, stringy girl with ash-blonde hair, gray eyes, an oval face, and a straight nose.

Of the three, Marjorie alone was serene. Helen was intensely fearful; Sybil Ann, listless to the point of neurasthenia.

Marjorie was vivacious and quick to laugh. She enjoyed many things—parties and the theater, fairs and travel, most especially games of intellectual competition, from which Sybil almost invariably withdrew. Marjorie had no hesitation in expressing annoyance or impatience, but she never showed anger. Most remarkably, Marjorie Dorsett neither was depressed in the present nor gave evidence of having been depressed in the past. Through some special immunity she had emerged unscathed from the battering in Willow Corners.

Marjorie enjoyed making wry little jokes and was also something of a tease. Asked, for instance, whether she knew any of the other selves, she raised her eyebrows, rolled her eyes coyly, and bantered, "I'll never tell!" A moment later she grinned. "But maybe the answer is yes," she said. Then she added cryptically, "I like helping these other people."

"They laugh or cry," Marjorie reported, "and I often hear them mumbling beside me, heads close together. It's quite a hum, and it always was—ever since I came."

Marjorie Dorsett never spoke Sybil's name. When referring to the person who bore that name, Marjorie resorted to "you know who."

Dr. Wilbur couldn't understand why Marjorie, who didn't paint and who was interested in neither art nor religion, had been on the scaffold of the Omaha church with Sybil.

Helen, who seemed unassertive in manner, was nevertheless ambitious, determined "to be sombody, to do things in my own way, and to make you, Dr. Wilbur, proud of me."

At the mention of Hattie, Helen broke away from the couch, where she had been seated quietly, to clamber on all fours toward and then under the desk. Her arms folded over her breasts, her head bent over her neck, her eyes wide with terror, Helen sat huddled in a heap. Her teeth were chattering noisily.

"Helen?" the doctor, placing a hand on the patient's shoulder, asked gently.

"She's in this room," Helen screamed, beginning to tremble even more violently than before. "Behind the curtains."

"Who?"

"Mother."

"There's nobody here, Helen, but you and me."

"I never want to see my mother again."

"You never will."

"Never?" Her teeth ceased to chatter, and the terror departed from her eyes. As the doctor helped the patient from under the desk and on to her feet, Helen remarked in a suddenly realistic tone that broke the reenacted terror of childhood: "My muscles are cramped."

As in the instance of Marjorie, Helen, who neither painted nor had any special religious concern, seemed to have occupied an anachronistic place on the scaffold.

Sybil Ann shrank into the consulting room. She didn't speak to the doctor but whispered. After the introductions were over, Sybil Ann sat silently, staring into vacancy. It was as if she were erasing herself from the scene, almost as if, by implication, she were saying, "I'm not fit to occupy space. Excuse me for living."

When Sybil Ann was in command, moreover, the body itself underwent a marked change. It seemed literally to grow smaller. That first time she appeared, as the body seemed to shrink, the trim gray suit Sybil Ann was wearing seemed to stretch. On the other selves the suit fit perfectly. On Sybil Ann, it assumed the proportions of a sack. Within the recesses of the expanding gray suit Sybil Ann seemed to be hiding.

Out of the awkward enveloping silence there did finally come words with measured tread. Sybil Ann told Dr. Wilbur: "I have to force myself even to move my eyeballs. It's so easy just to stare."

This fragile personality, Dr. Wilbur learned later, seldom ate, slept little, and generally evinced only slight interest in her surroundings. Often she would say: "I don't feel anything." When she was in one of her better moods, she enjoyed libraries and museums, preferred music to painting. On the very rare occasions when she herself painted, she invariably produced a dreary picture of solitary characters with faces either covered or turned away. On the Omaha scaffold she had brought a measure of gloom to the faces of the beasts.

Characteristically, Sybil Ann assumed command of the body when "everything was too much." The "takeover," however, was a response to, rather than the means of coping with, the given situation; of all the

303

selves the most profoundly depressed was Sybil Ann, who could sit for hours as mute and unmoving as the pelican on the piano in the Dorsett home in Willow Corners.

When, at the end of the first visit to Dr. Wilbur's consulting room, Sybil Ann finally rose to leave, she walked at a slow, dragging pace. "It's an effort," she said wearily, "to put one foot ahead of the other, and I have to keep thinking about it—or I stop."

Noting Sybil Ann's great lassitude and weakness, Dr. Wilbur diagnosed her as suffering from neurasthenia, a type of neurosis resulting from emotional conflicts that usually are characterized by fatigue, depression, worry, and often, localized pains without apparent objective causes. Sybil Ann, Dr. Wilbur also felt certain, was an identification with Hattie Dorsett in her catatonic phase on the farm.

Clara, who had been in the consulting room during the reliving of the episode on the Omaha church scaffold during the Christmas holidays of 1957, continued silently to follow the running dialogue about religion, which extended through the rest of December and the early months of 1958. In March she presented herself to Dr. Wilbur with terse autobiographical information. "I'm twenty-three. I never had a mother. I just exist." She proceeded to explicate her religious role in the Dorsett conglomerate of selves.

"I know more about religion than the others do," Clara Dorsett said. "I was in the sandbox with Ruthie, at church school with Sybil and the others. Religion is as important to me as it is to Mary, even more important, I sometimes think. I believe in God without reservation, in the Bible as the revelation of His Truth, in Satan, who is His antithesis."

Suddenly the room was like a chalice in which the wine of wrath is contained. Clara was pacing the floor, uttering a vehement indictment: "Sybil's such a deplorable character. Honest, it's disgusting. The thing about it is that she gets the idea that she's going to try. She can't do anything!"

"You sound as if you don't like Sybil," the doctor said.

"I don't," Clara replied bluntly.

Self against self in a woman divided. "Why not?" the doctor asked.

"Why should I?" Clara replied resentfully. "The only thing I want to do, she keeps me from doing."

"What do you want to do?" the doctor asked.

"Oh, it isn't anything spectacular," Clara explained. "I like to study and learn. She stands in my way."

"What do you like to study?"

"Music and English. Especially history, medical things—chemistry, zoology," Clara replied.

"So does Sybil," the doctor was quick to point out.

"No, she doesn't," Clara said contemptuously. "A big steel wall goes up, and she just can't study. Can't do anything, in fact. It wasn't always that way. But that's how it is now."

"Why, Clara?" the doctor asked, to ascertain how much this newcomer really knew about Sybil.

"Anger," Clara replied authoritatively.

"I have some good drills for hacking that wall of anger down," the doctor asserted. "Clara, will you help me?"

"Why should I?" Clara's pique had become even more pronounced. "What has she ever done for me?"

"Then," the doctor suggested artfully, "help me take a whack at that wall—not for Sybil but for yourself."

"For me?" Clara drew up her shoulders in dismay. "I'm afraid, Doctor, I don't see the connection."

"Clara, can't you see that if you help me help Sybil to get well, she will no longer stand in the way of your doing the things you want to do?" The doctor's tone was urgently insistent. "Can't you see that in helping Sybil you will be helping yourself?"

"Well," Clara hesitated, "Sybil's still so far away from everything. I couldn't reach her if I tried."

"Try, Clara!" The doctor's urging had become an entreaty. "For your own sake, Clara," the doctor said softly. "Tomorrow morning when Sybil wakes up, I'd like all you girls to do something."

"The boys, too?" Clara asked.

"Yes, all of you," the doctor replied.

"What?" Clara wanted to know. "Go to church? It's Sabbath tomorrow."

"No, I don't want you to go to church," the doctor replied firmly. "Just sleep late and then tell Sybil that the reason she can't do all the things she'd like to do is that the complications of the illness are holding her back."

Clara, who had been pacing as she talked, came to an abrupt stop. "But, Doctor," she protested, "you told Sybil that she could manage school in spite of the illness, even though the analysis was consuming much of her time."

"Yes," the doctor explained, "I did tell her that. But that was before I knew how much pain had to be dealt with. At that time I thought that the basic trauma was the grief over the grandmother's death—that it was because of that that Sybil dissociated into other selves. I also thought that grief was kept alive because Sybil, who had been absent for two years, had never had the opportunity to get it out of her system. I didn't know then how much pain there had been or how complicated the roots were of Sybil's case."

"You know," Clara replied confidentially, "Sybil's worried because she lost several years of things, and she's afraid that you'll find out."

"That's ridiculous," the doctor averred. "Sybil knows I know about those lost years."

"She keeps reliving the past," Clara reported. "She keeps thinking her mother is going to hurt her." Clara paused. Then she added, "I'm glad I never had a mother."

The doctor allowed the comment to go unnoticed, as she replied, "We're going to free Sybil of the past."

"Yes, she wants to be free," Clara replied edgily. "Wants to forget everything and not face anything."

"She'll have to face it all before she can be free of it," the doctor replied. "But she can do it. She has great stamina, great courage. All of you have."

"Courage?" Clara asked with a sarcastic overtone. "She can't do anything. Can't face anything. You call that courage?"

306

"She has great ability and is gifted in many things," the doctor replied with conviction. "When we hack that wall of anger down, she'll be free to realize herself."

Clara shook her head gravely. "There never was a drill that could do that," she said.

"My drill," the doctor maintained, "will do that—on one condition."

"Condition?" Clara seemed puzzled.

"We can tear the wall down, Clara," the doctor replied firmly, "if you and the others will work with me." Clara looked even more perplexed. "Tomorrow," the doctor continued, "when you tell Sybil about the analysis, also begin telling her the various things you know."

"Things? What things?" Clara asked uncertainly.

"What you have learned, feel, remember . . . ." the doctor coaxed.

"I remember a great many things about the Church," Clara reminisced. "The incidents in the Willow Corners church are vivid."

"Tell Sybil."

"What's the use?" Clara shrugged. "Sybil's not a good listener. That big wall, you know."

"We're going to demolish that wall," the doctor replied. "All of us working together." The doctor looked at Clara unflinchingly. "Then Sybil will be able to do the things you want her to do. She won't interfere with your studies anymore."

"Well, I don't want to help her," an uncompromising Clara replied. "Why should I?"

"Then, why don't you get together with the others?" Dr. Wilbur persevered. "You can all do the things you enjoy. You can do them together."

Clara rose to her feet, began to pace once again. Then with a wry smile, she turned to the doctor. "You never saw such a pack of individualists," Clara said. "They all want to have things their own way."

"Try!" The doctor renewed her entreaty.

Clara laughed. "You should hear us squabble. I can feel them now. The Peggys are just simmering."

"Clara, listen." The doctor was now standing close to the patient. "What I'm asking of you is for your own good, for the good of all of you. I've already mentioned

307

it to some of the others. All of you must work together. All of you must try to reach Sybil. That, Clara, is the only way you're going to be able to persuade Sybil to do the things that don't interfere with your own self-realization. Don't you see what's at stake? Won't you try to see?"

The room reverberated with menace as Clara replied: "Sybil doesn't have to live!"

Standing in Dr. Wilbur's consulting room the next day was Nancy Lou Ann Baldwin. The traffic noises emanating from the street below that made their way into the room were to Nancy the dread sounds of explosion; for she lived on the outer rim of terror.

"I don't like things to blow up," Nancy remarked now. "Exploding, always exploding. It's just as bad as a bomb when you're little and your mother throws blocks at you, things hit you, you get all tied up, and you get dizzy and you see little spots running around. And there is noise, an awful banging, as bad as a bomb when you're little. The worst of it is mother is not dead."

"Your mother is buried in Kansas City. There are no explosions that will injure you now." The doctor's words of assurance were an incantation.

"I don't see how you know that," Nancy protested. "Mother can be buried in Kansas City and exploding in my mind at the same time. Besides, there are many other kinds of explosions I can name, and I can't see how you can prevent them. You can't keep the gas main or a furnace from blowing up."

"Your house doesn't have a gas furnace." The doctor struck a realistic, practical note to allay the terror.

Nancy's fey reply as her lips briefly curled in amusement was, "Well, I suppose it has to be a big poof to be an explosion." Terror returned as she added: "But you can't keep the world itself from blowing up. And that will be a big poof."

"The world is not going to blow up, Nancy," said Dr. Wilbur.

"Why, then, have they built civil defense shelters?" Nancy replied promptly. "Why do we see signs of the end everywhere? Satan will destroy the world and

308

God will make it perfect, so there will be no more sin. In the final war, in Armageddon, everything will be destroyed, according to prophecy."

"The time has not come." Dr. Wilbur was determined to free Nancy of her obsession.

"Before the end, prophecy tells us," Nancy continued, heedless of the interruption, " 'The rivers will dry up, and they will be as blood.' Before the end, prophecy also tells us, the Catholics will come into power and control the government and men's minds. We're seeing both things happening. Everywhere we read about rivers that have been polluted. Pollution is the blood of which prophecy speaks. And since you can't live very long without water, we all shall die as prophecy predicts. The prophecy about the Catholics is also being fulfilled. The Catholics started a long time ago by building schools and colleges. But they couldn't do much until 1936 or 1939, I'm not sure which. Anyway, they couldn't do much before the Vatican was recognized as a free state, with a right to speak out. And the Catholics have become more powerful since that time.

"The time will come, Dr. Wilbur, when, if you don't worship the Catholic priests, popes and cardinals, it'll be for you the way it was for the Jews under the Nazis. The Catholics are going to get more and more powerful, and if we're smart, we won't let any Catholic run for president. If they get in, they will assume control of education. They want a Catholic commissioner of education even more than they want a president. By controlling the children, they know they can also control the parents. They won't lose a single chance to enslave us all."

Nancy moved restlessly and apprehensively around the room. She turned to the doctor, saying: "I never will be a Catholic. I will never, never do what they order me to do, and I'm afraid of what they'll do. I don't want to be shut up in a prison. But I won't do what they will demand of me."

The hidden pathways of hysteria were no longer hidden. The crescendo of powerful feeling filled the small room with the mounting sweep of a full orchestra. Nancy collapsed onto the couch. "Doctor"—the words were being wrung out slowly—"sometimes I'm so frightened by all this that I'd rather die right now."

Dr. Wilbur answered quietly, softly, "Why should you want to die? There would be too much to give up. Loving people. Making things. Enjoying music, art, nature." Then the doctor added pointedly, meaningfully: "Getting together with Sybil and finding yourself."

The mood was broken. Terror was replaced by anger and defensiveness. "Why are you cornering me?" Nancy asked.

"My dear, I'm not cornering you," the doctor replied reassuringly. "I'm just trying to make you see that there is no reason for you to die."

"No reason?" Nancy replied thoughtfully. "There are private reasons, public reasons."

"What are the private reasons?" the doctor asked quietly, fully aware that, despite the turbulence of the outcry, this was her first encounter with Nancy.

"Oh," Nancy replied, "all of us are trying to get Sybil to do things, and it doesn't work. Being linked with Sybil is a constant frustration. It makes me angry, frightened. And sometimes I feel as if I'd like to curl up like a baby, free of responsibility. But then I'm very close to the Peggys, and you know how they feel about Sybil. Sybil makes Peggy Lou just simmer all the time."

Suddenly shifting into a relaxed, casual mood Nancy explained, "I'm so close to the Peggys I took both their middle names. But they use the name Dorsett. I don't. I'm Nancy Lou Ann Baldwin. Miss Baldwin was a teacher Sybil pretended to be at the time I came."

"What are the other private things that worry you, Nancy?" the doctor wanted to know. "What do you want to do that you can't?"

"Walk on legs that are not weak," was the surprising reply. "I want to go places and do things. One can't, you know, with Sybil."

"We can fix it so you can," the doctor promised.

"I'm afraid we can't," Nancy replied bluntly. "But just now I'm even more troubled by public concerns." The terror had returned to her eyes. "The Catholics," she warned, "will sneak in when we least suspect. They'll catch us."

"They won't catch me because I'm not afraid of them, and I don't believe as you do. I believe . . ."

"There isn't that much time left," Nancy interrupted hysterically. Then, quieter, she repeated, "I'd like to die. But God doesn't let me. You see I'd have to do it to me, and suicide is just as wrong as if I followed the Catholics' orders. It would give my soul to the devil either way."

"Now, Nancy . . ." The doctor tried to break the mood by injecting another point of view.

But Nancy cut her short. "And I don't want the devil to win!"

"Nancy," the doctor replied, changing the subject completely, "if you and Clara and some of the others —especially Marcia—would join Sybil . . ."

"Clara has the same trouble about religion that I do," Nancy interrupted again. "Her worry's the same as mine. I'm sure when she talked to you yesterday, she must have told you the same things that . . ."

This time it was the doctor who interrupted. "If you and Clara help Sybil to be strong and do the things Sybil wants to do," the doctor remarked pointedly, "then there will be another person to help maintain the democracy you're afraid the Catholics will take away." Absorbed in her own thoughts, Nancy replied in a different vein, "you're always supposed to be prepared for the day the Catholics destroy our democracy. You have to look out for it!"

"Nancy," the doctor insisted in a firm, strong voice, "God gives us our brains to use . . ."

"Sure." Again Nancy had broken into the doctor's words. "And He gave us the prophecies to know how to use our brains to get ready for the struggle against Catholic assumption of power."

"Now Nancy . . ." the doctor began.

"He did!" Nancy insisted vehemently.

"God gave us our brains to use," Dr. Wilbur explained. "You should not waste them in unfounded worry."

Nancy protested: "But He said to turn from the

powers of darkness unto the powers of light, and that means to follow Him."

"Now in this country we have consistently had freedom of religion and freedom of worship," Dr. Wilbur reminded Nancy.

"It has failed," Nancy replied.

"Because our government is a government of the people," the doctor continued, "you and I are just as much a part of our government as anyone else and . . ."

"I know those things," Nancy interrupted sharply.

"Now that means," the doctor affirmed, "that if you're so afraid of our losing our democracy, you and Clara should join Sybil so that Sybil can do all of the things that she is capable of doing to help other people to turn from the powers of darkness."

"Excuse me, Dr. Wilbur," a voice that was not Nancy's interrupted. "I think I should say something here."

"Yes, Vicky?" The doctor knew the voice well.

"Well, you'll excuse me for saying it because you know I don't say anything anymore except when it is absolutely necessary. But I think you're making a mistake in telling Nancy that. You see, Sybil has the same fears and worries that Nancy and Clara have. As a matter of fact, even though Marcia thinks she's breaking away from religion, she has those same fears too."

"Yes?"

"And I've been trying to help Nancy, Clara, Marcia, and Sybil. It's been better. You said to me one time, 'Vicky, why don't you help Sybil?' and I've been doing that. But if Nancy and Clara join Sybil now, with this great fear that they have, it would add that fear to those Sybil already has. I'm afraid it will be too much fear in one place. That's one reason that I've stopped encouraging Nancy and Clara to come closer. Why bring them closer when they aren't bringing us more strength? They have hold of the wrong things: not only extreme worries about religion but also depression and suicide ideas—more than they'd ever tell you and much more than they've said here. I don't want them to bring these things to Sybil because I'm not sure that even I

312

am strong enough to fight all of that. I won't say anymore. I just don't think it is sensible to try to bring Nancy and Clara closer to Sybil at this time."

"It would be a mistake, Vicky," Dr. Wilbur informed her co-analysand, "if I weren't going to do anything to change the worries of Nancy and Clara. Right? But I have every intention of doing so. Now if Nancy will let me talk for a little while longer, I think I can straighten out a few things."

"All right," Vicky replied, "I'll let Nancy come back. But please, Dr. Wilbur, remember my caution. It's more than a caution. It's a warning."

As Dr. Wilbur realized that five new selves had been revealed, she looked back to the time when, after first meeting Vicky, she had pored over the literature of multiple personality. She had then speculated that Sybil's case was more complex than that of either Miss Beauchamp or of Doris Fisher. Now she *knew* that the case of Sybil Dorsett, precipitated not by one trauma but by a multiplicity of traumas, was the most complex ever reported.

The multiple roots of Sybil's complexity—the schizophrenic mother aided and abetted by the peripheral, passive father, the naive and hypocritical environment, and the hysteria engendered by the fundamentalist faith, particularly as exemplified by Grandpa Dorsett—had been dissected and interpreted. But the doctor still did not know when the first dissociation had taken place, though she did know that not all the selves had emerged during the first dissociation and that all who so far had presented themselves had been in existence by the time Sybil was twelve years old. Whether, with fourteen alternating selves in evidence, there were still selves to come, the doctor could not determine.

Even though evidence of mental illness on both sides of the family suggested a possible genetic factor, Dr. Wilbur was certain that the illness had been environmentally induced. Dr. Wilbur knew that the analysis must continue to uproot specific incidents of environmental abuse in order to alleviate the illness.

The selves, the doctor was now convinced, were not

conflicting parts of the total self, struggling for identity, but rather defenses against the intolerable environment that had produced the childhood traumas. Sybil's mind and body were possessed by these others—not invading spirits, not dybbuks from without, but proliferating parts of the original child. Each self was younger than Sybil, with their ages shifting according to the time of the particular trauma that each had emerged to battle.

With the revelation of the five new selves, the strategy of treatment remained what it had been before—to uproot and analyze the traumas, thus rendering unnecessary the defense against each particular trauma and the self who did the defending. Integration would be accomplished by getting the various selves to return to Sybil, the depleted, waking self, the acquisitions and modes of behavior that they had stolen from the original Sybil. They had to return the knowledge, the experiences, and the memories that had become theirs in the third of the total Sybil's life that *they* and not Sybil had lived.

A stepped-up onslaught on the underlying traumas was now clearly indicated, an onslaught during which each self would have to be analyzed as a "person" in her and his own right. Ultimately, of course, all would have to be integrated with waking Sybil. Integration, however, was still a distant goal, the more distant because of the complicating emergence of new selves. The glimmers of integration that had already occurred had been short-lived.

Dr. Wilbur also realized soberly that there were risks to be faced. The very act of facing an uprooted trauma, by intensifying the pain, often functioned as a setback. There was no assurance that uprooting the trauma would lead to partial integration of the self who defended against it. Sybil might be torn further apart by the very therapy intended to cure her. But the illness was so severe, the need for integration so great, that all possible risks were warranted in a newly intensified struggle.

22

The Clock Comprehensible

Peggy Lou and Peggy Ann, Vicky and Mary, Marcia and Vanessa, Mike and Sid, Marjorie and Ruthie, Helen and Sybil Ann, Clara and Nancy. These fourteen alternating selves had drifted in and out of Dr. Wilbur's office, each with her or his own emotions, attitudes, tastes, talents, ambitions, desires, modes of behavior, speech patterns, thought processes, and body images. Twelve of the selves were female; two, male. All were younger than Sybil.

Each was different from the others and from Sybil; each knew of Sybil's existence and of the existence of the other selves. Sybil, however—and this was the great irony of her predicament—had not known about the others, until Dr. Wilbur had told her about them. The irony was compounded by the fact that even after the doctor had alerted Sybil to the truth, Sybil had refused to meet the others on tape, had refused to come closer to them, to accept them. In late 1957 and early 1958, the names Peggy Lou, Peggy Ann, Vicky, Marcia, Vanessa, Mary, Mike, Sid, Marjorie, Ruthie, Helen, Sybil Ann, Clara and Nancy were still, as far as Sybil was concerned, merely the products of Dr. Wilbur's intellectual presentation. Dr. Wilbur had met them, but Sybil had not. Sybil believed the doctor, but empirically the others were still unreal.

What continued to be real to Sybil, as it had been before the label *multiple personality* had been attached to her condition, was the fact that she lost time. In late 1957 and early 1958 Sybil was still promising herself that she would not lose time, and the promise in adult-hood as in childhood still carried the overtone of "I will be good, not evil." When, despite her promise she again lost time, she simply resolved anew that it would not happen again. Only when time passed that was not lost did she feel that she was getting better.

November and December, 1957, had been such a time. Not once during this period had Sybil suffered the anguish of finding herself in a strange situation without knowing how she had gotten there. Both Sybil and Dr. Wilbur had dared to hope that they were entering the promised land of integration.

The promised land disappeared, however, on the morning of January 3, 1958, when Dr. Wilbur opened the door to her waiting room at the time of the Dorsett appointment. Nobody was there. And it wasn't until five days later that the morning mail brought a clue to Sybil's possible whereabouts.

The letter, addressed to Dr. Wilbur at her former office—607 Medical Arts Building, 17th and Dodge Streets, Omaha, Nebraska—and forwarded from there held a clue. Written in a childish scrawl and dated January 2, 1946, the letter, which was on the stationery of the Broadwood Hotel in Philadelphia, read:

Dear Dr. Wilbur,
    You said you would help me. You said you liked me. You said I was good. Why don't you help me?
                                Peggy Ann Dorsett.

It had been fourteen years since Dr. Wilbur had left Omaha, and Peggy Ann's writing there indicated serious confusion. The tone of the letter was petulant, the mood one of disappointment and dissatisfaction with the way the analysis was going. The Philadelphia postmark contributed further to the doctor's disappointment. The hope she had shared with Sybil in November and December was shattered.

Inaction on the doctor's part was no longer possible even though that had been the course she had chosen when neither Sybil nor any of the others had kept the

January 3 appointment, the course that the doctor had followed during similar episodes. Action, the doctor always feared, might trigger a chain of events that would make Sybil Dorsett a name in police records and could land Sybil in a mental hospital. Determined to protect her patient against both eventualities, the doctor had again not called the police.

Despite the fact that five days had elapsed since Peggy Ann had written her letter from Philadelphia, the doctor decided to try calling the Broadwood Hotel. She hesitated only because of not knowing for whom to ask. The name in the hotel registry could be Peggy Ann Dorsett or Peggy Ann Baldwin, since Peggy Ann used both names. It could also be Sybil Dorsett, a name that, following Vicky's lead, the other personalities often used. Indeed, Sybil could have registered under any of her fifteen selves' names. Perhaps it was a newcomer. Dr. Wilbur didn't presume to know whether there were other selves yet to come.

"The Broadwood. Good morning." The Broadwood reservation desk was on the line.

"Good morning," said the doctor. "Do you have a Miss Dorsett registered?"

"Room 1113," the reservation clerk replied. "One moment, please."

"Don't bother with 1113," the doctor said with sudden caution. Not knowing which Miss Dorsett she would find, she made a swift decision. "Will you please give me the hotel matron?" It was better, the doctor reasoned, not to speak to Peggy Ann in her confused state.

"I'm a physician," Dr. Wilbur told the matron a moment later. "One of my patients—a Miss Dorsett in room 1113—is not well. I wonder whether you would be good enough to look in on her and let me know how she is. I'd appreciate your not telling her that I've talked with you." The doctor gave her phone number to the matron, asked the woman to reverse the charges when calling back, and sat down to wait.

Fifteen minutes later the matron's call came. "Dr. Wilbur?"

"Yes."

"This is Mrs. Trout at the Broadwood in Philadelphia."

"Yes. How is she?"

"Fine, Doctor, fine. She looked pale and thin but fine. Looked very pretty in her pajamas with their orange and green stripes. She was sitting at the bedside table, doing a pencil sketch on our letterhead."

"Did Miss Dorsett say anything?" Dr. Wilbur asked.

"Not much. She just said that she was going out soon to walk around and do some sketching. 'Don't go out,' I begged her. 'This is no weather to monkey around with. The weather man predicted a terrible storm.' She said she'd see. She was pale, but she didn't seem sick to me, Doctor. Really she didn't."

Dr. Wilbur thanked Mrs. Trout, waited a few minutes, and then decided to telephone the Broadwood to persuade Peggy Lou to come home; for although Peggy Ann had written the letter, Mrs. Trout had evidently spoken to Peggy Lou. It was Peggy Lou who drew in black and white, Peggy Lou who would buy the pajamas Mrs. Trout had described. What seemed probable was that Peggy Lou and Peggy Ann had taken the trip together, as they often did—Peggy Lou as Sybil's defense against anger and Peggy Ann as the defense against fear.

There was nobody in room 1113, however, when the doctor put in her call. Later, when she succeeded in reaching Mrs. Trout, who was then doing desk duty because the night desk clerk had been delayed in the storm, Mrs. Trout said, "Miss Dorsett's out in that storm. I begged her not to go out because a storm was coming. But she said she could take care of herself." At 10:15 P.M. the doctor, again trying to reach room 1113, was told that Miss Dorsett had checked out.

The doctor could only hope that Sybil would "come to" as herself and return safely or that the alternating personality who took over would return, or even that Vicky, as she had done during some of the many other blackouts Sybil had experienced in the course of the analysis, would somehow manage to telephone the doctor. But no call came.

The next morning the doctor, stepping into the waiting room to place some magazines on an end table, found the slender form of Sybil Dorsett waiting. Not knowing which personality it was, the doctor, using no name, simply said, "Come in."

There was an awkward silence.

"I've done it again," the patient said sadly. "It is going to be even harder to tell you than I had thought."

"Sybil?" the doctor asked.

"Sybil. I 'came to' in a Philadelphia street in a hideous warehouse district. This was even worse than some of the other blackouts. A real nightmare. And after we thought it would never happen again. Oh, Doctor, I'm so ashamed."

"Relax before you talk about it," the doctor said reassuringly.

"I always promise myself it won't happen again, that I'll start over again. But this time I really hoped. How many times have I started over again?"

"I don't know how many times," the doctor replied. "Will you please quit trying? It won't do any good at all. Why start over? Why not go on from where you are?"

"I don't know what was done in my name," Sybil blurted. "Maybe mayhem. Murder."

"Sybil," the doctor replied firmly, "I've told you again and again that none of the others go against your ethical code."

"You've told me," Sybil replied anxiously. "But do you really know? We can't be sure."

"Sybil," the doctor ventured for what in the course of over three years was easily the hundredth time, "I should like you to hear the other selves on tape."

"No." Sybil shook her head decisively. "The only thing I want to hear about these others, as you call them, is that they no longer exist."

"It will reassure you," the doctor persisted. "When the Peggys tell me their story of Philadelphia, why don't I tape it? Then you can hear for yourself."

"The Peggys?" Sybil asked in consternation. "You know they were the ones? How can you possibly know that?"

319

"Peggy Ann wrote me from the Broadwood," the doctor replied in a direct, factual manner.

"The Broadwood?" Sybil answered in shocked surprise. "You know I was there?"

"You found yourself in Philadelphia because the Peggys took you there. They are part of you, a part over which you have no control. But we're going to change that when we bring you girls together."

"Philadelphia proves I'm not getting any better," Sybil replied brokenly. "I'll never be well."

"You know that I want to help you," the doctor said gently. "You know that I have known about these problems for more than three years now, and you know that they are part of your illness."

"Yes, yes," Sybil replied anxiously. "You've told me that many times."

"And when you feel otherwise," the doctor said pointedly, "you are needlessly suspicious and frightened."

"Not strange?" Sybil blurted.

"No, not strange," the doctor replied emphatically. "Likable?"

"Yes, Sybil. Very likable. I like you. I don't know if you realize how much." The doctor had responded to the bid for approval with the genuine emotion of her growing fondness for her patient.

There was a suggestion of tears in Sybil's eyes—the tears that in the first year and a half of the analysis she had not been able to shed. Sybil asked quietly, "You still think I can get well?"

"With all my heart I think it, Sybil. With all my mind. And with all my experience as a psychoanalyst."

Sybil's slender hand moved into Dr. Wilbur's hand, as doctor and patient sat together on the couch. "Then," Sybil asked in a low, stilted voice, "why am I getting worse?"

"In analysis," the doctor replied objectively, "the further you go, the closer you get to the core conflicts. The closer you get to the core conflicts, the more you have to face in terms of resistance and in terms of the conflicts themselves."

320

"But I'm not facing anything," Sybil pointed out bitterly. "I'm running away."

"It's not you—waking Sybil, representing the conscious mind—but the others, who belong to the unconscious, who are running away," the doctor explained.

"You call them the unconscious and say they are part of me," Sybil replied thoughtfully. "But you also say they can take me where they please. Oh, Doctor, I'm afraid, terribly afraid. It's a predicament to which I've never become accustomed. These others drive me, possess me, destroy me."

"It's not possession, Sybil," the doctor declared emphatically. "Not some invasion from without. It comes from within, and it can be explained not by the supernatural but in very natural terms."

"It doesn't seem very natural to me," Sybil was quick to answer.

"Not natural in the sense of being common to lots of people," the doctor conceded. "But natural because it can be explained in terms of your own environment. All the personalities are younger than you. There is a reason for that. When your mother told you, 'You have so much,' she was creating a distortion because you didn't have the things that you needed for growing up. Consequently, you couldn't grow up and be all one person. You had to leave bits and parts behind. You didn't know you were doing it. You didn't know about these other selves. You still haven't met them, still refuse to meet them on tape, so you are not directly aware of them. You still don't really accept them except as a sort of intellectual exercise."

Sybil's mouth twitched uneasily.

"I have not yet been able to determine the precise ages of the selves, but some of them are little girls," Dr. Wilbur continued, "walking around in your woman's body. When the Peggys fled to Philadelphia, they were running away from your mother. They deny that your mother was theirs, but it is a surface denial. Deeply etched within them are fear and anger against your mother. Fear and anger make them take flight, break loose from the feeling of entrapment your mother created for them. And because the Peggys and some of the others are little girls, in a sense they keep you a little girl."

"Not only crazy," Sybil replied with bitter irony, "but immature?"

The doctor put her arm around Sybil and spoke with intensity: "Nobody ever said you were crazy, except you yourself, and I want you to banish that word from your vocabulary in relationship to yourself. Your mother interfered with your growing up. You didn't succumb totally to your mother because you had a core of strength that made your life different from hers. And when you found out that your mother was wrong, you began to be able to do the things with yourself that you wanted to do—even though there were bits and pieces from the past, forming other selves, that made you unlike other people and afraid of what you were."

The doctor's eyes held Sybil's as she said, "Sick, yes, but not schizophrenic. Your mother was schizophrenic. Her perception was totally different from yours. You told me once that she could not see the whole of a building but only a part; that when you heard the opera *Hansel and Gretel,* she could only see the candy canes on the door, not the door itself or the set as a whole. You see wholes. Yes, you are fragmented, but yours is not the fragmentation of a schizophrenic. Your kind of fragmentation is the result not of perception but of dissociation. Don't ever call yourself crazy again. You are sane, sane enough to have survived the torture chamber in which your mother trapped you and to have made so much of yourself with the terrible childhood you had to hold you back. Now tell me about your experiences in Philadelphia. Talking will help."

When Sybil told the January 2 to 7, 1958, Philadelphia story from her point of view, the doctor wished she could also talk to Peggy Ann and Peggy Lou to get their side of the story. There was at this stage of the analysis no way, however, of summoning the Peggys. The doctor just had to wait for them to appear spontaneously. That did not occur until a month later.

Meantime, Sybil returned to school. But she continued to live in terror about what might have or perhaps actually had happened in Philadelphia. She did not and could not accept Dr. Wilbur's assurance that these creatures within her were incapable of evil. Since the inception of the analysis, they had taken her, not only to Philadelphia but also to Elizabeth, Trenton, Altoona, and even San Francisco. Where they had taken her before the analysis began she often did not know. These others controlled her purse, transported her body, acted without her will. She always learned only *after* the event what the others had wrought. And always there was the fear that what had been wrought was worse, far worse, than what Dr. Wilbur had told her.

Even if these others did nothing wrong in a legal or criminal sense, the chiaroscuro of their actions was causing experience to be so constantly changing and recomposing that—whatever the apparent intention of any action she herself initiated or proposed to take— these others were the victors, acting in the limelight of her despair.

Then came the day, a month after the return from Philadelphia, when the doctor said, "I have Peggy Lou and Peggy Ann on tape. When you hear what they did in Philadelphia, you will be greatly relieved." The doctor was deliberately casual but had grave doubts that, after the persistent, intense refusal to listen, Sybil would now agree. Just getting her to listen was the prime problem.

Sybil's irises became dilated with fear.

"Well?" the doctor asked.

Sybil did not reply.

"Sybil, this can be a turning point in the analysis."

"I don't see how," Sybil replied. Her words were muted, her throat obviously constricted.

"It is only by getting to know the others that you can make them part of you—that you can make their experiences your experiences, their memories, your memories."

"I don't want any part of it. Doctor, why are you torturing me?"

"If this were a physical illness," the doctor explained, "you would not tear up the prescription for a medicine that could tide you over a crisis, help to make you well."

"I don't really think the analogy is apt," Sybil replied doggedly.

"It is more apt than you realize," the doctor insisted. "These other selves are not your illness but the symptoms of your illness. They possess you, overwhelm you, subvert your intentions and desires. It is only by coming closer to these others that you can move toward a more normal life."

Sybil's lips curled in an ironic smile. "It sounds so easy," she said. "But, Doctor, you and I know that easy is just what it is not."

"Nobody ever said it was easy," the doctor replied. "But I can assure you that getting well will be infinitely more difficult if you don't get to know—and accept—these others."

"Philadelphia proved to me that I'll *never* get well," Sybil answered darkly. She rose from her chair and went to look out the window, abstracted.

"Sybil," the doctor called, "resistance is doing you no good."

"That nasty word again," Sybil replied as she turned to face the doctor.

"All patients put up resistance," the doctor assured her.

"But," Sybil replied, with a twisted curve of her lip, "I'm not just a patient. I'm patients." The stress on the "s" carried a terrifying overtone. "At least that's what you tell me. And I'm supposed to listen and face the fact that I'm a freak."

"Sybil, Sybil," the doctor urged, "you're distorting the truth. The others are part of you. We all have different parts of our personalities. The abnormality lies not in the division, but in the dissociation, the amnesia, and the terrible traumas that gave rise to the others."

"A euphemism," Sybil answered sadly. "By others you mean *other people*. I don't want to meet them. Why should I?"

"I've already told you why," the doctor asserted.

"I'll tell you again. Because listening will *really* do some good. It is a crucial step in getting well."

Sybil was silent, and the doctor realized that it was going to be even harder than she had anticipated. "It's going to have to take place eventually," the doctor urged. "Why not now? After all, you gave me permission to do the taping. It's not just for me."

"I'm afraid," Sybil said. A chill ran through her body.

"Listening will lessen the fear."

"But will my listening stop the blackouts?" Sybil asked desperately.

"Ultimately, yes," the doctor replied decisively. "The better you get to know the other selves, the closer we will come to making you one."

Sybil slumped into a chair and looked at the doctor warily. The irises of her eyes were even more dilated than before. She clutched the chair and, fully aware of the possible consequences, murmured, "All right."

The doctor rose from the chair at the head of the couch, reached into a desk drawer, and, with a tape in one hand and the other hand on the recorder, looked directly at Sybil. "Shall I start the tape?" the doctor asked. There was momentary silence. Then Sybil nodded.

The doctor's hands were on the recorder. The wheels turned. Sybil, who was now huddled in a corner of the couch, thought: The wheels that turn against me.

The voice on tape was saying, "I heard the crash of glass in the chemistry lab. It reminded me of Lulu and the pickle dish. I jist had to run to the door with Sybil . . ."

"My mother's voice," Sybil screamed. "How did you get my mother's voice?" Sybil rushed to the window. For a moment the doctor thought Sybil had become Peggy Lou, but as the voice on the tape was saying, "I rushed to the door with Sybil, walked with her to the elevator," Sybil, in a voice clearly hers and without the physical changes accompanying Peggy Lou's presence, repeated, "It's my mother's voice. Turn it off, I can't stand it. You'll drive me crazy. I'm not ready."

The doctor snapped off the recorder. Sybil turned

from the window, seated herself on the chair, and stared into space.

"It's not your mother's voice," the doctor said quietly. "It's the voice of Peggy Lou. Shall I play more to reassure you?" And even though Sybil did not reply, the doctor once again set the tape in motion.

Peggy Lou's voice was saying, "I could feel Sybil clutching our zipper folder. She was mad because the elevator didn't come. I took over. I was the one who stepped into the elevator. Yes, I was!"

"What does this mean?" Sybil asked frantically. "Turn that thing off." The doctor did as she had been instructed. "*Our* zipper folder," Sybil murmured as she began to pace the room. "She thinks she has joint possession with me. Oh, Dr. Wilbur, Dr. Wilbur, what shall I do?"

"Let's just listen," the doctor urged as the wheels again began to move, now assuming the frightening motion of revelation as Peggy Lou's words flooded the room.

"I left the lab," Peggy Lou was saying, "because I didn't want to be scolded for breaking the glass. I hadn't broken it. No I hadn't. But I didn't break it when Lulu said I did neither. That time I was punished. Yes, I was. It wasn't fair."

"Turn it off, turn that thing off," Sybil pleaded. Then in the silence that followed, Sybil, who was overwhelmed by feelings of uncanniness, began to reminisce softly. "I haven't thought of that pickle dish in years and years. But I remember now. Mother did punish me even though Lulu broke it. But how does this Peggy Lou know about it?"

"Peggy Lou is part of you. She defended you against the anger you felt at being unjustly punished," the doctor replied.

"I don't want her to defend me. I don't want to have anything to do with her," Sybil replied bitterly.

"Sybil," the doctor cautioned, "you're setting up all sorts of resistances that will do you no good."

"That nasty word again." Sybil made an effort to smile, but the attempt froze.

"It's because of the pickle dish," Dr. Wilbur explained, "that Peggy Lou goes around breaking glass."

"Well, I wish she'd stop," Sybil replied with irritation. "I have to pay for the glass Peggy Lou breaks. I can't afford Peggy Lou."

"As we remove the trauma connected with the pickle dish," the doctor insisted, "Peggy Lou will stop. When you are able to get angry in your own right, Peggy Lou will become one with you. Ready for more?" The doctor turned on the recorder. Peggy Lou's voice resumed.

"The chemistry lab smelled funny. It made me think of the old drugstore in Willow Corners, where I live. That's where Sybil's mother found us just after we came home from the farm. I was awful mad. I jist had to get away."

"Stop it. Please, please." The entreaty was frantic.

The doctor did as she was bidden, and in the silence that ensued Sybil murmured, "The old drugstore. I remember it. Old Dr. Taylor. Music. Wonderful music." Momentarily lost in recollection, Sybil grew calmer.

Seizing the moment of calm, the doctor explained, "You see, Peggy Lou shares your memories. She also has memories about which you know nothing, for which you are amnesic. When all of these memories return, we shall have made progress toward making you one."

The doctor turned on the recorder, and Peggy Lou resumed, "When I was in the subway and on the train to Philadelphia, I kept thinkin' that Sybil wouldn't do the things I wanted her to do. I wanted money for art supplies. She said we needed it for laboratory fees. I like the chemistry all right, but it makes me mad because Sybil works so hard on the formulas. She wouldn't have to work so hard if I helped with the multiplication. I learned it in school, but she didn't. I could help her if I felt like it. But I don't. I want to do the things I enjoy. That's what I thought on the way to Philadelphia. We hadn't been any place in quite a while. And I'm mad about that. Real mad. You see, I love to travel, but that Sybil will never go anyplace. So I went to Philadelphia to get even."

This time the doctor herself brought the tape to a halt.

"Is that all?" Sybil asked.

"No, but let's rest a minute," the doctor replied.

Sybil seemed calmer, capable for the first time during this session of responding not with her emotions but with her mind.

"There's so much to absorb," she said quietly. "What was that about the formulas?"

"You know, Sybil," the doctor explained, "that it was Peggy Lou who took over from the third to the fifth grade. I've told you that she learned the multiplication tables. When you have trouble with them, that's the reason. If we can get Peggy Lou and you to the point where she will let you have the knowledge that she has and you don't, you'll no longer have difficulty. We must break down the wall between you. That is what I mean by moving toward integration."

"Yes, I see," Sybil agreed. "This brings what you've been saying into sharper focus."

Once again the recorder was turned on, and Sybil was listening to Peggy Lou's voice, saying, "So I thought I'd go to the Broadwood and draw and sketch and enjoy myself. But when I got there, I looked at what I had with me and all I had was our zipper folder. I told them at the desk that my luggage would be coming along the next day, and they believed me. So I went with the bellboy up to room 1113. I liked the room because it had real high ceilings and cream-colored walls and there was a wonderful view out the window, and the room was very warm and very quiet. I locked the door after the bellboy left, put the zipper folder, my mittens, and my scarf on the dresser. But I didn't take off my coat. I stood by the window a long time. Then I realized that I didn't have any pajamas. That was great because I could go out and shop and have lots of fun. I wanted to get the wildest pair of pajamas I could find—the kind that would keep Sybil awake at night and that would make her mother say, 'You have no taste. Cultured, refined people dress quietly.'

"Well, I got into the subway and went to a department store I like real well, got pajamas with bold stripes, and that was really great. Peggy Ann went with me."

"The pajamas. The mittens. The red scarf. The zipper folder," Sybil echoed, her expression growing taut with the terrifying recollection.

Peggy Lou's voice continued. "I went back to the hotel and up to my room," Peggy Lou was saying, "washed my clothes, took a bath, washed my hair, got into my beautiful pajamas, turned on TV and sang along with the TV set. Television is company. Then I went to bed. Later in the night the people in the next room turned on the radio so loud I woke up and couldn't sleep no more. Boy was I mad!. So I got up and looked out the window. Across the street was the Roman Catholic High School for Boys and an old building that used to be the *Philadelphia Morning Record*. The subway station was outside the hotel. In the distance I could see the red and green lights on the bridge. I looked out the window a long time and finally didn't hear the radio going anymore, so I went back to bed.

"When I awoke, the fog of the night before was gone from the air, and the sun was shining. I was awful glad to see the sun, and I stood by the windows a long time looking at the reflections on the buildings and on the bridge. Near the bridge was a large church with a very tall, slender steeple. It stood out darkly against the hazy buildings across the river behind it. I liked this scene and returned to look at it several times while I was dressing. I called room service and ordered a big breakfast because Sybil never gives us enough to eat. The waiter was very nice, and we got friendly. While I was eating, I sat in the big chair near the window and put crumbs on the windowsill. Pigeons and other birds came and ate the crumbs. I shared my cocoa and toast with the birds. I decided that I would do that every day as long as I was in this room.

"Then I went out and walked along the streets. I hadn't gone very far when I saw an old, dark-red brick building. I walked up the steps and into the Academy of Fine Arts. I saw some lithograph prints on exhibit. They were black and white like my drawings, so I looked at them. Then I went up the stairs to see what was in the galleries above. I spent so much time at this museum that I got acquainted with one of the guards. We talked about art, and I got along very well with him.

"I also spent half a day at the Betsy Ross House. I went to the medical school museum, where I saw a brain of a forty-eight-year-old man with a bullet wound in his head and a brain of a thirty-eight-year-old woman who had had a stroke. And there were a lot of little babies in glass jars. Those jars were awful interesting. I had lots of fun in Philadelphia.

"In the street and in the hotel room I spent a lot of time sketching. I loved sketching on the hotel stationery. The paper was free, so I didn't have to buy any. My strokes were also free as I drew the woman standing alone on a cliff. I did her in black. I was happy.

"I was happy in Philadelphia. I went where I pleased, sketched, slept ten hours a day, spent three or four hours a day eating. It was the same kind of feeling that I had several times before and I was sure no one would tell me what to do ever again. And then there was the day when I was caught in a snowstorm. The wind was on my back, and snow was all around me. I had no overshoes or gloves, and my ears ached with the cold. The coat I was wearing wasn't warm enough. When I turned around to come back, I had the wind all the way. The woman who came into the hotel room and asked me how I was had warned me not to go out, and I should have listened. But I didn't. But when the wind whipped me, I wasn't so sure. I felt like smashing one of the windows in the ugly building I was passing. I stopped and put my hand on the glass. It was smooth and cold. When I touched it, I thought I heard someone say very quietly, 'But you don't want to break the glass. You said you wouldn't anymore.' I whirled around and expected to see you, Doctor. You weren't there.

But I didn't want to break the glass whether you were there or not because I wasn't angry anymore. I was cold, very cold. I thought: I'll let Sybil have the body. I was too tired to think about it then, but I suppose that was another way of getting even."

A click signaled the end of the tape. And in the room there was silence. "Red and green lights on the bridge," Sybil mused more to herself than to the doctor. "Large church with a very tall, slender steeple. I didn't notice them. The zipper folder, the mittens, red scarf, the pajamas. The waiter, the woman at the desk. I guessed right even though I had not met Peggy Lou."

Then, turning directly to the doctor, Sybil said, with composure: "Peggy Lou feeding the birds is like St. Francis of Assisi."

"You see," the doctor said. "Peggy Lou is no monster."

"Yes, she seems to have quite a lot of aesthetic feeling," Sybil concurred. "The drawing of the woman on the cliff is quite good. You told me that she always paints in black and white."

"She sees the world in black and white. No grays for Peggy Lou," said the doctor.

"Let Sybil have the body?" Sybil asked. "What an odd thing to say. As if the body were hers!"

"You see, Sybil," the doctor explained, "this account of the Philadelphia trip, revealing at what point an alternating personality in command of the body relinquishes it, gives us real insight into the dynamics of multiple personality. It is evident, you see, that, exhausted by the storm, Peggy Lou turned the body over to you because she preferred not to be."

"She has the choice?" Sybil asked somewhat wistfully.

"Oh, yes," the doctor replied. "Once the alternating self has acted out the emotions that at any given time have triggered her, there is no longer any reason for her to function. Philadelphia was Peggy Lou's way of acting out in the present what you and she had repressed in the past. By doing exactly as she pleased for five days, she exhausted the angry, hostile feelings that had been awakened in the chemistry lab. When you are unable to handle such feelings, Peggy Lou does it for you."

And so in Willow Corners and Elderville Peggy Lou had been the runaway who didn't run. Only in Philadelphia, some three decades later, had flight taken place. Her mother, whom Peggy Lou refused to acknowledge as hers but from whom she was forever in flight, was the key from the past on which the present action turned.

When the glass had crashed in the chemistry class, the sound had evoked two episodes from the past. In the old drugstore in Willow Corners Sybil had rested her elbow on the counter. A bottle of patent medicine crashed to the floor, and there had come Hattie's accusing voice: "You broke it." In the Anderson kitchen in Elderville, cousin Lulu had accused Sybil of breaking the pickle dish that Lulu had shattered. Again there had been Sybil's mother's accusation: "You broke it."

In the chemistry class, as in the old drugstore in Willow Corners and in the Anderson kitchen in Elderville, Sybil's head had throbbed and the room seemed to swirl. In all three incidents the physical reactions and the emotions were the same.

The next day Sybil listened to the tape of Peggy Ann. It was interesting that Peggy Ann was free of Peggy Lou's verbal mannerisms and grammatical errors. "I was walking toward Seventeenth and Dodge Streets," Peggy Ann's voice was saying, "so I could find out where Dr. Wilbur had gone. I walked several blocks, and none of the signs had numbers on them, so I turned and started another way to find streets with numbers. I thought if I could just find Sixteenth Street, Omaha's main street, I could then find Seventeenth. I walked and walked until I was very tired and very cold, but I could not find the streets with numbers on them. I began to get cross and agitated and felt like smashing a window. 'But you don't want to break the glass,' I heard. 'You said you wouldn't anymore.' I whirled around to see who had spoken to me. I wanted to talk to her, so I started down the street after her, but I could not find her. I felt sad again and very lonely. I wanted to find the only person I liked. Then I remembered I liked Dr. Wilbur best of all, and I was looking for her. I wanted to tell her about the hands and the music and the boxes. I didn't know just what about these, but they are what I thought I wanted to talk about. And I wanted to ask her why I wasn't getting better when she said I would. I was afraid."

"Dr. Wilbur is right here," the doctor's voice declared on the tape.

"Dr. Wilbur went away," Peggy Ann was insisting.

"Can't you see that I am Dr. Wilbur?"

"Dr. Wilbur went away and left us helpless."

"Where were you when Dr. Wilbur left you?"

"Omaha."

"Where are you now?"

"Omaha."

The tape had come to an end. It seemed curious to the doctor that Peggy Ann had assumed the burden of the broken glass, which really belonged to Peggy Lou. But then the two selves were so closely allied that they often shared the same experiences and even adopted as their own the emotions of the other. Anger and fear, as exemplified by the Peggys, were not disconnected.

The doctor then turned to Sybil, who had been silent during Peggy Ann's recital. "She has robbed me of my past," Sybil finally said. "They both have. Peggy Lou as well as Peggy Ann."

"The past," the doctor replied with conviction, "as we move toward integration, will no longer trouble you. Your mother's hands won't frighten you. We'll resolve the conflicts, and the thieves will return to you what they have stolen."

The doctor then explained that Peggy Ann was the terrified, frightened part of Sybil and that she had brought that fear home with her from Philadelphia.

"But Peggy Ann didn't even know she had been in Philadelphia," Sybil replied thoughtfully. "What a mix up in the emotions to have produced anything like this."

"Well," the doctor replied, "I also have tapes of the other selves. Shall we start listening tomorrow?"

"You've said there are fourteen besides me," Sybil replied. "That will take forever." Changing the subject, Sybil repeated what had been the source of her terror in the previous session: "Peggy Lou has my mother's voice."

"That's interesting," the doctor remarked. "You know, Peggy Lou insists that your mother was not hers."

"Peggy Lou," Sybil replied wistfully, "had all the advantages. She can deny what I have to face." Then in a sudden burst of curiosity long repressed Sybil asked, "Where did she come from? How was she created? Questions, questions, questions. But no answers."

"There are many answers," the doctor averred, "that I, too, don't have yet."

Then Sybil, suddenly less conciliatory, affirmed, "Well, I'm not going to listen to the others for a long time. They'll only make me miserable. Why should I?"

The doctor reminded Sybil: "Knowing is better than not knowing. It is important, as I've told you before, for you to remember and to accept as your own the things that happen to the fourteen other selves. As your own, Sybil, because they are part of you. Recognizing this is one of the first steps toward getting well."

23

The Retreating White Coat

When Sybil awoke the next morning, her thoughts had not fully been extricated from the dream that had propelled her into awakening.

In that dream her parents and she had had to leave

town unexpectedly because to stay would have meant doom. On sudden inspiration she had decided to take her parents to another town to inspect a house, in which they could have lived and been safe. She had been very proud to have been able to introduce her father to the owners of this house and prove to him that she really had known these people. It had been, in fact, the same feeling of satisfaction that she had experienced when her father had confirmed what she had told Dr. Wilbur.

Then she had been standing in the large living room of the house in the other town, face to face with the children of these people she had known—seven sets of twins and one singleton lined up in a row. Four sets of twins had had dark brown hair; the other three sets, blonde hair. The one singleton standing apart from the others had had hair identical to Sybil's.

"How about introducing your brothers and sisters to me?" Sybil had asked one of the older children.

Suddenly, however, the parents and their fifteen children had started to move out, and Sybil and her parents had begun to move in. As Sybil realized that the introduction to these children, who, all but one, were standing in a row in twosomes, had not taken place, she had awakened.

But that was a dream. In waking life Sybil continued resolutely to resist meeting the children—Marcia and Vanessa, Mike and Sid, Ruthie and Marjorie, Peggy Lou and Peggy Ann—who were twosomes. So resolute was the resistance that Dr. Wilbur decided to take the matter up with her co-analysand.

"Vicky," the doctor confided the week that Sybil had heard the Peggys on tape, "I told Sybil about you and the others. It doesn't seem to make any difference. I can't get Sybil to accept your existence. I can't get her to remember the things that happen to you."

"I'm afraid," Vicky replied, "I can offer no solution. But maybe it will help if I tell you a little about what living with the others is like."

The doctor nodded.

"I'm in the center," Vicky explained, "Sybil is at my right. Sybil has her back turned to all of us."

"I see," the doctor replied. "But tell me, Vicky, is there any connection between Sybil and the rest of you?"

Vicky paused thoughtfully, then said, "Yes, way underneath, so far underneath that Sybil doesn't remember about it. She doesn't want to remember because it hurts."

"And," observed the doctor, "she has split off what hurts, removed herself from it, relegated it to the others?"

"I suppose you could say that," Vicky replied pensively. "You see, I'm a whole person, Sybil is not. Don't ever tell her. It's bothering her. It's part of her complex."

What was Vicky trying to say? Dr. Wilbur wondered. The manifest content was obvious: Sybil was a depleted personality; Vicky, a fuller one. But there was something more than that.

"You know, Vicky," the doctor replied slowly, "you've just made a very important statement. What you're saying is that Sybil is not a whole person because parts of her have been siphoned off to the other selves. Am I correct?"

"Correct," Vicky answered.

"There must have been a multitude of dissociations occurring over the years that produced these others in the first place."

"Correct," said Vicky.

"The dissociations must have been caused by traumas —the result of intolerable realities against which each of the selves had to defend Sybil."

"So far you have a perfect score," said Vicky.

"But," the doctor added, "I've wondered when it all began. There must have been a time before the first dissociation, a time when Sybil was a whole person."

"How did it happen?" Vicky mused. "Who was in existence? I was in a way. Would it help if I told you about the first time I came?"

"You don't mean the time in the sixth grade after Danny Martin left Sybil?" the doctor asked.

"That," Vicky explained, "was when I decided to enter the world as an active personality. It was *not* the first time I came."

"Tell me about the very first time," the doctor urged.

"I was in existence long before Sybil was in the sixth grade," Vicky explained. "We were three and a half when I first came."

Dr. Wilbur listened intently to Vicky's remarkable narrative:

"On a day in early September, 1926, we were driving over rutted roads with Sybil's parents. We were going from Willow Corners to Rochester, Minnesota. Minnesota was another state, and we were pretty excited about going there.

"The car pulled up in front of a red-brick building. Mr. Dorsett drove back to Willow Corners. Mrs. Dorsett took us into St. Mary's Hospital.

"The doctor made the diagnosis, follicular tonsillitis, but that wasn't all. He couldn't understand why we were malnourished—coming from a good family as we did. Oh, you should have seen Mrs. Dorsett's face when the doctor told her that she should feed her daughter better. But you and I know that it was the enemas and the laxatives after meals that caused the malnutrition.

"We liked it at St. Mary's. The doctor was tall and young. When he came into our room, he always picked us up, hugged us, and said, 'How's my big girl today?' He looked at our throat and then let us look at his.

"The doctor laughed, and we laughed too. We liked being with him.

"As he held us high in the air, we could see that one of his cufflinks was loose. We told him that we would fix it.

" 'Do you think you can?' he asked.

" 'I know I can,' we replied promptly, 'because I put my Daddy's in for him every Sabbath.'

" 'All right, honey,' the doctor said as he put us back into a sitting position.

"Nobody had ever called us *honey* before.

"Then we fixed the cufflink and turned it through that little hole in his shirt sleeve.

" 'That's wonderful,' the doctor said.

"When we left our room, we hoped he would come

back soon. But when he did come, he didn't look at our throat. He didn't pick us up. He just smiled and said, 'I have good news for you. You're going home.'

"Our arms went around his neck. We looked into his face and asked, 'Would you like to have a little girl?'

"He had liked the way we fixed his cufflink. We were sure he would like to have us do it all the time. We waited for him to say, 'Yes, I want a little girl.'

"He didn't say that. He didn't say anything. He just turned away from us, and we saw that white coat moving toward the door. The white coat faded into nothingness. Again rescue was gone."

Vicky paused. Fascinated by the narrative, Dr. Wilbur said nothing. Vicky explained, "When we came to the hospital, I was part of Sybil. But at the moment that the doctor left us, I was no longer part of her. As that white coat moved through that door, we were no longer one. I became myself."

Dr. Wilbur was not surprised that the first dissociation had occurred this early. There had, in fact, been a good deal of evidence to substantiate this possibility. Earlier the analysis had revealed that during a visit to the Anderson family home in Elderville when Sybil was four, she had become Marcia. Long before talking of the St. Mary's episode, Vicky had said, "Sybil was just a little girl when I came." And in reconstructing the powerful experience of the lost two years between the third and the fifth grades Sybil had made clear that this had not been the first dissociation.

That same week Dr. Wilbur talked to Sybil about the events Vicky had reported. At first Sybil had no recollection of them. Then suddenly she recalled: "I was sitting on the rug in the sunroom at home in Willow Corners. I was fourteen. Something about that was connected with what you just told me." After a pause she added, "All of a sudden, as I was sitting there, I began thinking of the doctor's white coat moving away from me. I realized that I did not remember anything after that. There was nothing. I remembered my parents' taking me to the hospital on a beautiful September day; I couldn't remember the drive from the hospital back to Willow Corners. The next thing I remembered after the doctor left me was being in the sunroom and wearing a dress I had never seen before. When I asked my mother where the dress came from, she replied, 'You know perfectly well Mrs. Engle made it.' But I didn't.

"From then on whenever I was afraid and there was no one to help me, I saw that white coat moving away from me."

Later during the same hour Peggy Lou talked about being afraid of white because of the "white coat that left us helpless."

"Us?" Dr. Wilbur asked. "Were you at St. Mary's?"

"I went there as part of Sybil," Peggy Lou replied. "But when that white coat left us, I became myself. Well, not exactly. Peggy Ann and I were one then. We were called Peggy Louisiana."

When Vicky returned a few days later, the analysis again revolved around the first dissociation. Vicky told Dr. Wilbur: "Sybil left the hospital in Rochester as the other Sybil—frightened, timid, withdrawn."

Smiling, Vicky added, "The Peggys and I remember leaving St. Mary's and coming home, but Sybil doesn't remember."

"Yes, she told me," the doctor replied quietly.

Although she who was still called Sybil ostensibly rode with her parents from Rochester to Willow Corners, in the car were two other children. Vicky and Peggy Louisiana became autonomous, alternating selves, and from that moment forward there was much that Sybil didn't see, much that was concealed from her and would remain concealed for thirty-nine years.

When the doctor denied her hope of rescue from without, the rescue came from within. The original child, Sybil, ceased to be.

These newcomers to existence contained between them everything that the new Sybil had lost. In Peggy Louisiana there had been invested all of the original child's assertiveness and hostility, all of her rage. To the one who would later be called Vicky had gone most of the original child's poise, confidence, capacity

339

to negotiate the world. In Vicky, too, was centered the continuity of memory and of seeing life whole.

Observing, recording, remembering, Vicky was nevertheless, at this stage, quiescent. It was Peggy Louisiana whom Hattie and Willard brought home that September day.

The original Sybil had been an active child, able at two to swing on a door, but as a result of oppression she had become shy and retiring. Returning from Rochester, Peggy took over the active behavior that had been subdued and lost in the original Sybil. Peggy walked on fences, played "follow the leader," and showed herself to be a daredevil. "The hospital did her a lot of good," Hattie told Willard. "She's better."

Dr. Wilbur could see that the larger part of what the original Sybil had been—much of her libido and many of her acquisitions and modes of behavior—had been relegated to other selves, created in this first dissociation. What remained as Sybil was a depleted personality, whose initial fear of her mother had expanded to include not only maternal figures but everybody. Driven by fear, this depleted personality had resolved never again to take the risk of involving herself with human beings. A mere waking self, drained of feeling, it was a self bereft, but it was also a self protected by powerful built-in defenses against the very forces that had divided her. Not wanting to go home from the hospital, the original child did not go home. She sent two internal defenders as her deputies to represent her.

For Sybil, the waking self, this was the beginning of time unremembered, of time stolen by those who came to defend her.

The original defenders, Peggy and Vicky, later produced progeny of their own. It was a very special family "tree," a genealogy of psychological functioning, emotional inheritance. By 1935, she who was known simply as Sybil and was then twelve had become all of the fourteen selves who had so far presented themselves in analysis.

Dr. Wilbur had established that Vicky's line consisted of Marcia, who had appeared in 1927, Mary

(1934), Vanessa (1935), and Sybil Ann, the precise date of whose arrival is not known; that Peggy's line consisted of Peggy Ann, into whom the original Peggy had developed; Peggy Lou, who appeared in 1926; Sid, who arrived early in 1928; and Mike, who made his entrance later that same year.

It had also become clear to the doctor that whereas Sybil lost everything with which Vicky and the original Peggy were endowed, Vicky and Peggy lost nothing that their descendants inherited. Vicky and Peggy retained as their own the emotions, characteristics, acquisitions, and modes of behavior that had infused the lives of their progeny.

Ruthie, Helen, Marjorie, and Clara, the doctor noted, were descended from neither Vicky nor Peggy nor directly from the original Sybil. These four were without antecedents.

The following day, Dr. Wilbur, alone in her study, thought of the night some four years earlier when she had first gone to the Academy of Medicine library to read about multiple personality. Since that night she had been searching for the time of the first dissociation and for the original trauma that had caused Sybil to proliferate into multiple selves. Now Dr. Wilbur knew that the first dissociation had taken place in St. Mary's Hospital when Sybil was three and a half, and that it had been spawned not by one trauma but by a succession of traumas induced by Hattie Dorsett, the taproot, aided and abetted by the powerful associated root of Willard Dorsett's failure to provide rescue. The trauma had been reinforced by Sybil's entrapment by religion, particularly as projected by a religiously hysterical grandfather.

Hysterics flourish in a naive social milieu and even better in an environment bedecked with the fire and brimstone of a fundamentalist faith.

It was now also possible for Dr. Wilbur to associate with these traumatizing events of childhood the pervading fears that Sybil and Peggy Lou had expressed in the early days of the analysis. The fear of getting close to people, evident in the first days of the analysis, was an extension of the fear of getting close to her mother. The hands the patient feared were her mother's hands, instruments of torture. The fear of music had many themes: the tying of Sybil to the piano leg while Hattie played; Hattie's obsessive virtuosity that denied Sybil's presence; Hattie's unrelenting harping when Sybil herself tried to play; Hattie's and Willard's frustration by music; Willard's use of the guitar as an ersatz solution to Sybil's psychological problem, combined with his insistence that she study the guitar instead of the violin.

Also clearly evident was the origin of the seething rage, repressed in Sybil but unbridled in Peggy Lou. Clear, too, was why Vicky, inventing a loving mother of her own by extending the loving mother of Sybil's pretend world, was a neurotic solution to the childhood dilemma. Falling into place as well was the fact that the feeling of entrapment, manifested from the very beginning of the analysis, was the heritage from the past: the reliving of the capture, control, imprisonment, and torture syndrome and the feeling of entrapment by religion.

What was also clear was that the fourteen alternating selves, who had started out constructively but who had become highly destructive to one another and to Sybil, would have to be integrated before the original child could be restored.

The doctor reached for one of the essays Sybil had written for her, a procedure prescribed as part of the therapy. Written immediately after the Philadelphia episode, it revealed a confusion and despair that made the promised land of integration, which had so recently beckoned, recede.

The letter read:

I have a few things to say, and I'm not sure I can say them when I get down there, and anyway I want to get them off my chest first so I won't talk all hour when what I really need is your help and some understanding on MY part. I NEED to know what I am fighting. Philadelphia really hit hard. I had thought for the first time with no doubts that the losing time part was gone forever. I'd had doubts before because I'd go a while without and then it would happen again, but after two whole months without losing out, well—? And you were disappointed in me. Now I'm as tightly bound as I've ever been. The tension is so great and the despair. Oh well, I just can't find any peace, that's all. But nothing matters as much as the "why" of it. You have said a number of things that have circled my brain again and again. You have talked of my fears. The fear CAN'T be any worse than the feelings I had the last few days. I feel stuck. I have read in Fenichel and in Alexander's books that this causes that symptom, and I have come to see quite a lot. But never do I read WHAT TO DO ABOUT IT. I am ready to fight or accept or whatever, but how do I make the inside me accept what the outside me hears? I have gathered from what you have said that this is what I need to do. I've tried and tried, but I can't seem to. All I do is panic. It is just these awful symptoms. I've had to lie down twice since I started writing this. I know it is only tension using up my energy, but knowing it doesn't seem to change it. The only thing that really helps is when you and I work out some problem or memory. Then I get some relief for a while before something else starts in again. I don't know what to do. I sometimes think what's the use? There's no way out. Integration? That's a great mirage. The other sense of the word is easier to achieve than this. The real trouble is that I have never been able to convince you of my inadequacies and worthlessness. Will we even be able to talk about it? When will I get back to your office as "me"? When will I make decisions as "me"? There *is* NO WAY OUT.

Was there?

24

Suicide

"Awoke as me," "stayed myself." These were the triumphs of Sybil's fragmented existence as, almost four years after the inception of the analysis, she continued to fall prey to the same archetypical event, reproduced in the same ritualistic form. Sybil, it might be said, lived in parentheses. Outside the brackets was approximately one third of her waking life.

When she woke as someone else or turned into one of the others later, Teddy Reeves, noting the transfiguration and accepting it as a routine aspect of life in the Dorsett-Reeves household, reported the event to Sybil.

Within a single week, in which the analysis had uncovered the first dissociation, Teddy had informed Sybil:

—"Mike was here for fifteen minutes at breakfast. I asked him what he liked to draw. He said cars, trains, buses."

—"Vanessa was here at 3:00 A.M. 'I'm going to dress and go outside,' Vanessa said. 'I have a class. It says so on the schedule I wrote this morning.' I made her go back to bed." (Sybil had observed: "Maybe Vanessa is closest to me of any of them. She usually continues the concern that I have begun. I'm the one who wrote the schedule of classes.")

—"Mary came at 2:00 A.M. and tried to talk me into going with her to some other city. When I said, 'Not now,' she cried as if her heart would break." (Sybil had remarked, "Mary cries with the tears I can't shed.")

344

What Teddy reported with words, Capri, Sybil's cat, revealed through action. Upon "coming to" Sybil became expert in inferring from the cat's behavior which of the other selves had been present. With Mary, Capri was quiet, lovable, wanting to be held and petted. With Marcia, Capri would rub against her face as a gesture of comfort.

But it was with Peggy Lou, in whose presence the cat became frisky, that Capri underwent the most complete transformation. Knowing instinctively that it was Peggy Lou, the cat would race around the apartment and make its frenetic way to Peggy Lou's lap or shoulder. "Nice old cat," Peggy Lou would say, holding the animal a bit too tightly. But Capri didn't mind. The cat, who had no hesitancy about scratching any of the others, wouldn't scratch Peggy Lou.

"Maybe," Sybil quipped, "Capri is multiple too."

The quip, although an accommodation to the facts of Sybil's grim existence, could not mask the fact that waking life, which since Philadelphia had once again become a series of fragmented vignettes, had become increasingly terrifying.

In dreams Sybil, who in waking life was remote from her feelings, came closer to the truth about herself, for sleeping Sybil was the total unconscious. In dreams Sybil was more nearly one than at any other time. "Sleep and forget" did not apply. To be awake was to forget; to be asleep was to remember. Her dreams reverted to the original events that had caused her to become multiple and that in waking life were reproduced in her other selves.

During the week in which Sybil had learned that she had been a multiple personality since the age of three and a half, for example, she dreamed that she was on an intercity train on her way to the end of the line. The train came to a sudden halt. Dragging herself from her seat, she walked to the back window of the train to ascertain the reason for the hiatus.

Through the window she could see, in process of construction, a huge platform with prominently displayed buttresses. Obviously the train would not be able to resume its journey until the platform, which her father was building, had been completed.

Inexplicably she then found herself outside the train and in a warehouse. Looking out of the warehouse window, she noticed a small yellow and white mass trying to drag itself around a doorsill into the open space. It was a kitten.

Sybil watched as the pathetic little kitten rubbed its nose along the bottom of the doorway in what seemed like a search for food. Its movements were circumscribed, halting. Is it paralyzed? she wondered. Then she realized it was dying of starvation.

A few feet away from the kitchen there was a hideous sight—the decapitated body of the mother cat. The head lay a few inches away from the torso.

Not far from what had been their mother three kittens huddled together. Sybil hadn't noticed them at first, but these three seemed even closer to starvation than the first kitten.

I'll take them home, Sybil thought, and she raced out of the warehouse and into the street. Maybe Capri will grow to like them, and we'll be a happy family.

But first, Sybil knew, she had to dispose of the mother cat. Picking up the head and then the body, she flung both parts into the river that ran alongside the warehouse. But the parts fell close to the shore, where the water was shallow, and Sybil blamed herself for not having thrown the dismembered parts of the dead mother cat with greater force, for it seemed entirely possible that they would float back to the shore.

Dismissing her fear, Sybil turned her attention to the group of three kittens. Bending over to pick them up, she was filled with sudden wonder at finding that underneath them were three kittens she had not seen before.

Out of nowhere she managed to happen on a pink and white plaid blanket, identical to one on her own bed. After placing the blanket in the bottom of a box, murmuring, "Poor little pussies," she placed the kittens on the blanket. As she was setting out for home in search of the person who would know how to make everything all right, she woke up.

Shaken by the dream, which showed an unconscious awareness that had not yet filtered into conscious life, Sybil was appalled, guilt-ridden. To Sybil the meaning of the dream was threatening.

Sybil saw the train as life, moving toward a destination but stopped by new work (analysis), which meant reversing its route (retracing childhood events) to become one. The various degrees of starvation among the kittens symbolized the years during which Sybil had tried to live and work normally only to discover that she had come to the end of the line (the train again) in maintaining the ruse of normality.

The kittens also symbolized Sybil. That they were plural rather than singular was a recognition that she was many. The first kitten, attempting to drag herself into the open spaces, was Sybil herself. The other kittens, discovered in separate groups, were the other selves. The first group symbolized the early appearance in the analysis (and in life) of Vicky and the Peggys, and the second group, the later appearance of the other selves, who were more deeply buried.

Some of the kittens were weaker than others, as were some of the selves. "Some, such as Vicky, Peggy, Marcia, Vanessa, Mary, Mike, and Sid," Dr. Wilbur had said, "are active; others like Sybil Ann are passive. All of them are strong or weak depending upon what emotion at the time there is to defend." Dr. Wilbur, of course, was the unnamed figure in the dream who would know how to make everything all right.

The act of saving the kittens seemed to Sybil not an act of personal solicitude on her part but, like the train, the analogue of the analysis that was attempting to save both her and all of the "kittens" in her still mysterious "family."

Sybil rose from the bed, started to dress, and tried to extricate herself from the realization that having to get rid of their (her) dead mother before she could take the kittens safely home meant only one thing— that only by ridding herself of her mother could she become well, strong, really a "family." *Family* was the euphemism Sybil used for becoming one.

As Sybil walked into the kitchen for breakfast, she

pushed the dream aside, unaware that her explication had overlooked the fact that the "new work" that blocked the train's passage—the free flow of life—which she had interpreted as "analysis," had in the dream been built by her father. The starving kittens could be interpreted as representing sexual starvation. The same events that had driven Sybil from a normal childhood had driven her, too, from a normal womanhood.

Most importantly, what Sybil didn't notice about the dream were her own emotions in disposing of the mother cat. With businesslike precision but without repugnance she had flung her mother into the river and had become disturbed only when there was danger that her mother would float back to shore.

Later that morning, during the hour with Dr. Wilbur, Sybil talked of the selves the kittens in the dream symbolized.

"I went to all the trouble of coming to New York," Sybil remarked resentfully, "and *they* have taken over the analysis. They've made friends with you, go on trips, make friends with people I'd like to know. And I'm left out."

Overriding Dr. Wilbur's explanations, Sybil refused to let the doctor come to the defense of the personalities, particularly of Vicky. When the doctor pointed out that by resenting her other selves, Sybil was avoiding the issue and that such avoidance in psychoanalytical terms was known as resistance, Sybil began to make a joke of it. "I know I'm indulging in that nasty word," Sybil kept saying. "Don't say it. But that Vicky you're so fond of is a blabbermouth. I can't have any secrets. She rushes to tell you everything. If she doesn't, one of those other midwesterners does. They give me no peace, no privacy, no freedom."

"Vicky is trying to help you," the doctor protested.

Sybil summoned enough nerve to reply, "I'd be better off without her help." Then Sybil added what she had said many times before: "I can't afford that Peggy Lou."

Then, taking stock of her current financial situation, Sybil explained, "I came to New York with five thousand dollars in savings. Three thousand have been spent on paying for the analysis and buying a few extras I hadn't been able to manage on what Dad sent me. But two thousand of the five thousand have been blown on Peggy Lou's broken glass."

The resentment Sybil bore toward Peggy Lou for the broken glass was deepened by other evidences of Peggy Lou's destructiveness. "The other night," Sybil went on, "I found that my charcoal sketches had been destroyed. Teddy said that Peggy Lou had done it. What's the matter with Peggy Lou? You said she worked in black and white. Doesn't she like black and white any more? Or is it me she doesn't like? If so, the feeling is mutual."

After she left the office, Sybil went to school. As she was leaving the chemistry lab, Henry, who sat next to her and whom she also knew from other classes, followed her to the elevator.

There was an affinity between them. Both were from the Midwest; both loved music and books; both were premed students (now that she had her Master's degree in art, Sybil had decided on a future that included both art and child psychiatry). Although Henry was eight years younger than Sybil, she was so youthful in appearance that she actually looked younger than he.

Henry walked Sybil home. When they reached the old brownstone, they stood talking. Reluctant to leave her, he offered to let her read his notes covering the classes she had missed while she was in Philadelphia. "I'll go over the stuff with you," he volunteered. She invited him in.

They worked, student to student, with no surface insinuations of sex. He would have liked to have had a beer, but he settled for iced tea, which she presented to him with the cookies Teddy had said that Mary had baked. Sybil enjoyed a pleasant two hours of wholeness.

As Henry was leaving and they were standing at the half-open door, the mood changed. No longer only a colleague, Henry put his hand gently on Sybil's shoulder and looked at her tenderly. "I want you to give me a date for the dance Wednesday night," he said softly.

Sybil panicked. Replying no, she shrank from Henry's touch.

"Don't you like me just a little bit?" he asked.

"Of course, I like you," she replied slowly.

"Well?" he asked.

"But I don't want to date anybody," she replied firmly.

"You're too nice for that," he protested. "Lots of people like you, and you shouldn't be like that. You're good company. It would be fun to go with you."

Sybil shook her head decisively. "No," she repeated. "No."

"Then how about dinner?" he asked.

"No," she replied. "Henry, please don't press me. We'll see each other in the lab. I value your friendship, but don't press."

"But why? I don't get it," he persevered.

There was an awkward pause. Then he asked: "What is it?"

In the silence that followed Sybil could feel internal pressures, the interference of the others, as she had come to call it. The pressure was there, although the meaning was obscure. Sybil did not know that Vicky was thinking, "He's nice. I can't see why she doesn't date him," or that Peggy Lou was fuming, "Just like her. She never does anything I enjoy doing."

"Sybil," Henry said as he tried to take her in his arms, "I like you. I've liked you for a long time. Why can't we see each other?"

Extricating herself from the embrace, Sybil reached for the door knob, hinting that she wanted Henry to go. "Are you sure?" he said.

"Very sure," she replied.

There were footsteps in the hall. Henry turned to see who it was, and as he did so, Sybil shut the door behind him and bolted the lock. The feeling she experienced as she did so was reminiscent of the moment in her dream in which, after placing the kittens on the blanket, she had closed the box. In the dream she had created an improvised perforation to leave room for air, but now the "box" that she had remorselessly shut tight was airless.

Here she was, on the other side of the door that she herself had closed, thirty-five years old and an old maid—excluded by the phalanx of the married, a third plate at their dinner tables. Isolated, with only Teddy near, she felt removed from the world. And Teddy's awareness of the strange circumstances of their joint domesticity was deeply disquieting.

When Sybil blacked out in the apartment or returned to it as one of the other personalities, almost inevitably Teddy was a witness. It was even more disturbing to face the fact that Teddy had built quite separate relationships with Vicky, the Peggys, Mike and Sid, Marcia and Vanessa, Mary, Sybil Ann and the other personalities. This knowledge deepened Sybil's uneasiness and gave loneliness a terrifyingly new dimension. What did these others tell Teddy? Privacy was impossible as long as unknown voices proclaimed secrets in the apartment.

Henry. Male companionship. Perhaps the father of the baby Sybil so urgently wanted but probably couldn't have. Whenever a man had entered her life, she had wanted his children even more than she had wanted him. And the desire for Henry, although deeply buried, *had* been there.

The dance? She couldn't have gone to the dance. Her religion didn't permit it. She couldn't have gone even if there were no religion to stand in her way.

Why not dinner? One thing would lead to another. If she allowed herself to become involved with Henry, he would come to know her well and learn all about her. Then he would reject her. She knew that she had to protect herself against such an eventuality. No man must come close until she was well. Well? She winced. Would she ever be well?

The mantel clock was striking eight. Teddy wouldn't be home for two hours. Sybil went out. As she walked, the buildings of the city seemed to stretch endlessly to the east. She kept on walking west.

Life had stopped while she had reversed her route. She still had a whole world to forge. So far the analysis was taking her backward, not forward. The ambition to become a doctor had been consistently frustrated by her blackouts in science classes, and the ambition was constantly receding. She couldn't bear to try and fail.

She could scarcely even endure just being awake. Waking, she knew one of the others might take over. Even when there wasn't an actual takeover, there was the everlasting internal pressure, the interference by the others. She felt alone, useless, futile. Convinced that she was never going to get better, Sybil was faced with self-recriminations and complaints.

Certain that her life had stopped while she retraced a path that uncovered only anguish, Sybil felt that she had indeed come to the end of the line. She didn't want to live this way.

She reached the Hudson River, brownish-green and deep. She envisioned herself in the water, sinking. Death would bring surcease.

Sybil walked closer to the river, but before she could actually reach it, her body turned, propelled by another's will. The body, controlled by Vicky, sought and found a phone booth in one of the apartment houses on Riverside Drive. After dialing, Vicky said in a firm, clear voice, "Dr. Wilbur, Sybil was going to throw herself in the Hudson River, but I didn't let her."

Part IV

Reentry

25

Beginning to Remember

At first Sybil had doubted that any mere medicine could produce any decisive changes, but when the few electric shock treatments for which she had asked to make her feel safer after her suicide attempt had effected no discernible difference in her feelings, she had agreed to sodium pentothal because she trusted Dr. Wilbur.

The doctor herself had suggested pentothal reluctantly because she believed that straight psychoanalysis was the treatment of choice in Sybil's case. But the intimations of suicide, the actual near-attempt, made it necessary to resolve, to some degree and over a short period of time, the intense anxiety and depression. From long experience Dr. Wilbur knew that abreaction—the emotional release or discharge resulting from recalling to awareness a painful experience that has been repressed because it was consciously intolerable—with pentothal was a markedly useful tool. By discharging and desensitizing painful emotions, pentothal often led to increased insights.

The first pentothal treatment, administered by vein, appreciably diminished Sybil's anxiety. In the sessions that followed, for fifty-six, sometimes seventy hours after receiving pentothal, Sybil came to know a sense of freedom that never before had been hers. Pentothal, a barbiturate that is both an anesthetic and a hypnotic, had conferred the sensation of feeling perfectly well— an experience Sybil had never had before. On the day after the treatment, there was always euphoria, which was due not only to the anti-anxiety effect of the barbiturate but also to the abreaction of severe trauma. Pentothal brought to the surface the deeply buried, debilitating hatred of her mother. Although Sybil could not yet accept this hatred, the fact that it was no longer buried paved the way to a later acceptance.

The freedom Sybil knew through pentothal the other selves also experienced. Now as never before the others had the opportunity both to be and to talk. Vicky had all the memories, her own and those of the other selves, including Sybil's. The other fourteen personalities had their own memories and some of the recollections of the other alternating selves and of Sybil.

Only Sybil possessed none of the memories of the others. But as pentothal unleashed some forgotten fragments of the past, the memories relating to the experiences of the others and the memories of events that Sybil had lived through as herself but had forgotten began to filter into awareness.

Memory didn't just *happen*. After the pentothal treatment Dr. Wilbur would confront Sybil with the deeply buried memories that returned during the pentothal "sleep" and vanished upon waking.

"Oh, I had forgotten all about that," Sybil would remark when, upon awakening, she was presented with the memory. Then after remembering the event for a time, she would lose it again. The doctor would then try again, until, very gradually, what had been remembered under pentothal began also to be remembered during normal living.

Aware of the new order, Sybil had the feeling of expansive sidewalks, wherever she stood, reaching beyond the painful present and the even more terrifying past. The sidewalks pointed toward the promised land of either being freed of the others or becoming one with them. Neither Sybil nor Dr. Wilbur knew which of the two forms getting well would take.

For the first time Sybil also began to experience the emotions attributable to each of the other selves.

Beginning to understand, too, what triggered dissociation, the patient now knew not only intellectually but emotionally that "When I'm angry, I can't be." Anger, of course, was Peggy Lou's province.

The impression Sybil herself had was that subsiding slowly was the gnawing conflict that had driven her to the Hudson River—and also away from it. More concerned now with "Who am I?" she informed the doctor, "Pentothal makes me feel that I am me." Yet although the conflict had ebbed, it had not disappeared. For the present the barbiturate bestowed a sense of release, and concurrently, the feelings of unreality that had been hers almost since time began for her were gradually replaced by a feeling of solidity. Always far away from her feelings, she was coming closer to them now.

Sailing along with the speed of a schooner in a gale, Sybil came to regard the weekly pentothal sessions as propitious winds. That Dr. Wilbur visited Sybil in her apartment when pentothal was administered brought additional comfort. Feeling more alive, more interested, Sybil redecorated the apartment, made it more attractive for her doctor-guest. The jab in the vein, the occasional inability to find a new vein after months had passed and so many veins had been pressed into service, the not-infrequent swelling of the injected part of the anatomy, the feeling of chill that sometimes ran through the patient, the hiccups ("I sound as if I'm drunk," Vicky said. "And here I am getting treatment when I'm not sick")— all of this physical discomfiture was there. None of it mattered, however, in the light of the bright new day sodium pentothal had brought. On sodium pentothal Sybil had even gained fifteen pounds.

Nirvana? No. The euphoria was often deflated, sometimes destroyed by the reawakened memories of childhood horrors that Sybil had so painstakingly buried.

"Your mother trapped you, and it's almost as if you have taken over trapping yourself," Dr. Wilbur would say. "But you're getting rid of your mother." Sybil had already done so in her dream about the mother cat, but she was horrified by the unnatural desire.

"I'm helping you to grow up," the doctor would continue. "You're getting better, and you're going to be able to use all your talents." The incantation, the exorcising of Hattie Dorsett, would proceed: "Your mother taught you not to believe in yourself. I'm going to help you do so. The numbers will come back. The music will come back. There will be an end to the painting blocks. You will do many things well."

"I'm so cold, so cold," Sybil would reply through chattering teeth.

Integration? Far from it. As the past flooded back, there was all the more reason to regress into the other selves, defenses against the past. Yet in the valley of dissociation there were also the first glimmers of coalescence.

There was a glimmer on a Friday night in the very height of spring. Seated on her bed after having awakened from a tranquil three-hour sleep following a sodium pentothal treatment, Sybil was thinking about the previous day, much of which had been blank. Suddenly action was etched into the blankness.

Was this memory? She did not know. If it was, it was memory of a different kind; for she was remembering not what she had done as Sybil but what—and this was the bewildering part of the recollection—*she* had done as Mary and Sybil Ann. Sybil was distinctly aware of two persons, each of whom knew what the other was doing and saying. Together these two persons went to the supermarket, bought groceries, and conversed about the prices of their purchases.

Perhaps the most extraordinary aspect of the recollection was that Sybil remembered that at one moment she had been Mary, at the next Sybil Ann, and that when she was the one, the other was a person beside her, to whom she could talk and express opinions and from whom she could seek advice.

Sybil could see herself *becoming* Sybil Ann. As Sybil Ann she had returned to the apartment and had been suddenly obsessed with the desire to go off on a trip. Somehow this trip had not eventuated, but while planning to go, she had looked at a purse on the dresser with Sybil Ann's eyes, thinking that she would take the purse with her and return it as soon as she got settled somewhere. Observing that the name on the identification card was Sybil I. Dorsett, Sybil in the person of Sybil Ann thought: that must be the owner. The memory of being Sybil Ann was so distinct that it had even included Sybil Ann's confusion as to who Sybil was.

This glimpse into the present was followed some weeks later by an even more confoundingly swift perception of the past.

At breakfast Teddy was saying, "I'd certainly like to know what Peggy Lou was talking about when she said that letters make words, words make sentences, and sentences make paragraphs."

"You're asking *me* what Peggy Lou meant?" Sybil replied. "Me? I'm the last one to ask. You know how Peggy Lou and I feel about each other."

"Peggy Lou also said something about little gray boxes in rows and that she had to watch and be careful, that she had to get away," Teddy went on. "I've been hearing about these letters, words, and boxes for several years now."

Sybil replied thoughtfully, "I haven't the faintest idea." But as she spoke, she looked up at the blank red wall just ahead and, although aware of herself as Sybil, at the same time she felt like a little girl. It was not a matter of being childlike but of *being a child*. Then Sybil found herself saying, "When I was a youngster, I was not allowed to listen to fairy tales or any stories that were not 'the truth.' Nor was I allowed to make up stories. But I liked to write, especially animal stories and poetry. When Mother and Dad made me promise I would stop, I devised a way to 'write' without writing. I would cut words and single letters in headings out of newspapers and put the letters in little gray boxes, which I took to school. Then I'd paste the words on sheets of heavy paper so that the letters made words, the words made paragraphs, and I could write without writing. You see?"

Bewildered, Teddy reminded her roommate, "But

you just said that you didn't have the faintest recollection."

"I didn't," Sybil replied calmly, "but then I did. You see I devised that technique when I was in the third and fourth grades, after my grandmother died."

The third and fourth grades, after her grandmother died? The calm vanished as Sybil realized what she had said.

Out of the mist hanging heavily over Sybil's two lost years (between the ages of nine and eleven) Peggy Lou's memories were becoming Sybil's. By responding to Peggy Lou's memory as if it were her own, the waking self that was called Sybil had been able to recall an incident from the childhood of the alternating self. And all at once Sybil realized that at that moment she felt not merely *like* Peggy Lou; she was *one* with her. Pentothal had ripped open the unused line of communication between Sybil and one of her other selves to restore a fragment of the lost years. Sybil, who had never been ten or eleven years old, had in a swift flashback become those ages. What had started as a casual breakfast conversation had become a milestone along the pathways of restoration of the original Sybil.

With the new feeling of being one with Peggy Lou there also came a wholly new attitude toward both Peggy Lou and the other selves. Sybil was now becoming able to distinguish what she did, as she put it, as "someone else" from what she did "as myself." The Sybil who in Vicky's description stood aside had now moved in closer.

Aware now of the others through the eyes of Dr. Wilbur and of Teddy *and* through her own experience, Sybil wondered, with humor, why with all these "gals and guys" around, the veil of aloneness that hung over her had not been lifted. "Let's give a party for ourselves," Mary whispered in the recesses of being. Sybil was amused.

By Christmas, 1958, Sybil had accepted her other selves with sufficient humor to include them in her Christmas greetings to Dr. Wilbur. A series of cards, attached to each other like the folds of an accordion, all designed and executed *only* by Sybil, read:

> To Our Dr. Wilbur:
> Multiple greetings—Sybil
> Love—Vicky
> Happy Holidays—Vanessa Gail
> Merry Christmas from Mary
> Glad Noel—Marcia and Mike
> Best wishes—Sybil Ann
> Happy New Year—Peggy

Dr. Wilbur was not unaware that the Christmas ball beside Peggy's "Happy New Year" was of broken glass; nor that Sybil had failed to send greetings from Clara, Nancy, Marjorie, Ruthie, Helen, Sid, and that Peggy Lou and Peggy Ann were represented by a single Peggy. That Sybil could move out of her longtime negation of the others to share the spirit of the season was in the nature of an analytical turning point.

Unfortunately, to Sybil pentothal became "magic" and Dr. Wilbur, the "magician" who could confer bliss. The dependency upon the doctor that Sybil developed during the pentothal treatments made Sybil feel both loved and important. Becoming demanding about pentothal, Sybil also acted as if she could control the doctor and, by controlling the doctor, Hattie Dorsett. Safely ensconced in this double dependency, Sybil relived the relaxation she had known at her mother's breast before being weaned and being confronted with the manufactured nipple that had supplanted the warm human one. Euphoric on all these counts, Sybil came to regard pentothal as ecstasy and salvation.

Dr. Wilbur, however, was becoming increasingly concerned about administering pentothal to Sybil. The doctor didn't like having to use the needle, didn't like Sybil's growing dependency and the fact that Sybil was using pentothal to circumvent problems. It was clear to the doctor, although certainly not to Sybil, that no mere medicine could change the underlying psychic problems or conflicts. Although pentothal, because of its abreactive effects, had proved valuable in uncovering buried memories and lost time, in bringing Sybil closer to her other selves and so mitigating against her depletion, it had made no dent in the basic traumas, the core distortions created chiefly by Hattie Dorsett and perpetuated through Sybil's own defensive maneuvers. Yet it was precisely upon the resolution of these traumas that ultimate recovery, the final healing and integration, depended.

What was most disquieting to the doctor was that while it conferred upon Sybil the freedom of feeling well, pentothal had also threatened to impose upon her the bondage of addiction. Feeling that the gains did not outweigh the risks, Dr. Wilbur decided to terminate this treatment.

Accordingly, the first weekend in early March, 1959, was bad not only for Sybil but for "everybody else," as she called her other selves. It was the weekend of the weaning from pentothal.

"What have I done that made Dr. Wilbur punish me by taking me off pentothal?" Sybil murmured to Teddy Reeves. "What have I done that made the doctor shut me out?"

"The doctor is going to come," the Peggys kept saying. "We just know that she is."

Marcia, shaking her head gravely, said, "No, the doctor isn't coming and will never come again."

Nancy said, "Who knows? She just might."

"No," Vicky observed. "Dr. Wilbur isn't coming. She isn't going to give in about the pentothal. The decision to stop it was for our own good. She said we were becoming powerfully addicted to it, psychologically speaking. I believe in her." ✍

Hearing someone walking up the stairs or in the hallway, Marcia and Vanessa, Mike and Sid, Nancy, Sybil Ann, Mary, and the Peggys, feeling a tremor of excitement, would pretend it was Dr. Wilbur. The receding footsteps would electrocute hope.

All weekend the Peggys nagged; Mary cried; Nancy, Vanessa, and Marcia stormed. Sybil, feeling her own despair compounded by that of the others, told Teddy, "I've sewed the last of the hem in the wall hanging.

I'm never going to do another thing around this place. Dr. Wilbur isn't coming anymore. What's the use?"

And Vicky told Teddy: "You can't really blame them. The end of pentothal is the greatest loss they've sustained since the death of their grandmother."

In the doctor's office on Monday Sybil demanded, "Just give me pentothal on the Wednesday night before the chemistry final on Thursday. Then I'll be in the best possible shape for writing the exam."

"No, Sybil. No," said the doctor.

"Pentothal was something I could count on," Sybil pleaded.

"You're of sterner stuff. We'll find other safer, stronger means."

"I can't stand it."

"What you're saying to me, Sybil, is that there are some things you feel that you can't deal with as Sybil. As of this moment, that's true. But it doesn't have to stay true, you see?"

"I don't see. You *want* me to dissociate," Sybil replied bitterly. "If I didn't, you'd miss seeing Vicky and all those other people you're so fond of."

"Sybil," the doctor answered, "you know this makes me think it's a good thing you're not a drinking girl. If you were, you'd be an alcoholic. The connection between bottles and breasts is very real. Pentothal brought you the relaxation of your mother's breast, just as alcohol does for the alcoholic. And it is perfectly clear that you have a powerful psychological addiction to pentothal. Improvement has not been great enough to justify the risk."

Rejected again, newly deprived of the sweet dependency pentothal had conferred, Sybil felt hopeless. The resistance she had built against facing her underlying problems had been ripped away, and she was terrified by knowing that now she would probably come closer to the real roots of her illness.

With this realization there came the stifling rage that Sybil used to feel when Hattie Dorsett punished her without cause. The doctor, Sybil felt, was as omnipotent as Hattie—and just as unfair. Now, as in the

363

past, Sybil believed, had come punishment, irrational, cruel, and utterly groundless.

Leaving the doctor's office, Sybil walked along a crazy, swaying sidewalk. When she got home, she took a Seconal and went to sleep. When she woke up, she buried her face in the pillow, unable to face the new day.

Why should she face it? she wondered. For what was she struggling so hard and alone? There was no way out. Of that Sybil was certain.

26

Independent Futures

During May, 1959, several of the selves made individual thrusts toward independent futures. At the same time Sybil, reacting to these thrusts, wondered whether she was moving forward or backward or, indeed, was moving at all.

That May morning the sun was streaming into the apartment as Mary awoke, stretched toward the once-confining partition, and realized with a mistlike recollection that she had done something recently that would render the partition unnecessary.

Suddenly, like moving pictures on a screen, the relevant scenes flashed before her. Dan Stewart, a real-estate agent, was asking her, as she stood with him on the front porch of a ranch house in Crompond, New York, "How large is your family?"

"I'm alone," had been her reply.

"More than enough space," he had laughed openly.

"And plenty of room for company. You can throw great weekend parties."

Paying what he had called "earnest money," she had written a check for five hundred dollars as a down payment on this house, which was priced at twenty-two thousand dollars.

She had been about to sign Mary Lucinda Saunders Dorsett, but then she had remembered that it was not she but Sybil who had the checking account.

"Sybil I. Dorsett?" the agent had remarked, examining the check. "Are you related to the Dorsetts of Glens Falls?"

"No," she had replied, "I'm from the Midwest."

"The closing," he had then told her, "will be in a couple of weeks. I'll call you."

By now fully dressed, Mary headed for the kitchen. "I'm going to pack and leave," she told Teddy at breakfast, "so as not to be in the way."

"I don't want you to go away," Teddy replied as she walked to Mary's end of the table to put a reassuring hand on Mary's shoulder. "I want you to stay right where you are. It's where you belong."

"As a little girl," Mary replied wistfully, "I always wanted a room of my own." She paused briefly, adding, "I didn't get it until I was nine. I've always wanted privacy but never had it. I sometimes used to think that I would be driven out of my home."

Teddy left for work but not without a reassuring reminder that the Morningside apartment was where Mary Lucinda Saunders Dorsett belonged.

Alone, Mary made a fire in the fireplace. Then, huddled in a heap near the fireplace with Capri beside her, she began sewing brownish violet draperies for the bedroom in the ranch house that would soon be her own.

Two days later Sybil, standing at her mailbox, placed in her purse an unopened letter from her father, noted with wry amusement a letter from the Book-of-the-Month Club addressed to Marcia Dorsett, and then opened a manila envelope from the bank. She was overdrawn. The check for forty-seven dollars she sent to Hartley's Pharmacy last night would bounce.

Sybil thumbed through the canceled checks. A check for five hundred dollars? She hadn't written a check for that amount. Evans Real Estate? She had never heard of them. In a less sophisticated stage of her multiplicity she would have regarded a check she hadn't signed as a mystery, but now she realized that one of the others had signed the check. Who? It really didn't matter. In dollars and cents terms they were all spelled Sybil I. Dorsett.

After Sybil received a telephone call from a Dan Stewart, informing her that the closing of "her" house was to take place, she panicked. At first Dr. Wilbur, who kept on saying, "When you are well, these things won't happen to you," wasn't helpful. The doctor did finally get a lawyer, however, who, by pleading "mental incompetence," rescued Sybil from the commitment made by Mary. Dr. Wilbur, who saw Mary's house largely as a flight from the primal scene, thought of it as having been spun of the same fabric that had made the boys build the partition and that propelled Peggy Lou in repeated flights in search of new places.

Curious about the role of the others, who, unlike Sybil, had been aware of the purchase, Dr. Wilbur talked over Mary's house with two worthy representatives: Vicky and Peggy Lou. Vicky said: "Mary wanted that house so badly that I decided to let her go through with the initial stages. I knew she wouldn't be able to have it in the end. But what was wrong with letting her have her dream fulfilled briefly? What she did was certainly no worse than taking a dress from a shop, wearing it, and then returning it. Lots of women do that. That's dishonest. What Mary did was not."

And Peggy Lou explained: "I was in on letting Mary buy that house; I helped her express her feelings because so many people have been cruel to Mary. It didn't hurt that Mr. Stewart to let Mary go through with buying that house."

To Dr. Wilbur's practical question: "But who is going to pay for it?" Peggy Lou replied assertively, "Sybil. It's up to her to work and take care of us."

Sybil herself thought longingly of the house that

Mary had bought and she herself had rejected. Mary's wish was her wish; Mary's action, the uninhibited voice of an unconscious Sybil.

The others had a strength in forging reality out of dreams that Sybil lacked. The lost house had many mansions, many barricades against remembrance of things past and to come. How sweet, Sybil thought, to be in a house, held and caressed in a house that was hers, in which the earth mother could gather her children to herself and call them one!

Peggy Lou was watching closely as Sybil, seated at her desk in the Morningside Drive apartment, wrote: "July 20, 1959. Dear Carol, I had hoped to be able to accept your invitation to spend a few weeks at your home in Denver. I should so love to be with you and Carl, reviving old times. Then, too, New York summers are sultry, and I do feel the need to get away. I even went so far as to check plane schedules. But, Carol, I've finally decided that I can't really make it this summer. There are too many reasons for having to remain New York-bound. Forgive me. We'll look hopefully to another time."

Later in the morning the letter was uppermost in Peggy Lou's thoughts as she thrashed her way through the streets, trying to wear down her emotions against the pavement.

Peggy Lou had counted on going to Denver and, when Sybil had called the airlines, had told Dr. Wilbur, "All of us are smiling inside." But now Sybil had spoiled everything. It isn't fair. It isn't fair, Peggy Lou iterated and reiterated as she quickened her steps to keep pace with her mounting fury.

There was also a feeling of betrayal. Waiting for a traffic light, Peggy Lou suddenly realized that she had come to the end of the line and could not, at least *would* not, continue to ride with Sybil. They had different destinations, different life-styles. Sybil doesn't have the same ideas I have, Peggy Lou protested. She thinks my ideas are wrong. And she's the one who runs things. I have to give her credit because there are some times that she does what I want her to do.

But that's over now. Sybil can never again be trusted.

Her betrayal, moreover, as Peggy Lou saw it, was both a failure on Sybil's part to do what Peggy Lou desired and a violation of an agreement—a contract among the selves, negotiated by Dr. Wilbur. The doctor had gotten Peggy Lou to agree not to go off on trips of her own if Sybil would promise to take Peggy Lou places.

Well, Peggy Lou thought, as once again she quickened her steps, Sybil hasn't kept her part of the bargain, but I have. I haven't gone anywhere out of town since Philadelphia. Peggy Lou made the momentous decision to change her status—to break free from being an alternating self confined to a body headed by an alien person.

The Grand Design, long dimly brooded upon but now fully hatched, was to break completely with Sybil and the other selves. Peggy Lou decided that she would assume command of the body and take it to a distant place, never to return.

In the past Peggy Lou had had to be angry in order to *be*. When the anger was extinguished, Sybil had returned. Peggy Lou had never before been reluctant to return the body to Sybil. The future would be different. Never again would the body belong to anybody but Peggy Lou.

She knew exactly what this would entail. Her existence had made Sybil's survival possible. Many were the times when Sybil, overwhelmed by rage, had decided that for her there never would be anything but suffering, no chance to accomplish anything without interference from her selves. At such times, asking, "What's the use?" Sybil had been close to suicide. By taking over the rage Peggy Lou had literally let Sybil live.

But now that she was going to be the only occupant of the body, now that she would no longer be an alternating self but the one self, whose existence would not depend only upon rage, it would be different. Sybil would not live.

Buoyed by the expectation of supremacy and the sweet feeling of revenge against Sybil, Peggy Lou

368

realized that there were practical matters that had to be considered before she could make this new life for herself. Everything had to be planned carefully so as to avoid being apprehended by the police or others who would search for a missing person.

She would take the two hundred dollars Sybil kept in a box in the apartment and leave New York at once. Those who pursued her would be looking for the legal entity called Sybil Dorsett, a conservatively dressed schoolteacher. Peggy Lou would therefore seek an occupation remote from teaching and would bedeck herself in the most flamboyant clothes that money could buy. The pursuers would look for Sybil Dorsett in the North or perhaps the Midwest. Peggy Lou therefore planned to go south.

As she turned into East 74th Street, she suddenly remembered that, before these thoughts had occurred to her, she had been on her way to keep an appointment with Dr. Wilbur. Peggy Lou decided to keep the appointment. She wanted to see the doctor for one last time.

Coming closer to the doctor's office, Peggy Lou marshaled her arguments, rehearsed what she would say. The essential thrust would be: I'm the one who lets Sybil live, and she doesn't do anything for me. The thought of having to take leave of the doctor, however, made Peggy Lou suddenly sad.

Her thoughts, as she approached the building where for five years she had been allowed to speak freely and to assert herself, reverted to a snowy day the previous winter, when, to get away from the frightening snow, she had gone to Grand Central Station to buy a ticket for some place warm. She hadn't been at the station very long when, standing beside her, was Dr. Wilbur.

Peggy, who didn't know that Sybil, "coming to" briefly in the station, had called Teddy and that Teddy had called Dr. Wilbur, couldn't understand how Dr. Wilbur had gotten there.

"Oh, Dr. Wilbur," Peggy Lou asked on first seeing the doctor, "where did you come from?"

Avoiding a direct answer, Dr. Wilbur said only, "We have to get you home to a warm bed."

And Peggy Lou, instead of being angry because the doctor had interfered with her plans, nestled up against the doctor, saying, "Oh, Dr. Wilbur, I'm so glad to see you." Together they had walked out of the station to the taxi stalls while Peggy Lou shivered with the cold. As the doctor wrapped her mink coat around her runaway patient, Peggy Lou had continued to shiver, but not from the cold. It was an exquisite pleasure to be enveloped in mink. And Dr. Wilbur had promised that some day Peggy Lou could have a sleeve of that mink coat as a souvenir.

Peggy Lou entered the doctor's office with mixed emotions. Then, suddenly helpless before the flood of powerful feelings that overwhelmed her, Peggy Lou told the doctor every last detail of the Grand Design for emancipation.

"What have I done to make you want to leave me?" the doctor asked softly. In reply Peggy Lou nestled closer and said, "Oh, Dr. Wilbur." The gesture and the tone were identical to what had transpired on the snowy day.

Now, too, in the cradle endlessly rocking was Peggy Lou, her resolution to break with the past to start a life of her own lullabied into inactivity. Having expended her fervor in the declaration, Peggy Lou did not have to perform the deed.

Vanessa stood in front of the mirror, in which Sybil never looked. The body Vanessa lived in was too slender for her taste. A little more flesh, a few rounded curves, breasts that were more voluptuous: these she would have liked to have had. Her hair—that beautiful dark chestnut red hair, flaming with her passions —was nearer to her heart's desire. She wished for new clothes, chic and alluring, in which she could face the world. How tired she was of the veil that hung between her and the world. It was as if she, along with the others, were facing life from behind a scrim.

Poor Sybil, Vanessa thought. She would enjoy life more if she didn't always have to be skimping to make ends meet. She hasn't held a job since she came to New York. Father's check just covers basic expenses.

Dr. Wilbur isn't being paid. Sybil doesn't have money for clothes, art supplies, travel. We don't make it any easier for her, always nagging for the things we want and often spending money on our own. The conscience that makes her feel guilty about indulging herself even in small pleasures when she's in debt doesn't help either. The rigidities, Vanessa reflected bitterly, are the bequest of the hypocrites of Willow Corners.

While carefully lining her lips with lipstick, which Sybil still didn't use, Vanessa suddenly had a brainstorm. Sybil wasn't earning anything. Peggy Lou and Marcia were spending, heedless of Sybil's caution. Vanessa at that moment took a decisive stand: she would become the breadwinner!

Remembering the Help Wanted sign in an Amsterdam Avenue laundromat, she decided that to work there would be ideal. Involving neither stress nor brainwork, the job would reawaken no old traumas.

Later that morning the laundromat job became Vanessa's. Discovering that they had a job, the others were pleased. Peggy Lou thought it was great fun, and the boys admitted to getting a "kick" out of operating the machines. Vicky thought that having a job was not only economically wise but also good therapy. Sybil herself agreed that this was the sort of job that made sense. But it was to Vanessa, who alternated with the others in performing the simple tasks the job required, to whom the job meant most.

When Sybil I. Dorsett received her first paycheck, Vanessa Dorsett visited a small dress shop on Broadway and bought two stunning but inexpensive costumes. Vanessa, through Dr. Wilbur, was even able to persuade Sybil to go to the theater.

In any case, from the middle of August, 1959, to the middle of October, Sybil had a job that Vanessa had secured. When, however, the job interfered with the demands of classes, by then in full swing, Sybil, with Dr. Wilbur's approval, resigned. Of the selves, Vanessa alone could not accept resignation from a job that had provided new clothes and the means to wash away the guilt and hypocrisy of the past. For Vanessa the two months in the laundromat had meant purification.

In the meantime, Marcia had a better solution than the laundromat. She wanted to turn her talents to cash. I could do so many things, she thought as she walked to the mailbox, if only everybody didn't get in the way.

She placed her key in the lock anxiously. Asking acceptance from the world at this moment were two of her most recent creative efforts. One was a pop tune, "On a Holidate for Two," for which she had written both words and music. Finding a copy of the song in a drawer, Sybil had wilted with embarrassment. What, Marcia had heard Sybil ask, would people think if I were to die and they were to find this childish tune among my belongings? Sybil, of course, had been against sending the song to a publisher. That was Sybil. Defeated before she starts. Marcia had sent the song in spite of Sybil.

Would there be a reply today? If they bought it, Marcia could then buy all the paints she liked, and she wouldn't have to use Sybil's money.

The essay sent to *Parents* magazine had been out for three weeks. There might be a reply by now. The essay was entitled "Can a Loving Mother Be Dangerous?" Key phrases lingered in memory: "This mother was ambivalent. This kind of consistently inconsistent love is dangerous to the trusting child. Can a loving mother cause her child to be a potential neurotic? Psychologists and psychiatrists tell us, 'Yes, it is possible.'"

There was no news about the song or the essay. But there was a letter from Marcia's book club. "When you enroll a friend," the letter read, "you get four free books." Marcia decided to enroll her friend: Sybil I. Dorsett.

Her friend had objected to having Marcia's name in the mailbox, but Marcia had held her own, telling Sybil through Dr. Wilbur that these days she got more mail than Sybil did. Marcia had won. There in the mailbox alongside "Dorsett" and "Reeves" was "Marcia Baldwin." Well, Marcia thought, I have to have some victories.

As she walked up the stairs to the apartment, Marcia brooded moodily about her status. She was the one who came to the fore when Sybil simultaneously felt hidden anger and feelings of rejection, the one who took over these feelings that Sybil could not endure. "Marcia," Vicky had said, "feels what Sybil feels, only more so." No wonder, Marcia reflected, since I'm so close to Sybil that when she's asleep, I can't even open my eyes. But I want to be somebody, a recognized identity. If I sell my song and my article, I'll insist on using my own name. The fame and money will be mine.

It's the same way with my painting. My style is so individual that my work cannot be confused with the paintings of the others. And I'm cleverer than most of them—except perhaps Vicky and Vanessa.

My very existence, Marcia thought as she opened her apartment door, is tenuous. When Sybil is happy, she doesn't need me or any of us.

Inside the apartment Marcia could sense that Teddy was uncomfortable with her. Teddy, Marcia realized, was afraid of her depressions and her suicidal impulses.

Marcia headed for her easel and began, as was characteristic, to paint in a great variety of colors. She left the easel abruptly, thinking, I have everything and nothing, so much talent and so fragile an existence.

As Dr. Wilbur had observed, Marcia was a seeming contradiction: on the one hand, highly productive; on the other, as destructive. Underlying the buoyancy and creativity was a dark quality connected with her tremendous need for a loving mother and a desire, equally great, to kill retrospectively the mother she did have. Marcia's basic existence derived from the death wish for her mother, expressed long ago when Marcia had wished for the little box to grow big. But the death wish alternated within Marcia with a death wish for herself. When Sybil had stood at the banks of the Hudson River, ready to jump, Marcia had been the propelling inner force.

I want to live without the hurting, choking, the crying, Marcia thought as she walked back to the easel. I want to belong. I want to make a name for myself in the world. I want to get up in the morning and feel good, and I want to get in bed at night and go to sleep and be able on awakening, whether or not Sybil is asleep, to open my eyes.

Seated at her desk on August 17, 1959, Sybil wrote Dr. Wilbur:

I am not going to tell you there isn't anything wrong. We both know there is. But it is not what I have led you to believe. I do not have any multiple personalities. I don't even have a "double" to help me out. I am all of them. I have been essentially lying in my pretense of them. The dissociations are not the problem because they do not actually exist, but there *is* something wrong or I would not resort to pretending to be like that. And you might ask me about my mother. The extreme things I told you about her were not true. My mother was more than a little nervous. At times she was flighty, clever, overanxious, but she did love me. She was overprotective and watched me all the time. I was not the interesting, charming person she was. My parents were better than a lot of parents are. We had a nice home, plenty to eat, and nice clothes. I had lots of toys and books. My parents interfered with my music and my drawing, but it was due to a lack of understanding, not a lack of caring. I had no reason to complain. Why I grew to be odd I do not know.

After writing the letter Sybil lost almost two days. "Coming to," she stumbled across what she had written just before she had dissociated and wrote to Dr. Wilbur as follows:

It's just so hard to have to feel, believe, and admit that I do not have conscious control over my selves. It is so much more threatening to have something out of hand than to believe that at any moment I can stop (I started to say "This foolishness") any time I need to. When I wrote the previous letter, I had

374

made up my mind I would show you how I could be very composed and cool and not need to ask you to listen to me nor to explain anything to me nor need any help. By telling you that all this about the multiple personalities was not really true but just put on, I could show, or so I thought, that I did not need you. Well, it would be easier if it *were* put on. But the only ruse of which I'm guilty is to have pretended for so long before coming to you that nothing was wrong. Pretending that the personalities did not exist has now caused me to lose about two days.

Three weeks later Sybil reaffirmed her belief in the existence of her other selves in a letter to Miss Updyke, the school nurse of undergraduate days.

When I had been in analysis for a few months, I wrote you that Dr. Wilbur had explained to me about multiple personalities and that the "blank spells," as I had always called them, were not blank in anything but my memory. I had been active, and another "person" had taken over and said or done the things that I had not been able to do for some reason—whether fear of consequences, lack of confidence, lack of money, or for the reason of getting away from problems and pressures too great for me to face as "myself."

The point I'm trying to make is really twofold: The "blank spells" I have had since I was just under four were spells in which I, as another of the fifteen personalities that have emerged from time to time, did things to act out the problems or troubles of the past or the present. Many of these started with my mother, who was catatonic at times, at other times laughing hysterically and joking very cleverly, dancing on the street or talking much too loudly in church or acting "silly" at a party, sometimes cruel and sometimes entirely unreachable. We are trying to undo what has been done and what you, in your aversion to my mother, seemed to sense.

As Miss Updyke read this letter, she recalled the

homeward journey during which, chameleon-like, Sybil had revealed a swift succession of what had then been dismissed as moods. At one point Miss Updyke recalled that Sybil had put her head in her companion's lap, but Sybil had later insisted, "I'd never do a thing like that."

The others, who had been denied in the past because of lack of knowledge and denied in the present because of shame, had been readmitted to awareness.

27

Prisoners in Their Body

Watching Mary take the first steps toward buying a house, Peggy Lou plan to usurp the selfhood, Vanessa purge herself at the laundromat, and Marcia storm the citadel of authorship, Sybil came to consider herself more and more the hostage of the selves she hadn't been able to deny. As far as Sybil was concerned, these acts were part of the interference she had tried to banish from her life through denial. Vicky, on the other hand, decided that, although these were actions of the parts and not of the whole, they were thrusts toward health. As she told Dr. Wilbur: "I try to keep Sybil safe from dangers and give her as many good days as the others will allow."

Actually the days free of interference were few: Sybil's closets, despite limited funds, continued to sport the clothes she hadn't bought; her paintings were completed in her "absence"; and medicine—because the others took individual doses—persisted in running out long before it was time to renew a prescription.

On one occasion she had "come to" in the apartment to discover that she had a bandage over one eye and looked like a Cyclops. On another occasion she had found herself wearing ice skates and stumbling over the living room floor.

Captive, she was often late for appointments because her captors had deliberately hidden her purse or her underwear. Or the captors would manage to take her somewhere just long enough to keep her from getting to her destination on time. She often failed exams because those who held her hostage had deliberately given incorrect answers or because a particular jailer—Peggy Lou—had withheld the essential mathematical and chemical formulas.

With fourteen alternating selves making spontaneous appearances in the world, the slender frame of Sybil Dorsett, roaming the streets of New York, often confounded comprehensibility.

Peggy Lou walked in the rain, went into a store on Broadway, picked up a glass dish, wanting to break it. Vicky said no.

"Do you want the dish?" the clerk asked.

"No," Peggy Lou replied, "I want to break it."

"Put the dish back," Vicky ordered.

Peggy Lou did. Together Peggy Lou and Vicky left the store, leaving the clerk to think that the customer had been talking to herself.

Both Peggy Lou and Mary suddenly became sick at the corner of Seventy-First and Lexington Avenue. Peggy Lou leaned against an apartment building.

"What's wrong?" a policeman asked.

"She's sick," Vicky replied.

"Who is?" the officer wanted to know.

"I am," replied Peggy Lou.

Peggy Lou and Vicky, halfway across Madison Avenue, with traffic coming toward them from both directions, came to a sudden halt.

"I'm going over to the gift shop over there," Peggy Lou said, moving forward.

"I don't want to," Vicky replied, turning and walking toward the side of the street from which they had come.

377

Remarked the traffic policeman, "For heaven's sake, lady, make up your mind."

For several months Sybil made repeated attempts to get to an art gallery to retrieve a painting that had been part of an art exhibit. Each time she tried, Marcia took her elsewhere. In the end not Sybil but Dr. Wilbur reclaimed the painting.

Marcia and Peggy Lou took Sybil to a coffee shop in lower Manhattan. Sybil "came to" to find herself penniless and too far from home to walk. Seizing a dime on a counter, intended as a tip, she telephoned Dr. Wilbur. Again the doctor resolved the problem. The next day Sybil returned to the coffee shop to pay her debt.

Ironically, the captors thought of Sybil not as their hostage but as their keeper, the hostess of their body. All complained that she didn't give them enough to eat, that she didn't provide their favorite foods—a difficult task since they had individual tastes.

When one was ill, the others, who were not ill, felt the ravages of the illness. After Sybil's bout with colitis, Vicky complained, "See how much skinnier I've gotten." When Sybil Ann or Nancy Lou Ann, because of depression, would take to their bed, the others would also be immobilized. Mary and Sybil Ann had seizures, which were profoundly disturbing to the others. In cold weather, when Peggy Lou impetuously went out with insufficient clothes, Vicky would protest that "that made me cold, too." Vicky would say, "My head aches when Mary cries."

Captive the captors were, too, because Sybil's social life did not always coincide with their individual needs. Although they liked some people in common, they also had individual predilections for both outsiders and each other. Marcia and Vanessa did things together, as did Mike and Sid, Marjorie and Ruthie, and the Peggys. Although not a team, Mary and Vanessa were special friends.

Among outsiders Vanessa claimed to like everybody who wasn't a hypocrite. Peggy Lou vented her spleen against what she called "showoffs like Sybil's mother." Vicky favored intelligent and sophisticated persons.

Both Mary and Sybil had a special fondness for children. Mary, indicating oneness rather than autonomy, remarked about a woman they all knew, "None of us liked her."

Excited by conversations about music, Peggy Lou often shut her ears in the course of other conversations. Bored by female conversation in general, Mike and Sid sometimes succeeded in making Sybil break an engagement or nagged throughout the visit.

"I'd like to get going on building the new bookcase," Mike confided in Sid during one visit in which they were held captive.

"I have some typing to do and want to get home," Sid replied.

Summarizing what it was like to be a prisoner in a social situation, Marjorie told Dr. Wilbur, "I go with Sybil when she visits her friends, but they talk about things they like and I don't care about—houses, furniture, babies. But when Laura Hotchkins comes, they talk about concerts, and I like that."

Of them all Nancy Lou Ann had the greatest interest in politics, an interest that was closely linked with the fulfillment of Biblical prophecy. As had already become apparent, these other people within Sybil had different religious attitudes and different tastes in books. They also had different vocabularies, handwriting, speech patterns, and different body images. Their reactions to sex were not the same. The fear of getting close to people, the result of Hattie Dorsett's abuses, permeated the sexual attitude of all of them. In Peggy Lou and Marcia, however, the fear became terror. In Vanessa it was somehow sublimated by a *joie de vivre,* and in Sybil Ann it was dissipated by a yielding lassitude.

Incipient, insidious jealousies often flared among the selves. Peggy Lou was furious that Vicky had an extensive knowledge of early American furniture. To get back at Vicky, Peggy Lou burned the midnight oil for countless hours, poring over books on this subject, memorizing page after page, until she could proudly prattle as an expert on the subject. Vicky looked on with an amused, tolerant smile.

379

Talents and ambitions among the selves were both the same and different. According to Vicky, Sybil was the best of the painters. Vicky had often taught with and sometimes for Sybil. Both Sybil and Vicky wanted to become doctors. When asked whether Sybil should study medicine, Peggy Lou replied, "It's hard for her to concentrate. But I could do it if I tried."

The selves alternated with each other, but they also co-existed. They obstructed some of Sybil's activities, but they cooperated in others. Sid had built the partition. As on the Omaha scaffold, there was harmonious joint painting. Peggy Lou, who didn't like to paint in oils, helped with an oil painting. Marcia talked enthusiastically of an abstract painting that "we all did together."

Marcia often went to chemistry classes and lab sessions when Sybil could not attend, taking notes for Sybil to study later and signing Sybil's name on the attendance sheet. Like a secretary signing her boss's signature in the boss's absence, Marcia often put her own initials under the signature of Sybil I. Dorsett.

None of the selves was essentially more intelligent than any other, although there were marked differences in what had been studied, learned, and absorbed. Although their ages fluctuated, each self had a prevailing age. Differences in the prevailing ages, in the quality of emotions, in the degree of activity and passivity, and, of course, in the traumas each of the selves defended accounted for vast differences in behavior. So clearly marked were these differences that when the various selves telephoned Dr. Wilbur she knew not only from the voice but also from the behavior described who was on the line.

"Dr. Wilbur, I'm in this bar with colored lights. Everyone is having fun," the voice said. "Why can't I have a beer?"

"Sure you can, Peggy Lou," the doctor replied.

"Wouldn't that be naughty?" Peggy Lou had reversed her position.

"No," the doctor said reassuringly, "lots of people drink beer."

"Well, no," Peggy Lou decided. "I'm going home."

Captor and captive, Sybil counted on Teddy Reeves to mediate among the selves, to report on their comings and goings, to bridge the void that existed between blacking out and coming to. A Greek chorus commenting on Sybil's fragmented action, Teddy also shared Sybil's interest in multiple personality.

In 1957, for instance, when the movie *Three Faces of Eve* was released, Sybil and Teddy saw it together because they had heard it was about a multiple personality.

In the movie Eve White changed into Eve Black, who, talking to the doctor, dropped her eyes coquettishly. Teddy grabbed hold of Sybil and whispered, "That's exactly what you do." Misunderstanding, Sybil thought that Teddy had meant that she was flirtatious.

"Is that the way I act with people?" Sybil asked in dismay.

"No," Teddy replied. "That's the way you look when you change from one to another. You have a sort of blank look just for a moment."

"The movie was exactly like Sybil," Teddy later told Dr. Wilbur.

"No," the doctor explained. "Sybil and Eve don't have the same kind of personality. The reasons for being multiple personalities are not the same. But I do agree that Sybil and Eve have the same blank look when they change."

Despite the closeness between Sybil and Teddy in extraordinary circumstances, their relationship began to quaver. Disquieting to Teddy had been Peggy Lou's assertiveness and Marcia's depressions. Sybil, disturbed by Teddy's disquietude, became increasingly lonely.

The tension did not come to a head, however, until one night in the late summer of 1959 when Teddy made some scathing remarks about the doctor. "She's exploiting you to satisfy her own personal needs," Teddy charged.

"I don't want to hear any more of this," Sybil replied angrily as she rose from the dinner table.

"Well, you never want to hear the truth," Teddy snapped.

Propelled by mounting anger, Peggy Lou stepped right into the context of the action. "I'm leaving," she announced.

"No, you're not," Teddy replied authoritatively. "You're not going to run away again. I'm going to keep you here whether you like it or not."

"You get out of my way," Peggy Lou warned, "or I might hit you."

"You wouldn't dare," Teddy challenged.

"You get out of my way, or you'll see," Peggy Lou threatened, heading for the door.

With Teddy trying to block the way, Peggy Lou rushed to a large bay window. Teddy grabbed hold of her wrist, clutching it tightly. Breaking away, Peggy Lou crawled on all fours and, her back to Teddy, wedged herself under a large dresser. Despite repeated attempts, Teddy failed to get Peggy Lou out. She finally appealed by phone to Dr. Wilbur.

Arriving on the scene within an hour, the doctor got down on the floor, calling, "Peggy Lou." No answer. "Peggy, it's Dr. Wilbur," the doctor repeated several times.

"Huh?" Peggy Lou, her back still turned and certain that she was being tricked, mumbled, "where did you come from?"

"I came from my house to see you."

"Where do you live?"

The doctor described her apartment and office.

"Is it really Dr. Wilbur?" Peggy Lou asked incredulously.

"Yes."

"Is that girl still here?" Peggy Lou wanted to know.

"Yes."

"Tell her to go away. I won't come out until she does."

Finally Dr. Wilbur was able to cajole Peggy Lou into emerging from the hideaway.

A few months later, "that girl" did go away.

"I don't usually let anyone get close to me," Sybil

remarked sadly to Dr. Wilbur. "I did you and maybe Teddy. But look what happened."

28

Journey to One

In the autumn of 1959 Dr. Wilbur faced the fact that the Dorsett analysis was following a halting path. Progress was slow and resistances, strong. Sybil showed signs of marked improvement for longer or shorter periods; then one of the other selves would slide into depression, conflict, trauma, fear, self-destructiveness. All accomplishment suffered, and some accomplishments failed. One obvious external failure was that Sybil dropped out of school—too sick to learn.

Progress had to be more rapid. New action was essential. This Dr. Wilbur felt with increasing assurance and intensity.

She reread the hypnotic sessions Dr. Morton Prince had conducted with Christine Beauchamp and consulted colleagues for their opinions of the Dorsett case. The typical comment was: "Just keep going. You're doing fine." The advice was to continue along the route she had been following. She decided that being a pioneer was not all that it was cracked up to be.

Pondering the grave problems confronting both her patient and herself, Dr. Wilbur knew that she was facing a professional crisis.

Her conviction that straight psychoanalysis was the treatment of choice in the Dorsett case remained firm, yet she was willing to experiment as long as there was no threat to her patient or the treatment situation.

The doctor was aware, too, that she had strong feelings about Sybil not only as a patient but also as a human being.

Dr. Wilbur was convinced also that the manifestations of the multiplicity and the physical diseases that Sybil suffered were rooted in overwhelming childhood experiences that could be permanently changed through analysis.

The question that arose was: can I find a way to speed up the process of integration? The experience with pentothal had shown conclusively that symptomatology having to do with specific traumas and conflicts could and did disappear when the trauma was revealed and the conflict explicated clearly to the waking self.

Dr. Wilbur knew that to reinstitute pentothal was too dangerous because of the potential for addiction. She sought other means.

Her patient was a hysteric. Since the time of Charcot and Freud hysterics were known to be readily hypnotizable. Dr. Wilbur decided at least to investigate the potential of this technique. Before she had become a psychoanalyst, she had used hypnosis successfully with other patients. Now she would experiment with hypnosis in analysis. Once again she decided that she was ready to pioneer.

Toward the end of a gloomy and unfruitful analytic hour in the autumn of 1959, Dr. Wilbur said softly, "Sybil, when you first came to me in New York, you asked me to promise that I would not hypnotize you. I agreed, but there were tremendous disturbances I didn't understand then. Now I believe that hypnosis can help us."

Sybil replied quietly, "I have no objection."

The journey toward becoming one entered a new, intensified phase. Now, enveloped by the womb-like comfort of the doctor's office, cradled by the leavening power of hypnotic slumber, Sybil went back in time. The other selves went both back and forward—forward so that, through gradual stages, all could reach Sybil's age. Integration, Dr. Wilbur knew, would be simpler if all the selves were of the same age. Their very existence indicated a wedding to the traumas of the past and an immaturity in the total personality, both of which made integration impossible.

Two-year-old Ruthie was the natural point of embarkation. "How are you?" the doctor asked after summoning her in one of the earliest hypnotic sessions. "Are you all right?"

"Yes."

"Do you remember me?"

"Yes."

"When did you see me last?"

"Brown chair."

"Yes. Have you ever been here? When were you here?"

"One day and one more day."

"Yes, and what does the room look like?"

"Chair."

"Yes. What color are the walls here?"

"Green."

"That's right. You know, Ruthie, you are two. Isn't that right? Would you like to be three?"

"Yes."

"In ten minutes I'm going to say it is five minutes of seven. Between now and that time, you are going to grow up one whole year. It's going to be all right, Ruthie. You're going to grow up, and later all the others are going to grow up too. Would you like to?"

"Yes. Then I can color."

"You may draw all you want and make things with the colored pencils and crayons. Or you may help Sybil paint."

"I can?"

"Whenever she paints, you can help her."

"Yes."

"Anything else you would like to do?"

"Everything."

"Then you will help everybody do everything. And you are growing, growing, growing. You will never be so young again. When you get to be three, you will stay there for a little while and then you are going to grow again. I want you to pick a nice day to be three—a day you enjoyed."

"Aunt Fay."

"All right, you pick a day in the summer when you visited your aunt Fay."

"She was my Mama."

"She wasn't really. You liked to pretend she was your Mama. That was because your Mama wasn't very satisfactory, and *we know* that. We are going to help you grow up so that you don't have to worry about your Mama ever again. Do you understand, dear?"

"Yes."

Ruthie became three, with the doctor's full knowledge that this was no mere mechanical process, no simple suggestion. Age progression could only advance as the traumas and conflicts were resolved. Age progression was being utilized as the means to an end.

Two months later the doctor told Ruthie, "In ten minutes you will be six, and it will be spring. Then I will help you to grow up, to catch up with the others. In ten minutes, you will be six. You will never be any younger than that, and as we go on, you will get older. You will find that as you get older, you can do more about the things you want to do and you will do less about the things that other people want you to do. You will grow up one year, two years, three years, and you will pick a day that was good."

"Can Daddy help me make a grocery store in the haystack?"

"Then it is summer?" the doctor assumed.

"Winter," Ruthie insisted.

"A haystack in the winter?"

"Uh. And there's snow on top of it. And you dig a hole in it and you put in the oatmeal box and empty cans and you make a store inside the haystack."

"All right. Now you are six years old."

"We're on the farm, and it's the winter time," Ruthie said.

This was the winter of Hattie Dorsett's catatonia and Sybil's camaraderie with her father. Ruthie had enjoyed the farm; she was free of her mother and close to her father.

"You are six years old and you will never again be less than that. I'm going to help you grow up to catch up to the others and finally to Sybil. Would you like that?"

"Yes."

"Now, when I touch your right elbow, I will ask to speak to Mike and Sid together. Sid. Mike."

"Hi."

"Hi. Would the two of you like to grow up?"

"Sure. I don't want to be a little sissy," Mike replied enthusiastically. "I want to grow up like Daddy and do what he can do."

"All right, both of you are going to start to become grown up. Now is there anything you would like to say to me before you are older?"

Mike posed a startling question: "You think the girls are going to kill us?"

"Do I think the girls are going to kill you?" the doctor repeated with disbelief.

"Yes," Mike replied apprehensively.

"The girls? Which girls?" the doctor asked in an attempt to elucidate what Mike really meant.

"Marcia and Vanessa," Mike replied cryptically.

"If they kill them, will we die, too?" Sid asked with concern.

"I don't know whom you mean by 'they,'" the doctor insisted.

"There's a rumor," Sid explained, "that the girls are going to kill each other, that the time is coming when some of them won't be."

"The time is coming," the doctor replied with emphasis, "when no one of you will be by yourself. All of you are going to work together. But now I want to get back to your question. Mike, are you listening? Sid? I want you to understand very clearly what I'm about to say. If Marcia and Vanessa were dead, you would be dead too. Therefore, you must help them to live and catch up with Sybil so they will not want to die."

"But they feel so bad," Sid said.

"Yes, I know," the doctor replied softly. Then with

387

intensity she added, "But you can help them to feel better. You can cheer them up. Nobody is going to kill anybody. And now you are getting older, older, older."

'Dr. Wilbur felt reassured by the age progression sessions, especially since genuine analysis was taking place. The boys had just revealed suicidal intent on the part of other selves as well as their own fear that integration would result in death for them.

Getting older was the order of becoming until, by April, 1960, no one of the selves was less than eighteen. Sybil, however, was thirty-seven and three months. Since identity of ages constituted an important step toward integration, Dr. Wilbur talked with Vicky on April 21 about taking this step.

"I'm overwhelmed," Vicky replied, "at the thought of being that old."

"Shall we do it, Vicky?"

There was silence.

The psychoanalyst thought for a moment. Then she tried another approach. "Vicky, you're the one who knows everything about everybody; you're the memory trace, the positive force in the Sybil complex. Shouldn't you be her age when already you have all the memories of the years that make her older than you? Isn't that equity?"

"I suppose." Vicky was not enthusiastic about approaching forty. Then, lightly tapping her index finger on an end table, she remarked, "Have I ever told you that Sybil would like to be me but doesn't know how?"

"Making you her age will make it easier for her," the doctor explained. "Shall we?"

Vicky said softly, "You're the doctor."

Then, when the patient was under an hypnotic spell, Dr. Wilbur asked, "Is everybody here?"

Someone said, "Yes."

"Ruthie," the doctor called.

"Yes," said Ruthie, now eighteen.

"Mike," the doctor then asked, "would you like to be thirty-seven?"

"Sure," said Mike.

"Sid?"

"Sure," Sid replied.

When the doctor put the same question to Peggy Lou, the reply was, "Yes, if I have to do it."

"Well, you don't have to do it," the doctor replied. "What is your reservation?"

"Well," Peggy Lou hesitated. "I'll miss my television programs."

"Thirty-seven-year-olds watch television," the doctor said, laughing.

"I don't want to have to study all the time," Peggy Lou added apprehensively.

"No, studying all the time isn't good for anybody," the doctor replied. "You won't have to do that."

Peggy Lou gave her consent.

Then the doctor asked Peggy Ann, who replied, "Yes, I guess so."

"You sound a little doubtful," the doctor remarked.

"Well, will I have to go to church?" Peggy Ann wanted to know.

"No, you won't have to go to church," the doctor replied reassuringly.

"Other grown-ups do," Peggy Ann declared.

"Sybil is grown up," the doctor pointed out, "and she doesn't go to church. You're eighteen now, and you don't go."

"Okay. Okay," Peggy Ann assented.

The doctor called on each of the selves. Nancy Lou Ann, Marcia, Vanessa, Clara, Marjorie, Helen, and Sybil Ann had no objections.

Mary, however, protested: "I feel so tired."

"If you were Sybil's age," the doctor argued, "you would not be as tired, and you would feel better because you would get help and support from the others. Wouldn't you like that?"

"Would you still be my friend?" Mary asked apprehensively.

"You bet your life," the doctor replied emphatically.

"You won't leave me?" Mary asked.

"I won't leave you," the doctor promised.

"Very well," Mary finally agreed.

"Vicky," the doctor asked, "are you ready?"

"I'll take the plunge," Vicky declared.

"Is everybody all set?" asked the doctor.

"Yes," Vicky replied, "we are ready."

"We are going to start now," the doctor announced decisively. "All of you are going to grow. You are going to keep right on growing. Fifteen minutes from now you will be thirty-seven and three months—Sybil's age."

"Thirty-seven is awfully old," Nancy Lou Ann demurred. "That's too old for anything."

"No, that's not too old to do anything," the doctor insisted. "I do lots of things, and I'm older than that." Then proceeding to the attempt at suggestion as part of the cure, Dr. Wilbur iterated and reiterated, her voice assuming the cadence of hypnotic incantation, "You are getting older, older, older; you are growing, growing, growing: 25, 28, 31, 33. In six minutes you will all be thirty-seven and three months."

Seconds ticking. Minutes passing. Waiting, Dr. Wilbur could not know that there was sudden rapture flowing swiftly through the senses that belonged to the fifteen selves of her patient. In every vein and fiber of Sybil there was a quickening newness, as she and her other selves moved to a new phase of healing. Still in their hypnotic sleep they could feel a fluctuant wave, buoying them with new strength.

The patient seemed relaxed. Finally the doctor proclaimed, "You are all thirty-seven and nine months and will never again be any younger. When you wake up, you will know that now you are all thirty-seven and nine months. You will all be the same age as the others."

Then the fear of losing out crept in. "Will you love us now that we're old?" Peggy Lou asked wistfully.

"I will always love all of you," was the answer.

"And be our friend as you were in the past?" asked Marcia.

"Just as much your friend."

"Things will be quite different," Vanessa remarked apprehensively.

"Whenever you have a difference of opinion," the doctor pointed out, "you will be able to discuss it with each other within yourself. You won't have to fight about it."

"Or run away," Peggy Lou added.

"You'll have more in common and will be able to share some of the things you enjoy," the doctor explained. "One of the reasons for conflict and the lack of communication among you has been the vast differences in your ages. If Marcia feels depressed, the rest of you will be able to cheer her up. If Sybil Ann is listless, the others will give her energy."

Marcia asked, "Does this mean we can't call you if we don't feel well?"

"No," the doctor replied earnestly, "it does not mean that." She knew that the underlying fear Marcia had expressed for all of them was: Will I be rejected if I get well? The end of treatment to these troubled selves implied loss of the doctor, who had also become a friend.

"Now you are going to wake up," the doctor began in hypnotic cadences. "One—stretch. You are waking up. Two—stretch, stretch, stretch. Now you may wake up. Three."

Sybil opened her eyes. She and the doctor looked at each other intently—their eyes mirroring the other's hopes. Finally, the doctor spoke: "How do you feel, dear?"

"Quieter," Sybil murmured. Then she added, "I will have more time to use, and everybody can use it."

"That's exactly right," the doctor replied with expectation. "Now you will go home, and you will have a good day. I'll see you in the morning." With added reassurance she remarked, "There are no little girls around now to keep you from getting here on time."

Through hypnotic age progression, Dr. Wilbur had metamorphosed what had been fixations in the past into viable parts of the present. The hope was that this would become the bedrock on which to erect the superstructure of integration, a way to open the pathways to the original Sybil—and to restore her.

391

29

They Are Me, Too

The next morning—April 22, 1960—Dr. Wilbur asked: "Sybil, would you like to meet the others?"

"If you want me to," was the acquiescent reply.

"I'll introduce you to Ruthie first," the doctor said when Sybil was in a deep hypnotic sleep. "Until a few months ago she was just two years old. When I touch your right elbow, I will ask for Ruthie."

Ruthie was summoned: silence. The doctor waited. Then Sybil's voice said quietly, "I see her."

The moment was loaded with meaning because this was the very first time that Sybil had had a visual impression of any of her other selves, the first time that they had existed for her within her *own* consciousness. The way Sybil "saw," moreover, was a reminder of Sybil's freedom from psychosis; for Ruthie had been perceived not as floating in space, not as the projected image of a hallucination but only in the mind's eye.

"You see her?" the doctor asked. "Now tell me: why did you leave her behind?"

"Because she had ideas of her own. She wouldn't do what I said." It was a curious concept, the expression of the yawning chasm between the directives of the conscious mind and their execution by the unconscious.

"What do you think about that now?" the doctor asked.

"I don't think that's right," Sybil replied, "because things change all the time." Then she added, "Ruthie has her arms out, and I think she wants me."

"What do you think of her?" The doctor's voice was

low. "Do you like her? Would you like to have Ruthie with you now?"

A breathing stillness, then Sybil's saying, "Yes, I want her. She belongs to me."

"Ruthie will be with you," the doctor replied, conferring connection.

"I want her," Sybil iterated.

"She is as old as you and can help you," the doctor explained.

"I want her help," Sybil admitted.

"Now, how do you feel?" the doctor asked.

Sybil, in scarcely more than a whisper, replied, "Happier!"

"Now, Sybil," the doctor continued, "the others are right here, and you'll have to choose the next one you want to meet."

"That would be Vicky," Sybil said without hesitation. "She has taught me some things even though I haven't met her."

"She has helped us a great deal, too," the doctor explained, "by telling us what the others didn't know or couldn't tell."

Then Sybil asked, "Is Vicky my friend?"

There was strong conviction in the doctor's answer: "Very much your friend. Now I'm going to ask Vicky to come. Vicky."

"Hi," said Vicky.

The introduction of sleeping selves, now jointly sharing the unconscious, was simple. "Vicky," the doctor said, "this is Sybil."

Silence, awkwardness. "Does she want to be friends?" Sybil asked.

The doctor put the question to Vicky, and from Vicky came the gracious reply: "I should like to very much."

The conferral of friendship: "There are no obstacles. Now you two girls go right ahead and be friends."

Suddenly tears flowed copiously. Sybil's tears. This depleted girl was crying now at the prospect of having a friend within her. Over the tears came the doctor's affirmation: "Vicky is part of you." Then the question: "Why, Sybil, did you leave Vicky behind?"

393

Sybil insisted, "I didn't. When I couldn't do something, Vicky did it for me. I didn't leave her."

More affirmation from the doctor: "Vicky's a part of you that is very likable."

"I have these two friends now," Sybil said. "They came toward me willingly." Then the avowal, the declaration of acceptance: "They are me, too."

More silence. Then Sybil said, "I would like to go home. That's what I wish."

"Very well," the doctor agreed. "I will explain to the others that you will meet them another time. And we will do no more today."

"Yes," Sybil agreed, "I would like to meet them just a little later." Instinctively Sybil knew that meeting each of the selves involved facing the conflicts and traumas that each defended. Quite wisely Sybil decided that meeting two selves was enough for one day.

"Turn aside, Sybil, and rest. I want to make some explanation to the others, and then you can go home."

"Peggy Ann," the doctor called.

"Yes," from Peggy Ann.

"Does everybody understand why Sybil isn't meeting you today?"

Unhesitatingly Peggy Ann replied: "We certainly do. It's all right with us. We have no special claims on Sybil. We did some things to hurt her. Peggy Lou and I took her to Philadelphia, Elizabeth, other places. We did some things."

"Do the others understand?" Dr. Wilbur asked.

"The boys are laughing," Peggy Ann replied. "They think it's funny."

"What?"

"All this about getting older and meeting Sybil. And I think it's funny that the boys are men now. Thirty-seven is a man."

"In their case, no," said the doctor. "I would hope that they will become a woman."

Puzzled, Peggy Ann responded only with an "Oh."

Then, returning to the original theme, the doctor said, "We will wait a little while and let Sybil become adjusted to the idea of meeting all of you. Is that okay?"

"It's okay," Peggy Ann replied.

"That's very kind of you, very good of you," the doctor said. "Sybil will understand how good you are when she gets to know you better."

"Oh, Doctor," Peggy Ann blurted. "I hope Sybil won't go around saying 'We' instead of 'I.'"

"Now," Dr. Wilbur said, changing the subject, "I'm going to touch your right elbow and ask to speak to Sybil."

"Yes?" from Sybil.

"I'd like to wake you up now," said the doctor. "When you are awake, you will know that you, Vicky, and Ruthie are together, that you will always be together, and that you will never need to be apart. Now you are going to wake up. One—stretch; you are waking up. Two—stretch, stretch, stretch. Now you may wake up. Three."

In all analyses periods of improvement tend to be followed by periods of regression; for every step forward there is at least one step backward. After Sybil had established an entente with Vicky and Ruthie, she continued to resist meeting the other selves. In July, 1960, a month after the entente, that meeting still had not taken place. Moreover, as Peggy Lou made clear to Dr. Wilbur, many of the old conflicts had returned to plague Sybil, who once again was suicidal.

A woman now, Peggy Lou began the session with, "I'm afraid I'll do something foolish. I worry about that."

"Yes?" Dr. Wilbur asked thoughtfully.

"I was a little girl for so long, and now I'm a woman. Some of my old ways are no longer appropriate."

"I wouldn't worry about that," the doctor replied. "From what I can see you're doing fine. Now I'd like to ask you a question."

"Yes?"

"Sybil felt happier when she met Ruthie and Vicky. But what has happened to the happiness?"

"All the old feelings," Peggy Lou replied knowingly,

"have come back. I thought it wasn't going to be like that anymore."

"She called me," the doctor confided.

"I know," Peggy Lou replied.

"I never really know whether to go or not when she calls," the doctor explained. "I sometimes think she feels guilty about having me come."

"She does," Peggy Lou agreed.

"I don't want to undermine her feeling about herself any more than I want to weaken your feeling about yourself. Have the old suicidal feelings come back?"

"Even more strongly than before," Peggy replied with concern. "Her fears drive her to it. The greatest fears she has now are facing religion and school. She tried to tell you yesterday but couldn't."

The fears were so powerful that they led to retrogression, even after the entente with Vicky and Ruthie.

"Sybil feels that is a lot to face," Peggy Lou explained. "I heard Vicky say to Sybil: 'Well, you take it one day at a time.' But Sybil dreads that things will get like they were in the time of tension."

"What is it about religion that terrifies Sybil so, especially when Mary is still defending Sybil against the most serious religious conflicts?"

"It's a terrible fear of finding out that there's nothing to it," Peggy Lou replied thoughtfully.

"Could she be afraid of finding out that she doesn't want to be in her religion?" the doctor asked.

"She'd fear that," Peggy Lou reported, "if it occurred to her."

"This would frighten her?" the doctor asked.

"There's a reason why she's afraid," Peggy Lou explained.

"Yes?"

"Well, you see," Peggy Lou continued, "she believes in God and that the Commandments are true. They say, 'Thou shalt not kill.' That makes it wrong for her to kill herself. Her life isn't her own."

"Yes?"

"And that's an inhibition, the last thing in the way

of self-destruction. If that were taken away . . . well, I don't know, Doctor, I really don't."

"Aren't there other things that keep her from doing it?"

"There are several things," Peggy Lou replied with conviction. "We are one reason. You see, now that she has gotten to like us, she feels a responsibility toward us and doesn't want to destroy us."

Peggy Lou had always exerted strong pressures to let Sybil live. But she did it in a new way now. She did it, too, in concert with the other selves. Now the life force resided less in the actions of the others than in Sybil's new reaction toward them.

"So," Peggy Lou went on, "the evidence piles up. Sybil's afraid to kill herself because of God, because of us, and also because of you. She doesn't want to hurt you. She can't hurt you, and she can't do what God doesn't want. But you see, if she found out there wasn't any God, there would be one restraint gone. She's not afraid of the punishment in itself. Sometimes she thinks that would be over quickly—that you can't burn forever. But she's afraid to find out that there is no God and there's nobody to stop her but you and us."

"Now, Peggy," Dr. Wilbur asked, "you would say then that she wants to believe in God and the Commandments?"

"Well," Peggy Lou replied, "there are some things that Sybil thinks you will think are silly. The truth of the matter is that she's afraid to find out that *she*'s the one who thinks it's silly. If she thought that, it could all collapse."

"So," the doctor asked, "is this why she is afraid to talk about religion?"

"And when things were bad, she used to ask God to help her, and she thought He did," Peggy Lou went on. "She believed it."

"Yes."

"Yet things were bad," Peggy Lou continued skeptically, "even while she was doing that. But she always thought there was an explanation. She had it all reasoned out. You kind of mixed it up for her, and she wants to straighten it out. She knows she can't get anywhere unless she does. All I can say is that she has to make up her mind about what she believes. I don't know what the others think. They're just standing there."

"Now, Peggy, will you and the others who can still stand aside from Sybil join me in making it possible for Sybil to go ahead and get things done?"

"Well, I should think so," Peggy Lou replied with intensity.

The new Peggy Lou was both objective about Sybil and on Sybil's side.

New York's sultry summer of 1960 brought unrelentingly high temperatures. While the nation girded itself for the Kennedy-Nixon campaign, the Dorsett case was reverberating with a private cataclysm.

Dr. Wilbur's brows were knitted in astonishment. Sybil had been hypnotized, Peggy Lou summoned. Expecting Peggy Lou's crisp "Hi," the doctor heard instead: "I say to myself Sybil."

The voice was not unlike Peggy Lou's, but the message confounded comprehension. "I say to myself Sybil"?

Fixing her gaze on her sleeping patient, the doctor said quietly, "But I called for Peggy Lou."

"You don't understand, Doctor," was the answer. "I am Peggy Lou, and I heard you. I am also Sybil. I'm Vicky, too."

A conglomerate? How come? Rapprochement had been achieved so far only among Sybil, Ruthie, and Vicky. Peggy Lou was one of the selves who still stood aside from Sybil. Yet without introduction and by her own volition Peggy Lou had moved into the tiny inner circle: "I am Peggy Lou, and I heard you. I am also Sybil. I'm Vicky, too."

The doctor called again for Peggy Lou.

"We hear you," was the reply. "And your surprise does not surprise us. But you will become accustomed to us. This is what we have become."

"Vicky," the doctor called.

"We are Vicky."

The doctor called, "Sybil."

"We are Sybil."

Peggy Lou, Vicky, and Sybil had spoken with one voice.

"All right," the doctor then said, "it is time to wake up. When you do, you will feel relaxed. You will not try to solve any problem. The others who are not yet part of you have told me, without my asking, that they are with you and are going to help you. When you wake up, you will not feel lonely. You'll feel a little more sure of yourself, a little more confident. You will go about your business without fear."

The patient awoke.

"Sybil?" the doctor asked.

"Yes," was the reply.

"Just Sybil?" from the doctor.

"Why do you say it that way?" Sybil asked. "Who else should there be? I'm really just me, and I'm not ready to hold hands with all those other people."

"How do you feel, dear?" the doctor asked.

"I feel better."

"Are you a little less scared?" the doctor continued.

"I think so."

"Do you think you can do what you want to do today?"

"I'll try to make buttonholes this afternoon," Sybil replied.

"It's going to be a good day for all of you," Dr. Wilbur predicted.

"I'm really just me," Sybil insisted.

"All of you are just you," the doctor replied prophetically.

The prophecy, however, was without any optimism as to when the integration would take place. What had happened in this session was spontaneous, spectacular, but the doctor could not be certain of the true significance. Peggy Lou had obviously joined sleeping Sybil, Vicky, and Ruthie, not through the assistance of hypnosis, but spontaneously. The doctor had not said, "Peggy Lou, I want you to meet Sybil." It was Peggy Lou herself who said, "I am Sybil and Vicky, too." Since the spontaneous merger had occurred in the hypnotic state, the joining was with sleeping Sybil, not waking Sybil. The doctor believed that the wisest course of action was to wait and see what would happen to this spontaneous integration.

Meantime, between July, 1960, and early January, 1962, analysis proceeded, traumas were resolved, and the massive residue from the past began to chip away. The two and a half years, however, were a period of watchful waiting for the major breakthrough that would make Sybil *one* person.

30

Hate Heals

On a day in early January, 1962, as Sybil and Dr. Wilbur were driving along the West Side Highway on one of their now frequent out-of-the-office visits, Sybil was listless, gloomy. Usually she enjoyed the nonprofessional moments with the doctor, but on this overcast day depression shrouded enthusiasm.

"You're down," the doctor ventured, "because you're angry and you've turned your anger against yourself. It's probably your mother."

"That doesn't make me feel any better," Sybil replied defensively. Turning to the window, she made clear that the matter was closed.

Dr. Wilbur's hands were on the steering wheel; her eyes were focused on the traffic ahead, but her thoughts were on the impenetrable void that still clearly separated the conscious from the unconscious Sybil. Virtually all of the other selves, representing the unconscious, had vigorously declared their hatred of

Hattie Dorsett, a hatred Sybil also had expressed in the dream about the mother cat. Neither the reactions of the other selves nor the behavior in the dream, however, had filtered into Sybil's conscious awareness.

Now, when the chasm between inner truth and outer awareness had become apparent, was the very moment, Dr. Wilbur decided, for a direct onslaught on this stranglehold suppressing Sybil's freedom to be one.

"Sybil," the doctor called, placing her hand on Sybil's shoulder.

"Yes?" Sybil replied hesitantly.

"Would you mind," the doctor asked, "if I hypnotize you to get at the source of your depression?"

"Here?" Sybil looked at the doctor incredulously.

"Here," was the decisive reply.

Against the background of honking horns and chugging cars, there then came the hypnotic chant. As consciousness faded and Sybil drifted off into sleep, she dug her fingernails into the car's upholstery and murmured, "When somebody is your mother, you're supposed to love her, honor her."

"Not when she doesn't earn your love or give you reason to honor her," said the doctor.

"I wanted to please her because she was my mother," Sybil pleaded in a low, strained voice. "But I never could. She said I was funny. I feel choked up, like crying, when I think of her. She tied me down. It hurt terribly. She was always doing things—hideous things." Sybil's voice quavered; her body shook.

"Sybil?" the doctor asked quietly.

"I got all mixed up," was the reply. "I never did understand. Put it way inside. A black strip with a round hole in it. I see it now."

Silence. A low moan of suffering. Dr. Wilbur held her breath. She knew that Sybil, like a surgeon pointing a knife at the crucial lesion, was poised on the threshold of traumatic revelation. Sybil's voice rose. "I told myself I loved mother and only pretended that I hated her. But it was no pretense." Sybil's voice broke. The crisis had passed. Sybil went on: "I really hated her—ever since I can remember."

Overpowering feelings of hatred flooded Sybil. "I

401

hate her," she gasped. "Whenever she hurt me, I saw myself put my hands around her throat. Other ways, too. Stab her. Lots of times I wanted to stab her. Figures of her filled with nails. Never did it at home. Sometimes at school, sometimes at the hardware store. But I wanted to do it. I wanted to. When she died, I thought for a moment I had killed her. I wanted to for so long. I wanted to kill my mother."

At this point Dr. Wilbur could see that the paroxysm of hatred, drained from the unconscious, was invading the conscious. The internal motion catapulted Sybil forward. Dr. Wilbur caught her before she could hit the dashboard, but the doctor could not—and would not even if she could—restrain the torrent of hatred. A crescendo of short, swift stabs: "I hate her. I hate that bitch. I want to kill my mother. Even if she is my mother. I want her *dead!* I hate her, do you hear? I HATE HER!"

Sybil's fists pummeled the dashboard. Turning inward, Sybil had reclaimed the anger she had denied since the time in St. Mary's hospital, when the original Sybil had ceased to be.

There was silence in the car, but from outside came the honking of horns, the sound of an auto careening because of a flat tire. Largely oblivious of outer things, Dr. Wilbur knew that the taproot of trauma that had triggered the original proliferation into multiple selves had been demolished. The doctor decided to wake Sybil up.

"I guess I didn't think much of my mother," was Sybil's first remark. Amazed that the patient had remembered, Dr. Wilbur countered: "On the contrary—you thought a great deal of her. And you wanted desperately to have her love you."

Smiling wryly, Sybil replied, "Wanting to kill your mother isn't very loving."

Even more startled than before at how much of what had been spoken under hypnosis had been remembered, the doctor knew that a milestone in the analysis had been reached. Not only had Sybil remembered what she had said under hypnosis, but she also had recalled and accepted as hers Mike's "killing" in effigy of

Hattie Dorsett. These two developments, supplementing the fundamental admission of hatred of Hattie, so crucial to recovery, had represented vital moves toward integration.

Now, for the first time since she was three and a half years old, Sybil could get angry. The need for the selves who dealt with anger had therefore diminished, and those selves were now partially integrated with Sybil. Now, too, that Marcia's death wish for mother had become Sybil's wish, it was possible for Marcia and Sybil to move closer. But most remarkable of all was that once the capacity to get angry had been restored to Sybil, the pathways had been cleared for other emotions. The very act of expressing rage against Hattie Dorsett had transformed Sybil into a woman no longer bereft of emotions. Sybil had begun to move away from depletion, toward wholeness.

Hattie Dorsett, who had not really died until Sybil killed her with hatred on the West Side Highway, was no longer the major obstacle to Sybil's return to health.

The liberation of Sybil was almost immediate. It revealed itself dramatically several weeks later during a visit to her father in Detroit. She was seated on the sofa in the sunroom when Willard joined her. At first, simply reminiscent, she half expected him to take refuge behind *Architectural Forum*. When, instead, he seated himself beside her, eager to talk, apparently receptive to what she would say, for the first time she had no inhibitions about talking to him.

"When I was six and you had neuritis," she heard herself saying in a gush of powerful recollections soon after the conversation had begun, "you let me be close to you for the first time." There was an involuntary twitching in Willard's face as he replied softly, "I didn't realize that this was so."

"When we went to the farm that winter," she continued unrelentingly, "our closeness was intensified. But when we left the farm and you returned to work and I began school, we became strangers again." Flustered, defensive, Willard Dorsett replied "I gave you everything. A good home, good clothes, toys. Guitar lessons. I did these things because I cared."

"Dad." Sybil paused to weigh her words; then, swept along by the assertiveness that had so recently been returned to her, she took the plunge. "You gave me a guitar when I wanted a violin," Sybil said. "Don't you realize now that you were working in a vacuum? That you never bothered to communicate with me?"

Willard drew himself up with a sharp, abrupt movement. "I did sense," he said, "that the guitar lessons made you nervous, but I certainly didn't know why." He paused reflectively. "I see a lot of things differently now. I always wanted to do the right thing for you, but I didn't know how."

Very much aware of his proximity and stunned that he had not tried to make her feel guilty because she had been direct with him for the first time in her life, Sybil decided to give voice to what had been buried deepest.

"Dad," she said, "there are things that happened to me when I was very little . . ." Willard Dorsett shut his eyes to stop the stream of his daughter's recollections, now flowing perilously close to the guilt that five years earlier in Dr. Wilbur's office he had accepted as his own. "Dad, are you all right?" Sybil asked anxiously.

Opening his eyes, he held up his hand in a gesture of entreaty, saying: "Sybil, say no more. I'm an old man now. Spare me because of my years if for no other reason."

"When I was very little, Dad," Sybil persisted despite the entreaty, "hideous things happened. You didn't stop them."

"The wheat crib. The buttonhook," Willard murmured. Then he looked directly at his daughter, imploring, "Forgive me."

This time it was Sybil who rose to her feet, pacing. Forgive the lost time, the lost years? The anger that so newly seethed in her precluded forgiveness. "Let the dead past remain buried," was as close as she came to conciliation. She was ready to forget, not in the old sense of retreating from what she couldn't face but in the altogether new way of not making an issue of what had been done long ago.

The moment passed, and her outer mood shifted. Willard and Sybil began to talk of less painful things and the pleasures in store for her during the visit. But before Frieda called to say that lunch was being served, Willard Dorsett for the very first time talked to his daughter about her blackouts. "If I gave you more money," he asked, "would the blackouts end?"

"Money always helps," Sybil said simply, "but after thirty-six years of having blackouts, more money is not directly the answer." Then she added, "But they are becoming less frequent. I'm getting better."

"While we're talking about money, Sybil," Willard went on, "I want you to know that if anything happens to me, you'll be taken care of. The new duplex I'm building will belong to you."

"Thanks, Dad," Sybil said, half daring to trust in the caring he had at long last expressed.

At this point Willard made a curious remark: "Tell me, Sybil, who are these people you talk to and think you know?" Startled, she scrutinized the man who for so many years had lived under the same roof with the Peggys, Vicky, Marcia, Vanessa, Mary, and the others.

"Dad," Sybil said, "you misunderstood what Dr. Wilbur told you about these other people. I don't talk to them or think I know them. I was unaware of their existence until Dr. Wilbur told me about them. I'm only now getting to know them, beginning to talk to them."

This declaration was too much for Willard to absorb. Groping for meaning, he managed to say, "There is so much about you, Sybil, I can't understand." Still profoundly perplexed he led her into the dining room for the lunch Frieda had prepared.

That night, in the guest room of her father's house, Sybil dreamed about the sunroom of the Dorsett home in Willow Corners. Hattie was dead, and Sybil had come expressly to visit her father. The only bed in the house—the familiar large white iron bed in which her parents had slept—was now placed in the sunroom. Since Sybil had to sleep somewhere and this was the only bed in the house, she was asleep on one side of it. Her father slept on the other side. Awaking suddenly, she saw a man's face at the window. The lips moved. To someone unseen the stranger was saying, "They are mating."

"Don't move your eyes, Dad," Sybil called aloud, waking him. "There's a man watching through the window. He thinks we're sleeping together." Then, observing that the accuser at the window had a camera, she covered her eyes with her arm to avoid being recognized in the photograph. "Dad," she pleaded, "please get me a glass of hot milk so I can sleep better." As her father silently complied, she studied the accuser's face so as to make an accurate sketch of him for the police. She was disturbed because the accuser at the window had blonde hair.

Carefully reaching her arms through the bars at the head of the bed, she felt for the phone on the floor.

"Operator," she said, "get me the police." She heard a voice answer, "They're gone for the night."

"Then please try the constable," Sybil persisted. "Gone for the night," the voice iterated in sepulchral tones. "But I have to have help," Sybil cried. "There's a man at my window."

"Does your father carry any insurance?" the voice queried.

"What has *that* got to do with it?" Sybil shouted.

"I'll call the insurance broker, madam," the voice replied obligingly. "If you have the number . . ."

Sybil suddenly found herself clutching a handful of small business cards of insurance companies. As she groped for a name, she found the print too small to read. "Number, please; number, please," hammered at her brain. "I can't read the numbers," she protested helplessly. "The cards keep slipping." Her hands tried vainly to control the cards, which, of their own momentum, kept shuffling themselves.

"Drop this call, please," the operator's voice finally said.

"Please," Sybil pleaded, "someone must help."

The shattering silence that followed told her the truth, a truth she had never before been able to face—

406

that nobody was going to avenge the accuser at the window or indeed ever come to her rescue in anything.

Three months later, a letter from Frieda Dorsett, dated April 12, 1962, arrived in Dr. Wilbur's office. It read:

My husband's doctor called me this noon and told me that Sybil's father would not last much longer. As I wrote before, Mr. Dorsett is suffering from terminal cancer.

The doctor suggested that I write you and let you know that he will be glad to talk to you and tell you the situation if you will call him. Enclosed is his card.

Neither Sybil nor her father has mentioned whether she is planning on coming home to see him. I have not suggested anything about it because I do not know whether she can get along without you. It seems they do not realize the seriousness of his illness. Mr. Dorsett keeps saying he will be better in a day or two. The doctors have given him enough medication to take away his pain, but it has also taken away his mind. He has not asked about Sybil's letters in over a week now, and they were always of great importance to him. The last time I tried to read one to him, he stopped me.

I will be glad to have Sybil come home if I can take care of her, but frankly that has worried me for a long time. You know I have to work and cannot stay with her during the daytime.

I will be glad to hear from you if you have anything to suggest.

Two weeks later Dr. Wilbur informed Sybil of Willard's death. Sybil took the news quietly, but Mary, who had loved her father unreservedly, did not. Sybil didn't want to go to the funeral, and it was Sybil's decision that prevailed. The night of the funeral, however, Sybil dreamed that she was at a party at which Dr. Wilbur told her that her father was dead. "He is not. He is not," Sybil heard her own protest. Then rushing to the sunroom, she found him alive and in bed, with people standing around him. She threw herself on the bed beside him, still protesting, "He is not dead. He is not dead."

But Willard was indeed dead for Sybil in a more devastating way than she could have remotely suspected. News from Frieda that Willard had left his daughter penniless confronted Sybil with the terrible truth, for which her dreams had already prepared her. "You see, Sybil," Dr. Wilbur said consolingly, "you have always had strong Oedipal feelings for your father, but you've also always hated him. The original Sybil hated both her mother and her father."

The hatred was buttressed by the irony of her father's words, which now returned to mock her: "If anything happens to me, you'll be taken care of."

Taken care of? With her allowance from her father now ended and no inheritance, Sybil found herself barely getting by. Fortunately, she already had her masters degree in art and had dropped out of the premedical program that had wed her to chemistry. There were therefore no tuition fees. The analysis, however, had to go unpaid—Dr. Wilbur's investment in the future of achieving the integration of Sybil. As far as Sybil was concerned, however, this was a loan that would be paid. For rent, food, clothes, and other necessities Sybil was dependent upon gifts from friends. These gifts she also regarded as loans. In addition, there were her own slim earnings from intermittent tutoring and sales of paintings (she no longer worked at the Westchester hospital). And there was the temporary job in the laundromat to which Vanessa had led her.

Meanwhile, the analysis, propelled by the momentum of the anger Sybil could now feel, made measurable strides. Vicky was effectively bringing the various selves together by telling them about the past and the present of the total Sybil Dorsett. "The gang," Vicky told Dr. Wilbur, "is getting chummy."

No longer were there two Peggys but a return to Peggy Louisiana. The consolidated Peggy, moreover, was accepting with humor the prospect of becoming one with Sybil. On a morning in May, 1962, wearing a trench coat and peering through the corners of her eyes, Peggy strode into the doctor's office, looked under desks and chairs, and finally announced in pontifical tones: "We must get to the bottom of these traumas. It takes good detective work, Dr. Wilbur— I mean Dr. Watson."

"Well, Mr. Holmes," Dr. Wilbur asked. "What shall we uncover today?"

Peggy replied: "The pieces, Dr. Watson, all the pieces that will solve this unusual case."

For three successive days Peggy continued to play the role of Sherlock Holmes while she cooperated in disinterring and eradicating the traumas of the past.

Then all of a sudden, just as Dr. Wilbur began to believe that integration was within easy grasp, Mary went into a severe depression.

Sitting in the doctor's office in early June, 1962, Mary was so depressed that she couldn't talk. The next day none of the selves turned up for the appointment. When Dr. Wilbur telephoned the apartment, there was no answer. When she finally managed to get into the apartment, she found Mary under the dresser, refusing to come out. Finally extricating Mary, the doctor put her to bed. The next day, when again no one kept the appointment, the doctor returned to the apartment to enact the same scene. There were many such repeat performances.

On one occasion Mary fumed: "I'm in here."

"Where?"

"A place of stone with no doors, no windows, curved and open above," Mary replied. "There isn't any way I can get up to the opening up there. There is no exit. I'm caught inside these walls."

At first Dr. Wilbur thought that the walls symbolized Mary's frustrated wish to have a home of her own.

"What is this place, Mary?" the doctor asked.

"It's shaped like an igloo," Mary answered.

Remembering Mary's earlier discussions of religion, in which she had talked of being caught "inside these walls," the doctor asked, "Could the igloo be the Church?"

"I don't know. I don't know," Mary sobbed.

When it became apparent that religion was the imprisoning igloo and that the igloo had formed a stranglehold on the progress of the analysis, Dr. Wilbur had to tear the igloo down stone after unyielding stone. This involved analyzing again the underlying religious problem. The more they concentrated on religion, however, the more depressed Mary became. The greater Mary's depression, the more depressed—and the more suicidal—became the total self. Marcia wanted to jump into the Hudson River. This time Vicky, who had protected Sybil on the earlier occasion, told Dr. Wilbur: "Marcia wants to jump into the river, and I think I'll let her."

"Wait till I get there," Dr. Wilbur urged. And though Vicky had responded to the contagion of Mary's intensely pervasive depression, Vicky waited.

The suicidal nightmare continued as Mary explained, "Even if you burn forever, you can only hurt for a little while," or, "I don't care if I don't go to heaven. The only reason I'd like to go there is to be with my grandmother, and if mother is there, she'll keep me from Grandma anyway." Then, weeping, Mary would talk of what she called "my sorrowful childhood" and the barren walls of the church in Willow Corners.

Peggy protested: "We want to do things, but Mary drags us down."

It was paradoxical that, with the liberation of Sybil from her mother that had taken place on the West Side Highway, there should still be so strong a desire for suicide among some of the other selves. Dr. Wilbur had always regarded Sybil's suicide wish as an expression of the hatred for her mother turned against herself. The doctor hypothesized, however, that Sybil's liberation had not affected Marcia, who had always carried the burden of that wish and who at the same time had, as Vicky explained, a greater need for her mother.

Mary, for her part, had not been deeply affected by

410

Sybil's liberation from her mother, for her mother was not one of Mary's major problems. This personality's chief concerns were with Grandma Dorsett and her father and the fundamentalist religion that had informed their lives. As long as Mary accepted Grandma's simple faith of living an exemplary life, Mary was serene. When, however, she had allowed herself to be overwhelmed by the church and the theology that Grandma eschewed but which her father and Grandpa Dorsett embraced, she had carried the burden of religious entrapment that in some measure most of the selves, including Sybil, shared. For Mary there could be no resolution, no diminution of her suicidal inclinations until she was freed of her religious conflict.

The years between 1962 and 1965 were torn by conflict. Year after year Mary remained trapped in her igloo; year after year there was the struggle between survival and suicide, between getting well and remaining ill. "We're all afraid to get well," Marcia confided in Dr. Wilbur. But there was also another fear—subtle, indefinable, existential—a fear that Mike and Sid had voiced earlier when they had asked, "Are they going to kill us?"

"Am I going to die?" each of the selves asked Dr. Wilbur. For some of the selves integration seemed synonymous with death. The doctor's assurances that, although one with Sybil, the individual selves would not cease to be seemed at best only partly convincing. "There are many things I have to do," Vanessa told Marcia. "You see, I won't be here very long." Even Sybil, misunderstanding what Dr. Wilbur meant by saying that Vicky was endowed with more of the original Sybil than was Sybil herself, remarked with intensity, "I don't want to die and yield to that blabbermouth."

Then two new developments occurred that made the promised land recede even further.

Dr. Wilbur had thought that Mike and Sid had been integrated shortly after the age progression to thirty-seven. It had seemed theoretically impossible

411

for thirty-seven-year-old "men" to find sustenance in a woman's body. It had seemed probable that they would just yield to the totality of being the male in every woman. But one day in 1964 there came the crisp, "I'm Mike, and I want to talk to you, Dr. Wilbur."

"Hi, Mike," the doctor replied. Well, she reasoned, she hadn't treated a multiple personality before, and she didn't really know what to expect. Why should she be surprised?

"I want to know something," Mike asked belligerently.

"What's that?"

"How long are you going on with this farce about integrating Sid and me with all these women?"

"But I explained to you long ago," Dr. Wilbur reminded her patient, "that you live in a woman's body and have to accept that fact."

"Then why did you make us men? A Godlike sort of thing to do. Doesn't it bother you?"

Mike was cornering the doctor in the way that some of the selves had complained that she cornered them. "I didn't make Sid and you men," she finally replied. "Just as you were never really boys, you're not men now." She added quietly: "You still don't have penises."

"It's a lie," Mike replied angrily. "A bare-faced lie. Like anything else, a penis exists in the eye of the beholder. In my mind's eye my penis exists. I'm a man among men." He held the doctor's eye fixedly and added: "I'm not going to be part of a woman. Sid isn't either."

"Where is Sid?" The doctor stalled for time.

"Right here," Sid answered. "I came with Mike. He spoke for both of us. Now that our dad is dead, we're the men in the family, and no sissy doctor is going to stand in the way."

"Sid," the doctor asked, "what have I done to make you speak this way? I thought we were friends."

"Then act like our friend," Mike responded. "Give us our freedom to be what we are."

"That is what I'm trying to do," Dr. Wilbur protested.

"Don't try to trick us with double meaning," Sid snapped. "Integrating us with that gang of women is not freedom. It's bondage."

"I've been their hostage long enough," Mike added ruefully. "The time for our freedom is at hand. Whether you like it or not, we're not going to be part of a woman. We're going to be men in our own right."

"You are what you are," said the doctor.

"Well, let me tell you something," Mike declared. "You're getting Sybil ready to go into the world on her own. You've encouraged her in her dream of being an independent woman and making a place for herself. A teacher? Maybe. But the big jobs in education are held by men. But Sid and I aren't going to help her as we did in the past. We're not going to build anything for her or play Mr. Fixit in her house. As far as that silly dream of being a doctor is concerned, she doesn't have what it takes. All these years of studying science subjects that haven't come naturally have gotten her nowhere. Medical schools are very selective about the women they take, and they're not going to settle for her. This is still a man's world, and women don't really have a chance. Doctor, it's time to wake up to the truth about Sybil Dorsett. She's a woman, and a woman can't wow the world."

Then they stalked out of the office. From the door Mike pronounced an ultimatum: "Give us our freedom, lady doctor. The world belongs not to you but to us!"

With Mike and Sid in revolt, with Mary still in the igloo, the time was out of joint. Once again Dr. Wilbur had to summon the patience of the previous eight years.

The next morning the patient was Sybil, fortified by Vicky, Peggy, and Ruthie, all of whom were close enough to give her strength. As in the beginning of the analysis, Sybil talked of music, although not in the same way. "I haven't played the piano since I was a child," Sybil said wistfully. "I lost all that. It bothers me."

"You will play," Dr. Wilbur promised in much the same tone that Dr. Taylor had used about the violin in

413

the old Willow Corners drugstore. "You will play beautiful music on the piano."

"How can you say that?" Sybil asked in perplexity.

"It may surprise you," Dr. Wilbur replied, "to know that one of your other selves does play beautifully. When you are one with her, she will return to you the ability to play the piano in the way that Peggy has returned the capacity to get angry."

Bewilderment shrouded Sybil's smile. "Which one?" she asked.

"Vanessa," Dr. Wilbur answered. "I'm going to have a talk with Vanessa and will try to persuade her to come closer. She's still pretty far from you. But, soon, Sybil, when all fifteen of you are one, it will be otherwise." Thinking of Mary, Mike, and Sid, the doctor hoped she was not being unduly optimistic.

In March, 1964, Mike and Sid were still recalcitrantly fighting integration, but Mary had stepped out of the igloo. In an analytic session she announced, "The church doesn't matter. What is important is to live a good, Christian life and love your fellow man." It was the very philosophy, Grandma Dorsett's philosophy, Mary had enunciated earlier in the analysis, but which had become obscured as the church had reached out to trap her.

With the problems carried by Marcia and Mary resolved, Sybil was now well enough to hunt for her first full-time job since coming to New York.

"Vanessa," Vicky told Dr. Wilbur, "doesn't think we have the right clothes for our reentry into the world."

Dr. Wilbur went shopping with Sybil and bought her several new outfits. Fortified with new costumes and the assertiveness that Peggy had returned to her, Sybil, who had difficulty in getting back into teaching because of not having taught in ten years, paced the pavements of New York to a variety of employment agencies.

Waking up at 4:45 A.M. on August 8, Sybil recognized that she had very definite "Peggy feelings." She closed her eyes and drifted for a few seconds to see if she could discover what Peggy wanted. Purple boats with green sails came into Sybil's mind's eye. She had once done a painting of sagebrush in Professor Klinger's class, but she had never had a very high regard for the combination of purple and green. Then Peggy said, "See, there are three pink flags on the ship." Sybil got out of bed. It was 5:00 A.M., too early to go job hunting. She decided to give Peggy the chalk and paper to make purple and green boats with pink flags. A dreadful mixture, Sybil thought, but why not please Peggy? At six Peggy's completed boats were sailing high. Peggy wanted to call the drawing *Pink Flags*; Sybil preferred *Of Ships and Sailing*, but in the end Sybil let Peggy have her way.

Later that morning Sybil visited the agencies, feeling calm and energetic. She attributed her happy mood to having allowed Peggy to color. That morning Sybil secured a job as a receptionist at a New York Hotel.

She had been working there for a week when Ramon Allegre asked her for a date. She accepted. From the first, her response to Ramon, an accountant on special assignment to the Gotham and soon to return to his native South America, was positive.

The day after their first date Dr. Wilbur left for a medical convention in Zürich and a vacation abroad. Accompanying the doctor to the airport, Sybil talked about Ramon. "I like him," she said with an unabashed forthrightness that the doctor had never seen her display toward any man. "He's asked me for another date tonight."

"He's rushing you," the doctor said smiling.

"Is that what you call it?" Sybil asked. "It's been so long since I've had a date, I've forgotten the vocabulary."

As Dr. Wilbur's plane shot up steeply into the air, Sybil watched until nothing was left. Then, finding a set of benches out in the cool air, Sybil sat down to enjoy the sights. She felt peaceful and not alone even though Dr. Wilbur was not beside her. The thought of Ramon contributed, too, to the feeling of well-being.

Was this euphoria? That word had never been in her vocabulary until this moment.

That night, after Sybil had returned to the apartment and before Ramon called for her, Sybil continued to feel as if the doctor were still with her. Dr. Wilbur had often said that this was how it should be, but the feeling hadn't come before. This time, however, Sybil really felt it. She was so pleased to have been able to tell the doctor about Ramon. Sybil knew that the togetherness that Sybil had enjoyed with the doctor outside the office had been an important, perhaps the most crucial, part of the therapy. And now Ramon. There was also peace in the thought of him—a man against whom she hadn't shut the door.

31

Ramon

Ramon Allegre had aroused feelings in Sybil that to her were entirely new. Always afraid to see the same person, man or woman, too many times for fear that the friend would discover her lapses of time or meet one of the other selves, habitually unable to make plans in advance since the morrow might not belong to her, Sybil had dared to be with Ramon in the course of eight weeks of continuous dating.

By day she had glimpses of him, preoccupied but not remote. At night and on weekends, they enjoyed concerts, theaters, art galleries, long walks in Central Park, and an occasional evening in the Morningside Drive apartment. Since Teddy's departure only two people had been admitted to closeness: Laura Hotchkins, a friend from Whittier Hall, and Flora Rheta

Schreiber, a friend and professional writer to whom Dr. Wilbur had introduced Sybil in 1962. Yet while Laura and Flora knew that Sybil was a multiple personality and Flora had met the other selves, Ramon knew nothing about Sybil's "condition." In seeing him, therefore, Sybil was declaring her confidence in her own ability to remain herself.

Indeed, while cooking dinner for Ramon one Thursday evening, Sybil suddenly realized that no longer was she what she had been—a depleted person, incapable of loving or of personal involvement. Shortly before meeting Ramon she had confided in Flora, whom Dr. Wilbur and she had brought close to the analysis, "I can't feel anything. How can you feel when you have such a mix-up in your emotions? You're too busy with the feelings complicating existence to have any others."

But now Sybil was no longer the shell of a self she had been when Stan—who had proposed a sexless marriage and had been comfortable with her just because she had not been intense—had wooed and rejected her.

It was different with Ramon. She was gripped with intensity of feeling. Was this love? The feeling was new, as new as the experience of solidity that had replaced the floating feelings of the past.

Was she well? she wondered. Was it health that had ripped away the heavy weight and had brought her to a metaphorical gate, through which she was reentering the world?

What lay beyond the gate? Sybil didn't know. She had glimpsed what she knew belonged to the world of well people, yet she also knew that she was still set apart. This was so even though, despite Dr. Wilbur's absence and an altogether new experience with Ramon, she had not once dissociated during these eight weeks. But some of her other selves still existed.

Vicky had told her, "Ramon's a nice person, but he's pushing too fast." Peggy had said, "He comes from Colombia. How exciting. It's a place I want to go." Vicky and Peggy were close to her now. Some of the others, however, had never been close, and they were fighting integration. Even though she had concealed the fact from Ramon, she *was* still a multiple personality.

As Sybil worked on preparations for dinner, she also admitted to herself that her depressions and suicidal feelings had not been put to rest by the euphoria of her romance. Even during these eight weeks there had been tugs of despair, desire for surcease. The surcease of death.

She went into the bedroom, started to dress, looked into the mirror. Until her meeting with Ramon, mirrors had been ruled out of her existence. Finally daring to look, she had not been displeased with what she saw. Lingering at the mirror, Sybil was also aware that the truth about herself that she had tried to conceal from Ramon was changing. At the age of forty-one she was waiting for him with the expectation of a teenager. For the very first time she was experiencing love.

The doorbell roused her. There stood Ramon, holding a bouquet of red roses. "Cara," he said as he kissed her, "I missed you." It had been precisely two hours since they had seen each other at the office, less than twenty-four hours since their last date.

"Ramon," she replied, "I missed you, too."

To Sybil, who often personified people, moods, and things in colors, who had described her lost two years as blue and had conceived of chickens with blue feet, Ramon seemed all brown, like the earth. He took her in his arms so easily, touched her so expressively, that she, to whom the slightest touch had once been abhorrent, did not withdraw.

"A new drawing, cara?" Ramon called as his eye rested on the mantel, where there was a brooding figure of black and white chalk. "A self-portrait?"

Sybil was embarrassed. It was Peggy's drawing of Sybil.

"The figure looks omnipotent," Ramon remarked. Silence.

"I've always liked that one," Ramon commented as he walked toward an abstract figure of blue on a background of darker blue. This time Sybil felt more comfortable, for that painting was her own.

"Notice the shading," she said. "All the shades of blue that are love."

"I never thought of love as blue," Ramon replied.

"Blue as the sky, the sea. I always have," was Sybil's answer.

Ramon studied the painting thoughtfully. "It does create the impression of love," he admitted. Then, looking at drawings and paintings in which figures of children predominated, he observed, "You seldom draw grown-ups. Have you declared war on the adult world?"

Sybil laughed. "Not exactly," she teased. "But one of my recurrent motifs is a large house in which many brothers and sisters stand in a row. I suspect it's because I'm an only child."

"That's just about the first thing you've told me about your past," he replied. "After eight weeks I didn't even know that."

The remark made Sybil uneasy. Circumspect and careful to withhold the truth about herself, she had repressed her entire autobiography.

"All I really know about you," Ramon continued, "is that you are my age and that, like me, you have never married. For the same reasons, I suspect. Both of us have been busy with other things."

The uneasiness had become acute. Sybil changed the subject, saying, "I better get the casserole out of the oven."

At dinner, Ramon, a Roman Catholic, said grace. Sybil found her thoughts wandering to Nancy's strong anti-Catholic feeling and Mary's entrapment in an anti-Catholic church. Nancy's problem had been resolved, and Nancy herself had disappeared. Resolved, too, had been Mary's religious conflicts. Unless these things had happened, Sybil mused, Ramon would not be sitting at this table.

After grace, Ramon remarked, "I had a letter from my little niece this morning. Would you like to see it?"

"I can't read Spanish," Sybil replied, but she took the letter readily. "There are more pictures than

419

words," she remarked, while examining it with delight. "Like me when I was six."

Although she had not met Ramon's niece, Sybil had grown fond of her and of her two brothers, of whom Ramon talked constantly. Sybil had come to think of them as Ramon's children because she knew that, after the death of their mother, Ramon's sister, and her husband in an automobile crash, Ramon had instituted adoption proceedings.

From the first, Ramon's strong family feeling had moved Sybil. As his story had unfolded, she had been deeply impressed, too, with the energy he had shown in realizing his rags-to-riches dream. Ramon, eldest of nine children, was the only one in the family to get an education. A scholarship saw him through a Catholic college in his native Bogotá. By working at night and studying during the day he had earned a degree from the Columbia University School of Business. An accountant now, he had secured a number of special assignments in first-class American hotels.

As Sybil returned his niece's letter to Ramon, he remarked, "You love children."

"As becomes a schoolteacher," Sybil temporized. "Even though it's been years since I've taught. I've been so involved with graduate work, you see." She felt uneasy at having allowed the threads of the past to become entwined with the present.

"You should have married," Ramon said. "You would make a wonderful mother."

The room was still. The many avowals of motherhood from Sybil's childhood flooded her thoughts. She heard herself saying to herself, "When I grow up, I'm going to have lots of children. They can play with each other. I'll be good to them. I'm going to let them do what they want to do. I won't hit them or tie them up or bury them in a wheat crib. I won't . . ."

She remembered how she had pretended that she was a mother, how she had planned for each of her fifty-odd dolls and for her paper dolls as well. Then she suddenly realized that in these games of pretense never once had she considered actually bearing or delivering a child. Ramon's ready-made family coincided with her early fantasy.

As she served coffee, she thought: I could love these children, I, who probably can never have children of my own.

"I can still see the little girl in you," Ramon remarked. Yes, Sybil thought, that little girl, those little girls, were around long past their time.

The conversation turned to books, music, and religion. "I used to have a confused set of ideas about religion," Sybil commented. "I'm over that now." And she thought: how good it is that Nancy, with her strong anti-Catholic feeling, has disappeared. Nancy would never have accepted Ramon, a Catholic, or let me accept him. Now the difference of faiths did not separate Sybil from Ramon.

Ramon turned on the radio for the market news. A newscaster was talking about a psychiatrist's testimony in a murder case. "*Complejos Americanos,*" Ramon said with irritation. "People with real troubles don't need what you Americans call a shrink. Latins and Europeans don't indulge in the silly luxury of psychiatry the way you Americans do."

Silence.

"Are you angry about something, cara? I didn't offend you?"

"Oh, no, Ramon." She looked at the brown hair, the dancing eyes. *Complejos Americanos.* American complexes? How little he understood. He could never understand the emotions that had complicated her existence.

Sybil arose from the table to kneel at the fireplace. "These October days can be chilling," she said as she lit a flame.

"Let me help you, cara," he replied, kneeling beside her.

She thought: I want him to make love to me. I want to have a baby of my own. If only I could. I'm scared. For eight weeks my fear has made him afraid. We've touched and kissed but that's all. I want more —I've got to have more.

Responding to her unspoken entreaty, Ramon

421

caressed her. Her head moved against his chest. He embraced her tightly. "When I have an erection," he told her, "I measure. It's seven inches. Good?"

She smiled nervously and recalled that she used to think that love hurt, that when people loved you they hit you and put flashlights in you and bottles. Then she dismissed these thoughts as recollections belonging to the era before she had come to terms with the past.

"Cara, I want you," Ramon murmured passionately.

"No, Ramon," she replied with a quiver of still surging desire as she extricated herself from his embrace.

He moved back toward her and began gingerly to unzip her dress.

She shook her head, pulled up her zipper, and seated herself on the sofa.

"I love you, Sybil," he said.

"I love you, too, Ramon. And that's why my answer is no."

"But I don't understand," he protested.

"I know you don't," she replied. "I'm afraid."

"Afraid of me, Sybil?" he asked, confounded. "I love you."

"I love you, too," she replied. "But I have reason to be afraid."

He looked at her in a manner that reflected both perplexity and tenderness. Anxious to advance his cause, he was also eager to protect Sybil against her fears. He quietly said, "Maybe it's not the right time." He put on his coat and walked to the door. "Tomorrow night," he said. "The opera. I'll call for you at six. We'll have dinner first, some place we haven't been before." He kissed her fingertips and was gone.

After the door had closed behind him, Sybil thought: what if he doesn't come back? What if he does?

The following Sunday morning Sybil and Ramon walked in Central Park. The solid rock they passed reaffirmed for Sybil her own solidity. The denuded trees reminded her of the leaves of herself that had fallen away. How many of the selves had merged was as hard to say as to count the leaves strewn in the pathway.

"Quiet today, *mi amor*," Ramon remarked.

"I was thinking of the fallen leaves," she replied, "and of the enduring rock."

"My little one is poetic," he answered.

"I wrote poetry as a child," she replied.

Ramon next suggested that they take a drive in a horse and carriage. "After all," he teased, "I'm a visitor in your country."

As they were driving, Ramon drew out of his pocket a small box wrapped in white paper and tied with a blue bow. "I have something for you," he said as he opened the package. She gasped as he uncovered a diamond and ruby ring, which he placed on her finger. "It will not be a long engagement," he said. "We will marry at once. You will go to Bogotá with me for the children. Then we will return to the United States with our family. Are you happy?"

Torn by conflicting feelings, Sybil was silent. She wanted these children more, if possible, than she wanted Ramon himself. If she were their mother, she would be good to them, would undo all that had been done to her. All that had seemed beyond grasp was now on her finger, symbolized by Ramon's ring. "You say nothing," Ramon said urgently. "Why do you say nothing?"

For a time the only sound was that of the horses' hoofs. "We won't stay in Bogotá long," Ramon explained. "You won't get homesick."

Homesick for what? she wondered. She was ready to go now. She wanted to marry Ramon, wanted to help care for those children. "I must have your answer at once. We don't have much time, cara," Ramon pleaded. "The children can't wait. They need a mother."

Conflicting emotions rendered Sybil incapable of replying. To Ramon she seemed serious, abstracted. She opened her lips as if to speak, then closed them again.

"Are you all right?" Ramon asked anxiously.

Sybil became tremulous. She didn't want to seal

her fate. "You must say yes," Ramon was insisting. "Yes has been in your eyes for many weeks."

Finally, in a low, broken voice, Sybil said, "I love you, Ramon. I want to marry you and help raise those children. But I cannot."

Baffled, he protested. "Why? There isn't anyone else to stand in the way."

Silence. She could not tell him that although there was no husband or lover to obstruct his path, there *were* people in the way. How he would mock her if she told him that she was a multiple personality. He was like the rest of the uncomprehending world. You could tell people about any other illness, even other mental illnesses, but this she had kept enshrouded from all but a very few.

"Your answer, cara?" Ramon was asking.

"Give me time, Ramon," Sybil pleaded.

"Sybil, we do not have time. It must be *now*. These children must have a mother. I want that mother to be the woman I love."

Time, Sybil agonized. Time has always betrayed me. She asked only, "But why isn't there any time?"

"Don't you see?" he said. "I cannot have these children unless I have a wife. And I cannot bring them here to live unless that wife is an American."

The urgency of Ramon's petition suddenly became terrifyingly clear. He wanted a mother for these children, but he wanted an American without complexes. Who would rear these kids? Not Sybil alone but Peggy, Marcia, Vanessa, Mary, Mike, and Sid. Ramon would never understand.

"It has to be now," Ramon spluttered.

The others were falling into place within her. She *was* getting well. But even though she had reached the threshold, she had not yet crossed it. The gift of time could rescue this love, but Ramon had given her an ultimatum: now or never.

"Marry me. You stay here. I'll go and bring the children," Ramon now offered.

"Ramon," Sybil replied desperately, "it's no use. I just can't marry you."

"For God's sakes, why?" he cried.

424

"I can't," she repeated.

Turning from him, she looked through the window, fighting her despair.

Then she returned the ring to the box and the box to Ramon.

"Woman of mystery," Ramon spluttered angrily. "Tell me the reason for the mystery, or I'll go away. You'll never see me again." At once his tone changed from anger to tenderness. "If it's something serious, something grave, you can tell me. I love you, Sybil. I will listen."

The "don't dare tell" of earlier days returned to plague her. But although she didn't dare tell, she was not running away from the truth about herself as she had in the past. She was indeed a woman of mystery to Ramon; the years of analysis, however, had made her no mystery to herself. Her unconscious stood clear, translucent, while that of most people was sealed in noncommunication. Her unconscious had paraded itself before her as perhaps no other human being's ever had.

"I will listen," Ramon insisted.

Ramon was so eager to reach her yet so incapable of understanding what it was he would reach. Ramon had not really penetrated, as she thought he had, the heavy veil of aloneness that hung between her and the world. The veil remained.

The carriage came to a halt. As Ramon helped Sybil out of the vehicle, she reveled in his touch.

Silence reigned during their taxi ride.

Then Sybil and Ramon stood at the entrance of the old brownstone. "Will you reconsider?" he asked. His face bore the shadow of gloom.

"I wish I could," she answered.

How do I handle this? was her inner plea. In the past I didn't handle crises; I let the others act for me. But I'm not the same. Now I'm capable of facing my own problems. I'm also able to see the distinction between romance and reality. Ramon loves me—but with strings attached. I love him, and I want the children. But he is turning time into the old betraying enemy.

Ramon's lips and cheeks turned white. He relapsed into gloom. Then he seemed to withdraw. "I wish you no ill," he said vacantly, "and all good. But unless you change your mind and let me know that you have, we shall not meet again."

"Must we part this way, Ramon?" she asked.

"The decision was yours, Sybil," he replied coldly. "But remember, it is also yours to undo."

The avalanche had begun, but the earth did not yet crash down. The crash came when he chided bitterly, "You've rejected not only me but those three children you claimed to love even without knowing them. But once again I tell you: you can still undo what you have done." He turned from her, walked a few steps, and returned. He put the box with the ring in her hand. "Take it anyway," he said. "It's your birthstone. And you like pretty things. Take it in memory of the life you rejected, of your refusal to live."

She fled into the house.

She had rejected Ramon, Sybil thought, as she herself had so often been rejected. At three and a half she asked a doctor in a hospital, "Would you like to have a little girl?" He had turned from her in the same way that she had just turned from Ramon. She had turned her back on three children the way a doctor long ago had done to one.

Yet in an instant she also realized that she had no reason to feel guilty for her actions. Ramon's efforts to inflict guilt feelings on her had *not* succeeded. That realization gave her strength.

Have I been using my being a multiple personality as a mask for the real fears that keep me from what I most desire? she asked herself. Am I really so moral, so noble as to sacrifice myself to protect Ramon and his children from my malady? But Sybil knew that her very salvation depended upon her commitment to her dawning health.

As if in confirmation of this sudden insight, the first thing she did in the apartment was to empty the vase of the now-withered roses Ramon had given her three days before.

The next morning Sybil thought of not going to work, but she made herself go. Conscience again, she thought. But Ramon was not there. His special assignment had been completed, she learned, and he was not returning to the hotel.

No time. Ramon had meant what he had said.

At the end of the week, finding it too painful to remain alone where Ramon and she had been together, Sybil gave up her job at the hotel.

Sybil was certain that Ramon did not harbor a spirit of vindictiveness toward her. Both by nature and principle he was superior to the mean gratification of hard feelings. He probably would never forgive her for having scorned his love, but that was another matter.

The memory was a lingering torture. It kept up a slow fire of remorse, a tremulous grief that would not ebb. She tried to propitiate her regret by an objective recollection of the practicality of his marriage suit and its implicit manipulation. Nevertheless, tears flooded her days. The remarks of the others still within her added to her distress. Vicky's: "He was a nice person. All of us liked him. You should have told him the truth." Peggy's: "He was great. We all wanted to marry him." The taunting of Vanessa: "You turned him down because underneath perhaps you didn't want him."

Dr. Wilbur, who returned shortly after Ramon had departed, was impressed with the growth in her patient. Sybil's letters had informed her, "This is the first time you've been away that I've managed to stay myself throughout." The psychiatrist who saw Sybil during this period verified Sybil's own account.

Moreover, both in the office and away from it during the first few weeks of the resumption of the analysis, Sybil seemed stronger, more confident. She had even gained weight, which in her case was always linked with an upswing in health, both mental and physical. There was a strong psychosomatic aspect of Sybil's *grande hystérie*.

The relationship with Ramon, however, troubled the doctor. The references to him in Sybil's letters had in no way indicated the seriousness of their relationship. She felt that if she had been in the country, the relationship could have been salvaged by her talking to Ramon.

Sybil, showing her new maturity, insisted, however, that it would have done no good because Ramon did not understand emotional problems or mental illness, and when Dr. Wilbur urged her to write to Ramon so that the doctor could talk with him, she replied: "I must first know when I will be well."

"You're so much better," the doctor replied. "You wrote me that you remained yourself in my absence. Did that continue to be true even after you parted with Ramon?"

"It did," Sybil replied confidently. "The others talked to me sometimes, especially at the end, but *I* ran things."

While Dr. Wilbur was absorbing the transformation in her patient, Sybil protested, "But you haven't answered my question. *When* will I be well?"

"Sybil, I don't know. You've shown health in your relationship with Ramon. But the boys are still fighting integration."

Sybil looked steadily at the doctor. "You've answered my question," Sybil replied. "If you had told me I'd be well in a month, two months, three months, I would have written Ramon and taken my chances on your making him understand. But time has betrayed me once again."

"If he loves you, he'll understand anyway," the doctor protested. "We can write him and try."

"No," Sybil replied quietly. "Ramon is a practical man. He won't wait for a neurotic."

As Sybil left the doctor's office, she felt lonesome to the core. In songs, she thought, people belonged, loved, lived, danced, marched. What Sybil had loved had been torn away.

She didn't hope to love again. Yet there was triumph in defeat. In the old days a crisis like this would have caused Sybil to dissociate. Now, however, she had not only remained herself but also continued to recognize the new feelings of solidity. The grief she

428

felt over Ramon, moreover, was real, as surely as the emotions of the past had seemed unreal. Although the grief was terrible, the new reality was good. For the first time, despite her grief, she felt solid enough to be able to defend her place in the world.

32

One

"Dead vines, old vines, barbs or briars," Marcia said under hypnosis in January, 1965. "I'm afraid of life and the world—afraid of going out into it. Afraid of being rejected, turned down, cast aside." It was a natural fear of reentry.

"I'm looking forward to being a well person among well people," Vanessa declared. "Life is for living, and I've waited too long."

"I think," Mike admitted during the same session, "Sybil's worth more than she thinks she is or Sid and I ever thought she was. People care about her— Flora, Flora's mother, and, of course, the lady doctor and Ramon."

"Maybe," Sid added, "Sybil can do the things Mike and I want to do but haven't been allowed to do. Maybe it's all right for a woman to build a partition. Maybe she *can* be the kind of woman she wants to be and do well in a career. With Mike's skill and my skill, with our enthusiasm, I'm sure she can. What she wants to do is all right with Mike and me. We like the new Sybil."

The new Sybil? Who am I? she asked herself. Who is she? Dr. Wilbur likewise asked. For although Sybil was not yet a whole person, she was no longer a mere waking self.

The only person to appear for the Dorsett appointment these days was this new Sybil. When Dr. Wilbur wanted to communicate with the other selves, she could do so only through hypnosis.

Shortly after Mary had come out of the igloo, Mary and Sybil Ann had been consolidated. Vanessa, always closer to Sybil than most of the other selves, had moved further in the same direction. Vanessa's passionate denunciation of hypocrisy had now in fact sharpened Sybil's awareness of it, both in the past and the present, thus providing the waking self with new insights. Marcia, who previously had voiced a patient's typical fear of getting well, had gotten well by joining Sybil. The joining had taken place after Marcia, too, had accepted the death wish for mother.

Peggy did not appear even when summoned. Peggy Lou and Peggy Ann had already been consolidated as Peggy; now the consolidation had gone even further. These keepers of the unintegrated past with its angry and fearful memories had returned to Sybil. After doing the portrait that Ramon had admired—the very last work to come from her—Peggy had ceased to exist as a separate entity. But her assertiveness was very much in the forefront of the new Sybil.

The newly emerging Sybil, however, was very different from what Dr. Wilbur had originally expected. Since Vicky had all the memories and possessed more of the original Sybil than waking Sybil, the doctor had thought it might be a good idea to do away with all the selves, including waking Sybil, and allow Vicky to be the one self. Yet the doctor had discovered that Vicky, like all the selves, existed for the express purpose of masking the feelings that the waking or central self could not bear to face.

The answer, therefore, had been to preserve the waking self as such while returning to it all the memories, emotions, knowledge, and modes of behavior of the other selves, thereby restoring the native capacities of the original child. It also meant returning to the waking self the experiences of the one-third of Sybil's life that the other selves alone had lived. This was pioneer work for Dr. Wilbur.

The doctor knew that all the selves had come close to Sybil. As Sybil changed, the other selves changed as well. There had previously been two levels of denial of Sybil's mother. Sybil had accepted Hattie Dorsett as her mother but had denied the hatred. The other selves had denied that the woman whom they hated was their mother. After Sybil, in that moment of purging in the car, had accepted the hatred, the other selves had come to accept Hattie and now acknowledged her as "our mother." Even Vicky, whose parents had never come from France to reclaim her, finally had come to admit, "Sybil's mother is also mine."

Sybil had begun to assume the behavior of the others. For example, what had been the exclusive preserve of Peggy Lou had become Sybil's capacity to draw black and white. In fact, an overlapping of painting styles had developed among all the selves. On the other hand, although Peggy had returned to Sybil the multiplication that had been learned in Miss Henderson's fifth-grade class, Sybil was still not proficient in its use.

In May and June, 1965, the use of hypnosis had tapered off even more, now almost solely confined to communicating with the selves, who could not otherwise be reached. The days of Sybil's dissociation and the spontaneous appearance of the secondary selves seemed over.

Sybil was in her apartment, writing résumés for a teachers' agency with which she had registered in hope of getting a job outside New York. She now felt able to manage without Dr. Wilbur and was eager to prove her independence. As Sybil was typing, her fingers suddenly went numb. Frightened, she called Dr. Wilbur, but without success. She called Flora. By the time Flora came on the line, Sybil felt numb all over. "I'm sick," she cried into the telephone. "If anything happens to me, sell the stamp album—see that Dr. Wilbur is reimbursed for the analysis." Sybil tried to say more, but the receiver dropped out of her hand. Her arms and legs moved involuntarily. Pitching forward, she hit the wall, crashed across the room, and even hit the ceiling. Then she fell into an inert heap on the floor.

It was there that Flora found her, black and blue, a terrifying sight. Finally able to speak, Sybil said triumphantly, "I watched all of it. I was aware of what was happening every minute of the time."

Rising to her feet, Sybil seemed taller than her normal self. A voice younger than Sybil's, light, lilting, and cheerful, exclaimed, "I'm the girl Sybil would like to be. My hair is blonde and my heart is light."

Then she was gone, and Sybil was there. "I must have blacked out," Sybil said. "Still? How can it be?"

Flora knew at once that the blonde self who had instantaneously emerged was not any one of the fifteen selves she had previously met. A new self at this stage of the analysis, when Sybil was nearly integrated? The immediate matter at hand, of course, was to get Sybil into bed, to apply cold compresses to the injuries, and to reach Dr. Wilbur. And then?

"It was a major gastrointestinal upset," Dr. Wilbur told Flora later that evening, "accompanied by a waking seizure and spasticity. All through it Sybil was aware of what was happening."

Then Flora told Dr. Wilbur about the blonde. "The dissociation was brief, perhaps no more than a minute," Flora said.

"Last February," Dr. Wilbur replied thoughtfully, "I met this blonde in the office, although I didn't realize it at the time. Sybil had been talking; then she looked blank for a minute, as she did in the old days. Then I heard the voice you described. It was only a minute, a mere flash."

The next day in the office Dr. Wilbur hypnotized Sybil. Mary Ann was the first to emerge. "We had a fit," she explained. "There's lots to have fits about. The people in the old church in Willow Corners—the barren, ugly church. We hate those people."

Vicky said, "In our room last night there was someone else."

"Blonde hair—that one, I saw her," Marcia added. "I don't know her name."

432

"Who does?" Vanessa asked.

"I suppose Vicky does," Marcia replied, "because I think Vicky knows her. Who is she?"

"A new girl but not new," Vicky replied.

Suddenly the newcomer spoke—stiltedly, strangely, with the cadences of a rehearsed speech. "I'm not really new," she said. "I've been around for nineteen years. I'm the girl Sybil would like to be. Born in tranquility, I've lived unseen. An adolescent while the others still remained essentially children, I've carried no childhood traumas. I never knew either Hattie or Willard Dorsett, never lived in Willow Corners, never attended the Willow Corners church. I came in Omaha. I enjoyed college, and I love New York. I would have joined sororities, would have had many dates, would have been a cheerleader at sports events, a campus leader in everything. I love life and living. The only thing that has stood in my way is that I wasn't free to be myself, to walk in the sun and face the world. But now that the others are about to face it, I shall go with them. Now that the others have shed their traumas, I will hold hands with the rest. My vitality will lend strength; my zest for living, buoyancy; my unscathed past, assurance. I, who have never been ill, will walk with Sybil in the unprotected world of well people."

"Welcome," said Vicky.

"You and I belong together, Victoria," the blonde, who still had given no name, replied. "Unlike the others, we were not cradled in traumas but in Sybil's wish. You and I are blonde—the only two of all sixteen of us who are. I understand there were a lot of blondes in Sybil's mother's family and that her mother glorified that hair color. We are blonde because Sybil wished to be blonde."

The blonde was a dream girl—the girl who had stood with Sybil at the mirror, throbbing with adolescent expectations, as they had waited for Ramon. And if her speech sounded unnatural, it was the affectation of a teen-ager, spouting her newly found knowledge and confidence.

"I've come to set Sybil free," the blonde announced.

433

"As she enters the world, she will throw away what were once Marcia's dead vines and walk with me among newly budding trees, not in the winter of life but in the springtime."

Silence. Dr. Wilbur tried to get the blonde to say more, but Vicky replied instead. "The blonde is Sybil's adolescence," Vicky said.

"Isn't this late?" Dr. Wilbur asked.

"She needs to be with Sybil now," Vicky replied.

"Is there anybody else?" the doctor asked, as if she were reliving the first days of the analysis.

"Why should there be?" Vicky seemed to shrug vocally. "We didn't expect the blonde, true. But as she told you, she has been around for nineteen years, although inactive. How could she have been active when Sybil, carrying the weight of childhood, bypassed adolescence in anything but a strictly physical, developmental sense?" Vicky paused. Then she added, "It was hard for Sybil to have a normal adolescence. She left so much of herself behind, fixed in childhood. Now that Sybil has scotched these childhood traumas, you should expect to find the lost adolescence returning in search of the gratification of maturity."

As Vicky's words trailed off, the lilting yet stilted voice of the blonde was heard again. "I held back," she said, "until Sybil fell in love. When I realized that Ramon wouldn't work out, I rose to protect the adolescent Sybil from heartbreak. She was an adolescent, you know, when she was with Ramon."

"If Sybil still wants to feel like an adolescent in love, there's no reason why she shouldn't," the doctor said. "People of all ages do this. She can function as an eighteen-year-old blonde at forty-two. Sybil can integrate you."

"She has," the blonde replied. "I'm no threat to the final healing. In fact, I will make the wheels of that healing turn faster."

"Have you been listening, Sybil?" Dr. Wilbur asked.

"I have," Sybil replied. "And I know that this part of me who gave no name is telling the truth."

The wish, personified by the dream girl, had brought

434

new youth to the unlived life, to the womanhood aborted by depletion and discontinuity.

Baffling, terrifying, life-renewing, the episode of the blonde's appearance proved to be the climax of Sybil's illness. After the event there were many days during which she just sat and absorbed the emotions, attitudes, knowledge, and experiences that since early June of that year the other selves had voluntarily shared with her. And while she took a new look at her emerging self, within her a tremendous reorganization of personality was taking place. The past blended with the present; the personalities of each of the selves with that of the others. The past returned, and with it the original child called Sybil, who had not existed as an entity since she was three and a half years old. Not everything came to a conscious level all at once, but the significant things that did were normal memory and a new sense of time. After thirty-nine years the clock was no longer incomprehensible.

A week after the July 7 crisis Sybil was talking animatedly to Dr. Wilbur about her plans to become an occupational therapist. They would involve leaving New York.

"The old fears seem to be gone," Dr. Wilbur remarked. "You sound well."

"Oh, I am, Doctor," Sybil replied, smiling. "I've thrown my last fit. But I was fully conscious of everything that was happening during it. It was not the same way out I took in the past." She added: "And the blonde? Well, I feel she is with me. I know that I will never dissociate again."

"You've never said that before," the doctor replied, "even during all this time when none of the others appeared."

"I didn't say it," Sybil averred, "because never before did I feel that it was so."

"We can tell," the doctor explained, "if all the memories of the others are now yours. Let's test it."

Through the several hypnotic sessions that followed Dr. Wilbur matched Sybil's memories alongside those of the selves who still had individual identities.

Not one of these selves had a single memory that Sybil did not also have.

Sybil's attitude toward these selves, moreover, had completely changed, from initial denial to hostility to acceptance—even to love. Having learned to love these parts of herself, she had in effect replaced self-derogation with self-love. This replacement was an important measure of her integration and restoration.

Three weeks after the July 7 crisis Dr. Wilbur hypnotized Sybil and called for Vicky Antoinette. "How are things going, Vicky?" the doctor asked. "What progress is there underneath?"

"I'm part of Sybil now, you know," Vicky replied. "She always wanted to be like me. Now we are one. I used to say, 'This or that event was before my time.' Now I say, 'It's after my time.' You see, I'm no longer completely free."

That was the last time that Dr. Cornelia B. Wilbur talked to Victoria Antoinette Scharleau.

On September 2, 1965, Dr. Wilbur recorded in her daily analysis notes on the Dorsett case: "All personalities one."

On September 30 it was moving day at the old brownstone. Sybil's furniture and paintings went to Pennsylvania, where she had obtained a job as an occupational therapist; she herself moved to Flora's apartment to spend the last two weeks in New York.

The Sybil who entered Flora's apartment was new not only to Flora but even to herself. She was not what had been waking Sybil. Neither was she any one of the fifteen other selves. She was *all of them.* Like Miranda in *The Tempest,* she seemed to be standing on the threshold of discovery, almost literally crying out, "O, wonder:/How many goodly creatures are there here:/How beauteous mankind is: O brave new world,/That has such people in't!"

The world seemed new because she was new, real because, for the first time in her adult life, she was a whole and real self. As she took off her coat, settled her bags, and sank into a chair, she was silent. Then she said, "I've been here before—yet I haven't."

"Who is the I?" Flora asked.

"The one who can feel," Sybil replied. "I have new feelings now, real feelings. It's not the way it used to be."

The "It's not the way it used to be" was the clue to the understanding that even though Sybil now had the feelings that for thirty-nine years the others had masked, her frame of reference was still that of the waking self.

Flora had prepared a snack, and as they ate, they talked for a while about impersonal things. Then apropos of nothing that had previously been said, Sybil remarked, "Memories make a person mature emotionally." Although stated as a generalization, it was obvious to Flora that Sybil was referring to herself and was saying in effect: now that the others have returned their memories to me, I have been able to mature emotionally; now that I'm whole, I'm mature.

Paradoxically, however, while this new Sybil seemed more mature, she also seemed younger than her forty-two years. The impression became even stronger when she remarked, "I'm discovering things that everybody else my age has known for a long time."

The next morning at breakfast Sybil said, "I hoped for a time when I would know what I was doing all the time I was doing it." Then she added with a compelling intensity, "Now I can account for every minute. When I wake up, I know what I did yesterday and can plan what I'm going to do today." She looked at Flora and Flora's mother and asked with fervor, "Do you know what it means to have a *whole* day ahead of you, a day you can call your own?"

At last, after thirty-nine years of having it otherwise, a day for her was all its hours. Before, time had to be done away with by relegating it to other selves. Now time presented the opportunity for self-realization.

Each morning as she planned the day ahead, her eyes sparkled and she betrayed an excitement that for anyone else would have been wholly out of proportion to the nature of the activity. The excitement continued with heightened awareness as the day unfolded and she did ordinary things—reading a book, watching television, talking.

437

"I see a name of some public figure in the newspaper," she remarked to Flora one evening. "Hear it again on television. Then someone talks about it. I always recognize it!" There was a reminiscent torment in her eyes as she added, "There were many times I couldn't do that—in the past." She lingered on the phrase *in the past* with the fascination one feels for a bygone horror. Then elucidating the isolation, the alienation of what it had been like to be a multiple personality, she explained, "I'd see the name in the newspaper, but by the time we ran into it again on television, it was often not I who saw it but one of the others. When it came up in conversation, still somebody else might have been there. The parts didn't go together."

Again she was using *I* as the frame of reference of the erstwhile waking self. Triumphantly she added, "Now the parts come together. The world seems whole."

Her expression became suddenly wistful as, looking fixedly at Flora, she remarked with earnestness, "I know it doesn't seem like anything to other people to be able to see a whole television program without interference from within, but to me it's revelation!"

Other insights continued to find expression. "It's quiet, very quiet around here," she said on another evening. "Come to think of it, I'm quiet, too, inside. There isn't any arguing with myself."

On yet another evening, when she returned with Flora and Flora's mother from a dinner engagement, Sybil summarized it with the supreme accolade by saying, "I was there all the time. I myself, Sybil. I see the food, recall every word of the conversation. All of it."

Simple things became momentous. One morning, for instance, when Sybil did the marketing, she discovered upon returning to the apartment that she had forgotten the orange juice. "It's wonderful," she observed humorously, "to be able to forget the way other people do!" More than humor, this statement was an avowal of inclusion—of being one with the human race.

One morning Sybil wanted to go to a store to buy

some material for a dress. Flora went with her. The store was crowded. Many women were standing at the dry goods counter. The saleswoman started to wait on a customer who had come in after Sybil. "I'm sorry, but I was here first," Sybil protested. Flora held her breath. In the past such assertive action would have been impossible for Sybil, would have had to come from one of the other selves, usually Peggy Lou. The only self who was present, however, was a newly confident Sybil.

Further indication of the success of the analysis followed. The saleswoman handed Sybil the receipt. Sybil scrutinized it, multiplying the number of yards by the cost per yard to see whether the total was correct. In the past Sybil would have appealed to her companion to check the accuracy of the receipt for her. But endowed with the knowledge Peggy Lou had hoarded since Miss Henderson's fifth-grade class and aided by a post-analytic phase of treatment during which Dr. Wilbur had taught the new Sybil how to use the knowledge the selves had returned to her, Sybil handled the transaction herself.

In the dress department Sybil decided on a brown dress with red and gold paisley print cuffs and belt. Leaving the store, she commented to Flora, "I got the brown dress for Sybil, but the paisley print for the Peggy part of me."

Outside the store Flora started to flag a taxi. Sybil stopped her, saying, "Let's take the bus." Recalling Sybil's intense terror of buses, Flora was very much aware of the significance of the remark. "Anybody can get on a bus and go places. It's so simple," Sybil remarked reassuringly. And on the bus Sybil gave voice to the thoughts that Flora had had while in the store. "I used to let other people do my arithmetic," Sybil said, "or I didn't do it at all. But now I can figure things out for myself. I can order the things I want, make change in a taxi, measure material for a dress or drapes, measure mats for framing pictures—do all the things I couldn't do before." Again there was a curious emphasis on the word *before*, accompanied also by a radiance at having expressed her new freedom.

There were still moments, of course, when Sybil demonstrated flashes of what used to be the other selves. The new Sybil would pace the living room, saying, "I'm going away. I'm going to build a new life. Everything's so exciting. There's so much to do, so many places to go." To Flora it rang of the time that Peggy Lou had planned to break with the others forever.

A dash of Vicky was in evidence when company came and Sybil would converse about early American furniture or would declare, "I don't see how anybody can be bored."

The blonde, who had so belatedly presented herself and had been so swiftly integrated, seemed omnipresent in the buoyancy of Sybil's new enthusiasm.

The new Sybil repaired a broken ceramic vase as Mike or Sid might have done, prepared a lamb stew that Mary used to make, and, what was most startling, played Chopin's Nocturne in B Minor. In the past only Vanessa could play the piano.

Shades of Nancy Lou Ann seemed to be present when Sybil confided in Flora, "I'm ashamed of having been narrow and bigoted. I don't fear Catholics now." And when Sybil added, "My fundamental religious beliefs are the same, but there is a modification that has removed the torment and puts the beliefs in a new perspective," it was as though she were saying, "Mary has come out of the igloo."

The selves as autonomous, independently entities were gone. But they *had* been successfully integrated and were now contributing their uniqueness as the various aspects of a rounded personality.

Naturally, although wholeness brought a sense of joyousness in being alive, a sense of wonder at having a whole day ahead, new confidence in negotiating with the world, and a balance stemming from a new maturity and a youthfulness withheld in chronological youth, Sybil's newly healed psyche was still somewhat fragile—not quite ready to trust itself. There were moments of panic, sharp but swiftly repressed eruptions of fears of the future. "I don't want to get sick again," she murmured from time to time. "I'm afraid of what might happen as the day moves toward night." Flora contemplated the poignancy of Sybil's fears and concluded how wonderfully normal it was for Sybil to be afraid, like everybody else, of old age.

Most painful of all to talk about was Ramon. Not until the night before Sybil left for her new job did she finally say, "I would have asked him to wait." In anguish she added, "If only I had known that I would soon be well." And Sybil, who once had been unable to cry, let the tears flow.

During the two weeks of Sybil's visit with Flora, Dr. Wilbur stayed close. There were daily phone calls to Sybil; on several occasions the doctor came to the apartment for dinner. Sybil and the doctor talked about their new plans. Sybil had secured a position as an occupational therapist in a Pennsylvania hospital for emotionally disturbed children. For Sybil it was to be an interim position until she could get into teaching.

On the evening of departure—October 15, 1965— doctor and former patient left Flora's apartment. Two women who had taken an eleven-year journey together began their separate journeys into the dawn of the new Sybil's new time. That there was a seventeenth self to supplant the depleted waking self was testament that truth is internal, the surface a lie. For buried in the depleted self, whom the world saw, had been this new woman, this whole woman, so long denied.

Epilogue:

The New Sybil's New Time

I, the Flora in the story and the author of the book, have stayed close to Sybil in the more than seven years since she left my apartment. In sharing excerpts from some of her letters to me, you will have a glimpse of the new Sybil in her new time.

November 4, 1965: "I wish you could see my house. Connie [Dr. Wilbur] said it was cheaper to buy than rent, and she lent me the money for the down payment —my guest room is fairly large. It is for you, Doctor Connie, and Laura in turn. See? I'm so thrilled to have my own place. Capri is here with me. Her favorite spot is the front window ledge. I sometimes wonder if she notices that I'm only me . . ."

January 20, 1966: "Have had time to read some books this past winter. *Friendship and Fratricide, The Search for Amelia Earhart, Papa Hemingway, The Jury Returns* (Nizer), *Other People's Money, The King in the Castle, The Chinese Looking Glass,* Bruce Catton's three volumes on the Civil War. Most of these books, like most of the magazine articles I've read, are about events and people that were in the news during the time that there were too many of me to be able to keep track of anything. These were things I heard about then only by remote control. There is so much to catch up with. Alger Hiss and Whittaker Chambers, for example, were just names to me."

September 25, 1966: "Just think, I've been here

almost a year now. It is the first continuous year of my life. It's amazing how days fit neatly into weeks and weeks into months that I can look back on and remember. Only missed one day of work so far (earache last winter). It's the greatest experience I've ever had, barring none. People just take it so much for granted, I think they miss the point.

"All has gone well. Not all easy, but no trouble. I even got a raise in salary after seven months. I was so surprised because I had not expected any since I had signed a contract for a set amount. I'm still looking forward to getting back into teaching, however. There's a good possibility.

"You asked if the private art classes I'd mentioned were for me or by me. Guess I thought I had told you about them before. You see, I visit with you in my mind often and then forget I have not told you things really. The classes are in oil painting and for adults. I teach them in the studio of my home. Get that. My home, not my house. At last Mary and the rest of them have a home, but there isn't any Mary or any of the others anymore. Just me."

January 8, 1967: "It is still a marvel to me how much a well person can accomplish; I'm so lucky."

January 14, 1967: "You will never guess what I finally got finished. The painting for over your davenport. It isn't the one I started for the two of you. I just did not have the heart to finish that after your mother died. I could not face the feelings of loss, as I am certain you understand. So I began an entirely different kind of painting. It is a casein (similar to and as permanent as oil) and is framed and ready to bring to you when we come to New York. Which, if Connie has not mentioned to you as yet, is to be something like two weeks for only a couple of days. She has appointments there, and I'm coming along to bring the picture (which, by the way, is one of mood and impression, not realism) and to see you and Laura and do a little shopping. See you soon . . ."

443

February 8, 1967: "Thank you for sending me the books. Stupid of me to forget them after all your trouble in getting them for me. Of course, Connie would say it was my unconscious not wanting to leave your place. Well, it was a short visit, but we can always hope for a next time. Really thought I'd left the books in a taxi when I got around to missing them much later. But I had no other thoughts about someone else's deliberately hiding them."

August 11, 1967: "Just have to write you a quickie this A.M., as you and Connie must be the first ones to know my big news—big to me, anyhow. Found out for certain yesterday that, as of September 1, I will be an Assistant Professor. Am so excited. They interviewed eighteen others, and I was sure I'd never have a chance, but the dean told me it was unanimous and no question after they interviewed me. Which helps my ego. Am I not lucky? More details and news soon . . ."

August 24, 1967: "Spent the weekend with Connie. She gave me a permanent, and I sewed a white nylon print summer dress, which she then 'hung' for me to hem. We washed and trimmed our three poodles. They don't like it very much. Mine whimpers, and her two try to bite us. More fun. Her color TV and stereo are marvelous, but we still find time to play Scrabble (our favorite). She won two out of three games as per usual. I'm busy in my own little swirl but love it. Wish you could see my mock orange bush in bloom. All kinds of flowers in my yard . . ."

November 20, 1968: "It's wonderful how well things are going. After a little over three years, there are times when I still can't believe how lucky I am. I can remember everything and can account for every minute of each day. You can well understand how reassuring it is for me to be just Sybil because you knew me when it was otherwise."

On June 6, 1969, Sybil wrote to say that she was coming to New York to represent her college at a convention. In the city that for eleven years had been her fragmented home she visited with me, but she also walked through the city alone. On July 2, 1969, from the vantage point of her present home, she recapitulated that visit: "When I walked along the streets of New York, many semi-forgotten memories came back, but all without exaggerated emotions. I just recalled old times, remembering what the feelings had been like but without reliving them. As I revisited familiar places, however, I became aware of memories that were not recollections of what had happened to me but rather to one of my former selves. There was the dress shop where Peggy Lou had shopped, the hotel where Marcia and Vanessa had spent a night, and a confrontation at the Metropolitan Museum of Art with Marian Ludlow, who had been Vicky's friend. Marian recognized me at once. Remembering her through Vicky, who was now part of me, I chatted with Marian, accepting her as *my* friend."

Each of the letters that followed continued to express a joyousness in being a normal person in a world through which she moved without incident in a time in which clocks no longer seemed capricious. The fears of the past had been put to rest.

At times, of course, there was a sort of wistful regret, expressed in a letter of May 28, 1970: "I would have accomplished much more than I have if things had been different during all those years. Yet I think I have an insight into and an understanding of my students that I wouldn't have had any other way. I will never forget that I was a multiple personality. But although I still recognize feelings associated with these former selves of mine, those feelings are like anybody else's—just different aspects of a person.

"And time? Time is so wonderful because it is always there. Something happened in class the other day that will amuse you. One of my students, who is a teacher, had been ill and had missed many classes. Struggling with an absence sheet, she couldn't figure out just how much time she had lost. 'Miss Dorsett,' she asked, 'were you ever unable to account for your time?' I

445

did a double take. 'Yes. Why, yes,' I replied as nonchalantly as I could."

Her statement made me recall my direct encounters with the thieves of Sybil's time: Peggy Lou, who had emerged spontaneously one day when I was having lunch with Sybil in the old brownstone; the blonde; and the time when Dr. Wilbur had hypnotized Sybil to present me to all the selves, asking them whether they would cooperate with me if I were to write this book. I had never met Vicky, but she said very politely, "I've known Flora for a long time." Ruthie had complained, "Sybil doesn't give us enough to eat," and Peggy Lou had remarked, "I can't understand why you want to write a book about Sybil of all people."

While Sybil was recalling having been a multiple personality from a distance, Dr. Wilbur was still living with multiple personality at close hand. In seven years the doctor had in fact diagnosed and treated six cases of multiple personality—five females and one male. None was psychoanalyzed, but all were treated with psychoanalytic psychotherapy and hypnosis. All were integrated, although one suffered a relapse and had to be integrated a second time.

These six ranged in age, at the time Dr. Wilbur first saw them, from twelve to thirty-three. Two had two selves each; three, four selves apiece; one, seven selves. All of the females except one, who was only twelve, were college-educated. None, however, was as bright or talented a person or as complicated a case as Sybil Dorsett, who continued to make medical history.

All had symptoms that followed as predictable a course as measles. Each had a central, or waking, self corresponding to waking Sybil and alternating selves of which the waking self had no knowledge and for whose memories and experiences she (he) was amnesic. In each of the six cases there was a "Vicky" character, who knew everything about all the selves and who served as a memory trace.

The causes of multiple personality, however, continue to remain elusive, although the evidence in these cases as well as in Sybil's points to at least one factor of common causation: an initial milieu (the nuclear family) that is restrictive, naive, and hysterical. For instance, a schoolteacher with four selves whom Dr. Wilbur treated at the hospital of the University of Kentucky Medical School was the daughter of a fire-and-brimstone spouting mountain minister. This bigoted father, so reminiscent of Sybil's grandfather Dorsett, didn't allow his children out of the house after dark because he firmly believed that when the sun went down, the Devil began to stalk the hills.

It can be postulated that the hysterical environment spawns a hysteric; the hysteric then becomes a multiple personality in order to assume identities that make it possible to escape from the restrictive standards of an oppressive milieu. What remains elusive, however, is why one person in that environment should seek this particular way out while another in the same environment does not.

What is clearly substantiated is that the escape, which is undertaken without the awareness of the waking self, far from being conscious, is a strategy of the unconscious mind. Clear, too, is that the selves, who are part of the strategy and who exist outside of the waking self's awareness, function as autonomous entities.

The autonomy, observed in the case of the selves of Sybil and reaffirmed through the direct observation of these other six cases by Dr. Wilbur and her colleagues, also held up under the scrutiny of objective measurements. The startling finding was that the waking self and each of the secondary selves of a given multiple personality *react like different people*.

Item: The four selves of a twenty-four-year-old, each of whom was independently given a psychological word association test, had totally different responses for individual words and for sets of words. From self to self there was indeed no leakage, no cross-fertilization of a single word association. Unmistakably, selves I, II, III, and IV were as independent in their responses as if they were four separate individuals.

447

Item: A battery of psychological and neurological tests was administered to the four selves of another patient (Jonah), a twenty-seven-year-old. The selves reacted with complete independence of one another. Even their EEGs (electroencephalograms) were unalike.

A study, which won an award from the Society for Experimental and Clinical Hypnosis, tabulates the results. Entitled "The Objective Study of a Multiple Personality," the article, which was published in the *Archives of General Psychiatry,* April, 1972, by Arnold M. Ludwig, MD, Jeffrey M. Brandsma, MD, Cornelia B. Wilbur, MD, Fernando Bentfeld, MD, and Douglas H. Jameson, MD, tabulated the EEG of Jonah and his secondary selves—Sammy, King Young, and Usoffa—thus:

Summary of Objective EEG Data (15-Minute Sample of Each Recording)

Data	Jonah	Trance	Sammy	King Young	Usoffa	Jonah
Alpha frequency mode*	10.5	9.5	9.5	9.5	10.5	10.0
Alpha range	9.5-10.5	9.0-10.0	9.0-10.0	8.5-10.0	9.0-11.0	9.0-10.5
Alpha amplitude mode†	20.0	20.0	20.0	30.0	15.0	20.0
Theta frequency mode*	5.0	4.0	4.0	4.0	4.0	5.0
Theta amplitude mode†	20.0	20.0	25.0	15.0	25.0	15.0
% time alpha‡	53.0	20.0	20.0	52.0	41.0	60.0
% time theta‡	31.0	76.0	75.0	18.0	45.0	8.0
% time low voltage‡	15.0	3.0	5.0	30.0	10.0	19.0
% time asleep‡	1.0	1.0	5.0	1.0	2.0	0.0
Movement & muscle activity (sec/min)	9.0	0.2	4.0	33.0	13.0	16.0
Eye movements/min	5.0	4.0	2.0	14.0	5.5	5.7

*Frequencies are given in cycles per second.
†Amplitudes are given in microvolts.
‡Percent time is the average number of seconds dominated by the indicated feature per 100 seconds of trace.

Even though Jonah's four selves could be substantiated through objective tests and clinical observation, thirteen army psychiatrists failed to spot the nature of his illness. That Dr. Wilbur, fresh from an eleven-year exploration of Sybil Dorsett, did make the diagnoses, not only of Jonah but also of five other cases in seven years, seems to indicate—just by the law of averages—that this illness occurs more frequently than is recognized by physicians. Not impossibly many persons who suffer from amnesia are in reality multiple personalities. At any rate, since the prognosis is very good when the multiple personality is recognized and properly treated, it is essential to develop further knowledge of this little explored, too often ignored field of medical knowledge.

Its importance is implicit in a statement of Freud, which appears in *The Interpretation of Dreams:*

The whole multiplicity of the problems of consciousness can only be grasped by an analysis of the thought-processes in hysteria. . . . Examples of every possible variety of how a thought can be withheld from consciousness or force its way into consciousnes under certain limitations are to be found included within the framework of psychoneurotic phenomena.

If you translate "thoughts" into "secondary selves," you have the analog of the seven multiple personalities, including Sybil Dorsett, whom Dr. Wilbur has treated.

During the Columbus Day weekend, 1972, Sybil, Dr. Wilbur, and I got together to celebrate the book's approaching completion. Sybil was marvelous—so well that it was hard to remember that she had once been otherwise. She is climbing the professional ladder with alacrity. Her colleagues respect her, and her students love her. She has many new friends, has her own home, drives her own car, and makes regular payments to Dr. Wilbur for the now-distant analysis. The several art exhibits of Sybil's work reflect the wholeness of an integrated artist in contrast to the medley of disparate styles of the past. In short, Sybil is leading the good life—a whole life.

During our weekend together I mentioned to Sybil that one of the typists of this book had become so involved with the story that she dreamed she was Sybil. Next morning at breakfast Sybil's lips curved in an impish smile as she announced, "I dreamed I was Sybil."

The Sybil about whom the typist dreamed seemed like someone other than the woman before me. The dream —or rather the nightmare—had receded so far into the past that at the breakfast table that October morning there was no question but that there were only three of us. Sybil was well, and as her friend I rejoiced in her story's happy ending.

Psychological
Index

451

453

hypnosis, 50, 384, 391, 400, 401, 402, 431, 446; age progression by, 385ff

hypocrisy, 129, 158, 181, 185, 186, 279, 295, 378; excessive propriety, as part of, 185

hysteria, 84, 87, 106, 309, 384, 446, 449; conversion symptoms, 165ff; genesis of, in environment, 314, 341. *See also* psychological symptoms

identifications, multiple, 287

identification with: aggressor (Mike), 288-289; father, 262; father, as Sid, 284, 288; grandfather Dorsett, as Mike, 284, 288; Jews, 275; males, 287

igloo, 409-410, 414

immaturity, 37, 43, 320, 395

incest, 188, 262, 405-406

incomprehensible thing, the. *See* terrible thing, the

injuries, physical. *See* abuses

insanity, 47

integration, 314, 316, 328, 333, 342, 343, 348, 360, 361-362, 384, 388, 391, 400, 403, 409, 432, 435-436, 440, 446; existential fear of, 411; mood improvement, 414; of Peggy Lou, 397-398; of Ruthie, 392-393; resistance to, by male personalities, 411-413; return of assertiveness, 414; spontaneous, 400

intercourse between parents, 183-189

internal injuries, 210, 275

Interpretation of Dreams (Freud), 449

IQ, 38, 278

James, Professor William, 109

Jekyll, Dr., 115

laughter, 195, 197, 198, 201, 209, 213, 224, 242, 248, 269, 286

lesbian feelings, 351, 381; of Sybil Ann, 381

lesbianism, encounter with, 205

listening, blockage to, 307

lobotomy, 48

lost time. *See* terrible thing, the

male cells, 288

male figures: Danny, 150ff, 164, 165, 278, 279, 336; Henry, 349ff; love for, 418; Ramon, 415, 416ff, 433-434, 441; Stan, 62ff, 417

male personalities, 283; environmental influences upon, 290; genesis of, 290

maleness, in every woman, 412

Mamie, 108, 109

manic depressive psychosis, 261

Marcia (Marcia Lynn Dorsett, sometimes Baldwin), 122-123, 177, 178, 179-180, 181, 186, 289, 296, 298, 312, 335, 338, 340, 345, 361, 362, 365, 371, 372, 373, 376, 378, 379-380, 387, 389, 390-391, 403, 405, 410, 411, 424, 430, 433, 434, 445; depression of, 381. *See also* alternating selves; alternations of personality

Marjorie (Marjorie Dorsett), 301, 302, 315, 335, 341, 361, 378, 389. *See also* alternating selves; alternations of personality

Mary (Mary Lucinda Saunders Dorsett), 123, 162-164, 165, 166, 168, 170, 171, 172, 173,

455

456

457

458

Vicky—Continued
  Scharleau), 100-101, 106, 107, 108, 111, 116, 117, 122, 127, 155ff, 156, 158, 159, 160, 161, 162, 164, 166, 167, 168, 169, 170, 171, 172, 173, 174, 177, 178, 180, 181, 185, 186, 202, 282, 286, 289, 298, 312, 313, 315, 317, 318, 335, 336, 337, 338, 339, 340, 341, 342, 347, 348, 350, 352, 356, 357, 360, 361, 362, 366, 371, 373, 376, 377, 378, 379, 380, 389, 390, 393, 394, 395, 396, 398, 399, 405, 408, 410, 411, 413, 414, 417, 427, 430, 431, 433, 434, 436, 440, 445, 446. *See also* alternating selves; alternations of personality

Vive, Louis, 108, 109
voyeurism, 203

waking self, the, 111, 321, 336, 341, 446; as "boss," 357; depletion of, 340, 341; Dorsett, Sybil Isabel, 23ff; recollection of behavior of alternating self, 357; recollection of memories of alternating self, 360; unawareness of alternating selves, 324
walking, delayed, 213

**BEST OF BESTSELLERS FROM
WARNER PAPERBACK LIBRARY**

AFTER CLAUDE by Iris Owens   (78-427, $1.50)
The hilarious story of a woman cast from her lover's bed, into a world that doesn't understand her. "A very funny book by an exhilarating talent and intelligence."—**New York Times**

THE CAMERONS by Robert Crichton   (79-258, $1.95)
"Built of the throbbing substance of life."—**L.A. Times.** Over five months on the bestseller lists. **The Camerons** is the story of a Scottish mining family trying to lift themselves from out of the mines, in a steadily mounting drama, as they face their neighbors in a fierce labor struggle. 1974's Paperback of the Year!

THE TOWER by Richard Martin Stern   (59-434, $1.75)
Soon to be a Spectacular Motion Picture! A bomb explodes! Fire roars upwards in New York's newest skyscraper trapping world-renowned dignitaries. "The suspense is kept very taut."—**New York Magazine**

XAVIERA GOES WILD
by Xaviera Hollander   (59-632, $1.75)
The all new adventures of the Happy Hooker. Follow Xaviera as she travels to the most swank, and most kinky resorts all over the Continent. Join in all the fun as Xaviera Goes Wilder than ever before!

 A Warner Communications Company

If you are unable to obtain these books from your local dealer, they may be ordered from the publisher.
Please allow 4 weeks for delivery.

WARNER PAPERBACK LIBRARY
P.O. Box 690
New York, N.Y. 10019

Please send me the books I have checked.
I am enclosing payment plus 15¢ per copy to cover postage and handling. N.Y. State residents add applicable sales tax.

Name ....

Address ....

City .... State .... Zip ....

_____ Please send me your free mail order catalog

GREAT READING FROM
WARNER PAPERBACK LIBRARY

STONE ISLAND by Peter Boynton   (78-518, $1.50)
The powerful journal of Helen Calder, a woman who has retreated
to a small town in Maine, provides the vehicle for this erotic, and
terrifying journey into the life and mind of a woman. "Brilliant . . .
profound"—*New York Times*

THE FIRST MS. READER   (78-352, $1.50)
How women are changing their lives—in work, sex, politics, love,
power, and life styles. An anthology of articles from *Ms.* magazine,
containing many articles from the preview issue now out of print.

DOWN AMONG THE WOMEN   (78-402, $1.50)
by Fay Weldon
Meet Wanda and her daughter Scarlet in their absurd, pathetic,
nightmarish and sometimes hilariously awful liaisons, their complex
and delicate servitude to men. It is "unnerving, yet fascinating"
(Pittsburgh Press) and "their stories are a microcosm of the female
world." *(New Directions for Women)* "Biting, powerful, sometimes
murderously funny"—*Washington Post*

ENJOY BEING A WOMAN   (76-162, $1.25)
by Dr. Allan Fromme
Noted psychotherapist and marriage counselor, Dr. Allan Fromme,
shows the modern woman how she can shed her guilt feelings and
learn more fully to appreciate life and its new freedoms. In
Enjoy Being A Woman, Dr. Fromme confronts women with the
realities of their own emotions and enables them to stop being
fearful of fulfilling human relationships.

W A Warner Communications Company

- -

If you are unable to obtain these books from your local dealer,
they may be ordered from the publisher.
Please allow 4 weeks for delivery.

WARNER PAPERBACK LIBRARY
P.O. Box 690
New York, N.Y. 10019

Please send me the books I have checked.
I am enclosing payment plus 15¢ per copy to cover postage and
handling. N.Y. State residents add applicable sales tax.

Name ....

Address ....

City .... State .... Zip ....

_____ Please send me your free mail order catalog

**MORE GREAT READING FROM
WARNER PAPERBACK LIBRARY**

THE SILENCE OF THE NORTH   (78-240, $1.50)
by Olive A. Fredrickson with Ben East
The true-life story of a courageous woman who fought bitter cold,
hunger and savage beasts, in the rugged Canadian wilderness, to
keep herself and her fatherless children alive.

HEDDA AND LOUELLA   (59-090, $1.75)
by George Eells
A dual biography of Hedda Hopper and Louella Parsons—two
women who clawed their way to the top and demanded the respect
that made them legends in their own time.

A HIGH OLD TIME   (76-286, $1.25)
by Lavinia Russ
How to enjoy being a woman over sixty. Here, in an easy and
humorous way, are the tips you need to aging gracefully: how
to act, what to wear, what to do, how to afford it, taking a trip,
dealing with relatives, the inner you!

SECOND WIVES' TALES   (75-193, 95¢)
by Amy Page Cassidy and Ruth Morton Fazio
A liberated primer on how to succeed with a divorced man. The
frank and fascinating rules of the game are all here: how to get
him to marry you, sexual games divorced men play, how to cope
with his alimony, what do men want in a second wife? and more.

W A Warner Communications Company

If you are unable to obtain these books from your local dealer,
they may be ordered from the publisher.
Please allow 4 weeks for delivery.

WARNER PAPERBACK LIBRARY
P.O. Box 690
New York, N.Y. 10019

Please send me the books I have checked.
I am enclosing payment plus 15¢ per copy to cover postage and
handling. N.Y. State residents add applicable sales tax.

Name ....

Address ....

City .... State .... Zip ....

_____ Please send me your free mail order catalog

BOOKS YOU WON'T WANT TO MISS
FROM WARNER PAPERBACK LIBRARY

HOW SHE DIED by Helen Yglesias   (76-093, $1.25)
The powerful Houghton Mifflin Literary Fellowship Award novel about the effects of a woman's terminal illness on her husband and best friend. "Superbly dramatic." —Newsweek

DANCERS AND LOVERS   (78-210, $1.50)
by Robert Wolfson
He was the greatest dancer since Nijinsky, but Russian property—watched over carefully on his Western tour. She was the prima ballerina of the Western world who wanted him to complete her fame. This is their intimate story.

UMBRELLA STEPS   (76-155, $1.25)
by Julie Gilbert
Prude is sixteen. Prude is rich. Prude is having an affair with her best friend's father. And more . . . Not since Francoise Sagan has love been seen from this angle. Shocking . . . Perceptive . . . Funny . . . Human.

CARMELA   (59-263, $1.75)
by Paul Gillette
The big bestselling novel of the girl from a little Italian town who became the greatest opera star of her time.

 A Warner Communications Company

If you are unable to obtain these books from your local dealer, they may be ordered from the publisher.
Please allow 4 weeks for delivery.

WARNER PAPERBACK LIBRARY
P.O. Box 690
New York, N.Y. 10019

Please send me the books I have checked.
I am enclosing payment plus 15¢ per copy to cover postage and handling. N.Y. State residents add applicable sales tax.

Name ....
Address ....
City .... State .... Zip ....
_____ Please send me your free mail order catalog